The
CHELSEA HOUSE LIBRARY
of LITERARY CRITICISM

_____The_____
CHELSEA HOUSE LIBRARY
of LITERARY CRITICISM

The
MAJOR AUTHORS EDITION
of the
NEW MOULTON'S LIBRARY *of* LITERARY CRITICISM

Volume 6

Bibliographical Supplement and Index

General Editor
HAROLD BLOOM

1989
CHELSEA HOUSE PUBLISHERS
NEW YORK
NEW HAVEN   PHILADELPHIA

MANAGING EDITOR
S. T. Joshi

ASSOCIATE EDITORS
Jack Bishop
Peter Cannon
Beth Heinsohn
Patrick Nielsen Hayden
Teresa Nielsen Hayden

ASSISTANT EDITORS
Marie Claire Cebrian
Susanne E. Rosenberg

EDITORIAL COORDINATOR
Karyn Gullen Browne

COPY CHIEF
Richard Fumosa

3 5 7 9 8 6 4 2

Library of Congress Cataloging in Publication
Data

The Major authors edition of the New
Moulton's library of literary criticism.
    (The Chelsea House library of literary criti-
    cism)
    Includes bibliographical supplement and in-
dex vol.
    1. English literature—History and criticism—
Collected works. 2. American literature—His-
tory and criticism—Collected works. I. Bloom,
Harold. II. Title: New Moulton's library of
literary criticism. III. Series.
PR85.M33   820'.9   84-27426
ISBN 0-87754-815-3 (v. 1)
        1-55546-776-8 (v. 6)

CONTENTS

PREFACE

This *Bibliographical Supplement and Index* concludes our series *The Major Authors Edition*. We have included bibliographies of the 66 authors covered in the series, a complete table of contents of each chapter in the series, and an index to critics.

In the *Author Bibliographies* for this series, we have listed every separate book publication—including pamphlets, broadsides, collaborations, and works edited or translated by the author—only for works published in the author's lifetime. We have been intentionally selective in listing posthumous works, citing only those editions of collected or selected works that are textually or historically important or contain previously unpublished or uncollected material. Offprints of periodical articles and facsimile editions have not been listed. Titles are those of the first edition, although where a work was published under a now unfamiliar title we have supplied the commonly known title in carets (e.g., ⟨Rasselas⟩ for Samuel Johnson's *The Prince of Abissinia*). Where a work was published with no title we have supplied one in carets. Works of doubtful authorship have been placed in square brackets; forgeries or works known to be spurious are not listed. In selected instances we have supplied dates of revised editions where these are significant (e.g., the first and second editions of Sidney's *Arcadia*, 1590 and 1593). Pseudonymous works are listed but the pseudonyms under which these works were published are not.

For plays we have listed date of publication, rather than date of production; unpublished plays are not listed. Periodicals edited by the author are not listed except where the author has written nearly the whole of the periodical (e.g., Johnson's *The Rambler*). All works by an author, whether in English or in other languages, have been listed; English translations of foreign-language works are not listed unless the author himself has done the translation. In some instances non-literary works—e.g., the artwork of William Blake—have also been listed.

This series is arranged chronologically by the death date of the author; the bibliographies have also been so arranged, and the bibliography for William Shakespeare, who occupies the whole of Volume 2 of the series, has been placed in its proper chronological sequence between Edmund Spenser and Sir Francis Bacon. Only in the case of Shakespeare have we listed every printing or edition of his work published during and just after his lifetime. For Geoffrey Chaucer, the only author in this series who wrote before the invention of printing, we have listed his works in order of writing (supplying conjectural dates of writing in carets), with a list of separate editions of these works and then a selective listing of collected and selected works.

The *Series Contents* list every item used in each chapter of the series, in the order in which the items appear; we have not, however, listed the sections (*Personal, General, Works*) into which the chapters are sometimes divided. If an item was used more than once it is listed for each time it is used.

In the *Index to Critics* we have given the name of the chapter and the page number on which the critic's work is cited. Although our series is numbered consecutively through the five volumes, a reader cannot be expected to know in which volume a given chapter or page appears. Hence an entry reading "Edgar Allan Poe 4:2277" refers to an item in the chapter on Edgar Allan Poe appearing in Volume 4, page 2277 of the series. A critic whose work appears more than once in a single chapter receives an entry for each appearance, although in rare cases two items by the same critic will appear on the same page.

S. T. Joshi

AUTHOR BIBLIOGRAPHIES

AUTHOR BIBLIOGRAPHIES

GEOFFREY CHAUCER (c. 1340–1400)

The Book of the Duchess ⟨1369⟩. Ed. Frederick J. Furnivall (1871); ed. Helen Phillips (1982).

The Romaunt of the Rose (translator) ⟨before 1370⟩. Ed. Frederick J. Furnivall (1911); ed. Stephen G. Nichols (1967); ed. Ronald Sutherland (1968).

The Parlement of Foules ⟨1377⟩. 1477 (William Caxton); 1530 (Wynkyn de Worde); ed. C. M. Drennan (1911); ed. Derek S. Brewer (1960).

The Hous of Fame ⟨c. 1380–1381⟩. 1484 (William Caxton); ed. Walter W. Skeat (1893); ed. C. M. Drennan (1921).

Boece de Consolacione (translator) ⟨c. 1381–1385⟩. 1478 (William Caxton); ed. Richard Morris (1868); ed. Frederick J. Furnivall (1886).

Troilus and Criseyde ⟨c. 1382–1385⟩. 1483 (William Caxton); 1517 (Wynkyn de Worde); 1526; ed. Robert Kilburn Root (1926); ed. Raymond Cullis Goffin (1935); ed. Georges Bonnard (1943); ed. Robert M. Lumiansky (1952); ed. Daniel Cook (1966); ed. Derek S. Brewer (1978); ed. Barry A. Windeatt (1984).

The Legend of Good Women ⟨c. 1385–1386⟩. Ed. Frederick J. Furnivall (1871–90; 3 vols.); ed. Walter W. Skeat (1889).

The Canterbury Tales ⟨begun 1386⟩. 1478 (William Caxton); 1492; 1498 (Wynkyn de Worde); ed. Thomas Morrell (1737); ed. Thomas Tyrwhitt (1775–78; 5 vols.); ed. Frederick J. Furnivall (1868–79; 36 parts in 9); ed. Alfred W. Pollard (1894; 2 vols.); ed. Walter W. Skeat (1908); ed. John Matthews Manly (1928); eds. John Matthews Manly, Edith Rickert et al. (1940; 8 vols.); ed. Arthur C. Cowley (1958); ed. John Halverson (1971); ed. Robert A. Pratt (1974); ed. Paul G. Ruggiers (1978); ed. Norman Francis Blake (1980); eds. A. Kent Hieatt and Constance Hieatt (1981); ed. Derek Pearsall (1985).

The Treatise on the Astrolabe ⟨1391⟩. Ed. A. E. Brae (1870); ed. Walter W. Skeat (1872); ed. Robert Theodore Gunther (1930).

Workes. 1526. 3 vols.

Workes. Ed. William Thynne. 1532.

Workes. Ed. John Stowe. 1561.

Workes. Ed. Thomas Speght. 1598.

Works. Eds. John Urry et al. 1721.

A Supplementary Parallel-Text Edition of Chaucer's Minor Poems (Containing Most of Those That Could Not Be Got into the Parallel-Text Edition). Ed. Frederick J. Furnivall. 1871–80. 2 vols.

Complete Works. Ed. Walter W. Skeat. 1894–97. 7 vols.

Works. Eds. Alfred W. Pollard, Mark Harvey Liddell, H. F. Heath, and William S. McCormick. 1898.

Collected Works. Ed. Alfred W. Pollard. 1928–29. 8 vols.

Complete Works. Ed. Fred Norris Robinson. 1933, 1957.

The Portable Chaucer. Ed. Theodore Morrison. 1949.

Complete Works. Ed. Kemp Malone. 1953.

Chaucer's Poetry: An Anthology for the Modern Reader. Ed. E. Talbot Donaldson. 1958.

Chaucer's Major Poetry. Ed. Albert C. Baugh. 1963.

Selections from the Tales of Canterbury and Short Poems. Ed. Robert A. Pratt. 1966.

Lyrics and Allegory. Ed. James Reeves. 1971.

Troilus and Criseyde and Selected Short Poems. Eds. Donald R. Howard and James Dean. 1976.

Complete Poetry and Prose. Ed. John H. Fisher. 1977.

Chaucer According to Caxton: Minor Poems and Boece, 1478. Ed. Beverly Boyd. 1978.

Poetical Works: A Facsimile of Cambridge University Library MS. Gg.4.27. Ed. Derek S. Brewer. 1979–81. 3 vols.

A Variorum Edition of the Works. Eds. Paul G. Ruggiers, Donald C. Baker et al. 1983– .

SIR PHILIP SIDNEY (1554–1586)

A Woorke concerning the Trewnesse of the Christian Religion by Philip of Mornay Lord of Pessie Marlie (translator; with Arthur Golding). 1587.

The Countesse of Pembrokes Arcadia. ⟨Eds. Fulke Greville, Lord Brooke, and Matthew Gwinne?⟩ 1590, 1593.

Syr P. S. His Astrophel and Stella. 1591.

The Defence of Poesie. 1595.

The Countesse of Pembrokes Arcadia: The Third Time Published with New Additions. 1598.

The Psalmes of David (translator; with others). Ed. S. W. Singer. 1823.

Miscellaneous Works. Ed. William Gray. 1829.

The Correspondence of Sir Philip Sidney and Hubert Languet. Ed. Steuart A. Pears. 1845.

Complete Poems. Ed. Alexander B. Grosart. 1873. 2 vols.

Defence of Poesie; Letter to Queen; Defence of Leicester. Ed. George E. Woodberry. 1908.

Complete Works. Ed. Albert Feuillerat. 1912–26. 4 vols.

Poems. Ed. William A. Ringler, Jr. 1962.

Selected Prose and Poetry. Ed. Robert Kimbrough. 1969.

Selected Poetry and Prose. Ed. David Kalstone. 1970.

Miscellaneous Prose. Eds. Katherine Duncan-Jones and Jan van Dorsten. 1973.

Selected Poems. Ed. Katherine Duncan-Jones. 1973.

CHRISTOPHER MARLOWE (1564–1593)

Tamburlaine the Great. 1590.

The Troublesome Raigne and Lamentable Death of Edward the Second. 1594.

The Tragedie of Dido Queene of Carthage (with Thomas Nashe). 1594.

The Massacre at Paris. c. 1594.

Epigrammes ⟨by John Davies⟩ *and Elegies* ⟨of Ovid (translator)⟩. c. 1595.

All Ovids Elegies ⟨Amores⟩ (translator). c. 1595–1600.

Hero and Leander (with George Chapman). 1598.

Lucans First Book Translated Line for Line. 1600.

The Tragicall History of D. Faustus. 1604.

The Famous Tragedy of the Rich Jew of Malta. 1633.

Works. Ed. Alexander Dyce. 1850. 3 vols.

Poems (with Robert Greene). Ed. Robert Bell. 1856.

Works. Ed. A. H. Bullen. 1885. 3 vols.

Christopher Marlowe. Ed. Havelock Ellis. 1887.

Works. Ed. C. F. Tucker Brooke. 1910.

Life and Works. Eds. Tucker Brooke et al. 1930. 6 vols.

Complete Plays. Ed. Irving Ribner. 1963.

Poems. Ed. Millar MacLure. 1968.

Complete Poems. Ed. Roma Gill. 1971.

Complete Works. Ed. Fredson T. Bowers. 1973. 2 vols.

Complete Plays and Poems. Eds. E. D. Pendry and J. C. Maxwell. 1976.

Complete Works. Ed. Roma Gill. 1987– .

EDMUND SPENSER (1552–1599)

The Shepheardes Calender. 1579.
Three Proper, and Wittie, Familiar Letters; Two Other, Very Commendable Letters (with Gabriel Harvey). 1580.
The Faerie Queene. 1590 [Books 1–3]; 1596 [Books 4–6]; 1609 [Books 1–12].
Muiopotmos. 1590.
Complaints. 1591.
Daphnaida: An Elegie upon the Death of the Noble and Vertuous Douglas Howard. 1591.
Prosopoia; or, Mother Hubbard's Tale. 1591.
Axiochus by Plato ⟨spurious⟩ (translator). 1592.
Colin Clouts Come Home Againe. 1595.
Amoretti and Epithalamion. 1595.
Fowre Hymnes. 1596.
Prothalamion; or, A Spousall Verse. 1596.
The Faerie Queen; The Shepheards Calendar; Together with Other Works. 1611 (First Folio).
Works. 1679.
Works. Ed. John Hughes. 1715. 6 vols.
Poetical Works. Ed. John Aikin. 1802. 6 vols.
Works. Ed. Henry John Todd. 1805. 8 vols.
Poetical Works. Ed. John Mitford. 1839. 5 vols.
Poetical Works. Ed. George S. Hillard. 1839. 5 vols.
Poetical Works. Ed. Francis J. Child. 1855. 5 vols.
Poetical Works. Ed. George Gilfillan. 1859. 5 vols.
Poetical Works. Ed. J. Payne Collier. 1862. 5 vols.
Complete Works. Eds. Richard Morris and John W. Hales. 1869.
Complete Works in Verse and Prose. Ed. Alexander B. Grosart. 1882–84. 9 vols.
Poems. Ed. W. B. Yeats. 1906.
Poetical Works. Eds. J. C. Smith and Ernest de Selincourt. 1909–10. 3 vols.
Works. Ed. W. L. Renwick. 1928–34. 4 vols.
Works: A Variorum Edition. Eds. Edwin Greenlaw, Charles Grosvenor Osgood, Frederick Morgan Padelford et al. 1932–57. 11 vols.
Selected Poetry. Ed. William Nelson. 1964.

WILLIAM SHAKESPEARE (1564–1616)

Venus and Adonis. 1593, 1594, 1596, 1599, 1602, 1617, 1620, 1627, 1630, 1636.
The Rape of Lucrece. 1594, 1598, 1600, 1616, 1617, 1624, 1632.
Henry VI. 1594, 1595, 1600, 1619.
Titus Andronicus. 1594, 1600.
The Taming of the Shrew. 1594.
Romeo and Juliet. 1597, 1599, 1609.
Richard III. 1597, 1598.
Richard II. 1597, 1598, 1608.
Love's Labour's Lost. 1598.
Henry IV. 1598, 1599, 1604, 1608, 1610, 1613.
The Passionate Pilgrim. 1599, 1612.
A Midsummer Night's Dream. 1600.
The Merchant of Venice. 1600.
Much Ado about Nothing. 1600.
Henry V. 1600, 1602.
The Phoenix and the Turtle. 1601, 1611.
The Merry Wives of Windsor. 1602, 1619.
Hamlet. 1603, 1604, 1611.
King Lear. 1608.

Troilus and Cressida. 1609.
Sonnets. 1609.
Pericles. 1609.
Othello. 1622.
Mr. William Shakespeares Comedies, Histories & Tragedies. Eds. John Heminge and Henry Condell. 1623 (First Folio), 1632 (Second Folio), 1663 (Third Folio), 1685 (Fourth Folio).
Poems. 1640.
Works. Ed. Nicholas Rowe. 1709. 6 vols.
Works. Ed. Alexander Pope. 1723–25. 6 vols.
Works. Ed. Lewis Theobald. 1733. 7 vols.
Works. Ed. Thomas Hanmer. 1743–44. 6 vols.
Works. Ed. William Warburton. 1747. 8 vols.
Plays. Ed. Samuel Johnson. 1765. 8 vols.
Twenty of the Plays of Shakespeare. Ed. George Steevens. 1766. 4 vols.
Plays and Poems. Ed. Edmond Malone. 1790. 10 vols.
The Family Shakespeare. Ed. Thomas Bowdler. 1807. 4 vols.
Pictorial Edition of the Works of Shakespeare. Ed. Charles Knight. 1838–43. 8 vols.
Works. Ed. J. Payne Collier. 1842–44. 8 vols.
Works. Ed. H. N. Hudson. 1851–56. 11 vols.
Works. Ed. Alexander Dyce. 1857. 6 vols.
Works. Ed. Richard Grant White. 1857–66. 12 vols.
Works (Cambridge Edition). Eds. William George Clark, John Glover, and William Aldis Wright. 1863–66. 9 vols.
A New Variorum Edition of the Works of Shakespeare. Eds. H. H. Furness et al. 1871– .
Works. Ed. W. J. Rolfe. 1871–96. 40 vols.
The Pitt Press Shakespeare. Ed. A. W. Verity. 1890–1905. 13 vols.
The Warwick Shakespeare. 1893–1938. 13 vols.
The Temple Shakespeare. Ed. Israel Gollancz. 1894–97. 40 vols.
The Shakespeare Apocrypha. Ed. C. F. Tucker Brooke. 1908.
The Arden Shakespeare. Eds. W. J. Craig, R. H. Case et al. 1899–1924. 37 vols.
The Yale Shakespeare. Eds. Wilbur L. Cross, Tucker Brooke, and Willard Highley Durham. 1917–27. 40 vols.
The New Shakespeare (Cambridge Edition). Eds. Arthur Quiller-Couch and John Dover Wilson. 1921–62. 38 vols.
The New Temple Shakespeare. Ed. M. R. Ridley. 1934–36. 39 vols.
Works. Ed. George Lyman Kittredge. 1936.
The Penguin Shakespeare. Ed. G. B. Harrison. 1937–59. 36 vols.
The New Clarendon Shakespeare. Ed. R. E. C. Houghton. 1938– .
The Arden Shakespeare. Eds. Una Ellis-Fermor et al. 1951– .
The Complete Pelican Shakespeare. Ed. Alfred Harbage. 1969.
The Complete Signet Classic Shakespeare. Ed. Sylvan Barnet. 1972.
The Oxford Shakespeare. Ed. Stanley Wells. 1982– .
The New Cambridge Shakespeare. Ed. Philip Brockbank. 1984– .

SIR FRANCIS BACON (1561–1626)

Essayes. 1597, 1612.
A Declaration of the Practices and Treasons Attempted and Committed by Robert Late Earle of Essex. 1601.
A Briefe Discourse, Touching the Happie Union of the Kingdomes of England, and Scotland. 1603.

Apologie, in Certaine Imputations concerning the Late Earle of Essex. 1604.
Certaine Considerations Touching the Better Pacification and Edification of the Church of England. 1604.
The Two Bookes of the Proficience and Advancement of Learning, Divine and Humane. 1605.
De Sapientia Veterum Liber. 1609.
The Charge Touching Duells. 1614.
Instauratio Magna ⟨Novum Organum⟩. 1620.
Historia Naturalis ⟨Historia de Ventis⟩. 1622.
The Historie of the Raigne of King Henry the Seventh. 1622.
De Dignitate et Augmentis Scientarum. 1623.
Historia Vitae et Mortis. 1623.
Apophthegmes New and Old. 1625.
Essays, Civil and Moral. 1625.
The Translation of Certaine Psalmes into English Verse. 1625.
Sylva Sylvarum; or, A Naturall History. 1626.
Considerations Touching a Warre with Spaine. 1629.
Certaine Miscellany Works. 1629.
The Use of the Law. 1629.
The Elements of the Common Lawes of England. 1630.
Operum Moralium et Civilium Tomus. 1638.
Cases of Treason. 1641.
The Confession of Faith. 1641.
A Speech concerning the Article of Naturalization of the Scottish Nation. 1641.
The Office of Constables. 1641.
Three Speeches. 1641.
A Wise and Moderate Discourse concerning Church-Affairs. 1641.
An Essay of a King. 1642.
The Learned Reading of Sir Francis Bacon. 1642.
Ordnances. 1642.
Remaines. 1648.
The Felicity of Queen Elizabeth. 1651.
A True and Historical Relation of the Poysoning of Sir Thomas Overbury. 1651.
Scripta in Naturali et Universali Philosophia. 1653.
Resuscitatio. Ed. William Rawley. 1657–70. 2 vols.
A Letter of Advice to the Duke of Buckingham. 1661.
A Charge at a Sessions Holden for the Verge. 1662.
Opera Omnia. 1665.
Baconiana. 1679.
Opera Omnia. Ed. Henry Wetston. 1684. 6 vols.
Letters. Ed. Robert Stephens. 1702.
Philosophical Works. Ed. Peter Shaw. 1733. 3 vols.
Law Tracts. 1737.
Works. 1740. 4 vols.
Works. Eds. James Spedding, Robert Leslie Ellis, and Douglas Denon Heath. 1857–74. 14 vols.
Selected Writings. Ed. Hugh G. Dick. 1955.

JOHN DONNE (1572–1631)

Pseudo-Martyr. 1610.
Conclave Ignati. 1611. Eng. tr. 1611.
An Anatomy of the World. 1611.
The First Anniversarie. 1612.
The Second Anniversarie. 1612.
A Sermon upon the XV. Verse of the XX. Chapter of the Booke of Judges. 1622.
A Sermon upon the XX. Verse of the V. Chapter of the Booke of Judges. 1622.
A Sermon upon the VIII. Verse of the I. Chapter of the Acts of the Apostles. 1622.

Encaenia: The Feast of Dedication. 1623.
Three Sermons upon Speciall Occasions. 1623.
Devotions upon Emergent Occasions. 1624.
A Sermon upon the Eighth Verse of the First Chapter of the Acts of the Apostles. 1624.
The First Sermon Preached to King Charles. 1625.
Foure Sermons upon Speciall Occasions. 1625.
A Sermon, Preached to the Kings M^{tie.} at Whitehall, 24. Febr. 1625. 1626.
Five Sermons upon Speciall Occasions. 1626.
A Sermon of Commemoration of the Lady Danvers (with George Herbert). 1627.
Deaths Duell. 1632.
Juvenilia; or, Certain Paradoxes and Problems. 1633.
Poems. 1633.
Six Sermons upon Speciall Occasions. 1634.
Sapientia Clamitans. 1638.
LXXX Sermons. 1640.
Biathanatos. 1647.
Fifty Sermons. 1649.
Essayes in Divinity. 1651.
Letters to Severall Persons of Honour. 1651.
Cabala: Mysteries of State. 1654.
A Collection of Letters Made by Sr Tobie Mathews, K^t. 1660.
XXVI Sermons. 1660.
Poetical Works. 1779. 3 vols.
Works. Ed. Henry Alford. 1839. 6 vols.
Poetical Works. Ed. James Russell Lowell. 1855.
Complete Poems. Ed. Alexander B. Grosart. 1872. 2 vols.
Poems. Ed. E. K. Chambers. 1896. 2 vols.
Poems. Ed. Herbert J. C. Grierson. 1912. 2 vols.
Sermons: Selected Passages. Ed. Logan Pearsall Smith. 1919.
Complete Poetry and Selected Prose. Ed. John Hayward. 1929.
Poetry and Prose. Ed. H. W. Garrod. 1946.
Divine Poems. Ed. Helen Gardner. 1952.
Sermons. Eds. George R. Potter and Evelyn M. Simpson. 1953–62. 10 vols.
The Anniversaries. Ed. Frank Manley. 1963.
Elegies and Songs and Sonnets. Ed. Helen Gardner. 1965.
Satires, Epigrams and Verse Letters. Ed. W. Milgate. 1967.
Complete Poetry. Ed. John T. Shawcross. 1967.
Selected Prose. Ed. Evelyn Simpson. 1967.
Complete English Poems. Ed. A. J. Smith. 1971.
Epithalamions, Anniversaries, and Epodes. Ed. W. Milgate. 1978.
Paradoxes and Problems. Ed. Helen Peters. 1980.
Complete English Poems. Ed. C. A. Patrides. 1985.
Selected Prose. Ed. Neil Rhodes. 1987.

GEORGE HERBERT (1593–1633)

Oratio Habita Coram Dominus Legatis. 1623.
Oratio qua Auspicatissimum Serenissimi Principis Caroli Reditum ex Hispaniis Celebravit. 1623.
A Sermon of Commemoration of the Lady Danvers (with John Donne). 1627.
The Temple: Sacred Poems and Private Ejaculations. 1633.
Hygasticon by Leonard Lessius (translator). 1634.
A Priest to the Temple; or, The Countrey Parson His Character, and Rule of Holy Life. 1652.
Remains. 1652.
Works. 1835–36. 2 vols.
Complete Works. Ed. Alexander B. Grosart. 1874. 3 vols.
English Works. Ed. George Herbert Palmer. 1905. 3 vols.
Works. Ed. F. E. Hutchinson. 1941.
Poems. Ed. Helen Gardner. 1961.

Latin Poetry: A Bilingual Edition. Eds. and trs. Mark McCloskey and Paul R. Murphy. 1965.
A Choice of Herbert's Verse. Ed. R. S. Thomas. 1967.
Selected Poems. Ed. Gareth Reeves. 1971.
George Herbert. Ed. W. H. Auden. 1973.
English Poems. Ed. C. A. Patrides. 1974.

JOHN WEBSTER (c. 1578–c. 1634)

The Malcontent (with John Marston). 1604.
The Famous History of Sir Thomas Wyat (with Thomas Dekker). 1607.
West-ward Hoe (with Thomas Dekker). 1607.
North-ward Hoe (with Thomas Dekker). 1607.
The White Divel. 1612.
Three Elegies on the Most Lamented Death of Prince Henry (with Cyril Tourneur and Thomas Heywood). 1613.
The Tragedy of the Dutchesse of Malfy. 1623.
The Devils Law-Case. 1623.
Monuments of Honor. 1624.
Appius of Virginia ⟨with Thomas Heywood?⟩. 1654.
A Cure for a Cuckold (with William Rowley ⟨and Thomas Heywood?⟩). 1661.
Works. Ed. Alexander Dyce. 1830. 4 vols.
Webster and Tourneur. Ed. John Addington Symonds. 1888.
Works. Ed. F. L. Lucas. 1927. 4 vols.
Three Plays. Ed. D. C. Gunby. 1972.
Selected Plays. Eds. Jonathan Dollimore and Alan Sinfield. 1983.

BEN JONSON (c. 1572–1637)

Every Man out of His Humor. 1600.
Every Man in His Humor. 1601.
The Fountaine of Self-Love; or, Cynthias Revels. 1601.
Poetaster; or, The Arraignment. 1602.
Part of King James His Royall and Magnificent Entertainment. 1604.
Sejanus His Fall. 1605.
Eastward Hoe (with George Chapman and John Marston). 1605.
Hymenaei; or, The Solemnities of Masque, and Barriers. 1606.
Volpone; or, The Foxe. 1607.
The Characters of Two Royall Masques, the One of Blacknesse, the Other of Beautie. 1608.
The Masque of Queenes. 1609.
The Case Is Alterd. 1609.
Catiline His Conspiracy. 1611.
The Alchemist. 1612.
Workes. 1616 (First Folio).
Lovers Made Men: A Masque. 1617.
The Masque of Augures. c. 1622.
Time Vindicated to Himselfe, and to His Honors. c. 1623.
Neptunes Triumph for the Returne of Albion. c. 1624.
The Fortunate Isles and Their Union. c. 1625.
Loves Triumph through Callipolis. 1630.
The New Inne; or, The Light Heart. 1631.
Chloridia: Rites to Chloris and Her Nymphs. 1631.
The Gypsies Metamorphos'd. 1640.
Workes. 1640 (Second Folio). 2 vols.
Works. 1692 (Third Folio). 2 vols.
Works. Ed. Peter Whalley. 1756. 7 vols.
Works. Ed. William Gifford. 1816. 9 vols.
Notes on Ben Jonson's Conversations with William Drummond. Ed. David Laing. 1842.
Ben Jonson. Ed. Brinsley Nicholson. 1893–94. 3 vols.

Complete Plays. Ed. Felix E. Schelling. 1906. 2 vols.
Works. Eds. C. H. Herford, Percy Simpson, and Evelyn M. Simpson. 1925–52. 11 vols.
Poems. Ed. Bernard H. Newdigate. 1936.
Selected Works. Ed. Harry Levin. 1938.
Poems. Ed. George Burke Johnston. 1954.
Complete Poetry. Ed. William B. Hunter, Jr. 1963.
Complete Masques. Ed. Stephen Orgel. 1969.
Plays and Masques. Ed. Robert M. Adams. 1979.
Complete Plays. Ed. G. A. Wilkes. 1981. 2 vols.
Complete Poems. Ed. George Parfitt. 1982.

RICHARD CRASHAW (c. 1613–1649)

Epigrammatum Sacrorum Liber. 1634.
Steps to the Temple. 1646.
Carmen Deo Nostro. 1652.
A Letter to the Countess of Denbigh, against Irresolution and Delay in Matters of Religion. 1653.
Poemata et Epigrammata. 1670.
Epigrammata Sacra Selecta. 1682.
Poetry. Ed. Peregrine Philips. 1785.
The Suspicion of Herod. 1834.
Poetical Works. Ed. George Gilfillan. 1857.
Complete Works. Ed. Alexander B. Grosart. 1872–73. 2 vols.
Delights of the Muses. Ed. J. R. Tutin. 1900.
Poems. Ed. A. R. Waller. 1904.
Poems English, Latin, and Greek. Ed. L. C. Martin. 1927.
Complete Poetry. Ed. George Walton Williams. 1970.

ROBERT HERRICK (1591–1674)

Hesperides; or, The Works Both Humane and Divine ⟨with Noble Numbers⟩. 1648.
A Song for Two Voices. c. 1700.
Select Poems from the Hesperides. Ed. John Nott. 1810.
Works. Ed. Thomas Maitland. 1823. 2 vols.
Hesperides. Ed. William Carew Hazlitt. 1869. 2 vols.
Complete Poems. Ed. Alexander B. Grosart. 1876. 3 vols.
Selections. Ed. Austin Dobson. 1882.
Hesperides and Noble Numbers. Ed. Alfred Pollard. 1891. 2 vols.
Poetical Works. Ed. George Saintsbury. 1893. 2 vols.
Lyric Poems. Ed. Ernest Rhys. 1897.
Poems. Ed. Thomas Bailey Aldrich. 1900.
Poems. Ed. John Masefield. 1906.
Poetical Works. Ed. Frederick W. Moorman. 1915. 2 vols.
Poetical Works. Ed. Humbert Wolfe. 1928. 4 vols.
Poetical Works. Ed. Leonard C. Martin. 1956.
Selected Poems. Ed. John Hayward. 1962.
Complete Poetry. Ed. J. Max Patrick. 1963.
Selected Poems. Ed. David Jesson-Dibley. 1980.

JOHN MILTON (1608–1674)

A Maske Presented at Ludlow Castle 1634 ⟨Comus⟩. 1637.
Epitaphium Damonis. c. 1640.
Of Reformation Touching Church Discipline in England, and the Causes That Hitherto Have Hindered It. 1641.
Of Prelatical Episcopacy, and Whether It May Be Deduc'd from the Apostolical Times. 1641.
Animadversions upon the Remonstrant's Defence, against Smectymnuus. 1641.
The Reason of Church-Government Urg'd against Prelaty. 1641.
An Apology against a Pamphlet Call'd A Modest Confutation of the Animadversions upon the Remonstrant against Smectymnuus. 1642.

The Doctrine and Discipline of Divorce. 1643.
Of Education. 1644.
The Judgement of Martin Bucer concerning Divorce (translator). 1644.
Areopagitica: A Speech for the Liberty of Unlicenc'd Printing. 1644.
Colasterion: A Reply to a Nameless Answer against the Doctine and Discipline of Divorce. 1645.
Poems. 1645.
Tetrachordon. 1645.
Poems Both English and Latin. 1645.
The Tenure of Kings and Magistrates. 1649.
Observations upon the Articles of Peace with the Irish Rebels. 1649.
Eikonoklastes. 1649.
Pro Populo Anglicano Defensio. 1651.
Pro Populo Anglicano Defensio Secunda. 1654.
Pro Se Defensio contra Alexandrum Morum. 1655.
The Cabinet Council. 1658.
A Treatise of Civil Power in Ecclesiastical Causes. 1659.
Considerations Touching the Likeliest Means to Remove Hirelings out of the Church. 1659.
The Readie and Easy Way to Establish a Free Commonwealth. 1660.
Brief Notes upon a Late Sermon Titl'd The Fear of God and the King *by Matthew Griffith.* 1660.
Paradise Lost. 1667.
Accedence Commenc't Grammar. 1669.
The History of Britain. 1670.
Paradise Regain'd; to Which Is Added Samson Agonistes. 1671.
Artis Logicae Plenior Institutio. 1672.
Of True Religion, Haeresy, Schism, Toleration, and What Best Means May Be Urg'd against the Growth of Popery. 1673.
Poems upon Several Occasions. 1673.
A Declaration. 1674.
Epistolarum Familiarum Liber. 1674.
Literae Pseudo-Senatus Anglicani. 1676.
Character of the Long Parliament. 1681.
A Brief History of Moscovia. 1682.
Republican Letters. 1682.
Letters of State from the Year 1649 till the Year 1659. 1694.
A Complete Collection of the Historical, Political, and Miscellaneous Works. Ed. John Toland. 1694–98. 3 vols.
Poetical Works. Ed. Patrick Hume. 1695.
Poetical Works. 1707. 2 vols.
Original Letters and Papers of State Addressed to Oliver Cromwell. Ed. John Nickolls. 1743.
Prose Works. Ed. Charles Symmons. 1806. 7 vols.
De Doctrina Christiana Libri. Ed. Charles Richard Sumner. 1825.
Poetical Works. Ed. John Mitford. 1832. 3 vols.
Works in Verse and Prose. Ed. John Mitford. 1841. 8 vols.
Poetical Works. Ed. George Gilfillan. 1853. 2 vols.
Poetical Works. Ed. David Masson. 1874. 3 vols.
A Common-place Book. Ed. A. J. Horwood. 1876.
Sonnets. Ed. Mark Pattison. 1883.
Poetical Works. Ed. H. C. Beeching. 1900.
Poetical Works. Ed. William Aldis Wright. 1903.
Poems. Ed. Herbert J. C. Grierson. 1925. 2 vols.
Works. Eds. Frank Allen Patterson et al. 1931–38. 18 vols.
Private Correspondence and Academic Exercises. Eds. and trs. Phyllis B. Tillyard and E. M. W. Tillyard. 1932.
Poetical Works. Ed. Helen Darbishire. 1952–55. 2 vols.
Complete Prose Works. Eds. Don M. Wolfe et al. 1953– . 8 vols.

The Cambridge Milton. Eds. John Broadbent et al. 1972– .
The Macmillan Milton. Eds. C. A. Patrides et al. 1972– .
Selected Prose. Ed. C. A. Patrides. 1974.

ANDREW MARVELL (1621–1678)

[*An Elegy upon the Death of My Lord Francis Villiers.* c. 1648.]
The First Anniversary of the Government under His Highness the Lord Protector. 1655.
The Character of Holland. 1665.
The Rehearsall Transpros'd. 1672 [Part 1]; 1673 [Part 2].
Mr. Smirke; or, The Divine in Mode. 1676.
An Account of the Growth of Popery and Arbitrary Government in England. 1677.
Remarks upon a Late Disingenuous Discourse by T. D. 1678.
A Short Historical Essay concerning General Councils. 1680.
Miscellaneous Poems. Ed. Mary Palmer (Marvell). 1681.
Works. Ed. Thomas Cooke. 1726. 2 vols.
Works. Ed. Captain Edward Thompson. 1776. 3 vols.
Complete Works. Ed. Alexander B. Grosart. 1872–75. 4 vols.
Poems and Satires. Ed. George A. Aitken. 1892. 2 vols.
Poems and Letters. Ed. H. M. Margoliouth. 1927. 2 vols.
Poems Printed from the Unique Copy in the British Museum, with Some Other Poems. Ed. Hugh Macdonald. 1952.
Selected Poems. Ed. Joseph H. Summers. 1961.
Latin Poetry. Eds. and trs. William A. McQueen and Kiffin A. Rockwell. 1964.
Selected Poetry. Ed. Frank Kermode. 1967.
Complete Poetry. Ed. George deForest Lord. 1968.
Poems and Letters. Ed. H. M. Margoliouth, rev. Pierre Legouis and E. E. Duncan-Jones. 1971. 2 vols.
Complete Poetry. Ed. Elizabeth Story Donno. 1972.
The Press, That Villainous Engine. 1984.

JOHN BUNYAN (1628–1688)

Some Gospel-Truths Opened According to the Scriptures. 1656.
A Vindication of the Book Called Some Gospel-Truths Opened. 1657.
A Few Sighs from Hell; or, The Groans of a Damned Soul. 1658.
The Doctrine of the Law and Grace Unfolded. 1659.
Profitable Meditations, Fitted to Mans Different Condition. c. 1661.
I Will Pray with the Spirit, and I Will Pray with the Understanding Also. 1663.
Christian Behaviour; or, The Fruits of True Christianity. c. 1663.
A Mapp Shewing the Order & Causes of Salvation & Damnation. c. 1663.
One Thing Is Needful; or, Serious Meditations upon the Four Last Things, Death, Judgment, Heaven and Hell; unto Which Is Added, Ebal and Gerizzim; or, The Blessing and the Curse; with Prison Meditations. c. 1665.
The Holy City; or, the New Jerusalem. 1665.
Prison Meditations. 1665.
The Resurrection of the Dead, and Eternall Judgement. c. 1665.
Grace Abounding to the Chief of Sinners. 1666.
A Confession of My Faith, and a Reason of My Practice. 1672.
A Christian Dialogue. c. 1672.
A New and Useful Confordance to the Holy Bible. c. 1672.
A Defence of the Doctrine of Justification, by Faith in Jesus Christ. 1672.
Difference in Judgment about Water-Baptism, No Bar to Communion. 1673.

The Barren Fig-Tree; or, The Doom and Downfall of the Fruitless Professor. 1673.

Peaceable Principles and True; or, A Brief Answer to Mr. D'Anvers and Mr. Paul's Books. c. 1674.

Light for Them That Sit in Darkness. 1675.

Instruction for the Ignorant. 1675.

Saved by Grace; or, A Discourse of the Grace of God. c. 1676.

The Strait Gate; or, Great Difficulty of Going to Heaven. 1676.

The Pilgrim's Progress from This World, to That Which Is to Come. 1678 [Part 1]; 1684 [Part 2].

Come, & Welcome, to Jesus Christ. 1678.

A Treatise of the Fear of God. 1679.

The Life and Death of Mr. Badman, Presented to the World in a Familiar Dialogue Between Mr. Wiseman, and Mr. Attentive. 1680.

The Holy War Made by Shaddai upon Diabolus for the Regaining of the Metropolis of the World; or, The Losing and Taking Again of the Town of Mansoul. 1682.

The Greatness of the Soul, and Unspeakableness of the Loss Thereof. 1683.

A Case of Conscience Resolved. 1683.

A Holy Life, the Beauty of Christianity. 1684.

Seasonable Counsel; or, Advice to Sufferers. 1684.

A Caution to Stir Up to Watch against Sin. c. 1684.

A Discourse upon the Pharisee and the Publicane. 1685.

Questions about the Nature and Perpetuity of the Seventh-Day-Sabbath. 1685.

A Book for Boys and Girls; or, Country Rhimes for Children ⟨*Divine Emblems*⟩. 1686.

Good News for the Vilest of Men; or, A Help for Despairing Souls. 1688.

The Advocateship of Jesus Christ Clearly Explained and Largely Improved. 1688.

A Discourse of the Building, Nature, Excellency, and Government of the House of God. 1688.

The Water of Life; or, A Discourse Shewing the Richness and Glory of the Grace and Spirit of God. 1688.

Solomon's Temple Spiritualiz'd; or, Gospel-Light Fetcht out of the Temple at Jerusalem. 1688.

The Acceptable Sacrifice; or, The Excellency of a Broken Heart. 1689.

Mr John Bunyan's Last Sermon. 1689.

Works. Ed. Charles Doe. 1692.

The Heavenly Foot-Man; or, A Description of the Man That Gets to Heaven. 1698.

Works. Ed. John Wilson. 1736–37. 2 vols.

A Relation of the Imprisonment of Mr. John Bunyan, Minister of the Gospel at Bedford, in November, 1660. 1765.

Works. Ed. George Whitefield. 1767–68. 2 vols.

Works. Ed. George Offor. 1853. 3 vols.

Entire Works. Ed. Henry Stebbing. 1859–60. 4 vols.

Selections. Ed. A. T. Quiller-Couch. 1908.

The Bedside Bunyan: An Anthology of the Writings of John Bunyan. Ed. Arthur Stanley. 1947.

God's Knotty Leg: Selected Writings. Ed. Henri Talon. 1961.

Miscellaneous Works. Eds. Roger Sharrock et al. 1976– .

JOHN DRYDEN (1631–1700)

Three Poems upon the Death of His Late Highnesse Oliver, Lord Protector of England, Scotland and Ireland (with Edmund Waller and Thomas Sprat). 1659.

Astraea Redux. 1660.

To His Sacred Majesty. 1661.

My Lord Chancellor, Presented on New-Years-Day. 1662.

The Rival Ladies. 1664.

The Indian-Queen. 1665.

The Indian Emperour. 1667.

Annus Mirabilis. 1667.

Secret-Love; or, The Maiden Queen. 1668.

*S*ʳ *Martin Mar-All.* 1668.

Of Dramatic Poesy: An Essay. 1668.

The Tempest; or, The Enchanted Island (adaptation; with Sir William D'Avenant). 1670.

Tyrannick Love; or, The Royal Martyr. 1670.

An Evening's Love; or, The Mock-Astrologer. 1671.

The Conquest of Granada by the Spaniards. 1672.

Marriage-à-la-Mode. 1673.

The Assignation; or, Love in a Nunnery. 1673.

Amboyna. 1673.

Notes and Observations on The Empress of Morocco (with Thomas Shadwell and John Crowne). 1674.

Aureng-Zebe. 1676.

The State of Innocence and Fall of Man. 1677.

All for Love; or, The World Well Lost. 1678.

Oedipus (with Nathaniel Lee). 1679.

Troilus and Cressida; or, Truth Found Too Late. 1679.

The Kind Keeper; or, Mr. Limberham. 1680.

Epilogue Spoke before His Majesty at Oxford. 1680.

The Spanish Fryar; or, The Double Discovery. 1681.

His Majesties Declaration Defended. 1681.

Absalom and Achitophel. 1681.

A Prologue Spoken at Mithridates King of Pontus ⟨by Nathaniel Lee⟩. 1682.

Prologue to The Loyal Brother ⟨by Thomas Southerne⟩. 1682.

The Medall: A Satyre against Sedition. 1682.

Mac Flecknoe. 1682.

Prologue to his Royal Highness. 1682.

Prologue to the Duchess on Her Return from Scotland. 1682.

Religio Laici; or, A Layman's Faith. 1682.

The Second Part of Absalom and Achitophel (with Nahum Tate). 1682.

Prologue to the King and Queen. 1683.

The Duke of Guise (with Nathaniel Lee). 1683.

The Vindication of The Duke of Guise. 1683.

Plutarch's Lives (editor). 1683–86. 5 vols.

Prologue ⟨by Thomas Otway⟩ *and Epilogue* ⟨by Dryden⟩ *to* Constantine the Great ⟨by Nathaniel Lee⟩. 1684.

Prologue to The Disappointment ⟨by Thomas Southerne⟩. 1684.

Miscellany Poems (with others). 1685.

Sylvae (with others). 1685.

Threnodia Augustalis. 1685.

Albion and Albanius. 1685.

A Defence of the Papers Written by the Late King of Blessed Memory, and Duchess of York, against the Answer Made to Them. 1686.

The Hind and the Panther. 1687.

A Song for St. Cecilia's Day. 1687.

Britannia Rediviva. 1688.

The Life of St. Francis Xavier by Dominick Bouhours (translator). 1688.

Don Sebastian, King of Portugal. 1690.

Amphitryon; or, The Two Socia's. 1690.

King Arthur; or, The British Worthy. 1691.

Works. 1691.

Eleonora: A Panegyrical Poem Dedicated to the Memory of the Late Countess of Abingdon. 1692.

Cleomenes, the Spartan Heroe. 1692.

The Satires of Decimus Junius Juvenalis, Together with the Satires of Aulus Persius Flaccus (translator; with others). 1693.

Works. 1693. 4 vols.

Examen Poeticum (with others). 1693.

Love Triumphant; or, Nature Will Prevail. 1694.

De Arte Graphica by C. A. Du Fresnoy (translator). 1695.

An Ode on the Death of Mr. Henry Purcell. 1696.

The Works of Virgil (translator). 1697.

Alexander's Feast; or, The Power of Musique. 1697.

The Pilgrim by John Fletcher (adaptation). 1700.

Fables Ancient and Modern (with others). 1700.

Works. 1701. 4 vols.

Poems on Various Occasions and Translations from Several Authors. 1701.

Comedies, Tragedies and Operas. 1701. 2 vols.

Dramatick Works. Ed. William Congreve. 1717. 6 vols.

Original Poems and Translations. Ed. Thomas Broughton. 1743. 2 vols.

Select Essays on the Belles Lettres. 1750.

Poems and Fables. 1753.

Original Poems. 1756. 2 vols.

Miscellaneous Works. Ed. Samuel Derrick. 1760. 4 vols.

Critical and Miscellaneous Prose Works. Ed. Edmond Malone. 1800. 4 vols.

Poetical Works. Ed. Thomas Park. 1806. 3 vols.

Works. Ed. Sir Walter Scott. 1808. 18 vols.

Poetical Works. Ed. H. J. Todd. 1811. 4 vols.

Poetical Works. Ed. John Mitford. 1832–33. 5 vols.

Poetical Works. Ed. Robert Bell. 1854. 3 vols.

Poetical Works. Ed. George Gilfillan. 1854. 2 vols.

Poetical Works. Ed. W. D. Christie. 1870.

Essays. Ed. C. D. Yonge. 1882.

Works. Ed. Sir Walter Scott, rev. George Saintsbury. 1882–93. 18 vols.

Satires. Ed. John Churton Collins. 1893.

Essays. Ed. W. P. Ker. 1900. 2 vols.

Dramatic Essays. Ed. W. H. Hudson. 1912.

Poetry and Prose. Ed. David Nichol Smith. 1925.

Dramatic Works. Ed. Montague Summers. 1931–32. 6 vols.

The Best of Dryden. Ed. Louis I. Bredvold. 1933.

Poems. Ed. Bonamy Dobrée. 1934.

Letters. Ed. Charles E. Ward. 1942.

Selected Poems. Ed. Geoffrey Grigson. 1950.

Prologues and Epilogues. Ed. William Bradford Gardner. 1951.

Poems and Prose. Ed. Douglas Grant. 1955.

Works. Eds. Edward Niles Hooker, H. T. Swedenberg, Jr., et al. 1956– .

Poems. Ed. James Kinsley. 1958. 4 vols.

Of Dramatic Poesy and Other Critical Essays. Ed. George Watson. 1962. 2 vols.

Literary Criticism. Ed. Arthur C. Kirsch. 1966.

Four Comedies. Eds. L. A. Beaurline and Fredson Bowers. 1967.

Four Tragedies. Eds. L. A. Beaurline and Fredson Bowers. 1967.

A Choice of Dryden's Verse. Ed. W. H. Auden. 1973.

DANIEL DEFOE (1660–1731)

[*A Letter to a Dissenter from His Friend at The Hague.* 1688.]

[*Reflections upon the Late Great Revolution.* 1689.]

[*The Advantages of the Present Settlement, and the Great Danger of a Relapse.* 1689.]

[*An Account of the Late Horrid Conspiracy to Depose Their Present Majesties K. William and Q. Mary.* 1691.]

A Compleat History of the Late Revolution. 1691.

A New Discovery of an Old Intreague. 1691.

Reflections upon the Late Horrid Conspiracy Contrived by Some of the French Court to Murther His Majesty in Flanders. 1692.

[*A Dialogue betwixt Whig and Tory.* 1693.]

The Englishman's Choice, and True Interest, in a Vigorous Prosecution of the War against France. 1694.

[*Some Seasonable Queries on the Third Head, viz.: A General Naturalization.* c. 1697.]

The Character of the Late Dr. Samuel Annesley. 1697.

Some Reflections on a Pamphlet Lately Publish'd. 1697.

An Essay upon Projects. 1697.

An Enquiry into the Occasional Conformity of Dissenters. 1697.

An Argument Shewing, That a Standing Army, with Consent of Parliament, Is Not Inconsistent with a Free Government. 1698.

A Brief Reply to the History of Standing Armies in England. 1698.

[*Some Queries concerning the Disbanding of the Army.* 1698.]

The Poor Man's Plea for a Reformation of Manners and Suppressing Immorality in the Nation. 1698.

The Interests of the Several Princes and States of Europe Consider'd. 1698.

Lex Talionis. 1698.

The Pacificator. 1700.

The Two Great Questions Consider'd. 1700.

The Two Great Questions Further Consider'd. 1700.

[*Reasons Humbly Offer'd for a Law to Enact the Castration of Popish Ecclesiastics.* 1700.]

The Six Distinguishing Characters of a Parliament-Man. 1700.

The Danger of the Protestant Religion Consider'd, from the Present Prospect of a Religious War in Europe. 1701.

The True-Born Englishman: A Satyr. 1701.

The Succession to the Crown of England, Considered. 1701.

The Free-Holders Plea against Stock-Jobbing Elections of Parliament Men. 1701.

A Letter to Mr. How. 1701.

The Livery Man's Reasons. 1701.

The Villainy of Stock-Jobbers Detected. 1701.

[*The Apparent Danger of an Invasion.* 1701.]

[*The Present Case of England, and the Protestant Interest.* 1701.]

Legion's Memorial. 1701.

Ye True-Born Englishmen Proceed. 1701.

The History of the Kentish Petition. 1701.

The Present State of Jacobitism Considered. 1701.

An Argument, Shewing that the Prince of Wales, Tho' a Protestant, Has No Just Pretensions to the Crown of England. 1701.

Reasons against a War with France. 1701.

Legion's New Paper. 1702.

The Original Power of the Collective Body of the People of England, Examined and Asserted. 1702.

The Mock-Mourners: A Satyr. 1702.

Reformation of Manners: A Satyr. 1702.

A New Test of the Church of England's Loyalty. 1702.

Good Advice to the Ladies. 1702.

The Spanish Descent. 1702.

An Enquiry into Occasional Conformity. 1702.

The Opinion of a Known Dissenter on the Bill for Preventing Occasional Conformity. 1702.

The Shortest-Way with the Dissenters. 1702.

A Brief Explanation of a Late Pamphlet, Entituled, The Shortest Way with the Dissenters. 1703.

A Dialogue between a Dissenter and the Observator. 1703.

King William's Affection to the Church of England Examin'd. 1703.

A Collection of the Writings of the Author of The True-Born Englishman. 1703.

More Reformation: A Satyr upon Himself. 1703.

The Shortest Way to Peace and Union. 1703.

A True Collection of the Writings of the Author of The True-Born Englishman. 1703–05. 2 vols.

A Hymn to the Pillory. 1703.

The Sincerety of the Dissenters Vindicated. 1703.

A Hymn to the Funeral Sermon. 1703.

The Case of Dissenters as Affected by the Late Bill Proposed in Parliament for Preventing Occasional Conformity. 1703.

An Enquiry into the Case of Mr. Asgil's General Translation. 1703.

A Challenge of Peace, Address'd to the Whole Nation. 1703.

Some Remarks on the First Chapter in Dr. Davenant's Essays. 1703.

Peace without Union. 1703.

The Dissenters Answer to the High-Church Challenge. 1704.

An Essay on the Regulation of the Press. 1704.

A Serious Inquiry into This Grand Question. 1704.

The Parallel. 1704.

A Review of the Affairs of France: and of All Europe. 1704–13. 9 vols.

The Lay-Man's Sermon upon the Late Storm. 1704.

Royal Religion: Being Some Enquiry after the Piety of Princes. 1704.

Moderation Mantain'd. 1704.

Legion's Humble Address to the Lords. 1704.

The Christianity of the High-Church Considered. 1704.

More Short-Ways with the Dissenters. 1704.

[The Address. 1704.]

The Dissenter Misrepresented and Represented. 1704.

A New Test of the Church of England's Honesty. 1704.

The Storm. 1704.

An Elegy on the Author of The True-Born English-man, *with an Essay on the Late Storm.* 1704.

[A True State of the Difference between Sir George Rook Knt and William Colepeper, Esq. 1704.]

A Hymn to Victory. 1704.

The Protestant Jesuite Unmask'd. 1704.

Giving Alms No Charity. 1704.

Queries upon the Bill against Occasional Conformity. 1704.

The Double Welcome: A Poem to the Duke of Marlbro. 1705.

Persecution Anatomiz'd. 1705.

The Consólidator; or, Memoirs of Sundry Transactions from the World in the Moon. 1705.

The Experiment; or, The Shortest Way with the Dissenters Exemplified. 1705.

A Hint to the Blackwell-Hall Factors. 1705.

Advice to All Parties. 1705.

The Dyet of Poland: A Satyr. 1705.

The Ballance; or, A New Test of the High-Fliers of All Sides. 1705.

The High-Church Legion; or, The Memorial Examin'd. 1705.

A Collection from Dyer's Letters. 1705.

Party-Tyranny. 1705.

An Answer to the L⟨or⟩d H⟨aver⟩sham's Speech. 1705.

Declaration without Doors. 1705.

A Hymn to Peace. 1706.

A Reply to a Pamphlet Entituled The L⟨or⟩d H⟨aver⟩sham's Vindication of His Speech. 1706.

The Case of Protestant Dissenters in Carolina. 1706.

Remarks on the Bill to Prevent Frauds Committed by Bankrupts. 1706.

Remarks on the Letter to the Author of the State-Memorial. 1706.

An Essay at Removing National Prejudices against a Union with Scotland. 1706. 4 parts.

An Essay on the Great Battle at Ramellies. 1706.

Jure Divino: A Satyr in Twelve Books. 1706.

A Sermon on the Fitting Up of Dr. Burges's Late Meeting House. c. 1706.

⟨Preface to⟩ De Laune's Plea for the Non-Conformists. 1706.

Daniel Defoe's Hymn for the Thanksgiving. 1706.

A True Relation of the Apparition of One Mrs. Veal. 1706.

A Letter from Mr. Reason, to the High and Mighty Prince of the Mob. 1706.

An Answer to My Lord Beilhaven's Speech. 1706.

The Vision: A Poem. 1706.

[Observations on the Fifth Article of the Treaty of Union. 1706.]

Considerations in Relation to Trade Considered. 1706.

A Seasonable Warning; or, The Pope and King of France Unmasked. 1706.

A Reply to the Scots Answer. 1706.

Caledonia: A Poem in Honour of Scotland, and the Scots Nation. 1706.

[The State of the Excise after the Union. 1706.]

[The State of the Excise &c. Vindicated. 1706.]

A Short Letter to the Glasgow-men. 1706.

The Rabbler Convicted. 1706.

The Advantages of Scotland by an Incorporate Union with England. 1706.

[A Letter concerning Trade, from Several Scots-Gentlemen That Are Merchants in England, to Their Country-men That Are Merchants in Scotland. 1706.]

An Enquiry into the Disposal of the Equivalent. 1706.

A Scots Poem. 1707.

A Fifth Essay, at Removing National Prejudices. 1707.

Two Great Questions Considered. 1707.

The Dissenters in England Vindicated. 1707.

Passion and Prejudice. 1707.

Proposals for Printing by Subscription a Compleat History of the Union. 1707.

[A Discourse upon an Union of the Two Kingdoms of England and Scotland. 1707.]

[Remarks upon the Lord Haversham's Speech in the House of Peers, Feb.15, 1707. 1707.]

A Short View of the Present State of the Protestant Religion in Britain. 1707.

[The True-Born Britain. 1707.]

A Voice from the South. 1707.

A Modest Vindication of the Present Ministry. 1707.

The Trade of Britain Stated. 1707.

An Historical Account of the Bitter Sufferings, and Melancholy Circumstances of the Episcopal Church in Scotland. 1707.

De Foe's Answer to Dyer's Scandalous News Letter. 1707.

Dyers News Examined as to His Swedish Memorial against the Review. 1707.

Reflections upon the Prohibition Act. 1708.

Advice to the Electors of Great Britain. 1708.

[A Memorial to the Nobility of Scotland. 1708.]

[Scotland in Danger. 1708.]

An Answer to a Paper concerning Mr. De Foe. 1708.

The Scot's Narrative Examin'd. 1709.

A Brief History of the Poor Palatine Refugees. 1709.

The History of the Union of Great Britain. 1709.

Parson Plaxton of Barwick. 1709.

A Letter to Mr. Bisset. 1709.

A Letter from Captain Tom to the Mobb. 1710.

A Reproof to Mr. Clark. 1710.

Advertisement from Daniel De Foe, to Mr. Clark. c. 1710.

A Speech without Doors. 1710.

The Age of Wonders. 1710.

Greenshields out of Prison and Toleration Settled in Scotland. 1710.

A Vindication of Dr. Henry Sacheverell. c. 1710.

Instructions from Rome, In Favour of the Pretender. c. 1710.

[*The Recorder of B⟨anbu⟩ry's Speech to Dr. Sach⟨eve⟩rell.* 1710.]

The Ban⟨bur⟩y Apes; or, The Monkeys Chattering to the Magpie. c. 1710.

A Collection of the Several Addresses in the Late King James's Time: Concerning the Conception and Birth of the Pretended Prince of Wales. c. 1710.

[*Dr. Sacheverell's Disappointment at Worcester.* 1710.]

[*A New Map of the Laborious and Painful Travels of Our Blessed High Church Apostle.* 1710.]

[*High-Church Miracles: or Modern Inconsistencies.* 1710.]

[*A Short Historical Account of the Contrivances and Conspiracies of the Men of Dr. Sacheverell's Principles, in the Late Reigns.* c. 1710.]

Four Letters to a Friend in North Britain. 1710.

[*Seldom Comes of Better; or, A Tale of a Lady and Her Servants.* 1710.]

[*A Letter from a Dissenter in the City of a Dissenter in the Country.* 1710.]

An Essay upon Publick Credit. 1710.

A New Test of the Sence of the Nation. 1710.

[*A Letter from a Gentleman at the Court of St. Germains.* 1710.]

A Condoling Letter to the Tattler. c. 1710.

[*Queries to the New Hereditary Right-Men.* 1710.]

An Essay upon Loans. 1710.

A Word against a New Election. 1710.

A Supplement to the Faults on Both Sides. 1710.

The British Visions. 1710.

Atalantis Major. 1710.

R⟨ogue⟩'s on Both Sides. 1711.

A Short Narrative of the Life and Actions of His Grace John, D. of Marlborough. 1711.

Vox Dei & Naturae. 1711.

Counter Queries. c. 1711.

[*The Quaker's Sermon.* 1711.]

[*Captain Tom's Remembrance to His Old Friends the Mob of London, Westminster, Southwark and Wapping.* 1711.]

A Seasonable Caution to the General Assembly. 1711.

[*A Spectators Address to the Whigs.* 1711.]

The Secret History of the October Club, from Its Original to This Time. 1711. 2 parts.

[*The Succession of Spain Consider'd.* 1711.]

Eleven Opinions about Mr. H⟨arle⟩y. 1711.

[*The Re-Representation; or, A Modest Search after the Great Plunderers of the Nation.* 1711.]

[*The Representation Examined: Being Remarks on the State of Religion in England.* 1711.]

Reasons for a Peace; or, The War at an End. 1711.

An Essay upon the Trade to Africa. 1711.

[*The Scotch Medal Decipher'd.* 1711.]

A Speech for Mr. D⟨und⟩asse Younger of Arnistown, If He Should Be Impeach'd. 1711.

A True Account of the Designs and Advantages of the South-Sea Trade. 1711.

An Essay on the South-Sea Trade. 1711.

The True State of the Case between the Government and the Creditors of the Navy. 1711

Reasons Why This Nation Ought to Put a Speedy End to This Expensive War. 1711.

Reasons Why a Party among Us, and Also among the Confederates, Are Obstinately Bent against a Treaty of Peace with the French at This Time. 1711.

Armageddon; or, The Necessity of Carrying On the War. 1711.

The Ballance of Europe. 1711.

[*Worcestershire-Queries about Peace.* 1711.]

An Essay at a Plain Exposition of That Difficult Phrase, A Good Peace. 1711.

The Felonious Treaty. 1711.

An Essay on the History of Parties, and Persecution in Britain. 1711.

A Defence of the Allies and the Late Ministry. 1712.

A Justification of the Dutch from Several Late Scandalous Reflections. 1712.

No Queen; or, No General. 1712.

The Conduct of Parties in England. 1712.

Peace or Poverty. 1712.

Some Queries Humbly Propos'd upon the Bill for Toleration to the Episcopal Clergy in Scotland. c. 1712.

A Letter from a Gentleman in Scotland, to His Friend at London. 1712.

[*The Case of the Poor Skippers and Keel-Men of Newcastle.* c. 1712.]

[*A Farther Case Relating to the Poor Keel-Men of Newcastle.* 1712.]

[*The History of the Jacobite Clubs.* 1712.]

[*Imperial Gratitude.* 1712.]

The Highland Visions; or, The Scots New Prophecy. 1712.

[*Plain English, with Remarks and Advice to Some Men Who Need Not Be Nam'd.* 1712.]

Wise as Serpents: Being an Enquiry into the Present Circumstances of the Dissenters. 1712.

The Present State of the Parties in Great Britain. 1712.

Reasons against Fighting. 1712.

The Present Negotiations of Peace Vindicated from the Imputation of Trifling. 1712.

The Validity of the Renunciations of Foreign Powers Enquired Into. 1712.

An Enquiry into the Danger and Consequences of a War with the Dutch. 1712.

A Further Search into the Conduct of the Allies and the Late Ministry as to Peace and War. 1712

The Justice and Necessity of a War with Holland. 1712.

An Enquiry into the Real Interest of Princes in the Persons of Their Ambassadors. 1712.

A Seasonable Warning and Caution against the Insinuations of Papists and Jacobites in Favour of the Pretender. 1712.

Hannibal at the Gates; or, The Progress of Jacobitism. 1712.

A Strict Enquiry into the Circumstances of a Late Duel. 1713.

Reasons against the Succession of the House of Hanover. 1713.

[*Not⟨tingh⟩am Politicks Examin'd.* 1713.]

The Second-Sighted Highlander. 1713.

And What if the Pretender Should Come? 1713.

An Answer to a Question That No Body Thinks Of, viz.: But What If the Queen Should Die? 1713.

An Essay on the Treaty of Commerce with France. 1713.

An Account of the Abolishing of Duels in France. 1713.

Union and No Union. 1713.

Mercator. 1713–14. 181 nos.

Considerations upon the Eighth and Ninth Articles of the Treaty of Commerce and Navigation. 1713.

Some Thoughts upon the Subject of Commerce with France. 1713.

The Trade of Scotland with France, Consider'd. 1713.

A General History of Trade. 1713. 4 parts.

The Honour and Prerogative of the Queen's Majesty Vindicated. 1713.

Memoirs of Count Tariff. 1713.

A Brief Account of the Present State of the African Trade. 1713.

[*Reasons concerning the Immediate Demolishing of Dunkirk.* 1713.]

[*A Letter from a Member of the House of Commons to His Friends in the Country, Relating to the Bill of Commerce.* 1713.]

Whigs Turn'd Tories, and Hanoverian-Tories, from Their Avow'd Principles, Prov'd Whigs; or, Each Side in the Other Mistaken. 1713.

A View of the Real Dangers of the Succession, from the Peace with France. 1713.

Extracts from Several Mercators. 1713.

A Letter to the Dissenters. 1713.

Proposals for Imploying the Poor in and about the City of London. 1713.

A Letter to the Whigs. 1714.

Memoirs of John, Duke of Melfort. 1714.

The Scots Nation and Union Vindicated. 1714.

Reasons for Im⟨peaching⟩ the L⟨or⟩d H⟨igh⟩ T⟨reasure⟩r, and Some Others of the P⟨resent⟩ M⟨inistry⟩. 1714.

[*A Letter to Mr. Steele.* 1714.]

The Remedy Worse Than the Disease. 1714.

The Weakest Go to the Wall; or, The Dissenters Sacrific'd by All Parties. 1714.

A Brief Survey of the Legal Liberties of the Dissenters. 1714.

The Schism Act Explain'd. 1714.

The Secret History of the White Staff. 1714–15. 3 parts.

Advice to the People of Great Britain. 1714.

A Secret History of One Year. 1714.

[*Tories and Tory Principles Ruinous to Both Prince and People.* 1714.]

[*Impeachment, or No Impeachment.* 1714.]

[*The Bristol Riot.* 1714.]

The Pernicious Consequences of the Clergy's Intermedling with Affairs of State, with Reasons Humbly Offer'd for Passing a Bill to Incapacitate Them from the Like Practice for the Future. c. 1714.

[*A Full and Impartial Account of the Late Disorders in Bristol.* 1714.]

The Secret History of the Secret History of the White Staff, Purse and Mitre. 1715.

Strike While the Iron's Hot. 1715.

Memoirs of the Conduct of Her Late Majesty and Her Last Ministry. 1715.

Treason Detected. 1715.

The Immorality of the Priesthood. 1715.

The Secret History of State Intrigues in the Management of the Scepter. 1715.

The Candidate: Being a Detection of Bribery and Corruption as It Is Just Now in Practice All over Great Britain. 1715.

A Reply to a Traiterous Libel, Entituled, English Advice to the Freeholders of Great Britain. 1715.

The Protestant Jubilee. 1715.

[*A Letter to a Merry Young Gentleman Intituled Tho. Burnet, Esq.* 1715.]

Burnet and Bradbury; or, The Confederacy of the Press and Pulpit for the Blood of the Last Ministry. 1715.

A View of the Present Management of the Court of France. 1715.

The Fears of the Pretender Turn'd into the Fears of Debauchery. 1715.

A Friendly Epistle by Way of Reproof from One of the People Called Quakers. 1715.

An Appeal to Honour and Justice, Tho' It Be of His Worst Enemies, by Daniel De Foe. 1715.

[*Some Reasons Offered by the Late Ministry in Defence of Their Administration.* 1715.]

The Family Instructor. 1715.

A Sharp Rebuke from One of the People Called Quakers to Henry Sacheverell. 1715.

An Apology for the Army. 1715.

The Second-Sighted Highlander. 1715.

Some Methods to Supply the Defects of the Late Peace. 1715.

[*A Remonstrance from Some Country Whigs to a Member of a Secret Committee.* 1715.]

[*The Happiness of the Hanover Succession.* 1715.]

An Attempt towards a Coalition of English Protestants. 1715.

An Account of the Riots, Tumults, and Other Treasonable Practices since His Majesty's Accession to the Throne (editor). 1715.

A Seasonable Expostulation with, and Friendly Reproof unto, James Butler. 1715.

[*His Majesty's Obligations to the Whigs Plainly Proved.* 1715.]

A Brief History of the Pacifick Campaign in Flanders Anno 1712, and of the Fatal Cessation of Arms. 1715.

Some Considerations on the Danger of the Church from Her Own Clergy. 1715.

A Letter from a Gentleman of the Church of England. 1715.

An Humble Address to Our Soveraign Lord the People. 1715.

The History of the Wars of His Present Majesty Charles XII King of Sweden. 1715.

An Account of the Conduct of Robert Earl of Oxford. 1715.

A Hymn to the Mob. 1715.

Hanover or Rome: Shewing the Absolute Necessity of Assisting His Majesty. 1715.

An Account of the Great and Generous Actions of James Butler (Late Duke of Ormond). 1715.

A View of the Scots Rebellion. 1715.

The Traiterous and Foolish Manifesto of the Scots Rebels. 1715.

Bold Advice; or, Proposals for the Entire Rooting Out of Jacobitism in Great Britain. 1715.

[*An Address to the People of England, Shewing the Unworthiness of Their Behavior to King George.* 1715.]

A Trumpet Blown in the North, and Sounded in the Ears of John Eriskine. 1715.

[*A Letter from One Clergy-Man to Another, upon the Subject of the Rebellion.* 1715.]

[*A Conference with a Jacobite, Wherein the Clergy of the Church of England Are Vindicated from the Charge of Hypocrisy and Perjury.* 1716.]

[*Proper Lessons for the Tories.* 1716.]

Some Account of the Two Nights Court at Greenwich. 1716.

[*The Case of the Protestant Dissenters in England.* 1716.]

[*The Address of the Episcopal Clergy to the Diocese of Aberdeen,*

to the Pretender, with Remarks upon the Said Address. 1716.]

[*The Address of the Magistrates and Town Council of Aberdeen, to the Pretender, with Remarks upon the Said Address.* 1716.]

Some Thoughts of an Honest Tory in the Country, upon the Late Dispositions of Some People to Revolt. 1716.

[*The Declaration of the Free-Holders of Great Britain, in Answer to That of the Pretender.* 1716.]

The Conduct of Some People, about Pleading Guilty, with Some Reasons Why It Was Not Thought Proper to Show Mercy to Some Who Desir'd It. 1716.

An Account of the Proceedings against the Rebels, and Other Prisoners, Tried before the Lord Chief Justice Jefferies. 1716.

The Proceedings of the Government against the Rebels, Compared with the Persecutions of the Late Reigns. 1716.

[*Remarks upon the Speech of James late Earl of Derwentwater, Beheaded on Tower-Hill for High-Treason.* 1716.]

An Essay upon Buying and Selling of Speeches. 1716.

Some Considerations on a Law for Triennial Parliaments. 1716.

The Triennial Act Impartially Stated. 1716.

Arguments about the Alteration of Triennial Elections of Parliament. 1716.

[*The Ill Consequences of Repealing the Triennial Act.* 1716.]

[*A Dialogue between a Whig and a Jacobite, upon the Subject of the Late Rebellion.* 1716.]

A True Account of the Proceedings at Perth. 1716.

Remarks on the Speeches of William Paul Clerk, and John Hall of Otterburn, Esq., Executed at Tyburn for Rebellion, the 13th of July 1716. 1716.

[*The Annals of King George.* 1716–17. 2 vols.]

The Layman's Vindication of the Church of England. 1716.

Secret Memoirs of the New Treaty of Alliance with France. 1716.

Secret Memoirs of a Treasonable Conference at S⟨omerset⟩ House. 1717.

[*Some National Grievances Considered.* 1717.]

The Danger of Court Differences; or, The Unhappy Effects of a Motley Ministry. 1717.

The Quarrel of the School-Boys at Athens. 1717.

[*Faction in Power; or, The Mischiefs and Dangers of a High-Church Magistracy.* 1717.]

An Impartial Enquiry into the Conduct of the Right Honourable Charles Lord Viscount T⟨ownshend⟩. 1717.

An Argument Proving That the Design of Employing and Enobling Foreigners Is a Treasonable Conspiracy. 1717.

[*An Account of the Swedish and Jacobite Plot.* 1717.]

A Curious Little Oration Deliver'd by Father Andrew. 1717.

An Expostulatory Letter to the B⟨ishop⟩ of B⟨angor⟩. 1717.

Fair Payment No Spunge. 1717.

What If the Swedes Should Come? 1717.

The Question Fairly Stated, Whether Now Is the Time to Do Justice to the Friends of the Government as Well as to Its Enemies? 1717.

Christianity No Creature of the State. 1717.

The Danger and Consequences of Disobliging the Clergy Consider'd. 1717.

[*Reasons for a Royal Visitation.* 1717.]

Memoirs of the Church of Scotland. 1717.

A Farther Argument against Enobling Foreigners. 1717.

The Conduct of Robert Walpole, Esq. 1717.

[*The Report Reported.* 1717.]

A Short View of the Conduct of the King of Sweden. 1717.

[*A General Pardon Consider'd.* 1717.]

Observation on the Bishop's Answer to Dr. Snape, by a Lover of Truth. 1717.

[*A Vindication of Dr. Snape.* 1717.]

A Reply to the Remarks upon the Lord Bishop of Bangor's Treatment of the Clergy and Convocation. 1717.

Minutes of the Negotiations of Monsr. Mesnager at the Court of England towards the Close of the Last Reign. 1717.

Memoirs of Some Transactions during the Late Ministry of Robert E. of Oxford. 1717.

A Declaration of Truth to Benjamin Hoadly. 1717.

[*A History of the Clemency of Our English Monarchs.* 1717.]

The Conduct of Christians Made a Sport of Infidels. 1717.

[*The Old Whig and Modern Whig Revived.* 1717.]

A Letter to Andrew Snape. 1717.

The Case of the War in Italy Stated. 1717.

Considerations on the Present State of Affairs in Great-Britain. 1718.

The Defection Farther Consider'd. 1718.

Some Persons Vindicated against the Author of the Defection. 1718.

Memoirs of the Life and Eminent Conduct of That Learned and Reverend Divine Daniel Williams, D.D. 1718.

Mr. de la Pillonniere's Vindication. 1718.

The New British Inquisition; or, The Racking of Mr. Pillonniere. 1718.

[*A Brief Answer to a Long Libel.* 1718.]

A Letter from the Jesuits to Father de la Pillonniere. 1718.

[*A Golden Mine of Treasure Open'd for the Dutch.* 1718.]

Miserere Cleri; or, The Factions of the Church. 1718.

[*Some Reasons Why It Could Not Be Expected That the Government Wou'd Permit the Speech or Paper of James Shepheard.* 1718.]

[*The Jacobites Detected.* 1718.]

[*Dr. Sherlock's Vindication of the Test Act Examin'd.* 1718.]

[*A Brief Comment upon His Majesty's Speech.* 1718.]

A Vindication of the Press. 1718.

[*A Letter from Some Protestant Dissenting Laymen.* 1718.]

Memoirs of Publick Transactions in the Life and Ministry of His Grace the D. of Shrewsbury. 1718.

[*A Letter from Paris, Giving an Account of the Death of the Late Queen Dowager.* 1718.]

A History of the Last Session of the Present Parliament. 1718.

A Letter to the Author of the Flying-Post. 1718.

A Continuation of Letters Written by a Turkish Spy at Paris. 1718.

The History of the Reign of King George. 1718.

The Memoirs of Majr. Alexander Ramkins. 1718.

A Friendly Rebuke to One Parson Benjamin. 1719.

[*Observations and Remarks upon the Declaration of War against Spain.* 1719.]

[*Merry Andrew's Epistle to His Old Master Benjamin.* 1719.]

The Life and Strange Surprizing Adventures of Robinson Crusoe, of York, Mariner, Written by Himself. 1719.

A Letter to the Dissenters. 1719.

The Anatomy of Exchange-Alley. 1719.

Some Account of the Life and Most Remarkable Actions of George Henry Baron de Goertz. 1719.

The Just Complaint of the Poor Weavers Truly Represented. 1719.

The Farther Adventures of Robinson Crusoe: Being the Second and Last Part of His Life. 1719.

The Gamester. 1719. 2 nos.

A Brief State of the Question, between the Printed and Painted Callicoes and the Woollen and Silk Manufacture. 1719.

Charity Still a Christian Virtue. 1719.

The Dumb Philosopher; or, Great Britain's Wonder. 1719.

The King of Pirates: Being an Account of the Famous Enterprises of Captain Avery, the Mock King of Madagascar, with His Rambles and Piracies. 1719.

The Female Manufacturers Complaint. 1720.

An Historical Account of the Voyages and Adventures of Sir Walter Raleigh, with the Discoveries and Conquests He Made for the Crown of England. 1720.

The History of the Wars, of His Present Majesty Charles XII, King of Sweden, with a Continuation to the Time of His Death. 1720.

The Chimera; or, The French Way of Paying National Debts Laid Open. 1720.

[*The Case of the Fair Traders.* 1720.]

The Trade to India Critically and Calmly Consider'd. 1720.

The Case Fairly Stated between the Turky Company and the Italian Merchants. 1720.

[*The Compleat Art of Painting* by C. A. Du Fresnoy (translator). 1720.]

[*A Letter to the Author of the* Independent Whig. 1720.]

[*The History of the Life and Adventures of Mr. Duncan Campbell, a Gentleman.* 1720.]

Memoirs of a Cavalier; or, A Military Journal of the Wars in Germany, and the Wars in England, from the Year 1632 to the Year 1648. 1720.

The Manufacturer. 1719–20.

The Life, Adventures, and Pyracies of the Famous Captain Singleton. 1720.

Serious Reflections during the Life and Surprising Adventures of Robinson Crusoe, with His Vision of the Angelick World. 1720.

[*The South-Sea Scheme Examin'd.* 1720.]

A True State of the Contracts Relating to the Third Money-Subscription Taken by the South-Sea Company. 1721.

A Vindication of the Honour and Justice of Parliament. 1721.

Brief Observations on Trade and Manufactures. 1721.

The Case of Mr. Law, Truly Stated. 1721.

A Collection of Miscellany Letters, Selected out of Mist's Weekly Journal (editor). 1722. 4 vols.

The Fortunes and Misfortunes of the Famous Moll Flanders, Written from Her Own Memorandums. 1722.

Due Preparations for the Plague as Well for Soul as Body. 1722.

Religious Courtship: Being Historical Discourses, on the Necessity of Marrying Religious Husbands and Wives Only. 1722.

A Journal of the Plague Year: Being Observations or Memorial of the Most Remarkable Occurrences, as Well Public as Private, Which Happened in London during the Last Great Visitation in 1665. 1722.

A Brief Debate upon the Dissolving the Last Parliament. 1722.

An Impartial History of the Life and Actions of Peter Alexowitz, the Present Czar of Muscovy. 1722.

The History and Remarkable Life of the Truly Honourable Col. Jacque, Commonly Call'd Col. Jack. 1722.

[*A Memorial to the Clergy of the Church of England.* 1723.]

[*The Wickedness of a Disregard to Others.* 1723.]

[*Considerations on Publick Credit.* 1724.]

The Fortunate Mistress; or, A History of the Life and Vast Variety of Fortunes of Mademoiselle de Beleau, Afterwards Called the Countess de Wintselsheim, in Germany, Being the Person Known by the Name of the Lady Roxana, in the Time of King Charles II. 1724.

The Great Law of Subordination Consider'd. 1724.

A General History of the Robberies and Murders of the Most Notorious Pyrates, and Also Their Policies, Discipline and Government, from Their First Rise and Settlement in the Island of Providence, in 1717, to the Present Year 1724. 1724.

A Tour thro' the Whole Island of Great Britain, Divided into Circuits or Journies. 1724–26. 3 vols.

The Royal Progress. 1724.

A Narrative of the Proceedings in France. 1724.

A Narrative of All the Robberies, Escapes Etc. of John Sheppard: Giving an Exact Description of the Manner of His Wonderful Escape from the Castle in Newgate. 1724.

Some Farther Account of the Original Disputes in Ireland. 1724.

The History of the Remarkable Life of John Sheppard. 1724.

A New Voyage round the World. 1724.

[*An Epistle from Jack Sheppard.* 1725.]

The Life of Jonathan Wild. 1725.

Every-body's Business in No-body's Business. 1725.

The True and Genuine Account of the Life and Actions of the Late Jonathan Wild. 1725.

An Account of the Conduct and Proceedings of the Late John Gow, Alias Smith, Captain of the Late Pirates. 1725.

The Complete English Tradesman, in Familiar Letters. 1725.

A General History of Discoveries and Improvements, in Useful Arts. 1725–26. 4 parts.

A Brief Case of the Distillers. 1726.

A Brief Historical Account of the Lives of the Six Notorious Street-Robbers. 1726.

An Essay upon Literature. 1726.

The Political History of the Devil. 1726.

Unparallel'd Cruelty; or, The Tryal of Captain Jeane of Bristol. 1726.

The Friendly Daemon; or, The Generous Apparition. 1726.

The Four Years Voyages of Capt. George Roberts: Being a Series of Uncommon Events, Which Befell Him in a Voyage to the Islands of the Canaries, Cape de Verde and Barbadoes, from Whence He Was Bound to the Coast of Guiney. 1726.

Mere Nature Delineated; or, A Body without a Soul. 1726.

Some Considerations upon Street-Walkers. 1726.

The Protestant Monastery. 1726.

A System of Magick; or, A History of the Black Art. 1726.

The Evident Approach of a War, and Something of the Necessity of It, in Order to Establish Peace and Preserve Trade. 1727.

Conjugal Lewdness; or, Matrimonial Whoredom. 1727.

The Evident Advantages to Great Britain and Its Allies from the Approaching War, Especially in Matters of Trade. 1727.

A Brief Deduction of the Original Progress and Immense Greatness of the British Woolen Manufacture. 1727.

An Essay on the History and Reality of Apparitions. 1727.

A New Family Instructor. 1727.

Parochial Tyranny. 1727.

Some Considerations on the Reasonableness and Necessity of Encreasing and Encouraging the Seamen. 1728.

Augusta Triumphens; or, The Way to Make London the Most Flourishing City in the Universe. 1728.

A Plan of the English Commerce. 1728.

[*The Memoirs of an English Officer.* 1728.]

Atlas Maritimus and Commercialis. 1728.

The History of the Pyrates. 1728.

An Impartial Account of the Late Famous Siege of Gibraltar. 1728.

Second Thoughts Are Best; or, A Further Improvement of a Late Scheme to Prevent Street Robberies. 1728.

Street-Robberies, Consider'd: The Reason of Their Being So Frequent, with Probable Means to Prevent 'Em, Written by a Converted Thief; to Which Is Prefixed Some Memoirs of His Life. 1728.

Reasons for a War, in Order to Establish the Tranquillity and Commerce of Europe. 1729.

The Unreasonableness and Ill Consequences of Imprisoning the Body for Debt. 1729.

An Humble Proposal to the People of England, for the Encrease of Their Trade. 1729.

An Enquiry into the Pretensions of Spain to Gibraltar. 1729.

Some Objections Humbly Offered to the Consideration of the Hon. House of Commons, Relating to the Present Intended Relief of Prisoners. 1729.

The Advantages of Peace and Commerce; with Some Remarks on the East-India Trade. 1729.

Madagascar; or, Robert Drury's Journal, during Fifteen Years Captivity on That Island, Written by Himself, Digested into Order, and Now Published at the Request of His Friends (editor). 1729.

A Brief State of the Inland or Home Trade of England. 1730.

The Perjur'd Free Mason Detected, and Yet the Honour and Antiquity of the Society of Free Masons Preserv'd and Defended, by a Free Mason. 1730.

Fortune's Fickle Distribution. 1730.

An Effectual Scheme for the Immediate Preventing of Street Robberies. 1730.

Novels. Ed. Sir Walter Scott. 1810. 12 vols.

Novels and Miscellaneous Works. 1840–41. 20 vols.

Life and Recently Discovered Writings. Ed. William Lee. 1869. 3 vols.

The Compleat English Gentleman. Ed. K. D. Bülbring. 1890.

Romances and Narratives. Ed. George A. Aitken. 1895. 16 vols.

Of Royall Education: A Fragmentary Treatise. Ed. K. D. Bülbring. 1895.

Works. Ed. G. H. Maynadier. 1903–04. 16 vols.

Novels and Selected Writings. 1927–28. 14 vols.

A Review of the Affairs of France: and of All Europe. Ed. A. W. Secord. 1938. 22 vols.

Meditations. Ed. George H. Healy. 1946.

Letters. Ed. George H. Healy. 1955.

ALEXANDER POPE (1688–1744)

An Essay on Criticism. 1711.

Windsor-Forest. 1713.

Ode for Musick ⟨*Ode on St. Cecilia's Day*⟩. 1713.

Proposals for a Translation of Homer's Ilias. 1713.

The Narrative of Dr. Robert Norris. 1713.

The Rape of the Lock: An Heroi-comical Poem. 1714.

The Temple of Fame: A Vision. 1715.

A Key to the Lock; or, A Treatise Proving, beyond All Contradiction, the Dangerous Tendency of a Late Poem, Entituled, The Rape of the Lock, to Government and Religion. 1715.

The Dignity, Use and Abuse of Glass-Bottles. 1715.

The Iliad of Homer (translator). 1715 [Books 1–4]; 1716 [Books 5–8]; 1717 [Books 9–12]; 1718 [Books 13–16]; 1720 [Books 17–21]; 1720 [Books 22–24].

A Full and True Account of a Horrid and Barbarous Revenge by Poison on the Body of Mr. Edmund Curll, Bookseller. 1716.

To the Ingenious Mr. Moore, Author of the Celebrated Worm-Powder. 1716.

A Further Account of the Most Deplorable Condition of Mr. Edmund Curll, Bookseller. 1716.

A Roman Catholick Version of the First Psalm. 1716.

God's Revenge against Punning. 1716.

Pope's Miscellany (editor). 1717. 2 vols.

Three Hours after Marriage (with John Gay and John Arbuthnot). 1717.

The Court Ballad. 1717.

Works. 1717 [Volume 1]; 1735 [Volume 2].

A Complete Key to the Non-Juror. 1718.

Eloisa to Abelard. 1719.

Duke upon Duke. 1720.

The Works of John Sheffield, Duke of Buckingham (editor). 1723.

The Works of Shakespear (editor). 1723–25. 6 vols.

The Odyssey of Homer (translator). 1725 [Books 1–4]; 1726 [Books 5–9]; 1725 [Books 10–14]; 1726 [Books 15–19]; 1726 [Books 20–24].

The Discovery. 1727.

A Receipt to Make a Soop. 1727.

Miscellanies in Prose and Verse (with Jonathan Swift and John Arbuthnot). 1727 [Volumes 1–2]; 1732 [Volume 3].

The Dunciad. 1728.

Posthumous Works in Prose and Verse by William Wycherley (editor; with Lewis Theobald). 1728–29. 2 vols.

The Dunciad Variorum. 1729.

An Epistle to the Right Honourable Richard Earl of Burlington ⟨*Moral Essays 4*⟩. 1731.

Of the Use of Riches: An Epistle to the Right Honorable Allen Lord Bathurst ⟨*Moral Essays 3*⟩. 1733.

The First Satire of the Second Book of Horace (adaptation). 1733.

An Essay on Man. 1733 [Epistle 1]; 1733 [Epistle 2]; 1733 [Epistle 3]; 1734 [Epistle 4].

The Impertinent by John Donne (adaptation). 1733.

An Epistle to the Right Honourable Richard Lord Visc$^{t.}$ Cobham ⟨*Moral Essays 1*⟩. 1734.

The Second Satire of the Second Book of Horace (adaptation). 1734.

Sober Advice from Horace. 1734.

An Epistle to Dr. Arbuthnot. 1735.

Of the Characters of Women: An Epistle to a Lady ⟨*Moral Essays 2*⟩. 1735.

Letters (with Sir William Trumbull, Richard Steele, and Joseph Addison). 1735.

A Narrative of the Method by Which the Private Letters of Mr. Pope Have Been Procured and Published by Edmund Curll. 1735.

Ethic Epistles, Satires, &c. 1735.

New Letters (with others). 1736.

Poems: A Chosen Selection. 1736.

Works. 1736. 4 vols.

Horace: His Ode to Venus (adaptation). 1737.

Works in Prose. 1737 [Volume 1]; 1741 [Volume 2].

The Second Epistle of the Second Book of Horace (adaptation). 1737.

The First Epistle of the Second Book of Horace (adaptation). 1737.

The Sixth Epistle of the First Book of Horace (adaptation). 1738.

An Imitation of the Sixth Satire of the Second Book of Horace. 1738.

The First Epistle of the First Book of Horace (adaptation). 1738.

One Thousand Seven Hundred and Thirty Eight. 1738.

The Universal Prayer. 1738.

Poems and Imitations of Horace. 1738.

Selecta Poemata Italorum Qui Latine Scripserunt (editor). 1740. 2 vols.

Memoirs of the Extraordinary Life, Works, and Discoveries of Martinus Scriblerus (with John Arbuthnot). 1741.

The New Dunciad. 1742.

A Blast upon Bays; or, A New Lick at the Laureate. 1742.

Verses on the Grotto at Twickenham. 1743.

Last Will and Testament. 1744.

The Character of Katharine, Late Duchess of Buckingham and Normanby. 1746.

Works. Ed. William Warburton. 1751. 9 vols.

Works. Ed. Joseph Warton. 1797. 9 vols.

Works. Ed. William Lisle Bowles. 1806. 10 vols.

Works. Ed. Alexander Dyce. 1831. 3 vols.

Works. Ed. Robert Carruthers. 1853. 4 vols.

Works. Eds. Whitwell Elwin and William John Courthope. 1871–89. 10 vols.

Collected Poems. Ed. Bonamy Dobrée. 1924.

The Best of Pope. Ed. George Sherburn. 1929.

Prose Works. Eds. Norman Ault and Maynard Mack. 1936. Vol. 1 only.

Works (Twickenham Edition). Eds. John Butt et al. 1939–69. 11 vols.

Selected Poetry and Prose. Ed. W. K. Wimsatt. 1951.

Correspondence. Ed. George Sherburn. 1956. 5 vols.

Poetical Works. Ed. Herbert Davis. 1966.

JONATHAN SWIFT (1667–1745)

A Discourse of the Contests and Dissensions between the Nobles and the Commons in Athens and Rome. 1701.

A Tale of a Tub, Written for the Universal Improvement of Mankind; to Which Is Added an Account of a Battel between the Antient and Modern Books in St. James's Library. 1704.

Predictions for the Year 1708, by Isaac Bickerstaff Esq. 1708.

The Accomplishment of the First of Mr. Bickerstaff's Predictions: Being an Account of the Death of Mr. Partrige. 1708.

An Elegy on Mr. Patrige, the Almanack-Maker. 1708.

A Vindication of Isaac Bickerstaff Esq. 1709.

A Letter from a Member of the House of Commons in Ireland to a Member of the House of Commons in England, concerning the Sacramental Test. 1709.

Baucis and Philemon, Imitated from Ovid. 1709.

A Meditation upon a Broom-Stick. 1710.

The Virtues of Sid Hamet the Magician's Rod. 1710.

A Learned Comment upon Dr. Hare's Excellent Sermon Preach'd before the D. of Marlborough on the Surrender of Bouchain (with Mary de la Rivière Manley). 1711.

An Apology for the Tale of a Tub. 1711.

A Short Character of His Excellency T. E. of W⟨harton⟩. 1711.

Some Remarks upon a Pamphlet, Entitl'd, A Letter to the Seven Lords of the Committee Appointed to Examine Gregg. 1711.

Miscellanies in Prose and Verse. 1711.

A New Journey to Paris by Sieur de Baudrier (translator). 1711.

The Conduct of the Allies. 1711.

An Excellent New Song: Being the Intended Speech of a Famous Orator against Peace. 1711.

The W—ds—r Prophecy. 1711.

Some Advice Humbly Offer'd to the Members of the October Club, in a Letter from a Person of Honour. 1712.

The Fable of Midas. 1712.

Some Remarks on the Barrier Treaty between Her Majesty and the States-General. 1712.

A Proposal for Correcting, Improving, and Ascertaining the English Tongue. 1712.

Some Reasons to Prove, That No Person Is Obliged by His Principles, as a Whig, to Oppose Her Majesty or Her Present Ministry. 1712.

T–l–nd's Invitation to Dismal, to Dine with the Calves-Head Club. 1712.

Peace and Dunkirk. 1712.

A Hue and Cry after Dismal. 1712.

Dunkirk Still in the Hands of the French. 1712. Lost.

A Letter from the Pretender to a Whig-Lord. 1712.

*A Letter of Thanks from My Lord W****n to the Lord B^p of S. Asaph.* 1712.

Mr. C——n's Discourse of Free-Thinking. 1713.

Part of the Seventh Epistle of the First Book of Horace Imitated. 1713.

The Importance of the Guardian Considered. 1713.

A Preface to the B——p of S–r–m's Introduction to the Third Volume of the History of the Reformation of the Church of England. 1713.

The First Ode of the Second Book of Horace Paraphras'd. 1714.

The Publick Spirit of the Whigs. 1714.

A Rebus Written by a Lady, on the Rev. D—n S——t, with His Answer. c. 1714.

A Letter from a Lay-Patron to a Gentleman, Designing for Holy Orders. 1720.

A Proposal for the Universal Use of Irish Manufacture. 1720.

An Elegy on the Much Lamented Death of Mr. Demar. 1720.

Miscellaneous Works Comical and Diverting. 1720.

Run upon the Bankers. 1720.

The Bubble. 1721.

The Present Miserable State of Ireland. 1721.

Epilogue to Be Spoke at the Theatre-Royal This Present Saturday in the Behalf of the Distressed Weavers. 1721.

The Bank Thrown Down. 1721.

[*Subscribers to the Bank Plac'd According to Their Order and Quality.* 1721.]

[*A Letter to the K⟨ing⟩ at Arms from a Reputed Esquire, One of the Subscribers to the Bank.* 1721.]

[*The Wonderful Wonder of Wonders.* 1722.]

The Last Speech and Dying Words of Ebenezor Elliston. 1722.

The First of April. c. 1723.

Some Arguments against Enlarging the Power of Bishops in Letting of Leases. 1723.

A Letter to the Shop-Keepers, Tradesmen, Farmers, and Common People of Ireland, concerning the Brass Half-Pence Coined by Mr. Woods, by M. B. Drapier. 1724.

A Letter to Mr. Harding the Printer, by M. B. Drapier. 1724.

Some Observations upon a Paper, Call'd, The Report of the Committee of the Most Honourable the Privy-Council in England, Relating to Wood's Half-Pence, by M. B. Drapier. 1724.

A Serious Poem upon William Wood. 1724.

A Letter to the Whole People of Ireland, by M. B. Drapier. 1724.

To His Grace the Arch-Bishop of Dublin. 1724.

An Excellent New Song upon His Grace Our Good Lord Archbishop of Dublin. 1724.

Prometheus. 1724.

Seasonable Advice. 1724.

The Presentment of the Grand-Jury of the County of the City of Dublin. 1724.

A Letter to the Right Honourable the Lord Viscount Molesworth, by M. B. Drapier. 1724.

[*A Second Letter from a Friend to the Right Honourable —— ——.* 1725.]

His Grace's Answer to Jonathan. 1725.

Sphinx. 1725.

Fraud Detected; or, The Hibernian Patriot ⟨*The Drapier's Letters*⟩. 1725.

A Letter from D. S——t. to D. S⟨medle⟩y. 1725.

The Birth of Manly Virtue, from Callimachus. 1725.

A Riddle by the Revd. Doctor S——t to My Lady C⟨artere⟩t. 1725.

Cadenus and Vanessa. 1726.

Travels into Several Remote Nations of the World, in Four Parts, by Lemuel Gulliver, First a Surgeon, and Then a Captain of Several Ships ⟨*Gulliver's Travels*⟩. 1726. 2 vols.

[*A Letter to the Freemen and Freeholders of the City of Dublin.* 1727.]

[*Advice to the Electors of the City of Dublin.* 1727.]

Miscellanies in Prose and Verse (with Alexander Pope and John Arbuthnot). 1727. [Volumes 1–2]; 1732 [Volume 3].

A Short View of the State of Ireland. 1728.

An Answer to a Paper, Called, A Memorial of the Poor Inhabitants, Tradesmen, and Labourers of the Kingdom of Ireland. 1728.

The Intelligencer (with Thomas Sheridan). 1728. 20 nos.

The Journal of a Dublin Lady. 1729.

A Modest Proposal for Preventing the Children of Poor People from Being a Burthen to Their Parents, or the Country, and for Making Them Beneficial to the Publick. 1729.

On Paddy's Character of the Intelligencer. c. 1729.

An Epistle to His Excellency John Lord Carteret, Lord Lieutenant of Ireland. 1730.

An Epistle upon an Epistle from a Certain Doctor to a Certain Great Lord. 1730.

An Epistle to His Excellency John Lord Carteret; to Which Is Added an Epistle upon an Epistle: Being a Christmas-Box for Doctor D⟨ela⟩ny. 1730.

A Libel on D—— D—— and a Certain Great Lord. 1730.

A Panegyric on the Reverend D—n S——t. 1730.

To Doctor D–L—Y, on the Libels Writ against Him. 1730.

An Answer to Dr. D——ny's Fable of the Pheasant and the Lark. 1730.

Lady A–S–N Weary of the Dean. 1730.

An Apology to the Lady C—R—T on Her Inviting Dean S–F–T to Dinner. 1730.

A Vindication of His Excellency the Lord C——T, from the Charge of Favouring None but Tories, High-Churchmen and Jacobites. 1730.

An Excellent New Ballad; or, The True En——sh D—n to Be Hanged for a R–pe. 1730.

Horace, Book I. Ode XIV., Paraphrased and Inscribed to Ir——d. 1730.

Traulus. 1730. 2 parts.

With favour and fortune fastidiously blest. c. 1730.

Helter Skelter; or, The Hue and Cry after the Attornies, Going to Ride the Circuit. 1730.

The Place of the Damn'd. 1730.

A Proposal Humbly Offer'd to the P——t, for the More Effectual Preventing the Further Growth of Popery. 1731.

A Soldier and a Scholar; or, The Lady's Judgment upon Those Two Characters in the Persons of Captain —— and D—n S——T. 1732.

*Considerations upon Two Bills Sent Down from the R—— H—— the H—— of L—— to the H—ble H—— of C—— Relating to the Clergy of I*****D.* 1732.

An Examination of Certain Abuses, Corruptions, and Enormities in the City of Dublin. 1732.

An Elegy on Dicky and Dolly. 1732.

The Lady's Dressing Room; to Which Is Added a Poem on Cutting Down the Old Thorn at Market Hill. 1732.

The Advantages Propos'd by Repealing the Sacramental Test, Impartially Considered. 1732.

Quaeries Wrote by Dr. J. Swift in the Year 1732, Very Proper to Be Read (at This Time) by Every Member of the Established Church. c. 1732.

An Answer to a Late Scandalous Poem, Wherein the Author Most Audaciously Presumes to Cast Indignity upon Their Highnesses the Clouds, by Comparing Them to a Woman. 1733.

The Life and Genuine Character of Doctor Swift. 1733.

A Serious and Useful Scheme to Make an Hospital for Incurables; to Which Is Added a Petition of the Footmen in and about Dublin. 1733.

Some Considerations Humbly Offered to the Right Honourable the Lord-Mayor, the Court of Aldermen, and Common Council of the Honourable City of Dublin, in the Choice of a Recorder. 1733.

The Drapier's Miscellany. 1733.

The Presbyterians Plea of Merit in Order to Take Off the Test, Impartially Examined. 1733.

Advice to the Free-Men of the City of Dublin. 1733.

An Epistle to a Lady, Who Desired the Author to Make Verses on Her, in the Heroick Stile; Also a Poem, Occasion'd by Reading Dr. Young's Satires, Called, The Universal Passion. 1733.

On Poetry: A Rhapsody. 1733.

Some Reasons against the Bill for Settling the Tyth of Hemp, Flax, &c. by a Modus. 1734.

A Beautiful Young Nymph Going to Bed, Written for the Honour of the Fair Sex; to Which Are Added Strephon and Chloe, and Cassinus and Peter. 1734.

Miscellanies in Prose and Verse: Volume the Fifth. 1735.

A Collection of Poems, &c., Omitted in the Fifth Volume of Miscellanies. 1735.

The Furniture of a Woman's Mind. c. 1735.

Works. 1735. 4 vols.

Poetical Works. 1736.

Reasons Why We Should Not Lower the Coins Now Current in This Kingdom. 1736.

A Proposal for Giving Badges to the Beggars in All the Parishes of Dublin. 1737.

Works. 1738. 6 vols.

Political Tracts. 1738. 2 vols.

An Imitation of the Sixth Satire of the Second Book of Horace. 1738.

The Beasts Confession to the Priest, on Observing How Most Men Mistake Their Own Talents. 1738.

A Complete Collection of Genteel and Ingenious Conversation, According to the Most Polite Mode and Method Now Used at Court, and in the Best Companies of England, in Three Dialogues. 1738.

Verses on the Death of Doctor Swift. 1739.

Some Free Thoughts upon the Present State of Affairs, Written in the Year 1714. 1741.

Letters to and from Dr. Jonathan Swift from the Year 1714 to 1737. 1741.
Three Sermons. 1744.
Directions to Servants. 1745.
Works. 1746. 8 vols.
The Story of the Injured Lady. 1746.
A True Copy of the Late Rev. Dr. Jonathan Swift's Will. 1746.
Works. 1751. 14 vols.
Brotherly Love: A Sermon. 1754.
Works. Ed. John Hawkesworth. 1755. 12 vols.
The History of the Four Last Years of the Queen. 1758.
Works. 1763. 11 vols.
Sermons. 1763.
Letters Written by the Late Jonathan Swift, D.D., and Several of His Friends. Eds. John Hawkesworth and Deane Swift. 1768–69. 6 vols.
Works. 1768. 13 vols.
Works. 1772. 20 vols.
Works. Eds. John Hawkesworth et al. 1774. 15 vols.
Poetical Works. 1778. 4 vols.
The Beauties of Swift. 1782.
Works. Ed. Thomas Sheridan. 1784. 17 vols.
Miscellaneous Pieces, in Prose and Verse, Not Inserted in Mr. Sheridan's Edition of the Dean's Works. 1789.
Sermons. 1790. 2 vols.
Works. 1801. 19 vols.
Works. Ed. Sir Walter Scott. 1814. 19 vols.
Poetical Works. Ed. John Mitford. 1833–34. 3 vols.
Prose Works. Ed. Temple Scott. 1898–1909. 12 vols.
Unpublished Letters. Ed. George Birkbeck Hill. 1899.
The Journal to Stella. Ed. George A. Aitken. 1901.
Poems. Ed. W. E. Browning. 1910. 2 vols.
Correspondence. Ed. F. Erlington Ball. 1910–14. 6 vols.
Vanessa and Her Correspondence with Swift. Ed. A. M. Freeman. 1921.
Satires and Personal Writings. Ed. William Alfred Eddy. 1932.
Letters to Charles Ford. Ed. David Nichol Smith. 1935.
The Drapier's Letters to the People of Ireland. Ed. Herbert Davis. 1935.
Poems. Ed. Harold Williams. 1937. 3 vols.
Prose Works. Ed. Herbert Davis. 1939–68. 14 vols.
The Journal to Stella. Ed. Harold Williams. 1948. 2 vols.
An Enquiry into the Behaviour of the Queen's Last Ministry. Ed. Irvin Ehrenpreis. 1956.
Collected Poems. Ed. Joseph Horrell. 1956. 2 vols.
Correspondence. Ed. Harold Williams. 1963–65. 5 vols.
Poetical Works. Ed. Herbert Davis. 1967.
Complete Poems. Ed. Pat Rogers. 1983.
Jonathan Swift. Eds. Angus Ross and David Woolley. 1984.
Account Books. Eds. Paul V. Thompson and Dorothy Jay Thompson. 1984.

HENRY FIELDING (1707–1754)

The Masquerade. 1728.
Love in Several Masques. 1728.
The Temple Beau. 1730.
The Author's Farce and The Pleasures of the Town. 1730.
Tom Thumb: A Tragedy. 1730.
Rape upon Rape; or, The Justice Caught in His Own Trap. 1730.
The Letter-Writers; or, A New Way to Keep a Wife at Home. 1731.
The Welsh Opera; or, The Grey Mare the Better Horse. 1731.
The Genuine Grub-Street Opera. 1731.

The Lottery. 1732.
The Modern Husband. 1732.
The Old Debauchees. 1732.
The Covent-Garden Tragedy. 1732.
The Mock Doctor; or, The Dumb Lady Cur'd. 1732.
The Miser (adaptation). 1733.
The Intriguing Chamber Maid by Jean François Regnard (adaptation). 1734.
Don Quixote in England. 1734.
An Old Man Taught Wisdom; or, The Virgin Unmask'd. 1735.
The Universal Gallant; or, The Different Husbands. 1735.
Pasquin: A Dramatic Satire on the Times. 1736.
Tumble-down Dick; or, Phaeton in the Suds. 1736.
The Historical Register for the Year 1736; to Which Is Added a Very Merry Tragedy, Called, Eurydice Hiss'd; or, A Word to the Wise. 1737.
The Military History of Charles XII, King of Sweden by Gustavus Alderfeld (translator; with others). 1740. 3 vols.
Of True Greatness: An Epistle to the Right Honourable George Dodington, Esq. 1741.
ΤΗΣ ΟΜΗΡΟΥ VΕΡΝΟΝ-ΙΑΔΟΣ, ΡΑΨΩΔΙΑ ἡ ΓΡΑΜΜΑ Α' *(The Vernon-iad).* 1741.
An Apology for the Life of Mrs. Shamela Andrews. 1741.
[*The Crisis: A Sermon on Revel. xiv. 9, 10, 11.* 1741.]
The Opposition: A Vision. 1742.
The History of the Adventures of Joseph Andrews, and of His Friend Mr. Abraham Adams. 1742.
A Full Vindication of the Dutchess Dowager of Marlborough. 1742.
Miss Lucy in Town: A Sequel to The Virgin Unmask'd. 1742.
Plutus, the God of Riches by Aristophanes (translator; with William Young). 1742.
Some Papers Proper to Be Read before the Royal Society, concerning the Terrestrial Chrysipus. 1743.
The Wedding-Day. 1743.
Miscellanies. 1743. 3 vols.
The Adventures of David Simple by Sarah Fielding (revised by Fielding). 1744.
An Attempt towards a Natural History of the Hanover Rat. 1744.
A Serious Address to the People of Great Britain. 1745.
A Dialogue between the Devil, the Pope, and the Pretender. 1745.
The History of the Present Rebellion in Scotland. 1745. Lost.
Dramatick Works. 1745. 2 vols.
The Charge to the Jury. 1745.
The True Patriot; and the History of Our Own Times. 1745–46. 33 nos.
The Female Husband; or, The Surprising History of Mrs. Mary. 1746.
Art of Love by Ovid (translator). 1747.
Familiar Letters between the Principal Characters in David Simple (with Sarah Fielding). 1747.
[*A Compleat and Authentick History of the Rise, Progress, and Extinction of the Late Rebellion.* 1747.]
A Dialogue between a Gentleman of London, Agent for Two Court Candidates, and an Honest Alderman of the Country Party. 1747.
A Proper Answer to a Late Scurrilous Libel. 1747.
The Jacobite's Journal. 1747–48. 49 nos.
[*The Important Triflers.* 1748. Lost.]
The History of Tom Jones, a Foundling. 1749. 6 vols.
A Charge Delivered to the Grand Jury, at the Sessions of the Peace, Held for the City and Liberty of Westminster. 1749.
A True State of the Case of Bosavern Penlez. 1749.

An Enquiry into the Causes of the Late Increase of Robbers. 1751.

A Plan of the Universal Register Office (with John Fielding). 1752.

Amelia. 1752. 4 vols.

The Covent-Garden Journal. 1752. 72 nos.

Examples of the Interposition of Providence in the Detection and Punishment of Murder. 1752.

A Proposal for Making an Effectual Provision for the Poor. 1753.

A Clear State of the Case of Elizabeth Canning. 1753.

The Journal of a Voyage to Lisbon. 1755.

Works. Ed. Arthur Murphy. 1762. 4 vols.

The Fathers; or, The Good-Natur'd Man. 1778.

The Beauties of Fielding. 1782.

Works. Ed. Alexander Chalmers. 1806. 10 vols.

Works. Ed. Thomas Roscoe. 1840.

Works. Ed. James P. Browne. 1871–72. 11 vols.

Writings. Ed. David Herbert. 1872.

Works. Ed. Leslie Stephen. 1882. 10 vols.

Works. Ed. George Saintsbury. 1893. 12 vols.

Works. Ed. Edmund Gosse. 1898–99. 12 vols.

Complete Works. Ed. W. E. Henley. 1903. 16 vols.

Works. Ed. G. H. Maynadier. 1903. 12 vols.

Selected Essays. Ed. Gordon Hall Gerould. 1905.

Works. Ed. George Saintsbury. 1926. 12 vols.

Novels. 1926. 10 vols.

Works (Wesleyan Edition). Eds. Martin C. Battestin et al. 1967– .

LAURENCE STERNE (1713–1768)

To the Rev. Mr. James at Leeds. 1741.

Query upon Query: Being an Answer to J. S.'s Letter Printed in the York-Courant October 20, 1741. 1741.

An Answer to J. S.'s Letter, Address'd to a Freeholder of the County of York. 1741.

The Case of Elijah and the Widow of Zerephath. 1747.

The Abuses of Conscience. 1750.

A Political Romance, Addressed to —— ——, Esq; of York. 1759.

The Life and Opinions of Tristram Shandy, Gentleman. 1760 [Volumes 1–2]; 1761 [Volumes 3–4]; 1762 [Volumes 5–6]; 1765 [Volumes 7–8]; 1767 [Volume 9].

The Sermons of Mr. Yorick. 1760 [Volumes 1–2]; 1766 [Volumes 3–4]; 1769 [Volumes 5–7].

A Sentimental Journey through France and Italy. 1768. 2 vols.

Letters from Yorick to Eliza. 1773.

Letters to His Friends on Various Occasions. 1775.

Letters to His Most Intimate Friends. 1775. 3 vols.

Works. 1780. 10 vols.

Original Letters. 1788.

Seven Letters Written by Sterne and His Friends, Hitherto Unpublished. Ed. W. Durrant Cooper. 1844.

Works. Ed. James P. Browne. 1873. 4 vols.

Works. Ed. George Saintsbury. 1894. 6 vols.

Works and Life. Ed. Wilbur L. Cross. 1904. 12 vols.

Letter to the Rev. Mr. Blake. 1915.

Works. 1926–27. 7 vols.

Letters. Ed. Lewis Perry Curtis. 1935.

Works. Eds. Melvyn New and Joan New. 1976– .

THOMAS GRAY (1716–1771)

An Ode on a Distant Prospect of Eton College. 1747.

An Elegy Wrote in a Country Church Yard. 1751.

Designs by R. Bentley for Six Poems by Mr. T. Gray. 1753.

Poems. 1756.

Odes. 1757.

The Union. 1761.

Poems. 1768.

Ode Performed in the Senate-House at Cambridge, July 1, 1769. 1769.

A Catalogue of the Antiquities, Houses, Parks, Plantations, Scenes, and Situations in England and Wales. Ed. William Mason. 1773.

The Bard (with Latin tr. by R. Williams). 1775.

Poems. Ed. William Mason. 1775.

Poetical Works. 1782.

Poems. Ed. Gilbert Wakefield. 1786.

Poetical Works. Ed. Stephen Jones. 1799.

Works. Ed. Thomas James Mathias. 1814. 2 vols.

Works. Ed. John Mitford. 1816. 2 vols.

Letters. 1819–21. 2 vols.

Poems and Letters. 1820.

Correspondence of Thomas Gray and the Rev. Norton Nichols, with Other Pieces Hitherto Unpublished. Ed. John Mitford. 1843.

Correspondence of Thomas Gray and William Mason. Ed. John Mitford. 1853.

Select Poems. Ed. WIlliam J. Rolfe. 1876.

Works in Prose and Verse. Ed. Edmund Gosse. 1884. 4 vols.

Gray and His Friends: Letters and Relics. Ed. Duncan C. Tovey. 1890.

Letters. Ed. Duncan C. Tovey. 1900. 3 vols.

Essays and Criticisms. Ed. Clark Sutherland Northup. 1911.

Poems, with a Selection of Letters and Essays. Ed. John Drinkwater. 1912.

Correspondence. Ed. Paget Toynbee. 1915. 2 vols.

Correspondence. Eds. Paget Toynbee and Leonard Whibley. 1935. 3 vols.

Poems. Ed. Leonard Whibley. 1939.

Selected Letters. Ed. Joseph Wood Krutch. 1952.

Poems (with William Collins and Oliver Goldsmith). Ed. Roger Lonsdale. 1969.

TOBIAS SMOLLETT (1721–1771)

Advice: A Satire. 1746.

Reproof: A Satire; The Sequel to Advice. 1747.

The Adventures of Roderick Random. 1748. 2 vols.

The Adventures of Gil Blas by Alain René Le Sage (translator). 1748. 4 vols.

The Regicide; or, James the First, of Scotland. 1749.

The Adventures of Peregrine Pickle. 1751. 4 vols.

A Treatise on the Theory and Practice of Midwifery by William Smellie (editor). 1751.

An Essay on the External Use of Water. 1752.

[*A Faithful Narrative of the Base and Inhuman Arts That Were Lately Practiced upon the Brain of Habbakkuk Hilding.* 1752.]

The Adventures of Ferdinand Count Fathom. 1753. 2 vols.

Select Essays on Commerce, Agriculture, Mines, Fisheries, and Other Useful Subjects (translator). 1754.

A Collection of Cases and Observations in Midwifery by William Smellie (editor). 1754.

Travels through Different Cities of Germany, Italy, Greece, and Several Parts of Asia by Alexander Drummond (editor). 1754.

The History and Adventures of the Renowned Don Quixote by Cervantes (translator). 1755. 2 vols.

A Compendium of Authentic and Entertaining Voyages (editor). 1756. 7 vols.

The Reprisal; or, The Tars of Old England. 1757.

A Complete History of England. 1757–58. 4 vols.

The Modern Part of the Universal History (editor; with others). 1759–66. 44 vols.

Continuation of the Complete History of England. 1760–61, 1765. 5 vols.

The Works of M. Voltaire (translator; with others). 1761–66. 26 vols.

The Life and Adventures of Sir Launcelot Greaves. 1762. 2 vols.

A Collection of Preternatural Cases and Observations in Midwifery by William Smellie (editor). 1764.

[*The Orientalist.* 1764.]

Travels through France and Italy. 1766. 2 vols.

The Present State of All Nations (editor). 1768–69. 8 vols.

The History and Adventures of an Atom. 1769. 2 vols.

The Expedition of Humphry Clinker. 1771. 3 vols.

An Ode to Independence. 1773.

Select Works. 1775–76. 8 vols.

The Adventures of Telemachus, Son of Ulysses by François de Salignac de la Mothe Fénelon (translator). 1776. 2 vols.

Plays and Poems. 1777.

Miscellaneous Works. 1790. 6 vols.

Works. 1793–94. 10 vols.

Miscellaneous Works. Ed. Robert Anderson. 1796. 6 vols.

Works. Ed. John Moore. 1797. 8 vols.

Miscellaneous Works. Ed. Thomas Roscoe. 1841.

Works. Ed. David Herbert. 1870.

Works. Ed. James P. Browne. 1872. 8 vols.

Works. Ed. W. E. Henley and Thomas Seccombe. 1899–1901. 12 vols.

Works. Ed. George Saintsbury. 1899–1903. 12 vols.

Works. Ed. G. H. Maynadier. 1902. 12 vols.

Works. Ed. 1925–26. 11 vols.

Letters. Ed. Edward S. Noyes. 1926.

Letters: A Supplement to the Noyes Collection. Ed. Francesco Cordasco. 1950.

Letters. Ed. Lewis M. Knapp. 1970.

OLIVER GOLDSMITH (c. 1730–1774)

The Memoirs of a Protestant, Condemned to the Galleys of France for His Religion by Jean Marteilhe (translator). 1758. 2 vols.

An Enquiry into the Present State of Polite Learning in Europe. 1759.

The Bee. 1759. 8 nos.

The Mystery Revealed: Containing a Series of Transactions and Authentic Testimonials Respecting the Supposed Cock-Lane Ghost. 1762.

The Citizen of the World. 1762. 2 vols.

Plutarch's Lives (translator; with others). 1762. 7 vols.

The Life of Richard Nash, of Bath, Esq. 1762.

[*The Art of Poetry on a New Plan* (revised by Goldsmith). 1762. 2 vols.]

[*The Martial Review; or, A General History of the Late Wars.* 1763.]

An History of England in a Series of Letters from a Nobleman to His Son. 1764. 2 vols.

An History of the Lives, Actions, Travels, Sufferings, and Deaths of the Most Eminent Martyrs and Primitive Fathers of the Church. 1764.

The Traveller; or, A Prospect of Society. 1765.

The Geography and History of England. 1765.

Essays. 1765.

Edwin and Angelina: A Ballad. 1765.

The Vicar of Wakefield. 1766. 2 vols.

A Concise History of Philosophy and Philosophers by Jean H. S. Formey (translator). 1766.

Poems for Young Ladies in Three Parts: Devotional, Moral, and Entertaining (editor). 1767.

The Beauties of English Poesy (editor). 1767. 2 vols.

The Good Natur'd Man. 1768.

The Present State of the British Empire in Europe, America, Africa, and Asia (editor). 1768.

The Roman History from the Foundation of the City of Rome to the Destruction of the Western Empire. 1769. 2 vols.

The Deserted Village. 1770.

Life of Thomas Parnell, D.D. 1770.

Life of Henry St. John, Lord Viscount Bolingbroke. 1770.

The History of England from the Earliest Times to the Death of George II. 1771. 4 vols.

Threnodia Augustalis. 1772.

Dr. Goldsmith's Roman History, Abridged by Himself for the Use of Schools. 1772.

She Stoops to Conquer; or, The Mistakes of a Night. 1773.

Retaliation. 1774.

The Grecian History from the Earliest State to the Death of Alexander the Great. 1774. 2 vols.

An History of the Earth and Animated Nature. 1774. 8 vols.

An Abridgement of the History of England from the Invasion of Julius Caesar to the Death of George II. 1774.

The Comic Romance of Monsieur Scarron (translator). 1775. 2 vols.

Select Poems. 1775.

Poems. 1775.

Miscellaneous Works. 1775.

The Haunch of Venison: A Poetical Epistle to Lord Clare. 1776.

A Survey of Experimental Philosophy, Considered in Its Present State of Improvement. 1776. 2 vols.

Poems and Plays. 1777.

Poetical and Dramatic Works. 1780. 2 vols.

The Beauties of Goldsmith. 1782.

Poetical Works. 1784.

Poems. 1786.

Miscellaneous Works. 1791. 2 vols.

Miscellaneous Works. 1792. 7 vols.

Miscellaneous Works. Ed. Samuel Rose. 1801. 4 vols.

Miscellaneous Works. Ed. Washington Irving. 1825. 4 vols.

Poetical Works. Ed. John Mitford. 1831.

The Captivity: An Oratorio. 1836.

Works. 1848. 4 vols.

Poetical Works. Ed. Robert Aris Willmott. 1859.

Miscellaneous Works. Ed. David Masson. 1869.

Selected Poems. Ed. Austin Dobson. 1887.

Poems and Plays. Ed. Austin Dobson. 1889. 2 vols.

Plays. Ed. Austin Dobson. 1893.

The Good Natur'd Man and She Stoops to Conquer. Eds. Austin Dobson and George P. Baker. 1905.

Plays. Ed. Charles E. Doble. 1909.

Selected Essays. Ed. J. H. Lobban. 1910.

Complete Poetical Works. Ed. Austin Dobson. 1911.

The Bee and Other Essays, Together with the Life of Nash. 1914.

New Essays. Ed. Ronald S. Crane. 1927.

Collected Letters. Ed. Katharine C. Balderston. 1928.

The Grumbler: An Adaptation. Ed. Alice I. Perry Wood. 1931.

The Vicar of Wakefield and Other Writings. Ed. Frederick W. Hilles. 1955.

Collected Works. Ed. Arthur Friedman. 1966. 5 vols.
Poems (with Thomas Gray and William Collins). Ed. Roger Lonsdale. 1969.

DAVID HUME (1711–1776)

A Treatise of Human Nature. 1739–40. 2 vols.
An Abstract of A Treatise of Human Nature. 1740.
Essays Moral and Political. 1741–42. 2 vols.
A Letter from a Gentleman to His Friend Containing Some Observations on Religion and Morality. 1745.
Three Essays Moral and Political, Never Before Published. 1748.
Philosophical Essays concerning Human Understanding. 1748.
A True Account of the Behaviour and Conduct of Archibald Stewart. 1748.
An Enquiry concerning the Principles of Morals. 1751.
The Petition of the Bellmen. 1751.
Political Discourses. 1752.
Scotticisms. 1752.
Essays and Treatises on Several Subjects. 1753–56. 4 vols.
History of Great Britain. 1754–62. 6 vols.
Four Dissertations. 1757.
Two Essays. 1777.
Dialogues concerning Natural Religion. 1779.
Philosophical Works. 1825. 4 vols.
Letters. Ed. Thomas Murray. 1841.
Philosophical Works. Eds. T. H. Green and T. H. Grose. 1874–75. 4 vols.
Letters to William Strahan. Ed. George Birkbeck Hill. 1888.
Letters. Ed. J. Y. T. Greig. 1932.
Political Essays. Ed. Charles W. Hendel. 1953.
New Letters. Eds. Raymond Klibansky and Ernest C. Mossner. 1954.
Writings on Economics. Ed. Eugene Rotwein. 1955.
The Philosophy of David Hume. Ed. V. C. Chappell. 1963.
Ethical Writings. Ed. Alasdair MacIntyre. 1965.

SAMUEL JOHNSON (1709–1784)

A Voyage to Abyssinia by Father Jerome Lobo (translator). 1735.
London: A Poem in Imitation of the Third Satire of Juvenal. 1738.
Marmor Norfolciense; or, An Essay on an Ancient Prophetical Inscription, in Monkish Rhyme. 1739.
A Compleat Vindication of the Licensers of the Stage. 1739.
A Commentary on Mr. Pope's Principles of Morality by J. P. de Crousaz (translator). 1739.
The Life of Admiral Blake. 1740.
An Account of the Life of Mr. Richard Savage. 1744.
Miscellaneous Observations on the Tragedy of Macbeth. 1745.
A Sermon Preached before the Sons of the Clergy. 1745.
Prologue ⟨by Johnson⟩ *and Epilogue* ⟨by David Garrick⟩ *Spoken at the Opening of the Theatre in Drury-Lane 1747.* 1747.
The Plan of a Dictionary of the English Language. 1747.
The Vanity of Human Wishes: The Tenth Satire of Juvenal, Imitated. 1749.
Irene. 1749.
The Rambler. 1750–52. 208 nos.
A New Prologue Spoken by Mr. Garrick at the Representation of Comus. 1750.
An Essay on Milton's Use and Imitation of the Moderns, in His Paradise Lost. 1750.
A Dictionary of the English Language. 1755. 2 vols.
Proposals for Printing, by Subscription, the Dramatick Works of William Shakespeare. 1756.

The Idler. 1758–60. 104 nos.
The Prince of Abissinia ⟨Rasselas⟩. 1759.
Preface to His Edition of Shakespear's Plays. 1765.
The Plays of William Shakespeare (editor). 1765. 8 vols.
The False Alarm. 1770.
Thoughts on the Late Transactions Respecting Falkland's Islands. 1771.
Miscellaneous and Fugitive Pieces. Ed. Thomas Davies. 1773–74. 3 vols.
The Patriot. 1774.
A Journey to the Western Islands of Scotland. 1775.
Proposals for Publishing the Works of Mrs. Charlotte Lennox. 1775.
Taxation No Tyranny: An Answer to the Resolutions and Address of the American Congress. 1775.
Political Tracts. 1776.
Prefaces, Biographical and Critical, to the Works of the English Poets ⟨Lives of the English Poets⟩. 1779–81. 10 vols.
The Beauties of Johnson. 1781–82. 2 vols.
Poetical Works. Ed. George Kearsley. 1785.
Prayers and Meditations. Ed. George Strahan. 1785.
Debates in Parliament. Ed. George Chalmers. 1787. 2 vols.
Works. Ed. Sir Hawkins. 1787. 11 vols.
Letters. Ed. Hester Lynch Piozzi. 1788. 2 vols.
A Sermon for the Funeral of His Wife. 1788.
Sermons on Different Subjects. 1788–89. 2 vols.
The Celebrated Letter to Philip Dormer Stanhope, Earl of Chesterfield. Ed. James Boswell. 1790.
Works. Ed. Arthur Murphy. 1792. 12 vols.
An Account of the Life of Dr. Samuel Johnson ⟨Annals⟩. Ed. Richard Wright. 1805.
A Diary of a Journey into North Wales, in the Year 1774. Ed. R. Duppa. 1816.
Works. Ed. Francis Pearson Walesby. 1825. 9 vols.
Poetical Works. Ed. George Gilfillan. 1855.
The Six Chief Lives from Johnson's Lives of the Poets. Ed. Matthew Arnold. 1878.
Letters. Ed. George Birkbeck Hill. 1892. 2 vols.
Lives of the English Poets. Ed. George Birkbeck Hill. 1905. 3 vols.
Johnson on Shakespeare. Ed. Walter Raleigh. 1908.
Prose and Poetry. Ed. R. W. Chapman. 1922.
Selected Letters. Ed. R. W. Chapman. 1925.
The French Journals of Mrs. Thrale and Dr. Johnson. Eds. Moses Tyson and Henry Guppy. 1932.
The Queeney Letters: Being Letters Addressed to Hester Maria Thrale by Dr. Johnson, Fanny Burney, and Mrs. Thrale-Piozzi. Ed. the Marquis of Lansdowne. 1934.
Poems. Eds. David Nichol Smith and Edward L. MacAdam. 1941, 1974.
Letters. Ed. R. W. Chapman. 1952. 3 vols.
Works (Yale Edition). Ed. A. T. Hazen et al. 1958– .
Selected Writings. Ed. R. T. Davies. 1965.
Political Writings. Ed. J. P Hardy. 1968.
Selected Writings. Ed. Patrick Cruttwell. 1968.
Complete English Poems. Ed. J. D. Fleeman. 1971.
Early Biographical Writings. Ed. J. D. Fleeman. 1973.
Johnson as Critic. Ed. John Wain. 1973.
Samuel Johnson. Ed. Donald Greene. 1984.

EDWARD GIBBON (1737–1794)

Essai sur l'étude de la littérature. 1761.
Mémoires littéraires de la Grande Bretagne, pour l'an 1767 (with Georges Deyverdun). 1768.

Mémoires littéraires de la Grande Bretagne, pour l'an 1768 (with Georges Deyverdun). 1769.

Critical Observations on the Sixth Book of the Aeneid. 1770.

The History of the Decline and Fall of the Roman Empire. 1776 [Volume 1]; 1781 [Volumes 2–3]; 1788 [Volumes 4–6].

A Vindication of Some Passages in the Fifteenth and Sixteenth Passages of the History of the Decline and Fall of the Roman Empire. 1779.

Mémoire justificatif pour servir de réponse à l'exposé &c. de la cour de France. 1779.

Miscellaneous Works. Ed. John, Lord Sheffield. 1796 (2 vols.), 1814 (5 vols.).

[*Speech on the Day of Election of Members to Serve in Parliament for the Borough of Petersfield.* c. 1813.]

The Antiquities of the House of Brunswick. Ed. John, Lord Sheffield. 1814.

Memoirs. Ed. John, Lord Sheffield. 1827. 2 vols.

Private Letters. Ed. Rowland E. Prothero. 1896. 2 vols.

The History of the Decline and Fall of the Roman Empire. Ed. J. B. Bury. 1909–14. 7 vols.

Gibbon's Journal to January 28th, 1763. Ed. D. M. Low. 1929.

Le Journal de Gibbon à Lausanne, 17 août 1763–19 avril 1764. Ed. Georges A. Bonnard. 1945.

Miscellanea Gibboniana. Eds. Gavin R. de Beer, Georges A. Bonnard, and Louis Junod. 1952.

Letters. Ed. J. E. Norton. 1956. 3 vols.

The Autobiography of Edward Gibbon. Ed. Dero A. Saunders. 1961.

Gibbon's Journey from Geneva to Rome: His Journal from 20 April to 2 October 1764. Ed. Georges A. Bonnard. 1961.

Memoirs of My Life. Ed. Georges A. Bonnard. 1966.

English Essays. Ed. Patricia B. Craddock. 1972.

ROBERT BURNS (1759–1796)

Poems, Chiefly in the Scottish Dialect. 1786, 1787.

The Scots Musical Museum, Volumes 2–5 (editor). 1787–1803. 6 vols.

The Ayrshire Garland. c. 1789.

The Prayer of Holy Willie. 1789.

The Whistle. c. 1791.

An Address to the Deil. 1795.

Wham will we send to London Town. c. 1795–96.

Fy, let us a' to K(irkcudbright). c. 1795–96.

What will buy my Troggin? c. 1795–96.

An Unco' Mornfu Tale. 1796.

Elegy on the Year Eighty-eight. 1799.

The Jolly Beggars: A Cantata. 1799.

The Kirk's Alarm: A Satire. 1799.

Holy Willie's Prayer, Letter to John Goudie, and Six Favourite Songs. 1799.

Extempore Verses on Dining with Lord Daer. 1799.

The Inventory. 1799.

The Henpeck'd Husband ⟨etc.⟩. 1799.

The Merry Muses of Caledonia (editor). 1799.

Works. Ed. James Currie. 1800. 4 vols.

Poems Ascribed to Robert Burns. 1801.

Letters Addressed to Clarinda, &c. 1802.

The Beauties of Burns. 1802.

Reliques of Robert Burns. Ed. R. H. Cromek. 1808.

Prose Works. 1816.

Letters and Correspondence. 1817. 2 vols.

Letters. 1819. 2 vols.

Works, Including His Letters to Clarinda and the Whole of His Suppressed Poems. 1821. 4 vols.

Songs and Ballads. Ed. J. Barwick. 1823.

Poetical Works, Including Several Pieces Not Inserted in Dr. Currie's Edition. 1823. 2 vols.

Letters, Chronologically Arranged. 1828.

Works. Eds. James Hogg and William Motherwell. 1834–36. 5 vols.

Works. Ed. Allan Cunningham. 1834. 8 vols.

Poetical Works. 1839. 3 vols.

The Correspondence between Burns and Clarinda. Ed. W. C. M'Lehose. 1843.

Life and Works. Ed. Robert Chambers. 1851. 4 vols.

Poetical Works. Ed. George Gilfillan. 1856. 2 vols.

Poetical Works. Ed. Robert Aris Willmott. 1856.

Poems, Songs, and Letters. Ed. Alexander Smith. 1868.

Poetical Works. Ed. William Michael Rossetti. 1871.

Common Place Book. 1872.

Works. Ed. William Scott Douglas. 1877–79. 6 vols.

Poetical Works. Ed. George A. Aitken. 1893. 3 vols.

Complete Poetical Works. Ed. J. Logie Robertson. 1896. 3 vols.

Poetry. Eds. W. E. Henley and T. F. Henderson. 1896–97. 4 vols.

Burns and Mrs. Dunlop: Correspondence. Ed. William Wallace. 1898. 2 vols.

The Glenriddell Manuscripts. 1914. 2 vols.

Journal of a Tour in the Highlands Made in 1787. Ed. J. C. Ewing. 1927.

Letters. Ed. J. De Lancey Ferguson. 1931. 2 vols.

Common Place Book 1783–1785. Eds. James Cameron Ewing and Davidson Cook. 1938.

The Merry Muses of Caledonia. Eds. James Barke and Sydney Goodsir Smith. 1959.

Poems and Songs. Ed. James Kinsley. 1968. 3 vols.

RICHARD BRINSLEY SHERIDAN (1751–1816)

The Love Epistles of Aristaenetus (translator; with Nathaniel Brassey Halhed). 1771.

The Ridotto of Bath: A Panegyrick. 1771.

The Rival Beauties: A Poetical Contest. 1772.

A Familiar Epistle to the Author of the Heroic Epistle to Sir William Chambers. 1774.

The Rivals. 1775.

The Duenna. 1775.

Verses to the Memory of Garrick. 1779.

The School for Scandal. 1780.

A Trip to Scarborough: Altered from Vanbrugh's Relapse. 1781.

The Critic; or, A Tragedy Rehearsed. 1781.

A Short Account of the Situations and Incidents Exhibited in the Pantomime of Robinson Crusoe. 1781.

The Legislative Independence of Ireland Vindicated in a Speech of Mr. Sheridan's. 1785.

The Genuine Speech of Mr. Sheridan Delivered in the House of Commons on a Charge &c. against Warren Hastings Esq. 1787.

Speech in Bringing Forward the Fourth Charge against Warren Hastings, Esq., Relative to the Begums of Oude. 1787.

The Celebrated Speech of Richard Brinsley Sheridan in Westminster Hall on His Summing Up the Evidence in the Begum Charge against Warren Hastings. 1787.

Speech before the High Court of Parliament on Summing Up the Evidence on the Begum Charge against Warren Hastings. 1788.

St. Patrick's Day; or, The Scheming Lieutenant. 1788.

A Comparative Statement of the Two Bills for the Better Government of India. 1788.

The Glorious First of June (with others). 1794.
Dramatic Works. 1797.
Speech in the House of Commons on the Motion to Address His Majesty on the Present Alarming State of Affairs. 1798.
Speech in the House of Commons in Reply to Mr. Pitt's Speech on the Union with Ireland. 1799.
Pizarro: A Tragedy Taken from the German Drama of Kotzebue. 1799.
Speech in the House of Commons on the Motion for the Army Establishment for the Ensuing Year. 1802.
Speech in the House of Commons on the Army Estimates. 1802.
Death of Mr. Fox. 1806.
The Forty Thieves (with Charles Ward and George Colman the Younger). 1808.
Speeches. 1816. 5 vols.
Clio's Protest; or, The Picture Varnished, with Other Poems. 1819.
Works. Ed. Thomas Moore. 1821. 2 vols.
Dramatic Works. 1828.
Dramatic Works. Ed. Leigh Hunt. 1840.
Works. Ed. James P. Browne. 1873. 2 vols.
Sheridan's Plays Now Printed as He Wrote Them. Ed. W. Fraser Rae. 1902.
Plays. Ed. Edmund Gosse. 1905. 3 vols.
Plays. Ed. Joseph Knight. 1906.
Plays and Poems. Ed. R. Crampton Rhodes. 1928. 3 vols.
Letters. Ed. Cecil Price. 1966. 3 vols.
Dramatic Works. Ed. Cecil Price. 1973. 2 vols.

JANE AUSTEN (1775–1816)

Sense and Sensibility. 1811. 3 vols.
Pride and Prejudice. 1813. 3 vols.
Mansfield Park. 1814. 3 vols.
Emma. 1816. 3 vols.
Northanger Abbey and Persuasion. 1818. 4 vols.
Novels. 1833. 5 vols.
Letters. Ed. Edward, Lord Brabourne. 1884. 2 vols.
Novels. Ed. Reginald Brimley Johnson. 1892. 10 vols.
Charades &c., Written a Hundred Years Ago by Jane Austen and Her Family. 1895.
Love and Freindship. 1922.
Novels. Ed. R. W. Chapman. 1923. 5 vols.
The Watsons. 1923.
Five Letters to Her Niece Fanny Knight. 1924.
Letters. Ed. R. Brimley Johnson. 1925.
Lady Susan. Ed. R. W. Chapman. 1925.
Fragment of a Novel Written by Jane Austen January–March 1817 ⟨Sanditon⟩. Ed. R. W. Chapman. 1925.
Plan of a Novel. Ed. R. W. Chapman. 1926.
Letters to Her Sister Cassandra and Others. Ed. R. W. Chapman. 1932.
⟨*Juvenilia.*⟩ 1933 [Volume 1, ed. R. W. Chapman]; 1951 [Volume 3, ed. R. W. Chapman]; 1963 [Volume 2, ed. Brian Southam].
Three Evening Prayers. 1940.
Minor Works. Ed. R. W. Chapman. 1954.
Jane Austen's "Sir Charles Grandison." Ed. Brian Southam. 1980.
The Juvenilia of Jane Austen and Charlotte Brontë. Ed. Frances Beer. 1986.

JOHN KEATS (1795–1821)

Poems. 1817.
Endymion: A Poetic Romance. 1818.
Lamia, Isabella, The Eve of St. Agnes, and Other Poems. 1820.

Poetical Works of Coleridge, Shelley, and Keats. 1829.
Poetical Works. 1840.
Life, Letters, and Literary Remains. Ed. Richard Monckton Milnes, Lord Houghton. 1848. 2 vols.
Poetical Works. 1854.
Another Version of Keats's Hyperion ⟨*The Fall of Hyperion*⟩. Ed. Richard Monckton Milnes, Lord Houghton. 1857.
Letters to Fanny Brawne. Ed. H. Buxton Forman. 1878.
Poetical Works and Other Writings. Ed. H. Buxton Forman. 1883. 4 vols.
Letters and Poems. Ed. Jonathan Gilmer Speed. 1883. 3 vols.
Letters to His Family and Friends. Ed. Sidney Colvin. 1891.
Letters. Ed. H. Buxton Forman. 1895.
Complete Works. Ed. H. Buxton Forman. 1900–01. 5 vols.
Poems. Ed. Ernest de Selincourt. 1905.
Poetical Works. Ed. H. Buxton Forman. 1908.
The Keats Letters, Papers, and Other Relics. Ed. H. Buxton Forman. 1914.
Letters. Ed. Maurice Buxton Forman. 1931. 2 vols.
Anatomical and Physiological Note Book. Ed. Maurice Buxton Forman. 1934.
Complete Poems and Selected Letters. Ed. Clarence DeWitt Thorpe. 1935.
Poetical Works and Other Writings. Ed. H. Buxton Forman, rev. Maurice Buxton Forman. 1938–39. 8 vols.
Poetical Works. Ed. H. W. Garrod. 1939.
The Keats Circle: Letters and Papers 1816–1878. Ed. Hyder Edward Rollins. 1948. 2 vols.
Selected Letters. Ed. Lionel Trilling. 1951.
Poetical Works. Ed. H. W. Garrod, rev. John Jones. 1956.
Letters 1814–1821. Ed. Hyder Edward Rollins. 1958. 2 vols.
Selected Poems and Letters. Ed. Douglas Bush. 1959.
Poems. Ed. Miriam Allot. 1970.
Letters: A New Selection. Ed. Robert Gittings. 1970.
The Odes and Their Earliest Known Manuscripts. Ed. Robert Gittings. 1970.
Complete Poems. Ed. John Barnard. 1973.
Life and Letters. Ed. Joanna Richardson. 1981.
Complete Poems. Ed. Jack Stillinger. 1985.

PERCY BYSSHE SHELLEY (1792–1822)

Zastrozzi: A Romance. 1810.
Original Poetry by Victor and Cazire (with Elizabeth Shelley). 1810.
Posthumous Fragments of Margaret Nicholson (with Thomas Jefferson Hogg). 1810.
St Irvyne; or, The Rosicrucian: A Romance. 1811.
The Necessity of Atheism (with Thomas Jefferson Hogg). 1811.
A Poetical Essay on the Existing State of Things. c. 1811. Lost.
An Address to the Irish People. 1812.
Proposals for an Association of Those Philanthropists, Who Convinced of the Inadequacy of the Moral and Philosophical State of Ireland to Produce Benefits Which Are Nevertheless Attainable, Are Willing to Unite to Accomplish Its Regeneration. 1812.
Declaration of Rights. 1812.
The Devil's Walk: A Ballad. 1812.
A Letter to Lord Ellenborough. 1812.
Queen Mab: A Philosophical Poem, with Notes. 1813.
A Vindication of Natural Diet. 1813.
A Refutation of Deism: In a Dialogue. 1814.
Alastor; or, The Spirit of Solitude, and Other Poems. 1816.
A Proposal for Putting Reform to the Vote throughout the Kingdom. 1817.

An Address to the People on the Death of the Princess Charlotte, by the Hermit of Marlow. 1817. Lost.

History of a Six Weeks' Tour through a Part of France, Switzerland, Germany, and Holland (with Mary Shelley). 1817.

Laon and Cythna; or, The Revolution of the Golden City ⟨The Revolt of Islam⟩. 1818.

Rosalind and Helen: A Modern Eclogue with Other Poems. 1819.

The Cenci: A Tragedy. 1819.

Prometheus Unbound: A Lyrical Drama, with Other Poems. 1820.

Oedipus Tyrannus; or, Swellfoot the Tyrant. 1820.

Epipsychidion. 1821.

Adonais: An Elegy on the Death of John Keats. 1821.

Hellas: A Lyrical Drama. 1822.

Posthumous Poems. Ed. Mary Shelley. 1824.

Poetical Works of Coleridge, Shelley, and Keats. 1829.

The Masque of Anarchy. Ed. Leigh Hunt. 1832.

Poetical Works. Ed. Mary Shelley. 1839. 4 vols.

Essays, Letters from Abroad, Translations and Fragments. Ed. Mary Shelley. 1840. 2 vols.

Relics of Shelley. Ed. Richard Garnett. 1862.

Poetical Works. Ed. William Michael Rossetti. 1870. 2 vols.

The Daemon of the World. Ed. H. Buxton Forman. 1876.

Poetical Works. Ed. H. Buxton Forman. 1876–77. 4 vols.

Prose Works. Ed. H. Buxton Forman. 1880. 4 vols.

Select Letters. Ed. Richard Garnett. 1882.

Essays and Letters. Ed. Ernest Rhys. 1886.

The Wandering Jew (with Thomas Medwin). Ed. Bertram Dobell. 1887.

Poetical Works. Ed. George Edward Woodberry. 1892. 4 vols.

Poetical Works. Ed. F. S. Ellis. 1895. 3 vols.

Complete Poetical Works. Ed. Thomas Hutchinson. 1904.

Letters. Ed. Roger Ingpen. 1909. 2 vols.

Note Books. Ed. H. Buxton Forman. 1911. 3 vols.

A Philosophical View of Reform. Ed. T. W. Rolleston. 1920.

Complete Works. Eds. Roger Ingpen and Walter E. Peck. 1926–30. 10 vols.

The Shelley Notebook in the Harvard Library. Ed. George Edward Woodberry. 1929.

On the Vegetable System of Diet. Ed. Roger Ingpen. 1929.

Shelley and His Circle 1773–1822 (with others). Eds. Kenneth Neill Cameron, Donald H. Reiman et al. 1961– .

Letters. Ed. Frederick L. Jones. 1964. 2 vols.

The Esdaile Notebook: A Volume of Early Poems. Ed. Kenneth Neill Cameron. 1964.

Shelley's The Triumph of Life: A Critical Study Based on a Text Newly Edited from the Bodleian Manuscript. Ed. Donald H. Reiman. 1965.

Shelley's Prose; or, The Trumpet of a Prophecy. Ed. David Lee Clark. 1966.

Posthumous Poems: Mary Shelley's Fair Copy Book. Ed. Irving Massey. 1969.

Complete Poetical Works. Ed. Thomas Hutchinson, rev. G. M. Matthews. 1970.

Complete Poetical Works. Ed. Neville Rogers. 1972– . 4 vols. (projected).

Poetry and Prose. Eds. Donald H. Reiman and Sharon B. Powers. 1977.

GEORGE GORDON, LORD BYRON (1788–1824)

Fugitive Pieces. 1806.

Poems on Various Occasions. 1807.

Hours of Idleness. 1807.

Poems Original and Translated. 1808.

English Bards and Scotch Reviewers. 1809.

Childe Harold's Pilgrimage: A Romaunt. 1812 [Cantos 1–2]; 1816 [Canto 3]; 1818 [Canto 4].

The Curse of Minerva. 1812.

The Genuine Rejected Addresses. 1812.

Waltz: An Apostrophic Hymn. 1813.

The Giaour: A Fragment of a Turkish Tale. 1813.

The Bride of Abydos: A Turkish Tale. 1813.

Poetical Works. 1813. 2 vols.

The Corsair. 1814.

Ode to Napoleon Buonaparte. 1814.

Lara; Jacqueline. 1814.

Hebrew Melodies. 1815.

The Siege of Corinth; Parisina. 1816.

A Sketch from Private Life. 1816.

Fare Thee Well! 1816.

Poems. 1816.

The Prisoner of Chillon and Other Poems. 1816.

Monody on the Death of the Right Honourable R. B. Sheridan. 1816.

The Lament of Tasso. 1817.

Manfred: A Dramatic Poem. 1817.

Beppo: A Venetian Story. 1818.

On John William Rizzo Hoppner. 1818.

My Boat Is on the Shore. 1818.

Mazeppa. 1819.

Don Juan. 1819 [Cantos 1–2]; 1821 [Cantos 3–5]; 1823 [Cantos 6–8]; 1823 [Cantos 9–11]; 1823 [Cantos 12–14]; 1824 [Cantos 15–16].

Letter to the Editor of My Grandmother's Review. 1819.

The Irish Avatar. 1821.

Marino Faliero; The Prophecy of Dante. 1821.

Sardanapalus; The Two Foscari; Cain. 1821.

Letter to **** *****, on the Rev. W. L. Bowles' Strictures on the Life and Writings of Pope. 1821.

The Vision of Judgment. 1822.

Poetical Works. 1822–24. 16 vols.

The Age of Bronze. 1823.

Heaven and Earth. 1823.

The Island; or, Christian and His Comrades. 1823.

Werner. 1823.

The Deformed Transformed. 1824.

Parliamentary Speeches. 1824.

Correspondence of Lord Byron with a Friend. Ed. R. C. Dallas. 1825. 3 vols.

Letters and Journals. Ed. Thomas Moore. 1830. 2 vols.

Dramas. 1832.

Works, with Letters and Journals. Ed. John Wright. 1832–33. 17 vols.

Tales. 1837. 2 vols.

A Selection from the Works. Ed. Algernon Charles Swinburne. 1866.

Poetical Works. Ed. William Michael Rossetti. 1870.

A Political Ode. 1880.

Works. Eds. Ernest Hartley Coleridge and Rowland E. Prothero. 1898–1904. 13 vols.

Poems. Ed. Arthur Symons. 1904.

Correspondence. Ed. John Murray. 1922. 2 vols.

Poems. Ed. Herbert J. C. Grierson. 1923.

The Ravenna Journal. 1928.

Poetry and Prose. Ed. David Nichol Smith. 1940.

Byron: A Self-Portrait: Letters and Diaries 1798–1824. Ed. Peter Quennell. 1950. 2 vols.

Selected Poetry. Ed. Leslie A. Marchand. 1951.

His Very Self and Voice: Collected Conversations. Ed. Ernest J. Lovell, Jr. 1954.
Poems. Ed. Vivian de Sola Pinto. 1963–68. 3 vols.
Selected Poetry and Prose. Ed. W. H. Auden. 1966.
Selected Prose. Ed. Peter Gunn. 1972.
Letters and Journals. Ed. Leslie A. Marchand. 1973–82. 12 vols.
Complete Poetical Works. Ed. Jerome J. McGann. 1980–   .

WILLIAM BLAKE (1757–1827)

Poetical Sketches. 1783.
There Is No Natural Religion. c. 1788.
All Religions Are One. c. 1788.
The Book of Thel. 1789.
Songs of Innocence. 1789.
The French Revolution. 1791.
The Marriage of Heaven and Hell. 1793.
For Children: The Gates of Paradise. 1793.
To the Public. 1793. Lost.
Vision of the Daughters of Albion. 1793.
America: A Prophecy. 1793.
Songs of Innocence and Experience. 1794.
Europe: A Prophecy. 1794.
The First Book of Urizen. 1794.
The Book of Ahania. 1795.
The Book of Los. 1795.
The Song of Los. 1795.
Milton. 1804.
Jerusalem: The Emanation of the Giant Albion. 1804–c. 1820.
Exhibition of Paintings in Fresco. 1809.
Blake's Chaucer: The Canterbury Pilgrims. 1809.
A Descriptive Catalogue of Pictures, Poetical and Historical Inventions, Painted by William Blake. 1809.
For the Sexes: The Gates of Paradise. c. 1818.
Laocoon. c. 1820.
On Homer's Poetry; On Virgil. c. 1821.
The Ghost of Abel. 1822.
Poems. Ed. R. H. Shepherd. 1874.
Poetical Works. Ed. William Michael Rossetti. 1874.
Works. Eds. Edwin John Ellis and W. B. Yeats. 1893. 3 vols.
Poems. Ed. W. B. Yeats. 1893.
Poetical Works. Ed. John Sampson. 1905.
Letters. Ed. Archibald G. B. Russell. 1906.
Poems. Ed. Alice Meynell. 1911.
Writings. Ed. Geoffrey Keynes. 1925. 3 vols.
Prophetic Writings. Eds. D. J. Sloss and J. P. R. Wallis. 1926. 2 vols.
Letters to Thomas Butts 1800–1803. Ed. Geoffrey Keynes. 1926.
The Poems and Prophecies. Ed. Max Plowman. 1927.
Selected Poems. Ed. Basil de Selincourt. 1927.
Note-Book. Ed. Geoffrey Keynes. 1935.
The Portable Blake. Ed. Alfred Kazin. 1946.
Selected Poetry and Prose. Ed. Northrop Frye. 1953.
Letters. Ed. Geoffrey Keynes. 1956.
Poetry and Prose. Ed. David V. Erdman. 1965.
Poems. Ed. W. H. Stevenson. 1971.
Complete Poems. Ed. Alicia Ostriker. 1977.
Writings. Ed. G. E. Bentley, Jr. 1978. 2 vols.
Paintings and Drawings. Ed. Martin Butlin. 1981. 2 vols.

WILLIAM HAZLITT (1778–1830)

An Essay on the Principles of Human Action. 1805.
Free Thoughts on Public Affairs. 1806.

An Abridgment of The Light of Nature Pursued by Abraham Tucker (editor). 1807.
A Reply to the Essay on Population by the Rev. T. R. Malthus. 1807.
The Eloquence of the British Senate (editor). 1807. 2 vols.
A New and Improved Grammar of the English Tongue. 1810.
Memoirs of the Late Thomas Holcroft, Written by Himself and Continued ⟨by Hazlitt⟩ to the Time of His Death. 1816. 3 vols.
The Round Table: A Collection of Essays on Literature, Men, and Manners (with Leigh Hunt). 1817. 2 vols.
Characters of Shakespear's Plays. 1817.
A View of the English Stage. 1818.
Lectures on the English Poets. 1818.
A Letter to William Gifford, Esq. 1819.
Lectures on the English Comic Writers. 1819.
Political Essays, with Sketches of Public Characters. 1819.
Lectures Chiefly on the Dramatic Literature of the Age of Elizabeth. 1820.
Table-Talk; or, Original Essays. 1821–22. 2 vols.
Liber Amoris; or, The New Pygmalion. 1823.
Characteristics: In the Manner of Rochefoucault's Maxims. 1823.
Sketches of the Principal Picture-Galleries in England. 1824.
Select British Poets (editor). 1824.
The Spirit of the Age; or, Contemporary Portraits. 1825.
The Plain Speaker: Opinions on Books, Men, and Things. 1826. 2 vols.
Notes of a Journey through France and Italy. 1826.
The Life of Napoleon Buonaparte. 1828–30. 4 vols.
Conversations of James Northcote, Esq., R.A. 1830.
Literary Remains. Ed. Edward Bulwer-Lytton. 1836. 2 vols.
Sketches and Essays. Ed. William Hazlitt, Jr. 1839.
Winterslow: Essays and Characters Written There. Ed. William Hazlitt, Jr. 1850.
Collected Works. Eds. A. R. Waller and Arnold Glover. 1902–06. 13 vols.
New Writings. Ed. P. P. Howe. 1925–27. 2 vols.
Complete Works. Ed. P. P. Howe. 1930–34. 20 vols.
Selected Essays. Ed. Geoffrey Keynes. 1930.
Selected Writings. Ed. Ronald Blythe. 1970.
Letters. Eds. Herschel Moreland Sikes, Willard Hallam Bonner, and Gerald Lahey. 1978.

SIR WALTER SCOTT (1771–1832)

The Chase and William and Helen: Two Ballads from the German of Göttfried Augustus Bürger. 1796.
Goetz of Berlichingen, with The Iron Hand: A Tragedy, Translated from the German of Goethé. 1799.
An Apology for Tales of Terror (editor). 1799.
The Eve of Saint John: A Border Ballad. 1800.
Minstrelsy of the Scottish Border (editor). 1802. 2 vols.
Sir Tristrem: A Metrical Romance by Thomas of Ercildoune (editor). 1804.
The Lay of the Last Minstrel. 1805.
A Health to My Lord Melville. 1806.
Ballads and Lyrical Pieces. 1806.
Original Memoirs Written during the Great Civil War by Sir Henry Slingsby and Captain Hodgson (editor). 1806.
Works. 1806–08. 6 vols.
Marmion: A Tale of Flodden Field. 1808.
The Works of John Dryden (editor). 1808. 18 vols.
Memoirs of Capt. George Carleton (editor). 1808.
Queenhoo-Hall: A Romance by Joseph Strutt (editor). 1808. 4 vols.

Memoirs of Robert Car⟨e⟩y, Earl of Monmouth and Fragmenta Regalia by Sir Robert Naunton (editor). 1808.

[*The Life of Edward Lord Herbert of Cherbury, Written by Himself* (editor). 1809.]

A Collection of Scarce and Valuable Tracts (editor). 1809–15. 13 vols.

English Minstrelsy (editor). 1810. 2 vols.

A Lady of the Lake. 1810.

The Poetical Works of Anna Seward (editor). 1810. 3 vols.

[*The Ancient British Drama* (editor). 1810. 3 vols.]

The Vision of Dan Roderick. 1811.

Memoirs of Count Grammont by Anthony Hamilton, tr. Abel Boyer (editor). 1811. 2 vols.

The Castle of Otranto by Horace Walpole (editor). 1811.

Secret History of the Court of King James the First (editor). 1811. 2 vols.

[*The Modern British Drama* (editor). 1811. 5 vols.]

Glenfinlas and Other Ballads, etc. with The Vision of Dan Roderick. 1812.

Works. 1812. 8 vols.

Rokeby. 1813.

The Bridal of Triermain; or, The Vale of Saint John. 1813.

[*Memoirs of the Reign of King Charles the First* by Sir Philip Warwick (editor). 1813.]

Waverley; or, 'Tis Sixty Years Since. 1814. 3 vols.

The Works of Jonathan Swift (editor). 1814. 19 vols.

The Letting of Humours Blood in the Head Vaine by Samuel Rowlands (editor). 1814.

Guy Mannering; or, The Astrologer. 1815. 3 vols.

The Lord of the Isles. 1815.

The Field of Waterloo. 1815.

Memorie of the Somervilles by James, Lord Somerville (editor). 1815. 2 vols.

The Antiquary. 1816. 3 vols.

Tales of My Landlord ⟨*The Black Dwarf; Old Mortality*⟩. 1816. 4 vols.

Harold the Dauntless. 1817.

Rob Roy. 1818. 3 vols.

Tales of My Landlord: Second Series ⟨*The Heart of Mid-Lothian*⟩. 1818. 4 vols.

My Mither is of sturdy airn. 1818.

Tales of My Landlord: Third Series ⟨*The Bride of Lammermoor; A Legend of Montrose*⟩. 1819. 4 vols.

Description of the Regalia of Scotland. 1819.

The Visionary. 1819. 3 vols.

Ivanhoe: A Romance. 1820. 3 vols.

The Monastery: A Romance. 1820. 3 vols.

The Abbot. 1820. 3 vols.

Poetical Works. 1820 (12 vols.), 1830 (11 vols.).

Miscellaneous Poems. 1820.

Trivial Poems and Triolets by Patrick Carey (editor). 1820.

Memorials of the Haliburtons (editor). 1820.

Novels and Tales. 1820. 12 vols.

Kenilworth: A Romance. 1821. 3 vols.

Northern Memoirs Writ in the Year 1658 by Richard Franck (editor). 1821.

Ballantyne's Novelist's Library (editor). 1821–24. 10 vols.

The Pirate. 1822. 3 vols.

The Poetry Contained in the Novels, Tales, and Romances, of the Author of Waverley. 1822.

The Fortunes of Nigel. 1822. 3 vols.

Halidon Hill: A Dramatic Sketch. 1822.

Carle, Now the King's Come! 1822.

Peveril of the Peak. 1822. 4 vols.

Chronological Notes of Scottish Affairs from 1680 till 1701: Being Taken Chiefly from the Diary of Lord Fountainhall (editor). 1822.

Military Memoirs of the Great Civil War: Being the Military Memoirs of John Gwynne (editor). 1822.

Historical Romances. 1822. 6 vols.

Quentin Durward. 1823. 3 vols.

A Bannatyne Garland. c. 1823.

St. Ronan's Well. 1824. 3 vols.

Redgauntlet: A Tale of the Eighteenth Century. 1824. 3 vols.

Lay of the Lindsays (editor). 1824.

Novels and Romances. 1824. 7 vols.

Tales of the Crusaders ⟨*The Betrothed; The Talisman*⟩. 1825. 4 vols.

Auld Robin Gray: A Ballad by Lady Anne Barnard (editor). 1825.

Lives of the Novelists. 1825. 2 vols.

Woodstock; or, The Cavalier. 1826. 3 vols.

Provincial Antiquities of Scotland. 1826. 2 vols.

A Letter to the Editor of the Edinburgh Weekly Journal, *from Malachi Malagrowther, on the Proposed Change of Currency.* 1826.

A Second Letter to the Editor of the Edinburgh Weekly Journal, *from Malachi Malagrowther, on the Proposed Change of Currency.* 1826.

A Third Letter to the Editor of the Edinburgh Weekly Journal, *from Malachi Malagrowther, on the Proposed Change of Currency.* 1826.

Chronicles of the Canongate ⟨*The Highland Widow; The Two Drovers; The Surgeon's Daughter*⟩. 1827. 2 vols.

The Life of Napoleon Buonaparte. 1827. 9 vols.

The Bannatyne Miscellany, Volume I (editor; with David Laing). 1827.

Memoirs of the Marchioness de la Rochejaqulein (editor). 1827.

Miscellaneous Prose Works. 1827. 6 vols.

Tales and Romances. 1827. 7 vols.

⟨*Verses to Sir Cuthbert Sharp.*⟩ 1828.

Chronicles of the Canongate, Second Series ⟨*The Fair Maid of Perth*⟩. 1828. 3 vols.

Tales of a Grandfather: Being Stories Taken from Scottish History. 1828. 3 vols.

Religious Discourses by a Layman. 1828.

Proceedings in the Court-Martial Help upon John, Master of Sinclair, 1708 (editor). 1828.

My Aunt Margaret's Mirror; The Tapestried Chamber; Death of the Laird's Jock; A Scene at Abbotsford. 1829.

Anne of Geierstein; or, The Maiden of the Mist. 1829. 3 vols.

Waverley Novels (Magnum Opus Edition). 1829–33. 48 vols.

Tales of a Grandfather: Being Stories Taken from Scottish History: Second Series. 1829. 3 vols.

Memorials of George Bannatyne 1545–1608 (editor). 1829.

Tales of a Grandfather: Being Stories Taken from the History of Scotland: Third Series. 1830. 3 vols.

The House of Aspen: A Tragedy. 1830.

The Doom of Devergoil: A Melo-Drama; Auchindrane; or, The Ayrshire Tragedy. 1830.

The History of Scotland. 1830. 2 vols.

Letters on Demonology and Witchcraft. 1830.

Tales of a Grandfather: Being Stories Taken from the History of France: Fourth Series. 1831. 3 vols.

Trial of Duncan Terig and Alexander Bane Macdonald 1754 (editor). 1831.

Tales of My Landlord: Fourth Series ⟨*Count Robert of Paris; Castle Dangerous*⟩. 1832. 4 vols.

Letters of Scott Addressed to the Rev. R. Polwhele; D. Gilbert,

Esq.; Francis Douce, Esq.; &c. &c. Ed. R. Polwhele. 1832.

Tales and Romances. 1833. 7 vols.

Introductions, and Notes and Illustrations. 1833. 2 vols.

Poetical Works. Ed. John Gibson Lockhart. 1833–34. 12 vols.

Miscellaneous Prose Works. Ed. John Gibson Lockhart. 1834–36. 28 vols.

Waverley Novels (Fisher's Edition). 1836–39. 48 vols.

Waverley Novels (Abbotsford Edition). 1842–47. 12 vols.

Letters between James Ellis and Walter Scott, Esq. 1850.

Waverley Novels (Library Edition). 1852–53. 25 vols.

Poetical Works. Ed. George Gilfillan. 1857. 3 vols.

Memoirs of the Insurrection in Scotland in 1715 by John, Master of Sinclair (editor). 1858.

Poetical Works (Globe Edition). Ed. Francis Turner Palgrave. 1866.

Waverley Novels (Centenary Edition). Ed. David Laing. 1870–71. 25 vols.

Journal 1825–32. Ed. David Douglas. 1890. 2 vols.

Poetical Works (Aldine Edition). Ed. John Dennis. 1892. 5 vols.

Waverley Novels (Dryburgh Edition). 1892–94. 25 vols.

Waverley Novels (Border Edition). Ed. Andrew Lang. 1892–94. 48 vols.

Poetical Works. Ed. J. Logie Robertson. 1894.

Tales from Scott. Ed. Edward Sullivan. 1894.

Familiar Letters. Ed. David Douglas. 1894. 2 vols.

Poetical Works (Dryburgh Edition). Ed. Andrew Lang. 1895.

Waverley Novels (Edinburgh Waverley). 1901–03. 48 vols.

The Letters of Sir Walter Scott and Charles Kirkpatrick Sharpe to Robert Chambers 1821–45. 1904.

Waverley Novels (Soho Edition). 1904. 25 vols.

Waverley Novels (Oxford Scott). 1912. 24 vols.

Private Letter-Books: Selections from the Abbotsford Manuscripts. Ed. Wilfred Partington. 1930.

Sir Walter's Post-Bag: More Stories and Sidelights from the Unpublished Letter-Books. Ed. Wilfred Partington. 1932.

Waverley Novels (New Crown Edition). 1932. 25 vols.

Some Unpublished Letters of Sir Walter Scott from the Collection in the Brotherton Library. Ed. J. Alexander Symington. 1932.

Letters. Ed. Herbert J. C. Grierson. 1932–37. 12 vols.

Short Stories. Ed. David Cecil. 1934.

The Correspondence of Sir Walter Scott and Charles Robert Maturin. Eds. Fannie E. Ratchford and William H. McCarthy, Jr. 1937.

Private Letters of the Seventeenth Century. Ed. D. Grant. 1948.

Sir Walter Scott on Novelists and Fiction. Ed. Ioan Williams. 1968.

Journal. Ed. W. E. K. Anderson. 1972.

Selected Poems. Ed. Thomas Crawford. 1972.

The Prefaces to the Waverley Novels. Ed. Mark A. Weinstein. 1978.

SAMUEL TAYLOR COLERIDGE (1772–1834)

The Fall of Robespierre: An Historic Drama (with Robert Southey). 1794.

A Moral and Political Lecture Delivered at Bristol. 1795.

Conciones ad Populum; or, Addresses to the People. 1795.

The Plot Discovered; or, An Address to the People, against Ministerial Treason. 1795.

An Answer to a Letter to Edward Long Fox, M.D. 1795.

Ode on the Departing Year. 1796.

Poems on Various Subjects. 1796.

The Watchman. 1796. 10 nos.

Poems (with Charles Lamb and Charles Lloyd). 1797.

Fears in Solitude; to Which Are Added France, an Ode; and Frost at Midnight. 1798.

Lyrical Ballads (with William Wordsworth). 1798, 1800 (2 vols.).

Wallenstein: A Drama Translated from the German of Frederick Schiller. 1800. 2 parts.

Poems. 1803.

The Friend. 1809–10. 28 nos.

Omniana; or, Horae Otiosiores (with Robert Southey). 1812. 2 vols.

Remorse: A Tragedy in Five Acts ⟨Osorio⟩. 1813.

Christabel; Kubla Khan: A Vision; The Pains of Sleep. 1816.

The Statesman's Manual; or, The Bible the Best Guide to Political Skill and Foresight ⟨First Lay Sermon⟩. 1816.

Biographia Literaria; or, Biographical Sketches of My Literary Life and Opinions. 1817. 2 vols.

Blessed are ye that sow beside all waters! ⟨Second Lay Sermon⟩. 1817.

Sibylline Leaves. 1817.

Zapolya: A Christmas Tale. 1817.

A Hebrew Dirge ⟨Israel's Lament⟩ by Hyman Hurwitz (translator). 1817.

General Introduction to Encyclopaedia Metropolitana ⟨On Method⟩. 1818.

Remarks on the Objections Which Have Been Urged against the Principle of Sir Robert Peel's Bill. 1818.

The Grounds of Sir Robert Peel's Bill Vindicated. 1818.

Prospectus of a Course of Lectures. 1818.

The Tears of a Grateful People by Hyman Hurwitz (translator). 1820.

Aids to Reflection in the Formation of a Manly Character, on the Several Grounds of Prudence, Morality and Religion. 1825.

Poetical Works. 1828. 3 vols.

Poetical Works of Coleridge, Shelley, and Keats. 1829.

On the Constitution of the Church and State According to the Idea of Each, with Aids toward a Right Judgment on the Late Catholic Bill. 1830.

The Devil's Walk: A Poem, Edited with a Biographical Memoir and Notes by Professor Porson (with Robert Southey). Ed. H. W. Montagu. 1830.

On the Prometheus of Aeschylus. 1834.

Poetical Works. Ed. Henry Nelson Coleridge. 1834. 3 vols.

Specimens of the Table-Talk of the Late Samuel Taylor Coleridge. Ed. Henry Nelson Coleridge. 1835. 2 vols.

Letters, Conversations, and Recollections. Ed. Thomas Allsop. 1836. 2 vols.

Literary Remains. Ed. Henry Nelson Coleridge. 1836–39. 4 vols.

Confessions of an Inquiring Spirit. Ed. Henry Nelson Coleridge. 1840.

Poems. Ed. Sara Coleridge. 1844.

Hints towards the Formation of a More Comprehensive Theory of Life. Ed. Seth B. Watson. 1848.

Notes and Lectures upon Shakespeare and Some of the Old Poets and Dramatists, with Other Literary Remains. Ed. Sara Coleridge. 1849. 2 vols.

Essays on His Own Times, Forming a Third Series of The Friend. Ed. Sara Coleridge. 1850. 3 vols.

Poems. Eds. Derwent and Sara Coleridge. 1852.

Notes Theological, Political, and Miscellaneous. Ed. Derwent Coleridge. 1853.

Complete Works. Ed. W. G. T. Shedd. 1853. 7 vols.

Seven Lectures on Shakespeare and Milton. Ed. J. Payne Collier. 1856.

Osorio: A Tragedy, as Originally Written in 1797. Ed. R. H. Shepherd. 1873.

Lectures and Notes on Shakspere and Other English Poets. Ed. T. Ashe. 1883.

The Table-Talk and Omniana of S. T. Coleridge, with Additional Table-Talk from Allsop's Recollections. Ed. T. Ashe. 1884.

Poetical Works. Ed. Thomas Ashe. 1885. 2 vols.

Critical Annotations: Being Marginal Notes Inscribed in Volumes Formerly in the Possession of Coleridge, Part I. Ed. William F. Taylor. 1889.

Poetical Works. Ed. James Dykes Campbell. 1893.

Anima Poetae. Ed. Ernest Hartley Coleridge. 1895.

Letters. Ed. Ernest Hartley Coleridge. 1895. 2 vols.

Poems: A Facsimile Reproduction. Ed. James Dykes Campbell. 1899.

Complete Poetical Works. Ed. Ernest Hartley Coleridge. 1912. 2 vols.

Letters Hitherto Uncollected. Ed. W. F. Prideaux. 1913.

Coleridge on Logic and Learning. Ed. Alice D. Snyder. 1929.

Coleridge's Shakespearean Criticism. Ed. Thomas Middleton Raysor. 1930. 2 vols.

Unpublished Letters. Ed. Earl Leslie Griggs. 1932. 2 vols.

Select Poetry and Prose. Ed. Stephen Potter. 1933.

Coleridge on Imagination. Ed. I. A. Richards. 1934.

Miscellaneous Criticism. Ed. Thomas Middleton Raysor. 1936.

The Political Thought of Samuel Taylor Coleridge. Ed. R. J. White. 1938.

The Philosophical Lectures, Hitherto Unpublished. Ed. Kathleen Coburn. 1949.

The Portable Coleridge. Ed. I. A. Richards. 1950.

Inquiring Spirit: A New Presentation of Coleridge from His Published and Unpublished Prose Writings. Ed. Kathleen Coburn. 1951.

Coleridge on the Seventeenth Century. Ed. Roberta Florence Brinkley. 1955.

Collected Letters. Ed. Earl Leslie Griggs. 1956–71. 6 vols.

Notebooks. Ed. Kathleen Coburn. 1957–73. 3 vols. in 6.

Poems. Ed. John Beer. 1963.

Collected Works. Eds. Kathleen Coburn et al. 1969–   .

Coleridge on Shakespeare: The Text of the Lectures of 1811–12. Ed. R. A. Foakes. 1971.

Verse. Eds. William Empson and David Pirie. 1973.

Imagination in Coleridge. Ed. John Spencer Hill. 1978.

Selections. Ed. H. J. Jackson. 1985.

CHARLES LAMB (1775–1834)

Poems (with Samuel Taylor Coleridge and Charles Lloyd). 1797.

Blank Verse by Charles Lloyd and Charles Lamb. 1798.

A Tale of Rosamund Gray and Old Blind Margaret. 1798.

John Woodvil: A Tragedy. 1802.

[*The Book of the Ranks and Dignities of British Society.* 1805.]

The King and Queen of Hearts, with the Rogueries of the Knave, Who Stole the Queen's Pies. 1805.

Tales from Shakespear (with Mary Lamb). 1807. 2 vols.

Adventures of Ulysses. 1808.

Specimens of English Dramatic Poets Who Lived about the Time of Shakespear. 1808.

Mrs. Leicester's School (with Mary Lamb). 1809.

Poetry for Children (with Mary Lamb). 1809. 2 vols.

[*Beauty and the Beast; or, A Rough Outside with a Gentle Heart* (with Mary Lamb). 1811.]

Prince Dorus; or, Flattery Put Out of Countenance. 1811.

Mr. H——; or, Beware a Bad Name. 1813.

Works. 1818. 2 vols.

Elia. 1823.

Elia: Second Series. 1828.

Album Verses (with others). 1830.

Satan in Search of a Wife, with the Whole Process of His Courtship and Marriage, and Who Danced at the Wedding, by an Eye Witness. 1831.

The Last Essays of Elia. 1833.

Recollections of Christ's Hospital. 1835.

Letters. Ed. Thomas Noon Talfourd. 1837. 2 vols.

Works. Ed. Thomas Noon Talfourd. 1840.

Final Memorials of Charles Lamb: Consisting Chiefly of His Letters Not Before Published. Ed. Thomas Noon Talfourd. 1848.

Eliana: Being the Hitherto Uncollected Writings. Ed. J. E. Babson. 1864.

Complete Correspondence and Works. Eds. William Carew Hazlitt and Thomas Purnell. 1870. 4 vols.

Complete Works. Ed. R. H. Shepherd. 1874.

Mary and Charles Lamb: Poems, Letters and Remains. Ed. William Carew Hazlitt. 1874.

Life, Letters, and Writings. Ed. Percy Fitzgerald. 1876. 6 vols.

Works. Ed. Alfred Ainger. 1884–88. 4 vols.

Letters. Ed. William Carew Hazlitt. 1886. 2 vols.

The Lambs: Their Lives, Their Friends, and Their Correspondence. Ed. William Carew Hazlitt. 1897.

Lamb and Hazlitt: Further Letters and Records Hitherto Unpublished. Ed. William Carew Hazlitt. 1900.

Works. Ed. William Macdonald. 1903. 12 vols.

Works of Charles and Mary Lamb. Ed. E. V. Lucas. 1903–05. 7 vols.

Letters. Ed. Henry H. Harper. 1905. 5 vols.

Works of Charles and Mary Lamb. Ed. Thomas Hutchinson. 1908. 2 vols.

Lamb's Criticism: A Selection. Ed. E. M. W. Tillyard. 1923.

Some Lamb and Browning Letters to Leigh Hunt. Ed. Luther A. Brewer. 1924.

The Letters of Charles Lamb, to Which Are Added Those of His Sister Mary Lamb. Ed. E. V. Lucas. 1935. 3 vols.

Letters of Charles and Mary Ann Lamb. Ed. Edwin W. Marrs. 1975. 2 vols.

Lamb as Critic. Ed. Roy Park. 1980.

Selected Prose. Ed. Adam Phillips. 1985.

EMILY BRONTË (1818–1848)

Poems by Currer, Ellis, and Acton Bell (with Charlotte and Anne Brontë). 1846.

Wuthering Heights. 1847. 2 vols.

Wuthering Heights and Agnes Grey ⟨by Anne Brontë⟩, *with a Biographical Notice of the Authors, a Selection from Their Literary Remains, and a Preface by Currer Bell.* 1850.

The Life and Works of Charlotte Brontë and Her Sisters. 1872–73. 7 vols.

The Works of Charlotte, Emily, and Anne Brontë. Ed. F. J. S. 1893. 12 vols.

The Life and Works of the Sisters Brontë. Eds. Mrs. Humphry Ward and Clement K. Shorter. 1899–1903. 7 vols.

The Novels and Poems of Charlotte, Emily, and Anne Brontë. 1901–07. 7 vols.

The Works of Charlotte, Emily, and Anne Brontë. Ed. Temple Scott. 1901. 12 vols.

Poems by Charlotte, Emily, and Anne Brontë. 1902.
Poems. Ed. Arthur Symons. 1906.
The Brontës: Life and Letters. Ed. Clement K. Shorter. 1908. 2 vols.
Complete Works. Eds. Clement K. Shorter and W. Robertson Nicoll. 1910–11. 2 vols.
Complete Poems. Eds. Clement K. Shorter and C. W. Hatfield. 1923.
The Shakespeare Head Brontë (with Charlotte and Anne Brontë). Eds. Thomas J. Wise and John Alexander Symington. 1931–38. 19 vols.
The Brontës: Their Lives, Friendships, and Correspondence. Eds. Thomas J. Wise and John Alexander Symington. 1932. 4 vols.
Two Poems: Love's Rebuke, Remembrance. Ed. Fanny E. Ratchford. 1934.
Gondal Poems: Now First Published from the MS. in the British Museum. Eds. Helen Brown and Joan Mott. 1938.
Complete Poems. Ed. C. W. Hatfield. 1941.
Five Essays Written in French by Emily Jane Brontë. Tr. Lorine W. Nagel. Ed. Fanny E. Ratchford. 1948.
Complete Poems. Ed. Philip Henderson. 1951.
A Selection of Poems. Ed. Muriel Spark. 1952.
Gondal's Queen: A Novel in Verse. Ed. Fanny E. Ratchford. 1955.
Poems. Ed. Rosemary Harthill. 1973.
The Novels of Charlotte, Emily, and Anne Brontë. Eds. Hilda Marsden, Ian Jack et al. 1976–   .
Selected Poems (with Anne and Charlotte Brontë). Eds. Tom Winnifrith and Edward Chitham. 1985.
The Brontës: Selected Poems. Ed. Juliet R. Barker. 1985.

EDGAR ALLAN POE (1809–1849)

Tamerlane and Other Poems. 1827.
Al Aaraaf, Tamerlane, and Minor Poems. 1829.
Poems. 1831.
The Narrative of Arthur Gordon Pym of Nantucket. 1838.
The Conchologist's First Book. 1839.
Tales of the Grotesque and Arabesque. 1840. 2 vols.
Prospectus of The Penn Magazine. 1840.
The Murders in the Rue Morgue; The Man That Was Used Up. 1843.
Tales. 1845.
The Raven and Other Poems. 1845.
Mesmerism "in Articulo Mortis." 1846.
Prospectus of The Stylus. 1848.
Eureka: A Prose Poem. 1848.
Works. Ed. Rufus W. Griswold. 1850–56. 4 vols.
Tales of Mystery and Imagination. 1855.
Works. Ed. John H. Ingram. 1874–75. 4 vols.
Works. Ed. Richard Henry Stoddard. 1884. 8 vols.
Works. Eds. Edmund Clarence Stedman and George Edward Woodberry. 1894–95. 10 vols.
Complete Works. Ed. James A. Harrison. 1902. 17 vols.
Last Letters to Sarah Helen Whitman. Ed. James A. Harrison. 1909.
Complete Poems. Ed. J. H. Whitty. 1911.
Poems. Ed. Killis Campbell. 1917.
Letters. Ed. Mary Newton Stanard. 1925.
Best Known Works. Ed. Hervey Allen. 1931.
Complete Poems and Stories. Ed. Arthur Hobson Quinn. 1946. 2 vols.
Letters. Ed. John Ward Ostrom. 1948. 2 vols.
Selected Prose, Poetry, and Eureka. Ed. W. H. Auden. 1950.
Literary Criticism. Ed. Robert L. Hough. 1965.

Poems. Ed. Floyd Stovall. 1965.
Collected Works. Eds. Thomas Ollive Mabbott et al. 1969–   .
The Science Fiction of Edgar Allan Poe. Ed. Harold Beaver. 1976.

WILLIAM WORDSWORTH (1770–1850)

An Evening Walk: An Epistle in Verse. 1793.
Descriptive Sketches in Verse Taken during a Pedestrian Tour in the Italian, Grison, Swiss, and Savoyard Alps. 1793.
Lyrical Ballads (with Samuel Taylor Coleridge). 1798, 1800 (2 vols.).
Poems. 1807. 2 vols.
Concerning the Relations of Great Britain, Spain, and Portugal, to Each Other, and to the Common Enemy, at This Crisis; and Specifically as Affected by the Convention of Cintra. Ed. Thomas De Quincey. 1809.
The Excursion: Being a Portion of The Recluse. 1814.
Poems. 1815. 2 vols.
The White Doe of Rylstone; or, The Fate of the Nortons. 1815.
A Letter to a Friend of Robert Burns. 1816.
Thanksgiving Ode, with Other Short Pieces, Chiefly Referring to Recent Public Events. 1816.
Two Addresses to the Freeholders of Westmorland. 1818.
Peter Bell: A Tale in Verse. 1819.
The Waggoner: A Poem; to Which Are Added Sonnets. 1819.
The River Duddon: A Series of Sonnets; Vaudracour and Julia; and Other Poems; to Which Is Annexed A Topographical Description of the Country of the Lakes in the North of England. 1820.
Miscellaneous Poems. 1820. 4 vols.
The Little Maid and the Gentleman; or, We Are Seven. c. 1820.
Memorials of a Tour on the Continent 1820. 1822.
Ecclesiastical Sketches. 1822.
A Description of the Scenery of the Lakes in the North of England: Third Edition (Now First Published Separately) with Additions, and Illustrative Remarks upon the Scenery of the Alps. 1822.
Poetical Works. 1824. 4 vols.
Poetical Works. 1827. 5 vols.
Epitaph ⟨Ode to the Memory of Charles Lamb⟩. 1835.
Yarrow Revisited and Other Poems. 1835.
Poetical Works. 1836–37. 6 vols.
Complete Poetical Works; Together with A Description of the Country of the Lakes in the North of England. Ed. Henry Reed. 1837.
Sonnets. 1838.
Poems, Chiefly of Early and Late Years; Including The Borderers: A Tragedy. 1842.
Poems on the Loss and Re-building of St. Mary's Church, Cardiff (with others). 1842.
Verses Composed at the Request of Jane Wallas Penfold. 1843.
Grace Darling. 1843.
Kendal and Windermere Railway: Two Letters Reprinted from the Morning Post. 1845.
Poems. 1845.
Ode Performed in the Senate-House, Cambridge, at the First Commencement after the Installation of His Royal Highness the Prince Albert, Chancellor of the University. 1847.
The Prelude; or, Growth of a Poet's Mind. 1850.
Poetical Works (Centenary Edition). 1870. 6 vols.
Prose Works. Ed. Alexander B. Grosart. 1876. 3 vols.
Poems. Ed. Matthew Arnold. 1879.
Poetical Works. Ed. William Knight. 1882–86. 8 vols.
Complete Poetical Works. Ed. John Morley. 1888.

The Recluse. 1888.

Poetical Works (Aldine Edition). Ed. Edward Dowden. 1892–93. 7 vols.

Poetical Works. Ed. Thomas Hutchinson. 1895.

Prose Works. Ed. William Knight. 1896. 2 vols.

Poetical Works. Ed. Andrew J. Gorge. 1904.

Literary Criticism. Ed. Newell C. Smith. 1905.

Poems and Extracts Chosen for an Album Presented to Lady Mary Lowther, Christmas 1819 by Anne Finch, Countess of Winchilsea (editor). Ed. Harold Littledale. 1905.

Letters of the Wordsworth Family from 1787 to 1855. Ed. William Knight. 1907. 3 vols.

Poems. Ed. Newell Charles Smith. 1908. 3 vols.

The Law of Copyright. 1916.

Wordsworth and Reed: The Poet's Correspondence with His American Editor 1836–1850. Ed. Leslie Nathan Broughton. 1933.

The Early Letters of William and Dorothy Wordsworth. Ed. Ernest de Selincourt. 1935.

The Letters of William and Dorothy Wordsworth: The Middle Years. Ed. Ernest de Selincourt. 1937. 2 vols.

The Letters of William and Dorothy Wordsworth: The Later Years. Ed. Ernest de Selincourt. 1939. 3 vols.

Poetical Works. Eds. Ernest de Selincourt and Helen Darbishire. 1940–49. 5 vols.

Some Letters of the Wordsworth Family, Now First Published, with a Few Unpublished Letters of Coleridge and Southey and Others. Ed. Leslie Nathan Broughton. 1941.

Pocket Notebook. Ed. George Harris Healey. 1942.

The Critical Opinions of William Wordsworth. Ed. Markham L. Peacock, Jr. 1950.

Letters. Ed. Philip Wayne. 1954.

Selected Poetry and Prose. Ed. John Butt. 1964.

Literary Criticism. Ed. Paul M. Zall. 1966.

The Early Letters of William and Dorothy Wordsworth. Ed. Ernest de Selincourt, rev. Chester L. Shaver. 1967.

The Letters of William and Dorothy Wordsworth: The Middle Years. Ed. Ernest de Selincourt, rev. Mary Moorman and Alan G. Hill. 1969–70. 2 vols.

Prose Works. Eds. W. J. B. Owen and Jane Worthington Smyser. 1974. 3 vols.

Literary Criticism. Ed. W. J. B. Owen. 1974.

The Cornell Wordsworth. Eds. Stephen Parrish et al. 1975–   .

Poems. Ed. John O. Hayden. 1977. 2 vols.

The Letters of William and Dorothy Wordsworth: The Later Years. Ed. Ernest de Selincourt, rev. Alan G. Hill. 1978–83. 4 vols.

Selected Poetry and Prose. Ed. Geoffrey H. Hartman. 1980.

Letters: A New Selection. Ed. Alan G. Hill. 1984.

William Wordsworth. Ed. Stephen Gill. 1984.

JAMES FENIMORE COOPER (1789–1851)

Precaution. 1820. 2 vols.

The Spy: A Tale of the Neutral Ground. 1821. 2 vols.

The Pioneers; or, The Sources of the Susquehanna: A Descriptive Tale. 1823. 2 vols.

Tales for Fifteen; or, Imagination and Heart. 1823.

The Pilot: A Tale of the Sea. 1823. 2 vols.

Lionel Lincoln; or, The Leaguer of Boston. 1825. 2 vols.

The Last of the Mohicans: A Narrative of 1757. 1826. 2 vols.

The Prairie. 1827. 3 vols.

The Red Rover. 1827. 3 vols.

Notions of the Americans: Picked Up by a Travelling Bachelor. 1828. 2 vols.

The Wept of Wish Ton-Wish. 1829. 2 vols.

The Water-Witch; or, The Skimmer of the Seas. 1830. 3 vols.

Works. 1831–48. 18 vols.

The Bravo: A Venetian Story. 1831. 2 vols.

Letter to Gen. Lafayette, on the Expenditure of the United States of America. 1831.

The Heidenmauer; or, The Benedictines. 1832. 2 vols.

Novels and Tales. 1833–36. 10 vols.

The Headsman; or, The Abbaye des Vignerons. 1833.

A Letter to His Countrymen. 1834.

The Monikins. 1835. 2 vols.

Hints on Manning the Navy. 1836.

Sketches of Switzerland. 1836. 4 vols.

Gleanings in Europe (France). 1837. 2 vols.

Gleanings in Europe: England. 1837. 2 vols.

The American Democrat; or, Hints on the Social and Civil Relations of the United States. 1838.

Gleanings in Europe: Italy. 1838. 2 vols.

Homeward Bound; or, The Case. 1838. 2 vols.

Home as Found. 1838.

The Chronicles of Cooperstown. 1838.

The History of the Navy of the United States of America. 1839. 2 vols.

The Pathfinder; or, The Inland Sea. 1840. 2 vols.

Mercedes of Castile; or, The Voyage to Cathay. 1840. 2 vols.

The Deerslayer; or, The First War-Path. 1841. 2 vols.

The Two Admirals. 1842. 2 vols.

The Wing-and-Wing; or, Le Feu-Follet. 1842. 2 vols.

Le Mouchoir: An Autobiographical Romance. 1843.

The Battle of Lake Erie; or, Answers to Messrs. Burges, Duer, and Mackenzie. 1843.

Wyandotté; or, The Hutted Knoll. 1843. 2 vols.

Ned Myers; or, A Life before the Mast. 1843.

Afloat and Ashore; or, The Adventures of Miles Wallingford. 1844. 4 vols.

Satanstoe; or, The Littlepage Manuscripts. 1845. 2 vols.

The Chainbearer; or, The Littlepage Manuscripts. 1845. 2 vols.

Lives of Distinguished American Naval Officers. 1846. 2 vols.

The Redskins; or, Indian and Injin: Being the Conclusion of the Littlepage Manuscripts. 1846. 2 vols.

The Crater; or, Vulcan's Peak: A Tale of the Pacific. 1847. 2 vols.

Jack Tier; or, The Florida Reef. 1848. 2 vols.

Oak Openings; or, The Bee-Hunter. 1848. 2 vols.

The Sea Lions; or, The Lost Sealers. 1849. 2 vols.

The Ways of the Hour. 1850.

Works. 1855. 33 vols.

Novels. 1867–69. 32 vols.

Correspondence. Ed. James Fenimore Cooper. 1922. 2 vols.

New York: Being an Introduction to an Unpublished Manuscript Entitled The Tours of Manhattan. Ed. Dixon Ryan Fox. 1930.

The Lake Gun. 1932.

Representative Selections. Ed. Robert E. Spiller. 1936.

Letters and Journals. Ed. James Franklin Beard. 1960–68. 6 vols.

Writings. Eds. James Franklin Beard et al. 1980–   .

MARY SHELLEY (1797–1851)

History of a Six Weeks' Tour through a Part of France, Switzerland, Germany and Holland (with Percy Bysshe Shelley). 1817.

Frankenstein; or, The Modern Prometheus. 1818. 3 vols.

Valperga; or, The Life and Adventures of Castruccio, Prince of Lucca. 1823. 3 vols.

Posthumous Poems by Percy Bysshe Shelley (editor). 1824.

The Last Man. 1826. 3 vols.

The Fortunes of Perkin Warbeck: A Romance. 1830. 3 vols.

Lodore. 1835. 3 vols.

Falkner. 1837. 3 vols.

Poetical Works by Percy Bysshe Shelley (editor). 1839. 4 vols.

Essays, Letters from Abroad, Translations and Fragments by Percy Bysshe Shelley (editor). 1840. 2 vols.

Rambles in Germany and Italy in 1840, 1842 and 1843. 1844. 2 vols.

The Choice: A Poem on Shelley's Death. Ed. H. Buxton Forman. 1876.

Letters, Mostly Unpublished. Ed. Henry H. Harper. 1918.

Proserpine and Midas: Mythological Dramas. Ed. André Henri Koszul. 1922.

Harriet and Mary: Being the Relations between P. B., Harriet and Mary Shelley and T. J. Hogg as Shown in Letters between Them (with others). Ed. Walter Sidney Scott. 1944.

Letters. Ed. Frederick L. Jones. 1944. 2 vols.

Journal. Ed. Frederick L. Jones. 1947.

My Best Mary: Selected Letters. Eds. Muriel Spark and Derek Stanford. 1953.

Mathilda. Ed. Elizabeth Nitchie. 1959.

Shelley's Posthumous Poems: Mary Shelley's Fair Copy Book (editor). Ed. Irving Massey. 1969.

Collected Tales and Stories. Ed. Charles E. Robinson. 1976.

Letters. Ed. Betty T. Bennett. 1980– .

Journals. Eds. Paula R. Feldman and Diana Scott-Kilvert. 1987. 2 vols.

CHARLOTTE BRONTË (1816–1855)

Poems by Currer, Ellis, and Acton Bell (with Emily and Anne Brontë). 1846.

Jane Eyre: An Autobiography. 1848. 3 vols.

Shirley: A Tale. 1849. 3 vols.

Villette. 1853. 3 vols.

The Professor: A Tale. 1857. 2 vols.

The Life and Works of Charlotte Brontë and Her Sisters. 1872–73. 7 vols.

The Works of Charlotte, Emily, and Anne Brontë. Ed. F. J. S. 1893. 12 vols.

The Adventures of Ernest Alembert: A Fairy Tale. Ed. Thomas J. Wise. 1896.

The Life and Works of Charlotte Brontë and Her Sisters. Eds. Mrs. Humphry Ward and Clement K. Shorter. 1899–1903. 7 vols.

The Works of Charlotte, Emily, and Anne Brontë. Ed. Temple Scott. 1901. 12 vols.

Poems by Charlotte, Emily, and Anne Brontë. 1902.

The Brontës: Life and Letters. Ed. Clement K. Shorter. 1908. 2 vols.

Richard Cœur de Lion and Blondel: A Poem. Ed. Clement K. Shorter. 1912.

Saul and Other Poems. 1913.

Letters Recounting the Deaths of Emily, Anne and Branwell Brontë by Charlotte Brontë; to Which Are Added Letters Signed "Currer Bell" and "C. B. Nicholls." Ed. Thomas J. Wise. 1913.

The Love Letters of Charlotte Brontë to Constantin Heger. Ed. M. H. Spielmann. 1914.

The Violet: A Poem Written at the Age of Fourteen. Ed. Clement K. Shorter. 1916.

The Red Cross Knight and Other Poems. 1917.

The Swiss Emigrant's Return and Other Poems. 1917.

The Orphans and Other Poems (with Emily and Branwell Brontë). 1917.

The Four Wishes: A Fairy Tale. Ed. Clement K. Shorter. 1918.

Latest Gleanings: Being a Series of Unpublished Poems from Her Early Manuscripts. Ed. Clement K. Shorter. 1918.

Thackeray and Charlotte Brontë: Being Some Hitherto Unpublished Letters. Ed. Clement K. Shorter. 1918.

Napoleon and the Spectre: A Ghost Story. Ed. Clement K. Shorter. 1919.

Darius Codomannus: A Poem Written at the Age of Eighteen Years. 1920.

Complete Poems. Eds. Clement K. Shorter and C. W. Hatfield. 1923.

An Early Essay. Ed. M. H. Spielmann. 1924.

The Twelve Adventurers and Others Stories. Ed. C. W. Hatfield. 1925.

An Account of Her Honeymoon: In a Letter to Miss Catharine Winkworth. Ed. Thomas J. Wise. 1930.

The Spell: An Extravaganza. Ed. George Edwin MacLean. 1931.

The Shakespeare Head Brontë (with Anne and Emily Brontë). Eds. Thomas J. Wise and John Alexander Symington. 1931–38. 19 vols.

The Brontës: Their Lives, Friendships, and Correspondence. Eds. Thomas J. Wise and John Alexander Symington. 1932. 4 vols.

Legends of Angria: Compiled from the Early Writings. Eds. Fanny E. Ratchford and William Clyde DeVane. 1933.

The Miscellaneous and Unpublished Writings of Charlotte and Patrick Branwell Brontë. Eds. Thomas J. Wise and John Alexander Symington. 1936. 2 vols.

Tales from Angria. Ed. Phillis Bentley. 1954.

The Search after Hapiness. Ed. T. A. J. Burnett. 1969.

Five Novelettes. Ed. Winifred Gérin. 1971.

The Novels of Charlotte, Emily, and Anne Brontë. Eds. Hilda Marsden, Ian Jack et al. 1976– .

Two Tales. Ed. William Holtz. 1978.

Poems. Ed. Tom Winnifrith. 1984.

Poems: A New Text and Commentary. Ed. Victor A. Neufeldt. 1985.

Selected Poems (with Anne and Emily Brontë). Eds. Tom Winnifrith and Edward Chitham. 1985.

The Brontës: Selected Poems. Ed. Juliet R. Barker. 1985.

The Juvenilia of Jane Austen and Charlotte Brontë. Ed. Frances Beer. 1986.

WASHINGTON IRVING (1783–1859)

A Voyage to the Eastern Part of Terra Firma by François Depons (translator). 1806. 3 vols.

Salmagundi (with others). 1807–08. 20 nos.

A History of New York from the Beginning of the World to the End of the Dutch Dynasty. 1809. 2 vols.

Poetical Works of Thomas Campbell (editor). 1810. 2 vols.

The Sketch Book of Geoffrey Crayon, Gent. 1819–20. 7 parts.

Bracebridge Hall; or, The Humourists: A Medley. 1822. 2 vols.

Letters of Jonathan Old-Style, Gent. 1824.

Tales of a Traveller. 1824. 4 parts.

The Miscellaneous Works of Oliver Goldsmith (editor). 1825. 4 vols.

A History of the Life and Voyages of Christopher Columbus. 1828. 3 vols.

A Chronicle of the Conquest of Granada. 1829. 2 vols.

Voyages and Discoveries of the Companions of Columbus. 1831.

Poems by William Cullen Bryant (editor). 1832.

The Alhambra: A Series of Tales and Sketches of the Moors and Spaniards. 1832. 2 vols.

Complete Works. 1834.

The Crayon Miscellany ⟨*A Tour of the Prairies; Abbotsford and Newstead Abbey; Legends of the Conquest of Spain*⟩. 1835. 3 vols.

The Beauties of Washington Irving. 1835.

Astoria; or, Anecdotes of an Enterprise beyond the Rocky Mountains. 1836. 2 vols.

The Rocky Mountains; or, Scenes, Incidents, and Adventures in the Far West by Captain B. L. E. Bonneville (editor). 1837. 2 vols.

The Life of Oliver Goldsmith. 1840 (2 vols.), 1849.

Works. 1840. 2 vols.

Biography and Poetical Remains of the Late Margaret Miller Davidson. 1841.

Works (Author's Revised Edition). 1848–51. 15 vols.

A Book of the Hudson. 1849.

Mahomet and His Successors. 1850. 2 vols.

Wolfert's Roost and Other Papers. 1855.

The Life of George Washington. 1855–59. 5 vols.

Life and Letters. Ed. Pierre M. Irving. 1862–64. 4 vols.

Spanish Papers and Other Miscellanies. Ed. Pierre M. Irving. 1866. 2 vols.

Works. 1872. 28 vols.

Works (Hudson Edition). 1882. 27 vols.

Letters to Mrs. William Renwick, and to Her Son, James Renwick. 1915.

Letters to Henry Brevoort. Ed. George S. Hellman. 1915. 2 vols.

Journals. Eds. William P. Trent and George S. Hellman. 1919. 3 vols.

Notes and Journal of Travel in Europe 1804–1805. Ed. William P. Trent. 1921. 3 vols.

Abu Hassan. Ed. George S. Hellman. 1924.

The Wild Huntsman (adaptation). Ed. George S. Hellman. 1924.

An Unwritten Drama of Lord Byron. Ed. Thomas Ollive Mabbott. 1925.

Diary Spain 1828–1829. Ed. Clara Louisa Penney. 1926.

Notes While Preparing Sketch Book 1817. Ed. Stanley T. Williams. 1927.

Tour in Scotland 1817 and Other Manuscript Notes. Ed. Stanley T. Williams. 1927.

Letters from Sunnyside and Spain. Ed. Stanley T. Williams. 1928.

Journal (1823–1824). Ed. Stanley T. Williams. 1931.

Washington Irving and the Storrows: Letters from England and the Continent 1821–1828. Ed. Stanley T. Williams. 1933.

Journal 1803. Ed. Stanley T. Williams. 1934.

Journal 1828 and Miscellaneous Notes on Moorish Legend and History. Ed. Stanley T. Williams. 1937.

Contributions to The Corrector. Ed. Martin Roth. 1968.

Complete Works. Eds. Henry A. Pochmann, Herbert L. Kleinfeld, Richard Dilworth Rust et al. 1969–   .

THOMAS BABINGTON MACAULAY (1800–1859)

Pompeii: A Poem Which Obtained the Chancellor's Medal at the Cambridge Commencement, July 1819. 1819.

Evening: A Poem Which Obtained the Chancellor's Medal at the Cambridge Commencement, July 1821. 1821.

A Speech Delivered in the House of Commons on Lord John Russell's Motion for Leave to Bring In a Bill to Emend the Representation of the People in England and Wales. 1831.

Speech on the Second Reading of the Third Reform Bill. 1831.

Speech on the Anatomy Bill. 1832.

A Speech on the Second Reading of the East-India Bill. 1833.

A Penal Code Prepared by the Indian Law Commissioners (with others). 1837.

Speech at a Meeting of the Electors of Edinburgh. 1839.

Critical and Miscellaneous Essays. 1840–41. 3 vols.

A Speech Delivered in the House of Commons. 1841.

Lays of Ancient Rome. 1842.

Critical and Historical Essays. 1843. 3 vols.

Speech in the House of Commons on the Proposed Discriminating Duties on Sugar. 1845.

Speech Delivered in the House of Commons on the Bill for the Abolition of Scottish University Tests. 1845.

The History of England from the Accession of James II. 1849 [Volumes 1–2]; 1855 [Volumes 3–4]; 1861 [Volume 5].

Inaugural Address Delivered on His Installation as Lord Rector of the University of Glasgow. 1849.

Speeches. 1853. 2 vols.

Speeches Corrected by Himself. 1854.

The Indian Civil Service (with others). 1855.

Were Human Sacrifices in Use among the Romans? (with Sir Robert Peel and Lord Mahon). 1860.

Correspondence between the Bishop of Exeter and Thomas Babington Macaulay in January 1849 on Certain Statements Respecting the Church of England. 1860.

Critical, Historical, and Miscellaneous Essays. 1860. 6 vols.

Miscellaneous Writings. Ed. Thomas Flower Ellis. 1860. 2 vols.

Biographies Contributed to the Encyclopaedia Britannica. 1860.

Indian Education Minutes. Ed. H. Woodrow. 1862.

Works. Ed. Lady Trevelyan. 1866. 8 vols.

Works (Albany Edition). 1898. 12 vols.

Hymn: An Effort of His Early Childhood. Ed. Lionel Horton-Smith. 1902.

Works. 1905–07. 9 vols.

Marginal Notes. Ed. G. Otto Trevelyan. 1907.

Essay and Speech on Jewish Disabilities. Ed. Israel Abrahams and S. Levy. 1910.

What Did Macaulay Say about America? Ed. Harry Miller Lydenberg. 1925.

Lays of Ancient Rome and Other Historical Poems. Ed. George Macaulay Trevelyan. 1928.

Legislative Minutes. Ed. C. D. Dharker. 1946.

Prose and Poetry. Ed. G. M. Young. 1952.

Selected Writings. Eds. John Clive and Thomas Pinney. 1972.

Letters. Ed. Thomas Pinney. 1974–81. 6 vols.

HENRY DAVID THOREAU (1817–1862)

A Week on the Concord and Merrimack Rivers. 1849.

Walden; or, Life in the Woods. 1854.

Excursions. Ed. Ralph Waldo Emerson. 1863.

The Maine Woods. 1864.

Cape Cod. 1864.

Letters to Various Persons. Ed. Ralph Waldo Emerson. 1865.

A Yankee in Canada, with Anti-Slavery and Reform Papers. 1866.

Early Spring in Massachusetts: From the Journals. Ed. H. G. O. Blake. 1881.

Summer: From the Journal. Ed. H. G. O. Blake. 1884.

Winter: From the Journal. Ed. H. G. O. Blake. 1888.

Autumn: From the Journal. Ed. H. G. O. Blake. 1892.

Writings (Riverside Edition). Eds. Horace E. Scudder et al. 1893–94. 11 vols.

Poems of Nature. Eds. Henry S. Salt and Frank B. Sanborn. 1895.

Some Unpublished Letters of Henry D. and Sophia E. Thoreau. Ed. Samuel Arthur Jones. 1899.

Writings (Manuscript Edition). Eds. Bradford Torrey and Francis H. Allen. 1906. 20 vols.

The Transmigrations of the Seven Brahmas: A Translation from the Harivansa *of Langlois* (translator). Ed. Arthur Christy. 1931.

Collected Poems. Ed. Carl Bode. 1943, 1964.

Correspondence. Eds. Walter Harding and Carl Bode. 1958.

Consciousness in Concord: The Text of Thoreau's Hitherto "Lost Journal" (1840–1841). Ed. Perry Miller. 1958.

Huckleberries. Ed. Leo Stoller. 1970.

Writings. Eds. Walter Harding et al. 1971–   .

Selected Works. Ed. Walter Harding. 1975.

WILLIAM MAKEPEACE THACKERAY (1811–1863)

Flore et Zéphyr. 1836.

The Yellowplush Correspondence. 1838.

Reminiscences of Major Gahagan. 1839.

The Loving Ballad of Lord Bateman (with Charles Dickens). 1839.

An Essay on the Genius of George Cruikshank. 1840.

The Paris Sketch Book. 1840. 2 vols.

Comic Tales and Sketches. 1841. 2 vols.

The Second Funeral of Napoleon: In Three Letters to Miss Smith of London; and The Chronicle of the Drum. 1841.

The Irish Sketch-Book. 1843. 2 vols.

Jeames's Diary; or, Sudden Riches. 1846.

Notes of a Journey from Cornhill to Grand Cairo, by Way of Lisbon, Athens, Constantinople, and Jerusalem. 1846.

Mrs. Perkins's Ball. 1847.

Vanity Fair: A Novel without a Hero. 1847–48. 20 parts.

The Book of Snobs. 1848.

Our Street. 1848.

The History of Pendennis. 1848–50. 24 parts.

Doctor Birch and His Young Friends. 1849.

The History of Samuel Titmarsh and The Great Hoggarty Diamond. 1849.

Miscellanies: Prose and Verse. 1849–51. 2 vols.

The Kickleburys on the Rhine. 1850.

Stubbs's Calendar; or, The Fatal Boots. 1850.

Rebecca and Rowena: A Romance upon Romance. 1850.

The History of Henry Esmond, Esq. 1852. 3 vols.

The Confessions of Fitz-Boodle and Some Passage in the Life of Major Gahagan. 1852.

A Shabby Genteel Story and Other Tales. 1852.

Men's Wives. 1852.

The Luck of Barry Lyndon: A Romance of the Last Century. 1852–53. 2 vols.

Mr. Brown's Letters to a Young Man about Town. 1853.

The English Humourists of the Eighteenth Century. 1853.

The Newcomes: Memoirs of a Most Respectable Family. 1853–55. 24 parts.

The Rose and the Ring. 1855.

Miscellanies: Prose and Verse. 1855–57. 4 vols.

Ballads. 1856.

Christmas Books. 1857.

The Virginians: A Tale of the Last Century. 1857–59. 24 parts.

Mr. Thackeray, Mr. Yates, and the Garrick Club (with Edmund Yates). 1859.

The Four Georges: Sketches of Manners, Morals, Court, and Town Life. 1860.

Lovel the Widower. 1860.

The Adventures of Philip on His Way through the World; Shewing Who Robbed Him, Who Helped Him, and Who Passed Him By. 1862. 3 vols.

Roundabout Papers. 1863.

Miscellanies. 1864. 6 vols.

Denis Duval. 1864.

Works (Library Edition). 1867–69, 1885–86. 24 vols.

Early and Late Papers Hitherto Uncollected. Ed. James T. Fields. 1867.

The Orphan of Pimlico and Other Sketches, Fragments, and Drawings. Ed. Anne Thackeray ⟨Ritchie⟩. 1876.

Works (De Luxe Edition). 1878–86. 26 vols.

Etchings. 1878.

Works (Standard Edition). 1883–86. 26 vols.

Sultan Stork and Other Stories and Sketches (1829–1844). Ed. R. H. Shepherd. 1887.

A Collection of Letters 1847–1855. Ed. J. O. Brookfield. 1887.

Works. Ed. Horace E. Scudder. 1889. 22 vols.

Early Writings. Ed. Charles Plumptre Johnson. 1888.

Reading a Poem. 1891.

Works (New Century Library). 1899–1900. 14 vols.

The Hitherto Unidentified Contributions of W. M. Thackeray to Punch. Ed. M. H. Spielmann. 1899.

Writings in the National Standard *and* Constitutional. Ed. W. T. Spencer. 1899.

Stray Papers: Being Stories, Reviews, Verses, and Sketches (1821–1847). Ed. Lewis Melville. 1901.

Prose Works. Ed. Walter Jerrold. 1901–03. 30 vols.

Works. Ed. Lewis Melville. 1901–07. 20 vols.

Letters to an American Family. Ed. Lucy W. Baxter. 1904.

The New Sketch Book: Being Essays Now First Collected from the Foreign Quarterly Review. Ed. Robert S. Garnett. 1906.

Works (Oxford Edition). Ed. George Saintsbury. 1908. 18 vols.

Works (Centenary Biographical Edition). Ed. Anne Thackeray Ritchie. 1910–11. 26 vols.

Some Family Letters. 1911.

Unpublished Letters. Ed. Clement K. Shorter. 1916.

W. M. Thackeray and Edward FitzGerald, a Literary Friendship: Unpublished Letters and Verses. Ed. Clement K. Shorter. 1916.

Letters of Anne Thackeray Ritchie, with Forty-two Additional Letters from Her Father. Ed. Hester Ritchie. 1924.

Letters and Private Papers. Ed. Gordon N. Ray. 1945–46. 6 vols.

Contributions to the Morning Chronicle. Ed. Gordon N. Ray. 1955.

Illustrations. Ed. John Buchanan-Brown. 1979.

The Heroic Adventures of M. Boudin. Ed. Gordon N. Ray. 1984.

NATHANIEL HAWTHORNE (1804–1864)

Fanshawe. 1828.

Twice-Told Tales. 1837, 1842 (2 vols.).

Peter Pauley's Universal History (editor; with Elizabeth Hawthorne). 1837. 2 vols.

Time's Portraiture: Being the Carrier's Address to the Patrons of the Salem Gazette *for the First of January, 1838.* 1838.

The Sister Years: Being the Carrier's Address to the Patrons of the Salem Gazette *for the First of January, 1839.* 1839.

Grandfather's Chair: A History for Youth. 1841.

Famous Old People: Being the Second Epoch of Grandfather's Chair. 1841.

The Liberty Tree, with the Last Words of Grandfather's Chair. 1841.

Biographical Stories for Children. 1842.
The Celestial Rail-Road. 1843.
Mosses from an Old Manse. 1846. 2 vols.
The Scarlet Letter: A Romance. 1850.
The House of the Seven Gables: A Romance. 1851.
A Wonder-Book for Girls and Boys. 1852.
The Snow-Image and Other Twice-Told Tales. 1852.
The Blithedale Romance. 1852.
Life of Franklin Pierce. 1852.
Tanglewood Tales for Girls and Boys: Being a Second Wonder-Book. 1853.
The Marble Faun; or, The Romance of Monte Beni. 1860.
Our Old Home: A Series of English Sketches. 1863.
Pansie: A Fragment: The Last Literary Effort of Nathaniel Hawthorne. 1864.
Works. 1865–76. 23 vols.
Passages from the American Note-Books. Ed. Sophia Hawthorne. 1868. 2 vols.
Passages from the English Note-Books. Ed. Sophia Hawthorne. 1870. 2 vols.
Passages from the French and Italian Note-Books. Ed. Una Hawthorne. 1871. 2 vols.
Septimius Felton; or, The Elixir of Life. Eds. Una Hawthorne and Robert Browning. 1872.
Writings. Ed. George Parsons Lathrop. 1875–83. 25 vols.
The Dolliver Romance and Other Pieces. Ed. Sophia Hawthorne. 1876.
Doctor Grimshawe's Secret: A Romance. Ed. Julian Hawthorne. 1883.
Works (Riverside Edition). Ed. George Parsons Lathrop. 1883. 12 vols.
Complete Writings (Autograph Edition). 1900. 22 vols.
Twenty Days with Julian and Little Bunny: A Diary. 1904.
Love Letters. 1907. 2 vols.
Letters to William D. Ticknor. 1910. 2 vols.
Works. Ed. Charles Curtis Bigelow. 1923. 10 vols.
The Heart of Hawthorne's Journals. Ed. Newton Arvin. 1929.
Hawthorne as Editor: Selections from His Writings in the American Magazine of Useful and Entertaining Knowledge. Ed. Arlin Turner. 1941.
Works. Eds. William Charvat et al. 1963– .
Hawthorne's Lost Notebook 1835–1841. Ed. Barbara S. Mouffe. 1978.

CHARLES DICKENS (1812–1870)

Sketches by "Boz" Illustrative of Every-day Life and Every-day People. 1836. 2 vols.
Sunday under Three Heads. 1836.
The Village Coquettes: A Comic Opera. 1836.
The Strange Gentleman: A Comic Burletta. 1837.
The Posthumous Papers of the Pickwick Club. 1836–37. 20 parts.
Memoirs of Joseph Grimaldi (editor). 1838. 2 vols.
Sketches of Young Gentlemen. 1838.
Oliver Twist; or, The Parish Boy's Progress. 1838. 3 vols.
The Life and Adventures of Nicholas Nickleby. 1838–39. 20 parts.
The Loving Ballad of Lord Bateman (with William Makepeace Thackeray). 1839.
Sketches of Young Couples. 1840.
Master Humphrey's Clock ⟨*Old Curiosity Shop; Barnaby Rudge*⟩. 1840–41. 88 parts.
The Pic Nic Papers (editor). 1841. 3 vols.

American Notes. 1842. 2 vols.
A Christmas Carol in Prose: Being a Ghost-Story of Christmas. 1843.
The Life and Adventures of Martin Chuzzlewit, His Relatives, Friends and Enemies. 1843–44. 20 parts.
The Chimes: A Goblin Story of Some Bells That Rang an Old Year Out and a New Year In. 1845.
The Cricket on the Hearth: A Fairy Tale of Home. 1846.
Pictures from Italy. 1846.
The Battle of Life: A Love Story. 1846.
Dealings with the Firm of Dombey and Son Wholesale, Retail and for Exportation. 1846–48. 20 parts.
An Appeal to Fallen Women. 1847.
Works. 1847–67. 17 vols.
The Haunted Man and the Ghost's Bargain: A Fancy for Christmas Time. 1848.
Elegy Written in a Country Churchyard. c. 1849.
The Personal History, Adventures, Experiences and Observations of David Copperfield the Younger. 1849–50. 20 parts.
Mr. Nightingale's Diary: A Farce (with Mark Lemon). 1851.
Bleak House. 1852–53. 20 parts.
A Child's History of England. 1852–54. 3 vols.
Hard Times, for These Times. 1854.
Speech Delivered at the Meeting of the Administrative Reform Association. 1855.
Little Dorrit. 1855–57. 20 parts.
Novels and Tales Reprinted from Household Words (editor). 1856–59. 11 vols.
The Case of the Reformers in the Literary Fund (with others). 1858.
Speech at the Anniversary Festival of the Hospital for Sick Children. 1858.
Speech at the First Festival Dinner of the Playground and Recreation Society. 1858.
Works (Library Edition). 1858–59 (22 vols.), 1861–74 (30 vols.).
A Tale of Two Cities. 1859. 8 parts.
Christmas Stories from Household Words. 1859. 9 parts.
Great Expectations. 1861. 3 vols.
Great Expectations: A Drama. 1861.
The Uncommercial Traveler. 1861.
An Address on Behalf of the Printer's Pension Society. c. 1864.
⟨*Speech at the*⟩ *North London or University College Hospital: Anniversary Dinner in Aid of the Funds.* 1864.
Our Mutual Friend. 1864–65. 20 parts.
The Frozen Deep (with Wilkie Collins). 1866.
No Thoroughfare (with Wilkie Collins). 1867.
⟨*Speech at the*⟩ *Railway Benevolent Institution: Ninth Annual Dinner.* 1867.
Works (Charles Dickens Edition). 1867–75. 21 vols.
Christmas Stories from All the Year Round. c. 1868. 9 parts.
The Readings of Mr. Charles Dickens, as Condensed by Himself. 1868.
Address Delivered at the Birmingham and Midland Institute. 1869.
A Curious Dance round a Curious Tree (with W. H. Wills). 1870.
Speech as Chairman of the Anniversary Festival Dinner of the Royal Free Hospital. 1870.
The Mystery of Edwin Drood. 1870. 6 parts.
Speeches Literary and Social. Ed. R. H. Shepherd. 1870.
The Newsvendors' Benevolent and Provident Institution: Speeches in Behalf of the Institution. 1871.

Is She His Wife? or Something Singular: A Comic Burletta. c. 1872.

The Lamplighter: A Farce. 1879.

The Mudfog Papers, etc. 1880.

Letters. Eds. Georgina Hogarth and Mary Dickens. 1880–82. 3 vols.

Plays and Poems, with a Few Miscellanies in Prose Now First Collected. Ed. R. H. Shepherd. 1885. 2 vols.

The Lazy Tour of Two Idle Apprentices; No Thoroughfare; The Perils of Certain English Prisoners (with Wilkie Collins). 1890.

Works (Macmillan Edition). 1892–1925. 21 vols.

Letters to Wilkie Collins 1851–1870. Ed. Lawrence Hutton. 1892.

Works (Gadshill Edition). Ed. Andrew Lang. 1897–1908. 36 vols.

To Be Read at Dusk and Other Stories, Sketches and Essays. Ed. F. G. Kitton. 1898.

Christmas Stories from Household Stories *and* All the Year Round. 1898. 5 vols.

Works (Biographical Edition). Ed. Arthur Waugh. 1902–03. 19 vols.

Poems and Verses. Ed. F. G. Kitton. 1903.

Works (National Edition). Ed. Bertram W. Matz. 1906–08. 40 vols.

Dickens and Maria Beadnell: Private Correspondence. Ed. G. P. Baker. 1908.

The Dickens-Kolle Letters. Ed. Harry B. Smith. 1910.

Works (Centenary Edition). 1910–11. 36 vols.

Dickens as Editor: Letters Written by Him to William Henry Wills, His Sub-Editor. Ed. R. C. Lehmann. 1912.

Works (Waverley Edition). 1913–18. 30 vols.

Unpublished Letters to Mark Lemon. Ed. Walter Dexter. 1927.

Letters to the Baroness Burdett-Coutts. Ed. Charles C. Osborne. 1931.

Dickens to His Oldest Friend: The Letters of a Lifetime to Thomas Beard. Ed. Walter Dexter. 1932.

Letters to Charles Lever. Ed. Flora V. Livingston. 1933.

Mr. and Mrs. Charles Dickens: His Letters to Her. Ed. Walter Dexter. 1935.

The Love Romance of Dickens, Told in His Letters to Maria Beadnell (Mrs. Winter). Ed. Walter Dexter. 1936.

The Nonesuch Dickens. Eds. Arthur Waugh, Hugh Walpole, Walter Dexter, and Thomas Hatton. 1937–38. 23 vols.

Letters. Ed. Walter Dexter. 1938. 3 vols.

The New Oxford Illustrated Dickens. 1947–58. 21 vols.

The Heart of Dickens. Ed. Edgar Johnson. 1952.

Best Stories. Ed. Morton D. Zabel. 1959.

Speeches. Ed. K. J. Fielding. 1960.

Selected Letters. Ed. F. W. Dupee. 1960.

Letters (Pilgrim Edition). Eds. Madeline House, Graham Storey, Kathleen Tillotson et al. 1965–   .

The Clarendon Dickens. Eds. John Butt, Kathleen Tillotson, and James Kinsley. 1966–   .

Uncollected Writings from Household Words *1850–1859.* Ed. Harry Stone. 1968.

Complete Plays and Selected Poems. 1970.

Short Stories. Ed. Walter Allen. 1971.

Dickens in Europe: Essays. Ed. Rosalind Vallance. 1975.

The Public Readings. Ed. Phillip Collins. 1975.

Selected Short Fiction. Ed. Deborah A. Thomas. 1976.

Supernatural Short Stories. Ed. Michael Hayes. 1978.

Selected Letters. Ed. David Paroissien. 1985.

Dickens' Working Notes for His Novels. Ed. Harry Stone. 1987.

GEORGE ELIOT (MARY ANN EVANS) (1819–1880)

The Life of Jesus Critically Examined by David Friedrich Strauss (translator). 1846. 3 vols.

The Essence of Christianity by Ludwig Feuerbach (translator). 1854.

Scenes of Clerical Life. 1858. 3 vols.

Adam Bede. 1859. 3 vols.

The Mill on the Floss. 1860. 3 vols.

Silas Marner: The Weaver of Raveloe. 1861.

Romola. 1863. 3 vols.

Felix Holt, the Radical. 1866. 3 vols.

Novels. 1867–78. 6 vols.

The Spanish Gypsy. 1868.

Agatha. 1869.

How Lisa Loved the King. 1869.

Middlemarch: A Study of Provincial Life. 1872. 4 vols.

A Legend of Jubal and Other Poems. 1874.

Daniel Deronda. 1876. 4 vols.

Novels. 1876. 9 vols.

Works (Cabinet Edition). 1878–85. 24 vols.

Impressions of Theophrastus Such. 1879.

Essays and Leaves from a Note-Book. Ed. Charles Lee Lewes. 1885.

George Eliot's Life as Related in Her Letters and Journals. Ed. J. W. Cross. 1885. 3 vols.

Complete Poems. 1888.

Letters to Elma Stuart 1872–1880. Ed. Roland Stuart. 1909.

Early Essays. Ed. George W. Redway. 1919.

Letters. Ed. R. Brimley Johnson. 1926.

Letters. Ed. Gordon S. Haight. 1954–78. 9 vols.

Essays. Ed. Thomas Pinney. 1963.

Works. Ed. Gordon S. Haight. 1980–   .

A Writer's Notebook 1854–1879, and Uncollected Writings. Ed. Joseph Wiesenfarth. 1981.

Ethics by Benedict Spinoza (translator). 1981.

THOMAS CARLYLE (1795–1881)

Elements of Geometry and Trigonometry by A. M. Legendre (translator). 1824.

Wilhelm Meister's Apprenticeship: A Novel from the German of Goethe (translator). 1824. 3 vols.

The Life of Friedrich Schiller: Comprehending an Examination of His Life and Writings. 1825.

German Romance: Specimens of Its Chief Authors, with Biographical and Critical Notices (editor and translator). 1827. 4 vols.

Sartor Resartus: The Life and Opinions of Herr Teufelsdröckh. 1836.

The French Revolution: A History. 1837. 3 vols.

Critical and Miscellaneous Essays. Eds. Ralph Waldo Emerson et al. 1838. 4 vols.

Chartism. 1840.

On Heroes, Hero-Worship, and the Heroic in History. 1841.

Past and Present. 1843.

Oliver Cromwell's Letters and Speeches, with Elucidations. 1845. 2 vols.

Latter-Day Pamphlets. 1850. 8 parts.

The Life of John Sterling. 1851.

Occasional Discourse on the Nigger Question. 1853.

Collected Works. 1857–58. 16 vols.

History of Friedrich II. of Prussia, Called Frederick the Great. 1858–65. 6 vols.

Inaugural Address at Edinburgh, on Being Installed as Rector of the University There ⟨On the Choice of Books⟩. 1866.

Critical and Miscellaneous Essays. 1869. 6 vols.

Collected Works (Library Edition). 1869–71. 34 vols.

Collected Works (People's Edition). 1871–74. 37 vols.

Letters to Mrs. Basil Montagu and B. W. Procter. 1881.

Reminiscences. Ed. James Anthony Froude. 1881. 2 vols.

Last Words on Trades-Unions, Promoterism and the Signs of the Times. Ed. Jane Carlyle Aitken. 1882.

Reminiscences of My Irish Journey in 1849. Ed. James Anthony Froude. 1882.

The Correspondence of Thomas Carlyle and Ralph Waldo Emerson 1834–1872. Ed. Charles Eliot Norton. 1883. 2 vols.

The Correspondence of Thomas Carlyle and Ralph Waldo Emerson 1834–1872: Supplementary Letters. Ed. Charles Eliot Norton. 1886.

Early Letters 1814–1826. Ed. Charles Eliot Norton. 1886. 2 vols.

Correspondence between Goethe and Carlyle. Ed. Charles Eliot Norton. 1887.

Early Letters 1826–1836. Ed. Charles Eliot Norton. 1888. 2 vols.

Rescued Essays. Ed. Percy Newberry. 1892.

Last Words of Thomas Carlyle: Wotton Reinfred, a Romance; Excursion (Futile Enough) to Paris; Letters. 1892.

Lectures on the History of Literature; or, The Successive Periods of European Culture. Ed. J. Reay Greene. 1892.

Works (Centenary Edition). Ed. H. D. Traill. 1896–99. 30 vols.

Two Note Books from 23d March 1822 to 16th May 1832. Ed. Charles Eliot Norton. 1898.

Historical Sketches of Notable Persons and Events in the Reigns of James I. and Charles I. Ed. Alexander Carlyle. 1898.

Letters to His Youngest Sister. Ed. Charles Townsend Copeland. 1899.

Collectanea 1821–1855. Ed. Samuel Arthur Jones. 1903.

New Letters. Ed. Alexander Carlyle. 1904. 2 vols.

Carlyle and the London Library: Account of Its Foundation; Together with the Unpublished Letters to W. D. Christie. Ed. Frederic Harrison. 1907.

Love Letters of Thomas Carlyle and Jane Welsh Carlyle. Ed. Alexander Carlyle. 1909. 2 vols.

Letters of Thomas Carlyle to John Stuart Mill, John Sterling and Robert Browning. Ed. Alexander Carlyle. 1923.

Journey to Germany, Autumn, 1858. Ed. Richard Albert Edward Brooks. 1940.

Letters to William Graham. Ed. John Graham, Jr. 1950.

Carlyle's Unfinished History of German Literature. Ed. Hill Shine. 1951.

Carlyle: An Anthology. Ed. G. M. Trevelyan. 1953.

Letters to His Wife. Ed. Trudy Bliss. 1953.

Selected Works, Reminiscences and Letters. Ed. Julian Symons. 1955.

The Correspondence of Emerson and Carlyle. Ed. Joseph Slater. 1964.

Letters to His Brother Alexander, with Related Family Letters. Ed. Edwin W. Marrs, Jr. 1968.

Collected Letters of Thomas and Jane Welsh Carlyle. Eds. Charles Richard Sanders, Kenneth J. Fielding, Claude de L. Ryals et al. 1978–   .

The Correspondence of Thomas Carlyle and John Ruskin. Ed. George Allen Cate. 1982.

A Carlyle Reader. Ed. G. B. Tennyson. 1984.

Collected Poems of Thomas and Jane Welsh Carlyle. Eds. Rodger L. Tarr and Fleming McClelland. 1986.

RALPH WALDO EMERSON (1803–1882)

Letter to the Second Church and Society. 1832.

A Historical Discourse, Delivered before the Citizens of Concord, on the Second Centennial Anniversary of the Town. 1835.

Nature. 1836.

Original Hymn ⟨Concord Hymn⟩. 1837.

An Oration, Delivered before the Phi Beta Kappa Society ⟨American Scholar Address⟩. 1837.

⟨*Prospectus for Carlyle's* French Revolution.⟩ 1837.

An Address Delivered before the Literary Societies of Dartmouth College. 1838.

⟨*Prospectus for Carlyle's* Essays.⟩ 1838.

Critical and Miscellaneous Essays by Thomas Carlyle (editor; with others). 1838. 4 vols.

Essays and Poems by Jones Very (editor). 1839.

Essays. 1841.

The Method of Nature: An Oration, Delivered before the Society of the Adelphi. 1841.

Man the Reformer: A Lecture on Some of the Prominent Features of the Present Age. 1842.

Nature: An Essay, and Lectures on the Times. 1844.

Orations, Lectures, and Addresses. 1844.

The Young American: A Lecture Read before the Mercantile Library Association. 1844.

Essays: Second Series. 1844.

An Address on the Anniversary of the Emancipation of the Negroes in the British West Indies. 1844.

Poems. 1847.

⟨*Prospectus to the Town and Country Club.*⟩ 1849.

Town and Country Club Constitution. 1849.

Nature; Addresses, and Lectures. 1849.

Representative Men: Seven Lectures. 1850.

Memoirs of Margaret Fuller Ossoli (editor; with James Freeman Clarke and William Henry Channing). 1852.

English Traits. 1856.

Fourth of July Breakfast and Floral Exhibition, at the Town Hall, Concord: Ode. 1857.

Boston, Nov. 2, 1859. Dear Sir:—You are invited and urged to contribute and obtain contributions to aid the defense of Capt. ⟨John⟩ *Brown and his companions, on trial for their lives in Virginia* (with others). 1859.

The Conduct of Life. 1860.

Excursions by Henry David Thoreau (editor). 1863.

Letters to Various Persons by Henry David Thoreau (editor). 1865.

Complete Works. 1866–83. 3 vols.

Additional Testimonial in Favour of James Hutchison Stirling. c. 1866.

May-Day and Other Pieces. 1867.

Mrs. Sarah A. Ripley. 1867.

Address ⟨at the Dedication of the Soldier's Monument⟩. 1867.

Society and Solitude. 1870.

Prose Works. 1870–79. 3 vols.

Remarks on the Character of George L. Stearns. 1872.

Parnassus (editor). 1875.

Letters and Social Aims (with Ellen and James Eliot Cabot). 1876.

Remarks at the Centennial Celebration of the Latin School. 1876.

Works (Little Classic Edition). 1876–93. 12 vols.

Fortune of the Republic: Lecture Delivered at the Old South Church. 1878.

The Preacher. 1880.

Hymns for the Free Religious Association. 1882.

The Correspondence of Thomas Carlyle and Ralph Waldo Emerson. Ed. Charles Eliot Norton. 1883. 2 vols.

Works. 1883. 3 vols.

Complete Works (Riverside Edition). Ed. James Eliot Cabot. 1883–93. 12 vols.

The Senses and the Soul and Moral Sentiment in Religion. Ed. Walter Lewin. 1885.

The Correspondence of Thomas Carlyle and Ralph Waldo Emerson 1834–1872: Supplementary Letters. Ed. Charles Eliot Norton. 1886.

Two Unpublished Essays: The Character of Socrates; The Present State of Ethical Philosophy. 1896.

A Correspondence between John Sterling and Ralph Waldo Emerson. Ed. Edward Waldo Emerson. 1897.

Letters to a Friend 1838–1853. Ed. Charles Eliot Norton. 1899.

Correspondence between Ralph Waldo Emerson and Herman Grimm. Ed. Frederick William Holls. 1903.

Complete Works (Centenary Edition). Ed. Edward Waldo Emerson. 1903–04. 12 vols.

Journals. Eds. Edward Waldo Emerson and Waldo Emerson Forbes. 1909–14. 10 vols.

Records of a Lifelong Friendship 1807–1882: Ralph Waldo Emerson and William Henry Furness. Ed. Horace Howard Furness. 1910.

Uncollected Writings: Essays, Addresses, Poems, Reviews, and Letters. Ed. Charles C. Bigelow. 1912.

Uncollected Lectures. Ed. Clarence Gohdes. 1932.

Emerson-Clough Letters. Eds. Howard F. Lowry and Ralph Leslie Rusk. 1934.

Young Emerson Speaks: Unpublished Discourses on Many Subjects. Ed. Arthur Cushman McGiffert, Jr. 1938.

Letters. Ed. Ralph L. Rusk. 1939. 6 vols.

Early Lectures. Eds. Stephen E. Whicher, Robert E. Spiller, and Wallace E. Williams. 1959–72. 3 vols.

Dante's Vita Nuova (translator). Ed. J. Christy Mathews. 1960.

Journals and Miscellaneous Notebooks. Eds. William E. Gilman, Alfred R. Ferguson et al. 1960–82. 16 vols.

The Correspondence of Emerson and Carlyle. Ed. Joseph Slater. 1964.

Collected Works. Eds. Alfred R. Ferguson et al. 1971– .

Literary Criticism. Ed. Eric W. Carlson. 1979.

Emerson in His Journals. Ed. Joel Porte. 1982.

Essays and Lectures. Ed. Joel Porte. 1983.

Poetry Notebooks. Eds. Ralph H. Orth, Albert J. Von Franke, Linda Allardt, and David W. Hill. 1986.

HENRY WADSWORTH LONGFELLOW (1807–1882)

Manual de proverbes dramatiques (editor). 1830.

Elements of French Grammar by Charles Lhomond (translator). 1830.

Novelas españolas (editor). 1830.

Le Ministre de Wakefield by Oliver Goldsmith, tr. T. F. G. Hennequin (editor). 1831.

Syllabus de la grammaire italienne. 1832.

Saggi de' novellieri italiani d'ogni secolo (editor). 1832.

Outre-Mer: A Pilgrimage beyond the Sea. 1833–34. 2 nos.

Coplas de Don Jorge Manrique (translator). 1833.

Hyperion: A Romance. 1839. 2 vols.

Voices of the Night. 1839.

Poems on Slavery. 1842.

Ballads and Other Poems. 1842.

The Spanish Student. 1843.

The Waif: A Collection of Poems (editor). 1845.

The Poets and Poetry of Europe (editor). 1845.

Poems. 1845.

The Belfry of Bruges and Other Poems. 1846.

The Estray: A Collection of Poems (editor). 1847.

Evangeline: A Tale of Acadie. 1847.

Poems Lyrical and Dramatic. 1848.

Kavanagh: A Tale. 1849.

The Seaside and the Fireside. 1850.

Poems. 1850. 6 vols.

The Golden Legend. 1851.

The Song of Hiawatha. 1855.

Prose Works. 1857. 2 vols.

The Voices of the Night, Ballads, and Other Poems. 1857.

Poetical Works. 1858.

The Courtship of Miles Standish and Other Poems. 1858.

Tales of a Wayside Inn. 1863.

Noël. 1864.

Household Poems. 1865.

Complete Works. 1866. 7 vols.

The Divine Comedy of Dante (translator). 1867. 3 vols.

Flower-de-Luce. 1867.

Poetical Works. 1868.

The New-England Tragedies: I. John Endicott; II. Giles Corey of the Salem Farms. 1868.

The Building of the Ship. 1870.

Poetical Works. Ed. William Michael Rossetti. 1870.

The Alarm-Bell of Atri. 1871.

The Divine Tragedy. 1871.

Three Books of Song. 1872.

Christus: A Mystery. 1872. 3 vols.

Aftermath. 1873.

The Hanging of the Crane. 1875.

Morituri Salutamus: Poem for the Fiftieth Anniversary of the Class of 1825 in Bowdoin College. 1875.

The Masque of Pandora and Other Poems. 1875.

Poems of Places (editor). 1876–79. 26 vols.

Kéramos. 1877.

A Ballad of the French Fleet, October 1746. 1877.

Kéramos and Other Poems. 1878.

Poetical Works. 1878. 11 vols.

Early Poems. Ed. R. H. Shepherd. 1878.

Bayard Taylor. 1879.

From My Arm-Chair. 1879.

Ultima Thule. 1880.

In the Harbor: Ultima Thule, Part II. 1882.

Works. 1886. 11 vols.

Works. Ed. Samuel Longfellow. 1886–91. 14 vols.

Complete Poetical Works. Ed. Horace E. Scudder. 1893.

Poetical Works. 1904.

Poems. Ed. George Saintsbury. 1907.

Origin and Growth of the Languages of Southern Europe and of Their Literature: An Inaugural Address Delivered September 2, 1830. 1907.

Boyhood Poems. Ed. Ray W. Pettengill. 1925.

Poems. Ed. Louis Untermeyer. 1943.

Letters. Ed. Andrew Hilen. 1966–82. 6 vols.

The Shaping of Longfellow's John Endicott: *A Textual History, Including Two Early Versions.* Ed. Edward L. Tucker. 1985.

ANTHONY TROLLOPE (1815–1882)

The Macdermots of Ballycloran. 1847. 3 vols.

The Kellys and the O'Kellys; or, Landlords and Tenants: A Tale of Irish Life. 1848. 3 vols.

La Vendée: An Historical Romance. 1850. 3 vols.
The Warden. 1855.
Barchester Towers. 1857. 3 vols.
The Three Clerks. 1858. 3 vols.
Doctor Thorne. 1858. 3 vols.
The Bertrams. 1859. 3 vols.
The West Indies and the Spanish Main. 1859.
Castle Richmond. 1860. 3 vols.
Framley Parsonage. 1861. 3 vols.
The Civil Service as a Profession. 1861.
Tales of All Countries: First Series. 1861.
Orley Farm. 1861–62. 20 parts.
North America. 1862. 2 vols.
The Struggles of Brown, Jones and Robinson. 1862.
The Present Condition of the Northern States of the American Union. c. 1862.
Tales of All Countries: Second Series. 1863.
Rachel Ray. 1863. 2 vols.
The Small House at Allington. 1864. 2 vols.
Can You Forgive Her? 1864–65. 20 parts.
Miss Mackenzie. 1865. 2 vols.
Hunting Sketches. 1865.
The Belton Estate. 1866. 3 vols.
Travelling Sketches. 1866.
Clergymen of the Church of England. 1866.
The Last Chronicle of Barset. 1866–67. 32 parts.
Nina Balatha: The Story of a Maiden of Prague. 1867. 2 vols.
The Claverings. 1867. 2 vols.
Lotta Schmidt and Other Stories. 1867.
Linda Tressel. 1868. 2 vols.
Higher Education for Women. 1868.
British Sports and Pastimes (editor). 1868.
He Knew He Was Right. 1868–69. 32 parts.
Phineas Finn: The Irish Member. 1869. 2 vols.
Did He Steal It? 1869.
The Vicar of Bullhampton. 1869–70. 11 parts.
An Editor's Tales. 1870.
On English Prose Fiction as a Rational Amusement. 1870.
The Commentaries of Caesar. 1870.
Ralph the Heir. 1870–71. 19 parts.
Sir Harry Hotspur of Humblethwaite. 1871.
The Golden Lion of Granpere. 1872.
The Eustace Diamonds. 1873. 2 vols.
Australia and New Zealand. 1873. 2 vols.
Phineas Redux. 1874. 2 vols.
Lady Anna. 1874.
Harry Heathcote of Gangoil: A Tale of Australian Bush Life. 1874.
The Way We Live Now. 1874–75. 20 parts.
The Prime Minister. 1875–76. 8 parts.
The American Senator. 1877. 3 vols.
Christmas at Thompson Hall. 1877.
Chronicles of Barsetshire. 1878. 8 vols.
South Africa. 1878. 2 vols.
Is He Popenjoy? 1878. 3 vols.
Iceland. 1878.
How the "Mastiffs" Went to Iceland. 1878.
The Lady of Launay. 1878.
An Eye for an Eye. 1879. 2 vols.
Thackeray. 1879.
John Caldigate. 1879. 3 vols.
Cousin Henry. 1879. 2 vols.
The Duke's Children. 1880. 3 vols.
The Life of Cicero. 1880. 2 vols.
Dr. Wortle's School. 1881. 2 vols.

Ayala's Angel. 1881. 3 vols.
Why Frau Frohmann Raised Her Prices and Other Stories. 1882.
Lord Palmerston. 1882.
Marion Fay. 1882. 2 vols.
The Fixed Period. 1882. 2 vols.
The Two Heroines of Plumplington. 1882.
Kept in the Dark. 1882. 2 vols.
Not if I Know It. 1883.
Mr. Scarborough's Family. 1883. 3 vols.
The Landleaguers. 1883. 3 vols.
An Autobiography. 1883. 2 vols.
Alice Dugdale and Other Stories. 1883.
La Mere Bauche and Other Stories. 1883.
The Mistletoe Bough and Other Stories. 1883.
An Old Man's Love. 1884. 2 vols.
The Barsetshire Novels. Ed. Frederic Harrison. 1906. 8 vols.
The Noble Jilt. Ed. Michael Sadleir. 1923.
London Tradesmen. Ed. Michael Sadleir. 1927.
The Barchester Novels. Ed. Michael Sadleir. 1929. 14 vols.
Four Lectures. Ed. Morris L. Parrish. 1938.
The Tireless Traveller: Twenty Letters to the Liverpool Mercury *1875.* Ed. Bradford A. Booth. 1941.
Novels and Stories. Ed. John Hampden. 1946.
The Oxford Illustrated Trollope. Eds. Michael Sadleir and Frederick Page. 1948–54. 15 vols.
The Parson's Daughter and Other Stories. Ed. John Hampden. 1949.
The Spotted Dog and Other Stories. Ed. John Hampden. 1950.
Mary Gresley and Other Stories. Ed. John Hampden. 1951.
Letters. Ed. Bradford Allen Booth. 1951.
Letters to the Examiner. Ed. H. Garlinghouse King. 1965.
The Palliser Novels. 1973. 6 vols.
Complete Short Stories. Ed. Betty Jane Breyer. 1979–83. 5 vols.
Selected Works. Ed. N. John Hall. 1981. 62 vols.
Letters. Eds. N. John Hall and Nina Burgis. 1983. 2 vols.

EMILY DICKINSON (1830–1886)

Poems. Eds. Mabel Loomis Todd and T. W. Higginson. 1890.
Poems: Second Series. Eds. Mabel Loomis Todd and T. W. Higginson. 1891.
Letters. Ed. Mabel Loomis Todd. 1894 (2 vols.), 1931.
Poems: Third Series. Ed. Mabel Loomis Todd. 1896.
The Single Hound: Poems of a Lifetime. Ed. Martha Dickinson Bianchi. 1914.
Life and Letters. Ed. Martha Dickinson Bianchi. 1924.
Complete Poems. Ed. Martha Dickinson Bianchi. 1924.
Selected Poems. Ed. Conrad Aiken. 1924.
Further Poems Withheld from Publication by Her Sister Lavinia. Eds. Martha Dickinson Bianchi and Alfred Leete Hampson. 1929.
Poems (Centenary Edition). Eds. Martha Dickinson Bianchi and Alfred Leete Hampson. 1930.
Poems for Youth. Ed. Alfred Leete Hampson. 1934.
Unpublished Poems. Eds. Martha Dickinson Bianchi and Alfred Leete Hampson. 1935.
Bolts of Melody: New Poems. Eds. Mabel Loomis Todd and Millicent Todd Bingham. 1945.
Letters to Dr. and Mrs. Josiah Gilbert Holland. Ed. Theodora Van Wagenen Ward. 1951.
Poems. Ed. Louis Untermeyer. 1952.
Poems. Ed. Thomas H. Johnson. 1955 (3 vols.), 1960.

Letters. Eds. Thomas H. Johnson and Theodora Ward. 1958. 3 vols.
Selected Poems. Ed. James Reeves. 1959.
Selected Poems and Letters. Ed. Robert N. Linscott. 1959.
A Choice of Emily Dickinson's Verse. Ed. Ted Hughes. 1968.
Selected Letters. Ed. Thomas H. Johnson. 1971.
Manuscript Books. Ed. R. W. Franklin. 1981. 2 vols.
The Master Letters. Ed. R. W. Franklin. 1986.

MATTHEW ARNOLD (1822–1888)

Alaric at Rome. 1840.
Cromwell. 1843.
The Strayed Reveller and Other Poems. 1849.
Empedocles on Etna and Other Poems. 1852.
Poems. 1853.
Poems: Second Series. 1855.
Merope. 1858.
Oratio Anniversaria in Memoriam Publicorum Benefactorum Academiae Oxoniensis ex Instituto N. Domini Crewe. 1858.
England and the Italian Question. 1859.
Popular Education in France, with Notices of That of Holland and Switzerland. 1861.
On Translating Homer. 1861.
On Translating Homer: Last Words. 1862.
Oratio Anniversaria in Memoriam Publicorum Benefactorum Academiae Oxoniensis ex Instituto N. Domini Crewe. 1862.
A French Eton; or, Middle Class Education and the State. 1864.
Essays in Criticism. 1865.
On the Study of Celtic Literature. 1867.
Saint Brandon. 1867.
New Poems. 1867.
Schools and Universities on the Continent. 1868.
Poems. 1869. 2 vols.
Culture and Anarchy: An Essay in Political and Social Criticism. 1869.
St. Paul and Protestantism. 1870.
Friendship's Garland: Being the Conversations, Letters, and Opinions of the Late Arminius, Baron von Thunder-ten-Tronckh. 1871.
A Bible-Reading for Schools (editor). 1872.
Literature and Dogma: An Essay towards a Better Apprehension of the Bible. 1873.
Higher Schools and Universities in Germany. 1874.
God and the Bible: A Review of Objections to Literature and Dogma. 1875.
Isaiah XL–LXVI with the Shorter Prophecies Allied to It (editor). 1875.
Poems. 1877. 2 vols.
Last Essays on Church and Religion. 1877.
Selected Poems. 1878.
The Six Chief Lives from Johnson's Lives of the Poets (editor). 1878.
Mixed Essays. 1879.
Poems of Wordsworth (editor). 1879.
Geist's Grave. 1881.
Poetry of Byron (editor). 1881.
Letters, Speeches and Tracts on Irish Affairs by Edmund Burke (editor). 1881.
Irish Essays and Others. 1882.
Isaiah of Jerusalem in the Authorized Version (editor). 1883.
Discourses in America. 1885.
Poems. 1885. 3 vols.

Education Department: Special Report on Certain Points Connected with Elementary Education in Germany, Switzerland, and France. 1886.
Essays in Criticism: Second Series. 1888.
Civilization in the United States: First and Last Impressions of America. 1888.
Reports on Elementary Schools 1852–1882. Ed. Francis Sandford. 1889.
On Home Rule for Ireland. 1891.
Letters. Ed. George W. E. Russell. 1895. 2 vols.
Notebooks. 1902.
Works. 1903–04. 15 vols.
Letters to John Churton Collins. 1910.
Poetry and Prose. Ed. E. K. Chambers. 1930.
Letters to Arthur Hugh Clough. Ed. Howard Foster Lowry. 1932.
The Portable Arnold. Ed. Lionel Trilling. 1949.
Poetical Works. Eds. C. B. Tinker and H. F. Lowry. 1950.
Note-Books. Eds. Howard Foster Lowry, Karl Young, and Waldo Hilary Dunn. 1952.
Five Uncollected Essays. Ed. Kenneth Allott. 1953.
Poetry and Prose. Ed. John Bryson. 1954.
Complete Prose Works. Ed. R. H. Super. 1960–77. 11 vols.
Selected Essays. Ed. Noel Annan. 1964.
Poems. Ed. Kenneth Allott. 1965.
Selected Prose. Ed. P. J. Keating. 1970.
Matthew Arnold. Eds. Miriam Allott and Robert H. Super. 1986.

ROBERT BROWNING (1812–1889)

Pauline: A Fragment of a Confession. 1833.
Paracelsus. 1835.
Strafford: An Historical Tragedy. 1837.
Sordello. 1840.
Bells and Pomegranates. 1841 [*Pippa Passes*]; 1842 [*King Victor and King Charles*]; 1842 [*Dramatic Lyrics*]; 1843 [*The Return of the Druses*]; 1843 [*A Blot in the 'Scutcheon*]; 1844 [*Colombe's Birthday*]; 1845 [*Dramatic Romances and Lyrics*]; 1846 [*Luria and A Soul's Tragedy*].
Poems. 1849. 2 vols.
Christmas-Eve and Easter-Day. 1850.
Two Poems (with Elizabeth Barrett Browning). 1854.
Men and Women. 1855. 2 vols.
Selections from the Poetical Works. Eds. John Forster and Bryan Waller Procter. 1863.
Dramatis Personae. 1864.
Poetical Works. 1868. 6 vols.
The Ring and the Book. 1868–69. 4 vols.
Balaustion's Adventure. 1871.
Prince Hohenstiel-Schwangau, Saviour of Society. 1871.
Fifine at the Fair. 1872.
Red Cotton Night-Cap Country; or, Turf and Towers. 1873.
Aristophanes' Apology. 1875.
The Inn Album. 1875.
Pacchiarotto and How He Worked in Distemper, with Other Poems. 1876.
The Agamemnon of Aeschylus (adaptation). 1877.
La Saisiaz; The Two Poets of Croisic. 1878.
Dramatic Idyls. 1879–80. 2 vols.
Jocoseria. 1883.
Dramas. 1883. 2 vols.
Ferishtah's Fancies. 1884.
Parleyings with Certain People of Importance in Their Day. 1887.

Poetical and Dramatic Works. Ed. George Willis Cooke. 1887. 6 vols.

Poetical Works. 1888–94. 17 vols.

Asolando: Fancies and Facts. 1890.

Complete Poetic and Dramatic Works. Ed. Horace E. Scudder. 1895.

Poetical Works. Ed. Augustine Birrell. 1896. 2 vols.

Complete Works. Eds. Charlotte Porter and Helen A. Clarke. 1898. 14 vols.

Letters (with Elizabeth Barrett Browning). Ed. Robert Wiedemann Barrett Browning. 1899. 2 vols.

Works (Centenary Edition). Ed. Frederick G. Kenyon. 1912. 10 vols.

New Poems. Ed. Frederick G. Kenyon. 1914.

Complete Works. Ed. J. H. Finley. 1926. 6 vols.

Letters. Ed. Thurman L. Hood. 1933.

New Letters. Eds. William Clyde de Vane and Kenneth Leslie Knickerbocker. 1950.

Dearest Isa: Letters to Isa Blagden. Ed. Edward C. McAleer. 1951.

Letters to George Barrett (with Elizabeth Barrett Browning). Eds. Paul Landis and Ronald E. Freeman. 1958.

Browning to His American Friends: Letters between the Brownings, the Storys and James Russell Lowell. Ed. Gertrude Reese Hudson. 1965.

Learned Lady: Letters to Mrs. Thomas FitzGerald. Ed. Edward C. McAleer. 1966.

Complete Works. Eds. Roma A. King et al. 1969–   . 13 vols. (projected).

Letters (with Elizabeth Barrett Browning). Ed. Elvan Kintner. 1969. 2 vols.

Poetical Works 1833–1864. Ed. Ian Jack. 1970.

Browning's Trumpeter: The Correspondence of Robert Browning and Frederick J. Furnivall. Ed. William S. Peterson. 1979.

Poems. Ed. John Pettigrew. 1981. 2 vols.

Poetical Works. Eds. Ian Jack and Margaret Smith. 1983–   .

Correspondence (with Elizabeth Barrett Browning). Eds. Philip Kelley and Ronald Hudson. 1984–   .

HERMAN MELVILLE (1819–1891)

Typee: A Peep at Polynesian Life. 1846. 2 vols.

Omoo: A Narrative of Adventures in the South Seas. 1847.

Mardi: And a Voyage Thither. 1849. 2 vols.

Redburn: His First Voyage: Being the Sailor-Boy Confessions and Reminiscences of the Son-of-a-Gentleman, in the Merchant Service. 1849.

White-Jacket; or, The World in a Man-of-War. 1850.

Moby-Dick; or, The Whale. 1851.

Pierre; or, The Ambiguities. 1852.

Israel Potter: His Fifty Years of Exile. 1855.

The Piazza Tales. 1856.

The Confidence-Man: His Masquerade. 1857.

Battle-Pieces, and Aspects of the War. 1866.

Clarel: A Poem and Pilgrimage in the Holy Land. 1876. 2 vols.

John Marr and Other Sailors with Some Sea-Pieces. 1888.

Timoleon, etc. 1891.

Works (Standard Edition). 1922–24. 16 vols.

The Apple-Tree and Other Sketches. Ed. Henry Chapin. 1922.

Some Personal Letters and a Bibliography. Ed. Meade Minnigerode. 1922.

Journal up the Straits: October 11, 1856–May 5, 1857. Ed. Raymond Weaver. 1935.

Selected Poems. Ed. F. O. Matthiesen. 1944.

Complete Works. Ed. Howard P. Vincent. 1947–61. 6 vols.

Journal of a Visit to London and the Continent 1849–1850. Ed. Eleanor Melville Metcalf. 1948.

The Portable Melville. Ed. Jay Leyda. 1952.

Letters. Eds. Merrell R. Davis and William H. Gilman. 1960.

Writings. Eds. Harrison Hayford et al. 1968–   .

ALFRED, LORD TENNYSON (1809–1892)

Poems by Two Brothers (with Charles Tennyson). 1827.

Timbuctoo: A Poem Which Obtained the Chancellor's Medal at the Cambridge Commencement 1829. 1829.

Poems, Chiefly Lyrical. 1830.

Poems. 1833.

The Lover's Tale. 1833.

Poems. 1842. 2 vols.

The Princess: A Medley. 1847.

In Memoriam. 1850.

Ode on the Death of the Duke of Wellington. 1852.

The Charge of the Light Brigade. 1855.

Maud and Other Poems. 1855.

Stanzas on the Marriage of the Princess Royal. 1858.

Idylls of the King. 1859.

Ode for the Opening of the International Exhibition. 1862.

A Welcome. 1863.

Enoch Arden, etc. 1864.

A Selection from the Works of Alfred Tennyson. 1865.

The Holy Grail and Other Poems. 1870.

Works. 1870–77. 13 vols.

The Window; or, The Songs of the Wrens. 1871.

Gareth and Lynette, etc. 1872.

Works. 1872–73. 6 vols.

A Welcome to Her Royal Highness Marie Alexandrovna, Duchess of Edinburgh. 1874.

Works. 1874–81. 13 vols.

Queen Mary. 1875.

Harold. 1877.

Works. 1878–82. 12 vols.

Ballads and Other Poems. 1880.

Hands All Round: A National Song. 1882.

The Cup and The Falcon. 1884.

Becket. 1884.

Works. 1884–93. 10 vols.

Tiresias and Other Poems. 1885.

Gordon Boys' Morning and Evening Hymns (editor; with others). 1885.

Ode to the Opening of the Colonial and Indian Exhibition. 1886.

Locksley Hall Sixty Years After, etc. 1886.

Poetical Works. 1886–97. 17 vols.

Carmen Saeculare: An Ode in Honour of the Jubilee of Queen Victoria. 1887.

Demeter and Other Poems. 1889.

The Foresters: Robin Hood and Maid Marian. 1892.

The Death of Œnone, Akbar's Dream, and Other Poems. 1892.

Poetical Works. 1895–96. 23 vols.

Works (Farringford Edition). Ed. Eugene Parsons. 1902. 10 vols.

Works (Eversley Edition). Ed. Hallam Tennyson. 1907–08. 9 vols.

Patriotic Poems. 1914.

Alfred, Lord Tennyson and William Kirby: Unpublished Correspondence. Ed. Lorne Pierce. 1929.

The Devil and the Lady. Ed. Charles Tennyson. 1930.

Unpublished Early Poems. Ed. Charles Tennyson. 1931.

A Selection from the Poems. Ed. W. H. Auden. 1944.

Selected Poetry. Ed. Douglas Bush. 1951.

Poetical Works, Including the Plays. 1953.
Poems. Ed. Christopher Ricks. 1969.
Letters. Eds. Cecil Y. Lang and Edgar F. Shannon. 1981– .

WALT WHITMAN (1819–1892)

Leaves of Grass. 1855, 1856, 1860–61, 1867, 1871, 1876, 1881–82, 1891–92, 1897.
Walt Whitman's Drum-Taps. 1865.
Sequel to Drum-Taps. 1865.
Poems. Ed. William Michael Rossetti. 1868.
After All, Not to Create Only. 1871.
Democratic Vistas. 1871.
Memoranda during the War. 1875–76.
Two Rivulets, Including Democratic Vistas, Centennial Songs, and Passage to India. 1876.
Specimen Days and Collect. 1882–83.
November Boughs. 1888.
Complete Poems and Prose—1855–1888. 1888.
Good-Bye My Fancy. 1891.
Complete Prose Works. 1892.
Calamus: A Series of Letters Written during the Years 1868–1880. Ed. Richard Maurice Burke. 1897.
Complete Writings. Eds. Richard Maurice Burke, Thomas B. Harned, and Horace L. Traubel. 1902. 10 vols.
Criticism: An Essay. 1913.
The Gathering of the Forces: Editorials, Essays, Literary and Dramatic Reviews and Other Material Written by Walt Whitman as Editor of the Brooklyn Daily Eagle *in 1846 and 1847.* Eds. Cleveland Rodgers and John Black. 1920. 2 vols.
Uncollected Poetry and Prose. Ed. Emory Holloway. 1921. 2 vols.
The Half-Breed and Other Stories. Ed. Thomas Ollive Mabbott. 1927.
Rivulets of Prose: Critical Essays. Eds. Carolyn Wells and Alfred F. Goldsmith. 1928.
I Sit and Look Out: Editorials from the Brooklyn Daily Times. Eds. Emory Holloway and Henry S. Saunders. 1932.
New York Dissected: A Sheaf of Recently Discovered Newspaper Articles. Eds. Emory Holloway and Ralph Adimari. 1936.
Correspondence. Ed. Edwin Haviland Miller. 1961–77. 6 vols.
The Early Poems and the Fiction. Ed. Thomas L. Brasher. 1963.
Prose Works 1892. Ed. Floyd Stovall. 1963. 2 vols.
Leaves of Grass: Comprehensive Reader's Edition. Eds. Harold W. Blodgett and Sculley Bradley. 1965.
Daybooks and Notebooks. Ed. William White. 1978. 3 vols.
Leaves of Grass: A Textual Varorium of the Printed Poems. Eds. Sculley Bradley, Harold W. Blodgett, Arthur Golden, and William White. 1980. 3 vols.
Complete Poetry and Collected Prose. Ed. Justin Kaplan. 1982.
Notebooks and Unpublished Prose Manuscripts. Ed. Edward F. Grier. 1984. 6 vols.

WALTER PATER (1839–1894)

Studies in the History of the Renaissance. 1873.
Marius the Epicurean: His Sensations and Ideas. 1885. 2 vols.
Imaginary Portraits. 1887.
Appreciations; with an Essay on Style. 1889.
Plato and Platonism. 1893.
An Imaginary Portrait ⟨*The Child in the House*⟩. 1894.
Greek Studies. Ed. Charles L. Shadwell. 1895.
Miscellaneous Studies. Ed. Charles L. Shadwell. 1895.
Gaston de Latour: An Unfinished Romance. Ed. Charles L. Shadwell. 1896.

Essays from The Guardian. Ed. Thomas Bird Mosher. 1896.
Works. 1900–01. 9 vols.
Selections. Ed. Edward Everett Hale, Jr. 1901.
Uncollected Essays. Ed. Thomas Bird Mosher. 1903.
Sketches and Reviews. 1919.
Selected Essays. Ed. H. G. Rawlinson. 1927.
The Chant of the Celestial Sailors: An Unpublished Poem. 1928.
Selected Works. Ed. Richard Aldington. 1948.
Selected Prose. Ed. Derek Patmore. 1949.
Letters. Ed. Lawrence Evans. 1970.
Selected Writings. Ed. Harold Bloom. 1974.
Three Major Texts. Ed. William F. Buckler. 1986.

ROBERT LOUIS STEVENSON (1850–1894)

The Pentland Rising: A Page of History, 1666. 1866.
The Charity Bazaar: An Allegorical Dialogue. 1868.
An Appeal to the Clergy of the Church of Scotland, with a Note for the Laity. 1875.
An Inland Voyage. 1878.
Edinburgh: Picturesque Notes. 1879.
Travels with a Donkey in the Cévennes. 1879.
Deacon Brodie; or, The Double Life (with W. E. Henley). 1880.
The Surprise. 1880. 1 no.
To F. J. S. 1881.
Virginibus Puerisque and Other Papers. 1881.
Familiar Studies of Men and Books. 1882.
New Arabian Nights. 1882. 2 vols.
Not I and Other Poems. 1882.
Moral Emblems: A Collection of Cuts and Verses. 1882.
Moral Emblems: A Second Collection of Cuts and Verses. 1882.
A Martial Elegy for Some Lead Soldiers. 1882.
The Graver & the Pen; or, Scenes from Nature, with Appropriate Verses. 1882.
Robin and Ben; or, The Pirate and the Apothecary. 1882.
The Silverado Squatters: Sketches from a Californian Mountain. 1883.
Treasure Island. 1883.
We found him first as in the dells of day. 1883.
To the Thompson Class Club, "from Their Stammering Laureate." 1883.
Admiral Guinea (with W. E. Henley). 1884.
Beau Austin (with W. E. Henley). 1884.
A Child's Garden of Verses. 1885.
More New Arabian Nights: The Dynamiter (with Fanny Van de Grift Stevenson). 1885.
Prince Otto: A Romance. 1885.
Macaire (with W. E. Henley). 1885.
The Laureat Ste'enson to the Thamson Class. 1885.
The Strange Case of Dr. Jekyll and Mr. Hyde. 1886.
Kidnapped: Being Memoirs of the Adventures of David Balfour in the Year 1751. 1886.
Some College Memories. 1886.
The Merry Men and Other Tales and Fables. 1887.
Thomas Stevenson, Civil Engineer. 1887.
Memories and Portraits. 1887.
Underwoods. 1887.
Ticonderoga. 1887.
The Hanging Judge (with Fanny Van de Grift Stevenson). 1887.
Memoir of Fleeming Jenkin. 1887.
The Black Arrow: A Tale of the Two Roses. 1888.
The Misadventures of John Nicholson: A Christmas Story. 1888.
The Master of Ballantrae: A Winter's Tale. 1889.
The Wrong Box (with Lloyd Osbourne). 1889.

On Board the Old "Equator." 1889.
The South Seas: A Record of Three Cruises ⟨*In the South Seas*⟩. 1890.
Father Damien: An Open Letter to the Reverend Dr. Hyde of Honolulu. 1890.
Ballads. 1890.
Across the Plains, with Other Memories and Essays. 1892.
The Wrecker (with Lloyd Osbourne). 1892.
A Footnote to History: Eight Years of Trouble in Samoa. 1892.
Three Plays (with W. E. Henley). 1892.
The Beach of Falesá. 1892.
Island Nights' Entertainments. 1893.
Catriona: A Sequel to Kidnapped, *Being Memoirs of the Further Adventures of David Balfour at Home and Abroad.* 1893.
The Ebb-Tide: A Trio and Quartette (with Lloyd Osbourne). 1894.
Works. Ed. Sidney Colvin. 1894–98. 28 vols.
The Amateur Emigrant from the Clyde to Sandy Hook. 1895.
Vailima Letters: Being Correspondence Addressed to Sidney Colvin, November 1890–October 1894. 1895.
The Body-Snatcher. 1895.
Fables. 1896.
Weir of Hermiston: An Unfinished Romance. 1896.
Songs of Travel and Other Verses. 1896.
Familiar Epistle in Verse and Prose. 1896.
A Mountain Town in France: A Fragment. 1896.
Plays (with W. E. Henley). 1896.
St Ives: Being the Adventures of a French Prisoner in England (with A. T. Quiller-Couch). 1897.
Three Short Poems. 1898.
A Lowden Sabbath Morn. 1898.
Letters to His Family and Friends. Ed. Sidney Colvin. 1899. 2 vols.
R.L.S. Teuila. 1899.
The Morality of the Profession of Letters. 1899.
A Stevenson Medley. Ed. Sidney Colvin. 1899.
A Christmas Sermon. 1900.
Three Letters. 1902.
Some Letters. Ed. Horace Townsend. 1902.
Essays and Criticisms. 1903.
Prayers Written at Vailima. 1905.
Tales and Fantasies. 1905.
Essays of Travel. 1905.
Essays in the Art of Writing. 1905.
Essays. Ed. William Lyon Phelps. 1906.
Works. Ed. Edmund Gosse. 1906–07. 20 vols.
Collected Works. Ed. Charles Scribner and Sons. 1908–12. 31 vols.
Pan's Pipes. 1910.
Letters. Ed. Sidney Colvin. 1911. 4 vols.
Lay Morals and Other Papers. 1911.
Works. 1911–12. 25 vols.
Records of a Family of Engineers. 1912.
Memoirs of Himself. 1912.
The Flight of the Princess and Other Pieces. 1912.
Verses by R.L.S. Ed. L. S. Livingston. 1912.
Poems and Ballads. 1913.
Desiderata: 1895. 1914.
Letters to Charles Baxter. 1914.
Letters to an Editor. Ed. Clement K. Shorter. 1914.
Poetical Fragments. 1915.
An Ode of Horace: Book II, Ode III: Experiments in Three Metres (translator). 1916.
One the Choice of a Profession. 1916.

The Waif Woman. 1916.
Poems Hitherto Unpublished. Ed. George S. Hellman. 1916. 2 vols.
New Poems and Variant Readings. 1918.
Poems Hitherto Unpublished. Eds. George S. Hellman and William P. Trent. 1921.
Hitherto Unpublished Prose Writings. Ed. Henry H. Harper. 1921.
Confessions of a Unionist. Ed. Flora V. Livingston. 1921.
Works. Eds. Lloyd Osbourne and Fanny Van de Grift Stevenson. 1922–23. 26 vols.
The Manuscripts of Stevenson's Records of a Family of Engineers: *The Unfinished Chapters.* Ed. J. Christian Bay. 1929.
Henry James and Robert Louis Stevenson: A Record of Friendship and Criticism. Ed. Janet Adam Smith. 1948.
Collected Poems. Ed. Janet Adam Smith. 1950, 1971.
Silverado Journal. Ed. John E. Jordan. 1954.
RLS: Stevenson's Letters to Charles Baxter. Eds. De Lancey Ferguson and Marshall Waingrow. 1956.
From Scotland to Silverado. Ed. James D. Hart. 1966.
Complete Short Stories, with a Selection of the Best Short Novels. Ed. Charles Neider. 1969. 3 vols.
Travels to Hawaii. Ed. A. Grove Day. 1973.
Selected Short Stories. Ed. Ian Campbell. 1980.
An Old Song and Edifying Letters of the Rutherford Family. Ed. Roger C. Swearingen. 1982.
From the Clyde to California: Robert Louis Stevenson's Emigrant Journey. Ed. Andrew Noble. 1985.

JOHN RUSKIN (1819–1900)

Salsette and Elephanta. 1839.
Modern Painters. 1843 [Volume 1]; 1846 [Volume 2]; 1856 [Volumes 3–4]; 1860 [Volume 5].
The Seven Lamps of Architecture. 1849.
Poems. 1850.
The King of the Golden River; or, The Black Brothers: A Legend of Stiria. 1851.
The Stones of Venice. 1851–53. 3 vols.
Notes on the Construction of Sheepfolds. 1851.
Pre-Raphaelitism. 1851.
Giotto and His Works in Padua. 1853–60. 3 parts.
Lectures on Architecture and Painting. 1854.
The Opening of the Crystal Palace Considered in Some of Its Relations to the Prospects of Art. 1854.
Notes on Some of the Principal Pictures Exhibited in the Rooms of the Royal Academy. 1855–75. 6 nos.
The Harbours of England. 1856.
Notes on the Turner Gallery at Marlborough House. 1856.
Catalogue of the Turner Sketches in the National Gallery. 1857.
The Elements of Drawing. 1857.
The Political Economy of Art. 1857.
Cambridge School of Art: Mr. Ruskin's Inaugural Address. 1858.
The Oxford Museum (with Henry Acland). 1859.
The Unity of Art. 1859.
The Two Paths. 1859.
The Elements of Perspective. 1859.
Collected Works. 1861–63. 15 vols.
"Unto This Last": Four Essays on the First Principles of Political Economy. 1862.
Sesame and Lilies. 1865.
An Inquiry into Some of the Conditions at Present Affecting the Study of Architecture in Our Schools. 1865.
The Ethics of the Dust. 1866.

The Crown of Wild Olive. 1866.

Time and Tide, by Weare and Tyne. 1867.

First Notes on the General Principles of Employment for the Destitute and Criminal Classes. 1868.

The Queen of the Air: Being a Study of the Greek Myths of Cloud and Storm. 1869.

Samuel Prout. 1870.

Lectures on Art. 1870.

A Paper Read at the Royal Artillery Institution, Woolwich ⟨The Future of England⟩. 1870.

Catalogue of Examples Arranged for Elementary Study in the University Galleries. 1870.

Collected Works. 1871–80. 11 vols.

Fors Clavigera: Letters to the Workmen and Labourers of Great Britain. January 1871–December 1877 [Sections 1–84; monthly]; 1878–84 [Sections 85–96; intermittently].

Instructions in Elementary Drawing. 1872.

Munera Pulveris: Six Essays on the Elements of Political Economy. 1872.

Aratra Pentelici: Six Lectures on the Elements of Sculpture. 1872.

The Relation between Michael Angelo and Tintoret: Seventh of the Course of Lectures on Sculpture Delivered at Oxford 1870–71. 1872.

The Eagle's Nest: Ten Lectures on the Relation of Natural Science to Art. 1872.

The Sepulchral Monuments of Italy. 1872.

Love's Meinie: Lectures on Greek and English Birds. 1873–81. 3 parts.

The Poetry of Architecture. 1873, 1893.

Remarks Addressed to the Mansfield Art Night Class. 1873.

Ariadne Florentina: Six Lectures on Wood and Metal Engraving. 1873–76. 7 parts.

Val D'Arno: Ten Lectures on the Tuscan Art Directly Antecedent to the Florentine Year of Victories. 1874.

Social Policy Must be Based on the Scientific Principle of Natural Selection. 1875.

Mornings in Florence. 1875–77. 6 parts.

Proserpina: Studies of Wayside Flowers. 1875–79 [Parts 1–6]; 1882–86 [Parts 7–10].

Deucalion: Collected Studies of the Lapse of Waves, and Life of Stones. 1875–79 [Parts 1–6]; 1880–83 [Parts 7–8].

Letters to The Times *on the Principal Pre-Raphaelite Pictures in the Exhibition of 1854.* 1876.

The Art Schools of Mediaeval Christendom by A. C. Owen (editor). 1876.

Bibliotheca Pastorum (editor). 1876–85. 4 vols.

Guide to the Principal Pictures in the Academy of Fine Arts at Venice. 1877. 2 parts.

St. Mark's Rest: The History of Venice. 1877–79. 6 parts.

The Laws of Fiesole. 1877–78. 4 parts.

Notes by Mr. Ruskin on His Drawings by the Late J. M. W. Turner. 1878.

Notes on Samuel Prout and William Hunt. 1879.

Circular Respecting Memorial Studies of St. Mark's, Venice, Now in Progress under Mr. Ruskin's Direction. 1879.

Letters Addressed to the Clergy on the Lord's Prayer and the Church. Ed. F. A. Malleson. 1879.

Elements of English Prosody. 1880.

"Our Fathers Have Told Us": Sketches of the History of Christendom for Boys and Girls Who Have Been Held at Its Fonts ⟨The Bible of Amiens⟩. 1880–83. 5 parts.

Arrows of the Chase: Being a Collection of Scattered Letters Published Chiefly in the Daily Newspapers 1840–1880. Ed. Alexander Wedderburn. 1880. 2 vols.

Poems. Ed. J. O. Wright. 1882.

Catalogue of the Collection of Siliceous Minerals. 1883.

The Story of an Idea: Epitaph on an Etrurian Tomb by Francesca Alexander (editor). 1883.

The Art of England. 1883–84. 7 parts.

Catalogue of a Series of Specimens in the British Museum (Natural History) Illustrative of the More Common Forms of Native Silica. 1884.

Roadside Songs of Tuscany, tr. Francesca Alexander (editor). 1884–85. 10 parts.

The Pleasures of England. 1884–85. 4 parts.

The Storm Cloud of the Nineteenth Century. 1884. 2 parts.

Dame Wiggins of Lee and Her Seven Wonderful Cats (editor). 1885.

On the Old Road: A Collection of Miscellaneous Essays, Pamphlets, etc., etc., Published 1834–1885. Ed. Alexander Wedderburn. 1885. 2 vols.

Praeterita: Outlines of Scenes and Thoughts Perhaps Worthy of Memory in My Past Life. 1885–88. 28 parts.

Ulric the Farm Servant by Jeremias Gotthelf, tr. Julia Frith (editor). 1886–88. 9 parts.

Dilecta: Correspondence, Diary Notes, and Extracts from Books, Illustrating Praeterita. 1886 [Part 1]; 1887 [Part 2]; 1900 [Part 3].

Christ's Folk in the Apennine: Reminiscences of Her Friends among the Tuscan Peasantry by Francesca Alexander (editor). 1887–89. 2 vols.

Hortus Inclusus: Messages from the Wood to the Garden, Sent in Happy Days to the Sister Ladies of the Thwaite, Coniston ⟨Mary and Susie Beever⟩. Ed. Albert Fleming. 1887.

Two Letters concerning Notes on the Construction of Sheepfolds *Addressed to the Rev. F. D. Maurice.* 1889.

Ruskiniana. Ed. Alexander Wedderburn. 1890–92. 2 vols.

Poems. Ed. W. G. Collingwood. 1891. 2 vols.

Letters upon Subjects of General Interest. Ed. T. J. Wise. 1892.

Stray Letters to a London Bibliophile ⟨F. S. Ellis⟩. Ed. T. J. Wise. 1892.

Letters to William Ward. Ed. T. J. Wise. 1892. 2 vols.

Letters on Art and Literature. Ed. T. J. Wise. 1894.

Letters to Ernest Chesneau. Ed. T. J. Wise. 1894.

Letters Addressed to a College Friend ⟨Edward Clayton⟩ 1840–1845. 1894.

Letters to the Rev. F. J. Faunthorpe. Ed. T. J. Wise. 1894.

Verona and Other Lectures. Ed. W. G. Collingwood. 1894.

Letters to the Rev. F. A. Malleson. Ed. T. J. Wise. 1896.

Letters to Frederick J. Furnivall and Other Correspondents. Ed. T. J. Wise. 1897.

Works. Eds. E. T. Cook and Alexander Wedderburn. 1903–12. 39 vols.

Comments on the Divina Commedia. Ed. G. P. Huntington. 1903.

Letters to M. G. & H. G. ⟨Mary and Hellen Gladstone⟩. 1903.

Letters to Charles Eliot Norton. Ed. Charles Eliot Norton. 1904. 2 vols.

Poems. 1908.

An Ill-Assorted Marriage: An Unpublished Letter. Ed. Clement Shorter. 1915.

Letters to William Ward. Ed. Alfred Mansfield Brooks. 1922.

The Solitary Warrior: New Letters. Ed. J. Howard Whitehouse. 1929.

Letters to Francesca and Memoirs of the Alexanders. Ed. Lucia Gray Swett. 1931.

Letters to Bernard Quaritch 1867–1888. Ed. Charlotte Quaritch Wrentmore. 1938.

The Order of Release: The Story of John Ruskin, Effie Gray and John Everett Millais Told for the First Time in Their Unpublished Letters. Ed. Admiral Sir William James. 1948.

Selected Writings. Ed. Peter Quennell. 1952.

The Gulf of Years: Letters to Kathleen Olander. Ed. Rayner Unwin. 1953.

Letters from Venice 1851–1852. Ed. John Lewis Bradley. 1955.

Diaries. Eds. Joan Evans and John Howard Whitehouse. 1956–59. 3 vols.

The Lamp of Beauty: Writings on Art. Ed. Joan Evans. 1959.

Pigwiggian Chaunts. Ed. James S. Dearden. 1960.

The Contemptible Horse: The Text of John Ruskin's Letter to "My Dear Tinie" Written from the Bridge of Allan on 31 August 1857. Ed. Norman H. Strouse. 1962.

Letters to Lord and Lady Mount-Temple. Ed. John Lewis Bradley. 1964.

Ruskin Today. Ed. Kenneth Clark. 1964.

Literary Criticism. Ed. Harold Bloom. 1965.

Dearest Mama Talbot: A Selection of Letters Written to Mrs. Fanny Talbot. Ed. Margaret Spence. 1966.

The Froude-Ruskin Friendship as Represented through Letters. Ed. Helen Gill Viljoen. 1966.

The Winnington Letters: John Ruskin's Correspondence with Margaret Alexis Bell and the Children at Winnington Hall. Ed. Van Akin Burd. 1969.

Brantwood Diary. Ed. Helen Gill Viljoen. 1971.

Sublime and Instructive: Letters to Louisa, Marchioness of Waterford, Anna Blunden and Ellen Heeton. Ed. Virginia Surtees. 1972.

Ruskin in Italy: Letters to His Parents 1845. Ed. Harold I. Shapiro. 1972.

The Ruskin Family Letters: The Correspondence of John James Ruskin, His Wife, and Their Son, John, 1801–1843. Ed. Van Akin Burd. 1973. 2 vols.

Reflections of a Friendship: John Ruskin's Letters to Pauline Trevelyan 1848–1866. Ed. Virginia Surtees. 1979.

The Correspondence of Thomas Carlyle and John Ruskin. Ed. George Allen Cate. 1982.

Letters from the Continent 1858. Ed. John Hayman. 1982.

My Dearest Dora: Letters to Dorothy Livesey, Her Family and Friends 1860–1900. Ed. Olive Wilson. 1984.

The Correspondence of John Ruskin and Charles Eliot Norton. Eds. John Lewis Bradley and Ian Onsby. 1987.

OSCAR WILDE (1854–1900)

Ravenna. 1878.

Vera; or, The Nihilists. 1880.

Poems. 1881.

The Duchess of Padua: A Tragedy of the XVI Century. 1883.

The Happy Prince and Other Tales. 1888.

The Picture of Dorian Gray. 1891.

Intentions. 1891.

Lord Arthur Savile's Crime and Other Stories. 1891.

A House of Pomegranates. 1891.

Salomé. 1893.

Lady Windermere's Fan: A Play about a Good Woman. 1893.

The Sphinx. 1894.

A Woman of No Importance. 1894.

Oscariana: Epigrams. 1895.

The Soul of Man ⟨under Socialism⟩. 1895.

The Ballad of Reading Gaol. 1898.

The Importance of Being Earnest: A Trivial Comedy for Serious People. 1899.

An Ideal Husband. 1899.

Sebastian Melmoth. 1904.

De Profundis. 1905.

The Rise of Historical Criticism. 1905.

Wilde v. Whistler: Being an Acrimonious Correspondence on Art between Oscar Wilde and James A. McNeill Whistler. 1906.

Works. Ed. Robert Ross. 1908. 15 vols.

The Suppressed Portion of De Profundis. Ed. Robert Ross. 1913.

Resurgam: Unpublished Letters. Ed. Clement K. Shorter. 1917.

For Love of the King: A Burmese Masque. 1922.

Selected Works with Twelve Unpublished Letters. Ed. Richard Aldington. 1946.

Complete Works. Ed. Vyvyan Holland. 1948.

Essays. Ed. Hesketh Pearson. 1950.

Five Famous Plays. Ed. Alan Harris. 1952.

Selected Writings. Ed. Richard Ellmann. 1961.

Letters. Ed. Rupert Hart-Davis. 1962.

The Artist as Critic: Critical Writings. Ed. Richard Ellmann. 1969.

Complete Shorter Fiction. Ed. Isobel Murray. 1979.

More Letters. Ed. Rupert Hart-Davis. 1985.

STEPHEN CRANE (1871–1900)

Maggie: A Girl of the Streets. 1893.

The Black Riders and Other Lines. 1895.

The Red Badge of Courage: An Episode of the American Civil War. 1895.

George's Mother. 1896.

The Little Regiment and Other Episodes of the American Civil War. 1896.

The Third Violet. 1897.

The Open Boat and Other Tales of Adventure. 1898.

War Is Kind. 1899.

Active Service. 1899.

The Monster and Other Stories. 1899.

Whilomville Stories. 1900.

Wounds in the Rain: War Stories. 1900.

Great Battles of the World. 1901.

Last Words. 1902.

The O'Ruddy: A Romance (with Robert Barr). 1903.

Men, Women and Boats. Ed. Vincent Starrett. 1921.

Work. Ed. Wilson Follett. 1925–26. 12 vols.

Two Letters to Joseph Conrad. 1926.

Collected Poems. Ed. Wilson Follett. 1930.

A Battle in Greece. 1936.

Sullivan County Sketches. Ed. Melvin Schoberlin. 1949.

Love Letters to Nellie Crouse. Eds. Edwin H. Cady and Lester G. Wells. 1954.

Letters. Eds. R. W. Stallman and Lillian Gilkes. 1960.

Uncollected Writings. Ed. Olov W. Fryckstedt. 1963.

Complete Short Stories and Sketches. 1963.

War Dispatches. Eds. R. W. Stallman and E. R. Hagemann. 1964.

New York City Sketches. Eds. R. W. Stallman and E. R. Hagemann. 1966.

Poems. Ed. Joseph Katz. 1966.

Complete Novels. Ed. Thomas A. Gullason. 1967.

Notebook. Eds. Donald J. Greiner and Ellen B. Greiner. 1969.

The Portable Stephen Crane. Ed. Joseph Katz. 1969.

Works. Ed. Fredson Bowers. 1969–76. 10 vols.

Prose and Poetry. Ed. J. C. Levenson. 1984.

SERIES CONTENTS

SERIES CONTENTS

Volume 1

GEOFFREY CHAUCER

1. Thomas Usk, *Testament of Love* (c. 1387), *Works*, ed. William Thynne, 1532, Fol. 359b.
2. John Gower, *Confessio Amantis* (c. 1390), *Works*, ed. G. C. Macaulay, 1901, p. 466.
3. John Lydgate, *The Flower of Courtesy*, ed. William Thynne, c. 1400, Fol. 284b.
4. John Lydgate, *The Life of Our Lady*, c. 1410.
5. John Walton, "Translator's Preface" to *De Consolatione Philosophiae*, 1410.
6. Thomas Occleve, *The Regement of Princes*, 1412.
7. John Shirley, "Introduction" to *The Knight's Tale*, c. 1450.
8. Robert Henryson, *Testament of Cresseid*, c. 1475.
9. William Caxton, "Epilogue" to *Chaucer's Boethius*, 1478.
10. William Caxton, "Epilogue" to *The House of Fame*, 1483.
11. William Caxton, "Prohemye" to *The Canterbury Tales*, 2nd ed., 1484.
12. William Dunbar, *The Golden Targe* (c. 1503), *Poems*, ed. John Small, 1893, Volume 2, p. 10.
13. Gavin Douglas, "Translator's Prologue" to *Aenead: Eneados, Book I*, 1513.
14. Sir Thomas Wyatt, *How to Use the Court*, c. 1540.
15. "An Act for Thaduancement of True Religion and for Thabbolisshment of the Contrarie," *Statute 34 and 35 Henry VIII*, 1542–43, Ch. 1, Sec. 5.
16. Roger Ascham, *Toxophilus*, 1545.
17. Roger Ascham, *A Report . . . of the Affaires and State of Germany*, 1552.
18. Roger Ascham, *The Scholemaster*, 1570.
19. George Gascoigne, "Certayne Notes of Instruction," *The Posies of George Gascoigne, Esq.*, 1575.
20. Edmund Spenser, *The Shepheardes Calender*, 1579.
21. Sir Philip Sidney, *An Apology for Poetry* (c. 1579–80), 1595.
22. William Webbe, "A Discourse of English Poetrie" (1586), *Elizabethan Critical Essays*, ed. G. Gregory Smith, 1904, Volume 1, pp. 241–63.
23. Thomas Nashe, *To the Gentlemen Students of Both Universities*, 1589.
24. Richard Puttenham, *The Art of English Poesie*, 1589, pp. 49–50.
25. Edmund Spenser, *The Faerie Queene*, 1590–96, Book 4, Canto 2, Stanza 9.
26. Thomas Nashe, *Strange Newes of the Intercepting Certaine Letters*, 1592.
27. Edmund Spenser, "The Mutabilitie Cantos," *The Faerie Queene*, 1609.
28. Edward Foulis, "Prefatory Verse" to *The Loves of Troilus and Creseide*, tr. into Latin by Sir Francis Kynaston, 1635.
29. Samuel Pepys, *Diary*, 1663–64.
30. Sir John Denham, "On Mr. Abraham Cowley, His Death and Burial amongst the Ancient Poets," *Poems and Translations*, 1668, p. 89.
31. Joseph Addison, "To Mr. H. S⟨acheverell⟩, April 3, 1694" (1694), *Miscellany Poems*, ed. John Dryden, 1719, Volume 4, p. 288.
32. Alexander Pope, *An Essay on Criticism*, 1711.
33. John Hughes, *Essay on Allegorical Poetry*, 1715, pp. xxvi–xxvii.
34. Daniel Defoe, Letter to *Mist's Weekly Journal* (1718), *Daniel Defoe: His Life and Recently Discovered Writings*, ed. William Lee, 1869, Volume 2, p. 31.
35. Ambrose Phillips, "Introduction" to *The Cuckoo and the Nightingale* ⟨*The Boke of Cupide*⟩, *The Free-Thinker*, May 24, 1720.
36. Elizabeth Cooper, *The Muses' Library*, 1737.
37. George Ogle, "Letters to a Friend," *Gaultheris and Griselda: or the Clerk of Oxford's Tale; from Boccace, Petrarch and Chaucer*, 1739, pp. vii–viii.
38. Samuel Johnson, *Dictionary of the English Language*, 1755.
39. Joseph Warton, *Essay on the Genius and Writings of Pope*, 1756–82.
40. George Gordon, Lord Byron, "Memorandum Book, 30 November 1807," *The Life, Letters and Journal of Lord Byron*, ed. Thomas Moore, 1830, p. 49.
41. William Wordsworth, "Sonnet XXIII: Edward VI," *Ecclesiastical Sonnets*, 1822.
42. Ralph Waldo Emerson, "The American Scholar," 1837.
43. Leigh Hunt, *A Jar of Honey from Mount Hybla*, 1848, p. 122.
44. Ralph Waldo Emerson, *English Traits*, 1856.
45. Walter Savage Landor, "To Chaucer," *Heroic Idylls*, 1863, pp. 142–43.
46. Frederick Denison Maurice, "On Books" (1865), *The Friendship of Books and Other Lectures*, ed. Thomas Hughes, 1874, pp. 76–77.
47. Francis James Child, "Elision of Final Vowels," *On Early English Pronunciation*, ed. Alexander John Ellis, 1869, Pt. 1, Ch. 4, p. 360.
48. John Ruskin, "Letter 61," *Fors Clavigera*, 1876, pp. 21–22.
49. Gerard Manley Hopkins, Letter to Robert Bridges (1880), *The Letters of Gerard Manley Hopkins to Robert Bridges*, ed. Claude Colleer Abbott, 1935, pp. 106–7.
50. Gerard Manley Hopkins, Letter to R. W. Dixon (1881), *The Correspondence of Gerard Manley Hopkins and R. W. Dixon*, ed. Claude Colleer Abbott, 1953, pp. 66–67.
51. Algernon Charles Swinburne, "Wordsworth and Byron" (1884), *Miscellanies*, 1886, p. 152.
52. William Morris, "Feudal England," *Signs of Change*, 1888, pp. 73–75.
53. John Churton Collins, "The Predecessors of Shakspeare," *Essays and Studies*, 1895, pp. 106–7.
54. George Saintsbury, *The Earlier Renaissance*, 1901, pp. 231–36.
55. John Skelton, *Phillip Sparrowe* (c. 1508), *Poetical Works of John Skelton*, ed. Alexander Dyce, pp. 69–75.
56. John Foxe, "A Protestation to the Whole Church of England," *Ecclesiasticall History Contayning the Actes and Monuments of Thyngs Passed in Euery Kinges Tyme in This Realme*, 2nd enlarged ed., 1570, pp. 341, 965–66.
57. Robert Greene, *Greene's Vision*, 1592.
58. Thomas Speght, *Scholarly Edition of Chaucer* (1598), 2nd ed., 1602.
59. John Dryden, "Preface" to *Fables*, 1700.
60. Thomas Gray, *Commonplace Book*, c. 1760.
61. Thomas Warton, *The History of English Poetry* (1774–81), ed. Richard Price, 1840, Volume 2, pp. 129–216.
62. William Godwin, *Life of Chaucer*, 1803–04, Volume 1, pp. i–viii, 470–85; Volume 2, pp. 168–84; Volume 4, pp. 184–201.

63. William Blake, *Descriptive Catalogue* (1809), *Complete Writings*, ed. Geoffrey Keynes, 1966, pp. 556–75.

64. George Crabbe, *Preface to the* Canterbury Tales, 1812.

65. William Hazlitt, "Troilus and Cressida," *Characters of Shakespear's Plays*, 1817, pp. 89–92.

66. William Hazlitt, "On Chaucer and Spenser," *Lectures on the English Poets*, 1818.

67. Elizabeth Barrett Browning, "Mrs Browning on Chaucer" (1842), *Essays on Chaucer*, ed. Frederick J. Furnivall, 1868–94, pp. 157–64.

68. James Russell Lowell, *Conversations on Some of the Old Poets*, 1846, pp. 16–49.

69. Henry David Thoreau, "Friday," *A Week on the Concord and Merrimack Rivers*, 1849.

70. Leigh Hunt, *Stories in Verse*, 1855, pp. 1–19.

71. H. Simon, "Chaucer a Wicliffite," *Essays on Chaucer*, ed. Frederick J. Furnivall, 1868–94, pp. 229–46.

72. James Russell Lowell, "Chaucer" (1870), *Works*, Riverside ed., Volume 3, pp. 298–366.

73. William Minto, "Geoffrey Chaucer," *Characteristics of English Poets*, 1874, pp. 1–44.

74. Felix Lindner, "The Alliteration in Chaucer's *Canterbury Tales*" (1876), *Essays on Chaucer*, ed. Frederick J. Furnivall, 1868–94, pp. 199–205.

75. Adolphus William Ward, "Characteristics of Chaucer and His Poetry," *Chaucer*, 1879, pp. 146–88.

76. Matthew Arnold, "The Study of Poetry" (1880), *Essays in Criticism: Second Series*, 1888.

77. Algernon Charles Swinburne, "Short Notes on English Poets: Chaucer; Spenser; The Sonnets of Shakespeare; Milton" (1880), *Complete Works*, 1926, Volume 4, pp. 97–101.

78. George Dawson, "Chaucer," *Biographical Lectures*, ed. George St. Clair, 1887, pp. 205–16.

79. Henry Morley, *English Writers*, 1890, Volume 5, pp. 83–85, 186–282.

80. Bernhard ten Brink, "Prelude to Reformation and Renaissance," *History of English Literature*, tr. William Clarke Robinson, 1893, pp. 68–96.

81. W. P. Ker, "The Poetry of Chaucer," *Quarterly Review*, April 1895, pp. 521–48.

82. Frank Jewett Mather, "Introduction" to *The Prologue, The Knight's Tale and the Nun's Priest's Tale*, 1899, pp. ix–xlvii.

83. Peter Borghesi, *Boccaccio and Chaucer*, 1903, pp. 29–69.

84. Walter Raleigh, "Lecture on Chaucer" (c. 1903), *On Writers and Writing*, 1926, ed. George Gordon, pp. 108–19.

SIR PHILIP SIDNEY

1. Edmund Spenser, Title Page of *The Shepheardes Calender*, 1579.

2. Stephan Gosson, Dedication to *The Schoole of Abuse*, 1579.

3. Sir Francis Walsingham, Letter to Sir Henry Sidney (1586).

4. Fulke Greville (Lord Brooke), *On Sir Philip Sidney*, 1586.

5. Thomas Nashe, *Pierce Penilesse His Supplication to the Divell*, 1592.

6. Richard Barnfield, *The Affectionate Shepherd*, 1594.

7. Sir William Harbert, *A Prophesie of Cadwallader*, 1604.

8. Samuel Daniel, "A Funerall Poeme upon the Earle of Devonshire" (1606), *Works*, ed. Alexander B. Grosart, Volume 1, p. 176.

9. Anthony Stafford, *Niobe*, 1611, p. 112.

10. William Browne, *Britannia's Pastorals*, 1613, Volume 1, Book 2, Song 2.

11. Fulke Greville (Lord Brooke), *Life of Sir Philip Sidney*, c. 1628–52.

12. Sir Robert Naunton, *Fragmenta Regalia*, ed. Edward Arber, c. 1630, p. 34.

13. John Aubrey, "Sir Philip Sidney," *Brief Lives*, 1669–96.

14. Horace Walpole, *A Catalogue of the Royal and Noble Authors of England, Scotland, and Ireland*, 1758, Volume 2, p. 230.

15. Robert Southey, *For a Tablet at Penshurst*, 1799.

16. Thomas Campbell, *Essay on English Poetry*, 1819.

17. Percy Bysshe Shelley, *Adonais*, 1821, Stanza 45.

18. Charles Lamb, "Some Sonnets of Sir Philip Sydney," *London Magazine*, September 1823.

19. John Richard Green, *A Short History of the English People*, 1874, Ch. 7.

20. Edmund Gosse, "Sir Philip Sidney," *Contemporary Review*, November 1886, p. 638.

21. John Addington Symonds, *Sir Philip Sidney*, 1886, pp. 1, 199.

22. Donald G. Mitchell, *English Lands, Letters, and Kings: From Celt to Tudor*, 1889, p. 239.

23. Sir John Harrington, "Notes on the Book XVI," *Orlando Furioso in Heroical Verse*, 1591, p. 126.

24. George Peele, "Ad Maecenatem Prologus," *The Honour of the Garter*, 1593.

25. Sir Thomas Smithes, *Voiage and Entertainment in Rushia*, 1605.

26. Ben Jonson, "To Elizabeth, Countess of Rutland," *Epigrams*, 1616, No. 79.

27. Ben Jonson, *Conversations with William Drummond*, 1619.

28. Michael Drayton, "To My Most Dearely-Loved Friend Henery Reynolds, Esquire, of Poets and Poesie," *Elegies*, 1627.

29. Sir William Temple, "Of Poetry," 1690.

30. Edmund Waller, *At Penshurst*, c. 1636.

31. Richard Crashaw, "Wishes to His Supposed Mistress," *The Delights of the Muses*, 1646–48.

32. James Thomson, "Summer," *The Seasons*, 1727.

33. Alexander Pope, *Imitations of Horace*, 1737, *Ep.* II.i.98.

34. Nathan Drake, *Shakspeare and His Times*, 1817, Volume 1, p. 652.

35. William Gray, *Life of Sidney*, 1829, p. 36.

36. Robert Southey, Letter to Sir Egerton Brydges (1830), cited in Samuel Egerton Brydges, *Autobiography*, 1834, Volume 2, p. 267.

37. J. H. Hippisley, *Chapters on Early English Literature*, 1837, p. 250.

38. Robert Browning, *Sordello*, 1840, Book 1, ll. 68–71.

39. H. R. Fox Bourne, *A Memoir of Sir Philip Sidney*, 1862, p. 419.

40. George MacDonald, *England's Antiphon*, 1868, p. 77.

41. James Russell Lowell, "Spenser" (1875), *Prose Works*, Riverside ed., Volume 4, p. 276.

42. George Saintsbury, *A History of Elizabethan Literature*, 1887, pp. 40–43.

43. Edward Dowden, "Spenser, the Poet and Teacher," *Transcripts and Studies*, 1888, pp. 282–83.

44. W. E. Henley, "Sidney," *Views and Reviews*, 1890, p. 105.

45. Frederic Ives Carpenter, "Introduction" to *English Lyric Poetry, 1500–1700*, 1897, p. xliii.

46. Gabriel Harvey, *Pierces Supererogation* (1593), *Works*, ed. Alexander B. Grosart, Volume 2, pp. 100–101.

47. Francis Meres, *Palladis Tamia*, 1598, p. 96.

48. Peter Heylyn, *Description of Arcadia in Greece*, 1622.

49. J. Baudoin, *L'Arcadie de la Comtesse de Pembroke, mise en nostre langue*, 1624.

50. Fulke Greville (Lord Brooke), *Life of Sir Philip Sidney*, c. 1628–52.
51. William Cowper, *The Task*, 1785, Book 4.
52. William Godwin, "Of English Style," *The Enquirer*, 1797.
53. Charles Lamb, *Specimens of English Dramatic Poets*, 1808.
54. Thomas Zouch, *Memoirs of the Life and Writings of Sir Philip Sidney*, 1808.
55. Washington Irving, "The Mutability of Literature," *Sketch Book*, 1819–20.
56. George Ticknor, *History of Spanish Literature*, 1849–91, Volume 3, p. 106.
57. David Masson, *British Novelists and Their Styles*, 1859, p. 65.
58. Hippolyte Taine, *The History of English Literature*, tr. H. Van Laun, 1871, Book 2, pp. 164–66.
59. Anna Buckland, *The Story of English Literature*, 1882, p. 113.
60. Bayard Tuckerman, A *History of English Prose Fiction*, 1882, p. 98.
61. J. J. Jusserand, *The English Novel in the Time of Shakespeare*, 1890, p. 247.
62. Henry Kirke White, *Melancholy Hours* (c. 1806), *The Remains of Henry Kirke White*, ed. Robert Southey, 1807, Volume 2, p. 247.
63. Charles Lamb, "Some Sonnets of Sir Philip Sydney," *London Magazine*, September 1823.
64. Anna Brownell Jameson, *The Loves of the Poets*, 1829, Volume 1, pp. 251–55.
65. Henry Hallam, *Introduction to the Literature of Europe*, 1837–39, Pt. 2, Ch. 5, Par. 66.
66. Francis Turner Palgrave, *Golden Treasury*, 1861, p. 351.
67. Hippolyte Taine, *The History of English Literature*, tr. H. Van Laun, 1871, Book 2, pp. 168–72.
68. John Ruskin, "Letter XXXV," *Fors Clavigera*, 1873.
69. Alexander B. Grosart, "Memorial-Introduction" to *Complete Poems of Sir Philip Sidney*, 1877, Volume 1, p. lxi.
70. Mary A. Ward, "Sir Philip Sidney," *The English Poets*, ed. Thomas Humphry Ward, 1880, Volume 1, p. 344.
71. Hubert Hall, *Society in the Elizabethan Age*, 1886, p. 91.
72. George Saintsbury, A *History of Elizabethan Literature*, 1887, pp. 100–102.
73. Henry Olney, "Publisher to the Reader," *An Apology for Poetry*, 1595.
74. Horace Walpole, A *Catalogue of the Royal and Noble Authors of England, Scotland, and Ireland*, 1758, Volume 2, p. 232.
75. Oliver Goldsmith, *Essays*, 1773, No. 18.
76. Henry Hallam, *Introduction to the Literature of Europe*, 1837–39, Pt. 2, Ch. 7, Par. 35.
77. George P. Marsh, *The Origin and History of the English Language*, 1862, p. 547.
78. Paul Stapfer, *Shakespeare and Classical Antiquity*, tr. Emily J. Carey, 1880, p. 41.
79. Laura Johnson Wylie, *Evolution of English Criticism*, 1894, p. 12.
80. Sir Walter Ralegh, "An Epitaph upon the Right Honorable Sir Philip Sidney, Knight" (1586), A *Choice of Sir Walter Raleigh's Verse*, 1972, pp. 22–24.
81. Thomas Moffet, "A Sorrowful Lamentation" (1589), *Lessus Lugubris*, eds. and trs. Virgil Heltzel, Hoyt H. Hudson, 1940, pp. 99–105.
82. Thomas Nashe, "Preface" to *Astrophel and Stella* (1591), *Elizabethan Critical Essays*, ed. G. Gregory Smith, 1904, Volume 2, pp. 221–28.
83. William Hazlitt, *Lectures on the Literature of the Age of Elizabeth*, 1820.

84. H. R. Fox Bourne, "Authorship as Courtier," A *Memoir of Sir Philip Sidney*, 1862, pp. 321–52.
85. Henry Morley, A *First Sketch of English Literature*, 1873, pp. 391–426.
86. John Addington Symonds, "The *Defence of Poesy*," *Sir Philip Sidney*, 1886, pp. 156–70.
87. Walter Raleigh, *The English Novel*, 1894, pp. 49–64.
88. Duncan C. Tovey, "England's Helicon: More Lyrics from Elizabethan Songbooks," *Reviews and Essays in English Literature*, 1897, pp. 177–81.
89. Joel E. Spingarn, "The General Theory of Poetry," A *History of Literary Criticism in the Renaissance*, 1889, pp. 34–274.
90. Algernon Charles Swinburne, "Astrophel" (1894), *Works*, 1900, pp. 589–91.
91. Adolphus William Ward, "Sir Philip Sidney," *English Prose*, ed. Henry Craik, 1894, Volume 1, pp. 401–8.

CHRISTOPHER MARLOWE

1. Robert Greene, "To the Gentlemen Readers, *Health*," *Perimedes the Blacksmith*, 1538.
2. Robert Greene, *Groats-worth of Wit*, 1592.
3. Gabriel Harvey, A *New Letter of Notable Contents*, 1593.
4. George Peele, "Ad Maecenatem Prologus," *The Honour of the Garter*, 1593.
5. George Chapman, "Dedication to Lady Walsingham," *Hero and Leander: Begun by Christopher Marlowe and Finished by George Chapman*, 1598.
6. George Chapman, "Third Sestyad," *Hero and Leander: Begun by Christopher Marlowe and finished by George Chapman*, 1598, ll. 1–10, 183–98.
7. Frances Meres, *Palladis Tamia*, 1598.
8. *The Second Part of the Return from Parnassus*, 1598–1601.
9. William Vaughan, "Of Atheists," *The Golden Grove, Moralized in Three Bookes*, 1600, Volume 1, Ch. 3.
10. William Prynne, *Histrio-Mastix*, 1633, Fol. 556.
11. Ben Jonson, *Timber; or, Discoveries*, 1640.
12. William Winstanley, *The Lives of the Most Famous English Poets*, 1687, p. 134.
13. Anthony à Wood, *Athenae Oxonienses*, 1691–1721.
14. Joseph Ritson, *Observations on the Three First Volumes of the* History of English Poetry *in a Familiar Letter to the Author*, 1782.
15. Edward Phillips, *Theatrum Poetarum Anglicanorum*, 1675.
16. Charles Lamb, *Specimens of the English Dramatic Poets*, 1808.
17. Leigh Hunt, *Imagination and Fancy*, 1844, pp. 136–41.
18. George Henry Lewes, *The Life and Works of Goethe*, 1864, pp. 475–78.
19. Hippolyte Taine, *The History of English Literature*, tr. H. Van Laun, 1871, Book 1, pp. 234–44.
20. William Minto, *Characteristics of English Poets*, 1874, pp. 233–37.
21. Algernon Charles Swinburne (c. 1875), *Collected Works*, 1924, Volume 11, p. 711.
22. Adolphus William Ward, A *History of English Dramatic Literature* (1875), 1899, Volume 1, pp. 196–203.
23. George Saintsbury, A *History of Elizabethan Literature*, 1887, pp. 76–79.
24. Ernest Rhys, "At the Rhymer's Club," A *London Rose and Other Verse*, 1894, pp. 90–91.
25. W. J. Courthope, A *History of English Poetry*, 1897, Volume 2, pp. 404–21.
26. Notes and Documents (1593), *Revue Germanique*, 1913, pp. 570–78.
27. Thomas Warton, *The History of English Poetry*, 1774–81.

28. William Hazlitt, *Lectures on the Dramatic Literature of the Age of Elizabeth*, 1820, pp. 55–72.
29. Alexander Dyce, "Some Account of Marlowe and His Writings," *The Works of Christopher Marlowe*, 1850, Volume 1, pp. xv–xlviii.
30. Algernon Charles Swinburne, "Christopher Marlowe" (1883), *The Age of Shakespeare*, 1908, pp. 1–14.
31. Algernon Charles Swinburne, *The Works of George Chapman*, 1875, pp. lix–lxvi.
32. A. C. Bradley, "Christopher Marlowe," *The English Poets*, ed. Thomas Humphry Ward, 1880, Volume 1, pp. 411–17.
33. A. H. Bullen, "Introduction" to *The Works of Christopher Marlowe*, 1885, Volume 1, pp. xviii–xlv.
34. A. W. Verity, *The Influence of Christopher Marlowe on Shakespere's Earlier Style*, 1886, pp. 28–53.
35. Havelock Ellis, "Christopher Marlowe," *The Best Plays of the Old Dramatists: Christopher Marlowe*, 1887, pp. xxix–xlviii.
36. James Russell Lowell, "Marlowe," *The Old English Dramatists*, 1892, pp. 28–54.
37. John Churton Collins, "The Predecessors of Shakspeare," *Essays and Studies*, 1895, pp. 149–62.
38. Frederick S. Boas, "New Light on Marlowe and Kyd," *Fortnightly Review*, February 1899, pp. 212–18.
39. George Bernard Shaw, "The Spacious Times" (1896), *Dramatic Opinions and Essays*, 1909, pp. 36–43.

EDMUND SPENSER

1. Gabriel Harvey, *Marginalia* (1572), ed. G. C. Moore Smith, 1913, pp. 161–62.
2. Thomas Nashe, *To the Gentlemen Students of Both Universities*, 1589.
3. Michael Drayton, "Idea" (1593), *Works*, ed. William Hebel, 1931, Volume 1, p. 55.
4. Michael Drayton, "Endimion and Phoebe" (1595), *Works*, ed. William Hebel, 1931, Volume 1, p. 155.
5. Thomas Lodge, "The Induction" to "Phillis: Honoured with Pastorall Sonnets" (1593), *Complete Works*, ed. Edmund Gosse, Volume 2, p. 6.
6. Richard Barnfield, *A Remembrance of Some English Poets*, 1598.
7. William Camden, *Reges, Reginae, Nobiles, & Alij in Ecclesia Collegiata B. Petri Westmonasterij Sepulti*, 1600.
8. Ben Jonson, *Conversations with William Drummond*, 1619.
9. John Milton, "Il Penseroso," 1631, Book 2, ll. 116–21.
10. Francis Beaumont, "On Mr. Edm. Spenser, Famous Poet," 1653.
11. Thomas Fuller, *The History of the Worthies of England*, 1662.
12. Sir John Denham, "On Mr. Abraham Cowley," 1668.
13. John Dryden, "Of Heroique Playes," 1672.
14. Edward Phillips, *Theatrum Poetarum Anglicanorum*, 1675.
15. William Winstanley, *England's Worthies*, 1684, pp. 224–27.
16. Sir Richard Blackmore, "Preface" to *Prince Arthur* (1695), *Critical Essays of the Seventeenth Century*, ed. J. E. Spingarn, 1908, Volume 3, p. 238.
17. John Aubrey, "Edmund Spenser," *Brief Lives*, 1669–96.
18. William Hazlitt, "On the Character of Milton's Eve," *The Round Table*, 1816.
19. William Wordsworth, *The Prelude*, 1850, Book 1, ll. 166–85; Book 3, ll. 278–85.
20. Gabriel Harvey, *Marginalia* (1542–98), ed. G. C. Moore, 1913, pp. 122, 231–32.

21. Gabriel Harvey, *Three Proper, and Wittie, Familiar Letters*, 1580.
22. Thomas Nashe, *Pierce Penilesse His Supplication to the Divell*, 1592.
23. Gabriel Harvey, *Pierces Superorogation* (1593), *Works*, ed. Alexander B. Grosart, Volume 2, p. 93.
24. Samuel Daniel, "To the Right Honorable, the Lady Marie, Countess of Pembroke" (1594), *Complete Works*, ed. Alexander B. Grosart, Volume 3, pp. 26–27.
25. Francis Beaumont, Letter to Thomas Speght (1598).
26. Charles Fitzgeoffrey, *Affaniae; sive, Epigrammatum Libri Tres* (1601), *Poems*, ed. Alexander B. Grosart, p. xix.
27. Joshua Sylvester, *Bartas: His Deuine Weekes & Workes* (1605), *Complete Works*, ed. Alexander B. Grosart, p. 99.
28. William Browne, *Britannia's Pastorals*, 1616.
29. Ben Jonson, "The Golden Age Restored" (1616), *Works*, eds. C. H. Herford, Percy Simpson, Volume 7, p. 425.
30. Sir John Harrington, "Of Monsters, to My Lady Rogers" (1618), *Letters and Epigrams*, ed. Norman Egbert McClure, 1930, pp. 224–25.
31. Michael Drayton, "To the Reader," *The Legends of Robert Duke of Normandie* (1619), *Works*, ed. William Hebel, 1931, Volume 2, p. 382.
32. Ben Jonson, *Conversations with William Drummond*, 1619.
33. Michael Drayton, "To My Most Dearely-Loved Friend Henery Reynolds, Esquire, of Poets and Poesie," *Elegies*, 1627.
34. Sir Kenelm Digby, "A Discourse concerning Edmund Spenser," Harleian MSS., 1628.
35. Ben Jonson, *Timber; or, Discoveries*, 1640.
36. George Wither, *Halelviah*, 1641.
37. William D'Avenant, *A Discourse upon* Gondibert (1650), *Critical Essays of the Seventeenth Century*, ed. J. E. Spingarn, 1908, Volume 2, pp. 5–8.
38. John Dryden, Dedication to *The Spanish Friar*, 1681.
39. Nicholas Boileau, *The Art of Poetry*, trs. John Dryden, Sir William Soames, 1683.
40. Abraham Cowley, "Of Myself" (1688), *Essays, Plays and Sundry Verses*, ed. A. R. Waller, 1906, pp. 457–58.
41. John Dryden, *Discourse concerning the Original and Progress of Satire*, 1693.
42. Samuel Wesley, "An Epistle to a Friend concerning Poetry," 1700.
43. John Dennis, "The Grounds of Criticism in Poetry" (1704), *Critical Works*, ed. Edward Niles Hooker, 1939, Volume 1, p. 331.
44. Matthew Prior, "Preface" to *An Ode, Humbly Inscribed to the Queen*, 1706.
45. Joseph Addison, *The Spectator*, No. 62 (May 11, 1711).
46. Sir Richard Blackmore, *Essays upon Several Subjects*, 1716, pp. 41–42.
47. Joseph Spence, *Polymetis*, 1747, pp. 303–7.
48. William Wordsworth, "Preface" to *Lyrical Ballads*, 1800.
49. Samuel Taylor Coleridge, *Biographia Literaria*, 1817, Ch. 19.
50. Charles Lamb, "Sanity of True Genius" (1826), *The Last Essays of Elia*, 1833.
51. William Webbe, *A Discourse of English Poetrie*, 1586.
52. Sir Philip Sidney, *An Apologie for Poetrie*, 1595.
53. Francis Meres, *Palladis Tamia*, 1598.
54. Michael Drayton, "To the Reader," *Poems Lyrick and Pastorall*, 1605.
55. Michael Drayton, "To the Reader of His Pastorals," 1619.
56. John Milton, *Animadversations upon the Remonstrants Defence, against Smectymnuus*, 1641.
57. John Dryden, "Preface" to *Sylvae*, 1685.

58. John Dryden, "Dedication to the *Pastorals*," *The Works of Virgil*, 1697.
59. Alexander Pope, "A Discourse on Pastoral Poetry," 1704.
60. Samuel Johnson, *The Rambler*, No. 37 (July 24, 1750).
61. Gabriel Harvey, "To the Learned Shepherd," 1590.
62. Sir Walter Ralegh, "Two Visions vpon This Conceipt of the *Faery Queene*," 1590.
63. Sir John Harrington, *Orlando Furioso in Heroical Verse*, 1591, p. 373.
64. Gabriel Harvey, "Sonnet X: A More Particular Declaration of His Intention" (1592), *Works*, ed. Alexander B. Grosart, Volume 1, p. 244.
65. Gabriel Harvey, "A New Letter of Notable Contents" (1592), *Works*, ed. Alexander B. Grosart, Volume 1, p. 266.
66. Samuel Daniel, *The Poeticall Essayes* (1599), *Complete Works*, ed. Alexander B. Grosart, Volume 2, p. 175.
67. Unsigned, *The Return from Pernassus*, 1606, Volume 1, p. ii.
68. William Browne, *Britannia's Pastorals*, 1616.
69. Robert Burton, *The Anatomy of Melancholy*, 1621, pp. 519–37.
70. Henry Reynolds, "Mythomystes" (1632), *Critical Essays of the Seventeenth Century*, ed. J. E. Spingarn, 1908, Volume 1, p. 147.
71. John Milton, *The Reason of Church-Government*, 1641.
72. John Milton, *An Apology against a Pamphlet call'd A Modest Confutation of the Animadversation*, 1642.
73. John Milton, *Areopagitica*, 1644.
74. John Milton, *Eikonoklastes*, 1649.
75. Abraham Cowley, "To Sir William D'Avenant" (1650), *Poems*, ed. A. R. Waller, 1905, p. 42.
76. Thomas Rymer, "The Preface of the Translator" to Rapin's *Reflections on Aristotle's Treatise of Poesie*, 1674.
77. William Temple, "Of Poetry," 1690.
78. John Dryden, *Discourse concerning the Original and Progress of Satire*, 1693.
79. John Dryden, "Observations on the Art of Painting," 1695.
80. Matthew Prior, "Preface" to *Solomon on the Vanity of the World*, 1708.
81. Sir Richard Steele, *The Tatler*, No. 194 (July 4–6, 1710).
82. Joseph Addison, *The Spectator*, No. 183 (September 29, 1711).
83. Alexander Pope (1744), cited in Joseph Spence, *Anecdotes, Observations and Characters of Books and Men*, ed. S. W. Singer, 1820.
84. William Wordsworth, Dedication to *The White Doe of Rylstone*, 1815.
85. John Keats, Verses written in a copy of *The Faerie Queene*, at the end of Book 5, Canto 2, 1821.
86. John Ruskin, *Modern Painters*, 1856, Volume 3, Ch. 8.
87. E. K., "The Epistle" (1579), *The Poetical Works of Edmund Spenser*, 1807, Volume 8, pp. 7–15.
88. E. K., "The General Argument of the Whole Book," *The Shepheardes Calender*, 1579.
89. Sir Kenelm Digby, *Observations on the 22. Staffe in the 9th Canto of the 2d. Book of Spenser's Faery Queene*, 1628.
90. Richard Hurd, "Letters 7–12," *Letters on Chivalry and Romance*, 1762, pp. 55–120.
91. Thomas Warton, *Observations on the Faerie Queene of Spenser*, 1762.
92. Samuel Taylor Coleridge, "Spenser" (1818), *Literary Remains*, ed. Henry Nelson Coleridge, 1836, Volume 1, pp. 89–97.
93. William Hazlitt, "On Chaucer and Spenser," *Lectures on the English Poets*, 1818.
94. Leigh Hunt, *The Wishing-Cap* (1833), *Leigh Hunt's Literary Criticism*, eds. Lawrence Huston Houtchens, Carolyn Washburn Houtchens, 1956, pp. 446–56.
95. James Russell Lowell, "Spenser" (1875), *Among My Books: Second Series*, 1876, pp. 125–200.
96. Aubrey de Vere, "Spenser as a Philosophic Poet," *Essays*, 1887, Volume 1, pp. 48–100.
97. R. W. Church, "The *Faerie Queene*," *Spenser*, 1895, pp. 81–108.
98. R. E. Neil Dodge, "Spenser's Imitations from Ariosto," *PMLA*, 1897, pp. 151–98.
99. George Saintsbury, "Elizabethan Criticism," *A History of Literary Criticism and Literary Taste in Europe*, 1902, Volume 2, pp. 165–68.
100. W. B. Yeats, "Edmund Spenser," *Poems of Spenser*, 1906, pp. xxii–xliv.

SIR FRANCIS BACON
1. Earl of Essex, Letter to Francis Bacon.
2. Sir Francis Bacon, Letter to Sir Robert Cecil (May 1606).
3. Sir Dudley Carleton, Letter (May 11, 1606).
4. Ben Jonson, "Lord Bacons Birth-day," 1620.
5. Sir Francis Bacon, Letter to King James I (1621).
6. William Camden, *Annales Jacobi Regis*, 1603–23.
7. Ben Jonson, *Timber; or, Discoveries*, 1640.
8. Arthur Wilson, *The History of Great Britain: Being the Life and Reign of King James I*, 1653.
9. Thomas Fuller, *The Church History of Britain*, 1655.
10. Francis Osborne, *Historical Memoires of the Reigns of Queen Elizabeth and King James*, 1658.
11. Thomas Bushell, *Abridgment of the Lord Chancellor Bacon's Philosophical Theory in Mineral Prosecutions*, 1659.
12. Thomas Fuller, *The History of the Worthies of England*, 1662.
13. Thomas Sprat, *History of the Royal Society of London*, 1667.
14. Peter Heylyn, *Cyprianus Anglicus; or, The Life and Death of Archibishop Laud*, 1668.
15. Robert Stephens, "Introduction" to *Letters of Lord Bacon*, 1702.
16. Joseph Addison, *The Tatler*, No. 267 (December 23, 1710).
17. Alexander Pope, *An Essay on Man*, 1734, Ep. IV. 281–82.
18. David Hume, *History of England*, 1754–62.
19. John Lingard, *History of England*, 1819–30, Volume 9, pp. 183–85.
20. Basil Montagu, "The Life of Francis Bacon," *Bacon's Complete Works*, 1834, Volume 1.
21. Thomas Babington Macaulay, "Lord Bacon" (1837), *Critical, Historical, and Miscellaneous Essays*, 1860.
22. Isaac Disraeli, "Bacon," *Amenities of Literature*, 1841.
23. John Ruskin, *Modern Painters*, 1843–60, Pt. 5, Ch. 20.
24. Thomas Carlyle, *Historical Sketches of Notable Persons and Events in the Reigns of James I and Charles I*, 1844–98.
25. John, Lord Campbell, *Lives of the Lord Chancellors and Keepers of the Great Seal of England*, 1845–47, Volume 2.
26. William Hepworth Dixon, *Personal History of Lord Bacon*, 1860–61, p. 14.
27. Nathaniel Holmes, *The Authorship of Shakespeare*, 1866, pp. 110, 600.
28. Bernard Cracroft, *Essays, Political and Miscellaneous*, 1868.
29. James Spedding, *An Account of the Life and Times of Francis Bacon*, 1878, Volume 2, pp. 521–654.

30. Thomas Fowler, *Bacon*, 1881, p. 28.
31. Henry J. Nicoll, *Landmarks of English Literature*, 1882, p. 94.
32. Samuel R. Gardiner, *History of England*, 1883, Volume 1, p. 164.
33. Richard William Church, *Bacon*, 1884, pp. 1–225.
34. Asa Gray, *Letters*, 1884, Volume 2, p. 749.
35. Edwin Abbott Abbott, *Francis Bacon: An Account of His Life and Works*, 1885, pp. 81–82, 308.
36. Irving Browne, *Iconoclasm and Whitewash*, 1885, p. 12.
37. John Nicol, *Francis Bacon: His Life and Philosophy*, 1888, Pt. 1, p. 46.
38. Donald G. Mitchell, *English Lands, Letters, and Kings: From Celt to Tudor*, 1889, pp. 250–53.
39. Henry Morley, W. Hall Griffin, *English Writers*, 1895, Volume 11, p. 22.
40. George Brandes, *William Shakespeare: A Critical Study*, 1898, Volume 1, p. 309.
41. George Sandys, "Notes" to *Ovid's Metamorphosis*, 1621–26.
42. Isaac Gruter, Letter to William Rawley (1652), *Baconiana*, ed. Thomas Tenison, 1679.
43. Henry Stubbe, "Preface" to *Lord Bacon's Relation of the Sweating-Sickness Examined*, 1671, p. 5.
44. Joseph Addison, *The Tatler*, No. 267 (December 23, 1710).
45. Alexander Pope (1734–36), cited in Joseph Spence, *Anecdotes, Observations and Characters of Books and Men*, ed. S. W. Singer, 1820.
46. Horace Walpole, Letter to David Hume (July 15, 1758).
47. David Hume, *History of England*, 1754–62.
48. Edmund Burke, "Speech on the Impeachment of Warren Hastings," May 28, 1794.
49. Francis Horner, *Journal, Memoirs and Correspondence*, 1801, Volume 1, p. 168.
50. Nathan Drake, *Essays Illustrative of the* Tatler, Spectator, *and* Guardian, 1804, Volume 2, p. 18.
51. George Burnett, *Specimens of English Prose Writers*, 1807, Volume 2, p. 344.
52. Basil Montagu, "The Life of Francis Bacon," *Bacon's Complete Works*, 1834, Volume 1.
53. G. G. Gervinus, *Shakespeare Commentaries*, 1849–62, tr. F. E. Bunnètt, p. 884.
54. Abraham Mills, *The Literature and the Literary Men of Great Britain and Ireland*, 1851, Volume 1, p. 388.
55. Leigh Hunt, *Table Talk*, 1851, p. 84.
56. Frederick Denison Maurice, "The Friendship of Books" (1856), *The Friendship of Books and Other Lectures*, ed. Thomas Hughes, 1874, p. 11.
57. Bernard Cracroft, *Essays, Political and Miscellaneous*, 1868, Volume 2, p. 218.
58. George MacDonald, *England's Antiphon*, 1868, p. 93.
59. Frederic William Farrar, *Families of Speech*, 1869–73.
60. William Mathews, *Getting On in the World*, 1872, p. 245.
61. William Minto, *Manual of English Prose Literature*, 1872, p. 241.
62. Thomas Fowler, *Francis Bacon*, 1881, p. 202.
63. C. R. L. Fletcher, *The Development of English Prose Style*, 1881, p. 10.
64. Samuel R. Gardiner, *History of England*, 1883, Volume 3, pp. 396–98.
65. Richard William Church, *Bacon*, 1884, p. 29.
66. Alexander Bain, *Practical Essays*, 1884, p. 16.
67. Edwin Abbott Abbott, *Francis Bacon: An Account of His Life and Works*, 1885, pp. 447–53.
68. John Nicol, *Francis Bacon: His Life and Philosophy*, 1888, Pt. 1, p. 18.
69. Stopford A. Brooke, *English Literature*, 1896, p. 109.
70. Edmund Gosse, *A Short History of Modern English Literature*, 1897, pp. 130–32.
71. George Saintsbury, *A Short History of English Literature*, 1898, pp. 369–73.
72. Reuben Post Halleck, *History of English Literature*, 1900, pp. 124–25.
73. Nicholas Chamberlain, Letter to Sir Dudley Carleton (December 17, 1621), *Court and Times of James I*, ed. Thomas Birch, 1849, Volume 1, p. 214.
74. Edmond Malone, *Life of Sir Joshua Reynolds*, 1794.
75. Nathan Drake, *Essays Illustrative of the* Tatler, Spectator *and* Guardian, 1804, Volume 2, p. 20.
76. Dugald Stewart, "First Preliminary Dissertation," *Encyclopaedia Britannica*, 1815–21.
77. Basil Montagu, "The Life of Francis Bacon," *Bacon's Complete Works*, 1834, Volume 1.
78. Henry Hallam, *Introduction to the Literature of Europe*, 1837–39, Pt. 3, Ch. 4, Par. 34.
79. Ralph Waldo Emerson, "Milton" (1838), *Works*, Riverside ed., Volume 12, p. 152.
80. John, Lord Campbell, *Lives of the Lord Chancellors and Keepers of the Great Seal of England*, 1845–47, Volume 2.
81. George P. Marsh, *The Origin and History of the English Language*, 1862, p. 549.
82. Alexander Smith, *Dreamthorp*, 1863, pp. 31–32.
83. Noah Porter, *Books and Reading*, 1870, Ch. 19.
84. Henry Morley, *First Sketch of English Literature*, 1873, p. 465.
85. Leopold von Ranke, *A History of England*, 1875, Volume 1, p. 459.
86. Emelyn W. Washburn, *Studies in Early English Literature*, 1884, p. 202.
87. John Morley, "Aphorisms" (1887), *Studies in Literature*, 1891, p. 73.
88. John Earle, *English Prose*, 1890, p. 442.
89. Edgar Sanderson, *History of England and the British Empire*, 1893, p. 511.
90. Edmund Gosse, "Tennyson—and After," *Questions at Issue*, 1893, p. 190.
91. Lucy Aikin, *Memoirs of the Court and King James the First*, 1822, Volume 1, pp. 193–95.
92. John Quincy Adams, *Diary*, July 19, 1844.
93. John Richard Green, *Short History of the English People*, 1874, Ch. 9.
94. Sir Henry Wotton, Letter to Bacon (1622), *Reliquiae Wottonianae*, 1651.
95. Basil Montagu, "The Life of Francis Bacon," *Bacon's Complete Works*, 1834, Volume 1.
96. Sir David Brewster, *Memoirs of the Life, Writings, and Discoveries of Sir Isaac Newton*, 1855, Volume 2, p. 402.
97. Dora Greenwell (1860), cited in William Dorling, *Memoirs of Dora Greenwell*, 1885, p. 47.
98. Frederick Denison Maurice, *Moral and Metaphysical Philosophy*, 1862, Volume 2, p. 233.
99. John Richard Green, *Short History of the English People*, 1874, Ch. 9.
100. Samuel R. Gardiner, *History of England*, 1883, Volume 3, pp. 394–95.
101. William Nicolson, *The English Historical Library*, 1696–1714.
102. Henry St. John, Viscount Bolingbroke, "Letter 6" (1735–38), *Letters on the Study and Use of History*, 1752.
103. Horace Walpole, Letter to Robert Henry (March 28, 1783).

104. Nathan Drake, *Shakespeare and His Times*, 1817, Volume 1, p. 476.
105. Thomas Arnold, *Manual of English Literature*, 1862–67, p. 128.
106. William Minto, *Manual of English Prose Literature*, 1872, p. 249.
107. James Spedding, *An Account of the Life and Times of Francis Bacon*, 1878, Volume 2, p. 542.
108. Charles Kendall Adams, A *Manual of Historical Literature*, 1881–88, p. 8.
109. George Saintsbury, *History of Elizabethan Literature*, 1887, p. 209.
110. René Descartes, Letter to Father Mersenne (c. 1650).
111. Pierre Gassendi, *Syntagma*, 1658, tr. Craig B. Brush.
112. George Havers, *Another Collection of Philosophical Conferences*, 1664.
113. Thomas Sprat, *History of the Royal Society of London*, 1667.
114. Abraham Cowley, "Ode to the Royal Society," c. 1667.
115. Henry Oldenburg, "Preface" to *Philosophical Transactions of the Royal Society*, 1672.
116. Thomas Tenison, *Baconiana*, 1679.
117. Samuel Pufendorf, *Spicilegium Controversiarum*, 1680.
118. Robert Boyle, *New Experiments and Observations Touching Cold*, 1683.
119. John Evelyn, *Numismata*, 1697.
120. Jean le Rond d'Alembert, *Preliminary Discourse to the Encyclopedia*, 1751, trs. Richard N. Schwab, Walter E. Rex.
121. Etienne Bonnot de Condillac, *An Essay on the Origin of Human Knowledge*, tr. Thomas Nugent, 1756, Pt. 2, Sec. 2, Ch. 3.
122. Jean Sylvain Bailly, *Histoire de l'astronomie moderne*, 1775–85, Volume 2, Book 4.
123. Dugald Stewart, *Account of the Life and Writings of Thomas Reid*, 1803, Sec. 2.
124. Frederick Schlegel, *Lectures on the History of Literature*, 1815, p. 286.
125. Macvey Napier, "Lord Bacon" (1818), *Lord Bacon and Sir Walter Raleigh*, 1853, p. 14.
126. Sir David Brewster, Letter (April 26, 1824), cited in Margaret Brewster, *The Home Life of Sir David Brewster*, 1869, pp. 128–30.
127. Henry Hallam, *Introduction to the Literature of Europe*, 1837–39.
128. John, Lord Campbell, *Lives of the Lord Chancellors and Keepers of the Great Seal of England*, 1845–47, Volume 2.
129. Robert Leslie Ellis, "General Preface" to *Bacon's Philosophical Works*, 1857, Volume 1, pp. 63–64.
130. John William Draper, *History of the Intellectual Development of Europe*, 1863–76, Volume 2, pp. 258–60.
131. Johann Edward Erdmann, A *History of Philosophy*, tr. William S. Hough, 1865–76, Volume 1, pp. 682–83.
132. W. E. H. Lecky, *Spirit of Rationalism in Europe*, 1865, Volume 1, Ch. 4, Pt. 1.
133. Friedrich Überweg, A *History of Philosophy*, tr. George S. Morris, 1871–73, Volume 2, p. 33.
134. Edward Dowden, *Shakespere: A Critical Study of His Mind and Art*, 1875, p. 16.
135. Oscar Browning, *An Introduction to the History of Educational Theories*, 1881.
136. Richard William Church, Letter to Asa Gray (1883), *Life and Letters of Dean Church*, ed. Mary C. Church, 1894, p. 376.
137. George Croom Robertson, *Hobbes*, 1886, p. 18.
138. Thomas Humphry Ward, *The Reign of Queen Victoria*, 1887, Volume 2, p. 325.
139. John Nicol, *Francis Bacon: His Life and Philosophy*, 1889, Pt. 2, p. 242.
140. Alfred Weber, *History of Philosophy* (1872), tr. Frank Thilly, 1896, p. 298.
141. George Saintsbury, *Social England*, ed. H. D. Traill, 1895, Volume 4, p. 105.
142. George Chapman, Dedication to *The Georgicks of Hesiod*, 1618.
143. William Rawley, "The Life of Bacon," *Resuscitatio*, 1657–61.
144. François Marie Arouet de Voltaire, "Letter 12: On Chancellor Bacon" (1734), *Letters on England (Lettres Philosophiques)*, tr. Leonard Tancock, 1980, pp. 57–61.
145. Thomas Babington Macaulay, "Lord Bacon" (1837), *Critical, Historical, and Miscellaneous Essays*, 1860, Volume 3, pp. 436–95.
146. John Caird, "The Scientific Character of Bacon" (1880), *University Addresses*, 1898, pp. 128–56.
147. Richard William Church, "Bacon as a Writer," *Bacon*, 1884, pp. 209–27.
148. C. Stopes, "The History of the Heresy," *The Bacon-Shakspere Question Answered*, 1889, pp. 185–99.

JOHN DONNE

1. Inscription on Monument.
2. Henry King, "To the Memory of My Ever Desired Friend Doctor Donne," c. 1631.
3. Izaak Walton, *The Life of Dr. John Donne*, 1640.
4. Sir Richard Baker, A *Chronicle of the Kings of England*, 1641.
5. John Hacket, *Life of Archbishop Williams*, 1693, Par. 74.
6. Thomas Campbell, *Specimens of the British Poets*, 1819.
7. Anna Brownell Jameson, *The Loves of the Poets*, 1829, Volume 2, p. 94.
8. William Minto, "John Donne," *Nineteenth Century*, May 1880, p. 849.
9. J. B. Lightfoot, *Historical Essays*, 1895, pp. 221–23.
10. Augustus Jessopp, *John Donne, Sometime Dean of St. Paul's*, 1897, pp. 13, 18.
11. Edmund Gosse, *The Life and Letters of John Donne*, 1899, Volume 1, pp. 3, 11;, Volume 2, p. 290.
12. Izaak Walton, *The Life of Dr. John Donne*, 1640.
13. Henry Hallam, *Introduction to the Literature of Europe*, 1837–39, Pt. 3, Ch. 2, Par. 70.
14. Edwin P. Whipple, *The Literature of the Age of Elizabeth*, 1869, p. 237.
15. Anne C. Lynch Botta, *Hand-Book of Universal Literature*, 1860, p. 476.
16. William Minto, *Manual of English Prose Literature*, 1872, p. 253.
17. Augustus Jessopp, *Dictionary of National Biography*, 1888, Volume 15, p. 229.
18. John Donne, Letter to Sir Henry Goodyere (December 20, 1614), *The Works of John Donne*, ed. Henry Alford, Volume 6, 1839, p. 367.
19. Ben Jonson, "To John Donne," 1616.
20. Ben Jonson, *Conversations with William Drummond*, 1619.
21. Thomas Carew, "An Elegie upon the Death of Doctor Donne," c. 1631.
22. George Daniel, "A Vindication of Poesy," 1647.
23. John Dryden, *Discourse concerning the Original and Progress of Satire*, 1693.
24. Nathan Drake, *Literary Hours*, 1798–1820, No. 28.
25. Henry Kirke White, "Melancholy Hours" (c. 1806), *The Remains of Henry Kirke White*, ed. Robert Southey, 1807, Volume 2.
26. Samuel Taylor Coleridge, "Notes on Beaumont and

Fletcher" (1818), *Literary Remains*, ed. Henry Nelson Coleridge, 1836, Volume 2, pp. 291–92.

27. Robert Southey, *Specimens of the Later English Poets*, 1807, Volume 1, p. xxiv.
28. Thomas Campbell, *An Essay on English Poetry*, 1819.
29. Henry Hallam, *Introduction to the Literature of Europe*, 1837–39, Pt. 3, Ch. 5, Par. 39.
30. Elizabeth Barrett Browning, *The Book of the Poets* (1842), *Life, Letters and Essays of Elizabeth Barrett Browning*, 1863.
31. Hartley Coleridge, "Donne," *Sketches of the English Poets*, 1849.
32. Edwin P. Whipple, *The Literature of the Age of Elizabeth*, 1869, p. 231.
33. George Gilfillan, *Specimens with Memoirs of the Less-Known British Poets*, 1860, Volume 1, p. 203.
34. George L. Craik, *A Compendious History of English Literature and of the English Language*, 1861, Volume 1, p. 579.
35. Richard Chevenix Trench, *A Household Book of English Poetry*, 1868, p. 403.
36. Hippolyte Taine, *History of English Literature*, tr. H. Van Laun, 1871, Book 2, Ch. 1.
37. Robert Chambers, *Cyclopædia of English Literature*, 3rd ed. by Robert Carruthers, 1876.
38. Robert Browning, *The Two Poets of Croisic*, 1878.
39. Alfred Welsh, *Development of English Literature and Language*, 1882, Volume 1, p. 413.
40. Francis T. Palgrave, *The Treasury of Sacred Song*, 1889, p. 333, Note.
41. Edmund Gosse, *The Jacobean Poets*, 1894, pp. 47–48.
42. Edward Dowden, *New Studies in Literature*, 1895, pp. 90–91, 107–17.
43. Oswald Crawfurd, *Lyrical Verse from Elizabeth to Victoria*, 1896, p. 426.
44. Frederic Ives Carpenter, "Introduction" to *English Lyric Poetry, 1500–1700*, 1897, p. lviii.
45. David Hannay, *The Later Renaissance*, 1898, p. 220.
46. Sir Leslie Stephen, "John Donne," *National Review*, December 1899, p. 613.
47. Arthur Symons, "John Donne," *Fortnightly Review*, November 1899, p. 735.
48. Reuben Post Halleck, *History of English Literature*, 1900, p. 186.
49. William Hazlitt, "On Cowley, Butler, Suckling, etc.," *Lectures on the English Comic Writers*, 1819.
50. Unsigned, *Retrospective Review*, 1823, pp. 31–35.
51. Henry Alford, "Life of Dr. Donne," *The Works of John Donne*, 1839, Volume 1, pp. xvii–xxvi.
52. Unsigned, *Lowe's Edinburgh Magazine*, 1846, pp. 228–36.
53. John Alfred Langford, "An Evening with Donne," *Working Man's Friend*, December 1850, pp. 18–21.
54. George MacDonald, "Dr. Donne: His Mode and Style," *England's Antiphon*, 1868, pp. 114–24.
55. Edmund Gosse, "John Donne," *The Jacobean Poets*, 1894, pp. 51–67.
56. Felix E. Schelling, "Introduction" to *A Book of Elizabethan Lyrics*, 1895, pp. xxi–lxix.
57. J. B. Lightfoot, "Donne, the Poet-Preacher," *Historical Essays*, 1896, pp. 232–45.
58. George Saintsbury, "Introduction" to *Poems of John Donne*, ed. E. K. Chambers, 1896, Volume 1, pp. xi–xxxiii.
59. Edmund Gosse, *The Life and Letters of John Donne*, 1899, Volume 1, pp. 61–77, 263–69; Volume 2, pp. 329–44.
60. W. J. Courthope, "The School of Metaphysical Wit: John Donne," *A History of English Poetry*, 1903, Volume 3, pp. 147–68.
61. John W. Hales, "John Donne," *The English Poets*, ed. Thomas Humphry Ward, 1880, Volume 1, pp. 558–60.

GEORGE HERBERT

1. Edward Lord Herbert, *The Life of Edward Lord Herbert of Cherbury*, 1643.
2. Thomas Fuller, *The History of the Worthies of England*, 1662.
3. John Aubrey, "George Herbert," *Brief Lives*, 1669–96.
4. Izaak Walton, *The Life of Mr. George Herbert*, 1670.
5. Charles Cotton, "To My Old, and Most Worthy Friend Mr. Isaac Walton," cited in Izaak Walton, *The Life of Mr. George Herbert*, 1670.
6. John Dunton, *Athenian Mercury*, January 6, 1694.
7. John Reynolds, "To the Memory of the Divine Mr. Herbert," *A View of Death*, 1725, pp. 110–18.
8. Alexander B. Grosart, "George Herbert," *Leisure Hour*, 1873, p. 455.
9. Donald G. Mitchell, *English Lands, Letters, and Kings: From Elizabeth to Anne*, 1890, p. 119.
10. William Holden Hutton, *Social England*, ed. H. D. Traill, 1895, Volume 4, p. 34.
11. Robert Codrington, "On Herbert's Poems," 1638.
12. Henry Vaughan, "Preface" to *Silex Scintillans*, 1650.
13. Richard Baxter, "Prefatory Address" to *Poetical Fragments*, 1681.
14. Unsigned, "Preface" to *Select Hymns, Taken out of Mr. Herbert's Temple*, 1697.
15. Henry Headley, *Select Beauties of Ancient Poetry*, 1787.
16. Henry Neele, *Lectures on English Poetry*, 1827.
17. Ralph Waldo Emerson, "Ben Jonson, Herrick, Herbert, Wotton" (1835), *The Early Lectures of Ralph Waldo Emerson*, eds. Stephen E. Whicher, Robert E. Spiller, 1959, Volume 1, pp. 349–53.
18. John Ruskin, Letters to His Mother (April 13 and 20, 1845).
19. Robert Aris Willmott, "Introduction" to *The Works of George Herbert*, 1854.
20. George L. Craik, *A Compendious History of English Literature and of the English Language*, 1861, Volume 2, p. 19.
21. George MacDonald, *England's Antiphon*, 1886, pp. 174–76.
22. John S. Hart, *A Manual of English Literature*, 1872, p. 76.
23. Alexander B. Grosart, "George Herbert," *Leisure Hour*, 1873, p. 325.
24. Ralph Waldo Emerson, "Preface" to *Parnassus*, 1875, p. vi.
25. Wentworth Webster, *Academy*, July 8, 1882, p. 22.
26. George Saintsbury, *A History of Elizabethan Literature*, 1887, p. 372.
27. J. Howard B. Masterman, *The Age of Milton*, 1897, p. 108.
28. Louise Imogen Guiney, "Henry Vaughan," *A Little English Gallery*, 1894, p. 95.
29. Edmund Gosse, *A Short History of Modern English Literature*, 1897, p. 147.
30. George Herbert, "To Mr. Duncan," *The Life of George Herbert*, 1632.
31. Nicholas Farrer, "Preface" to *The Temple*, 1633.
32. John Polwhele, "On Mr. Herberts Devine Poeme *The Church*," c. 1633.
33. Izaak Walton, *Life of Dr. John Donne*, 1640, p. 37.
34. Christopher Harvey, "The Synagogue," 1640.

35. Richard Crashaw, "On Mr. G. Herbert's Booke Intituled *The Temple*," *Steps to the Temple*, 1646.
36. George Daniel, "An Ode upon the Incomparable Liricke Poesie Written by Mr. George Herbert; Entituled: *The Temple*," 1648.
37. James Duport, "In Divinum Poema (Cui Titulus Templum) Georgii Herberti," *Musae Subsecivae, seu Poetica Stromata*, 1676, pp. 357–58.
38. Samuel Taylor Coleridge, *Lectures and Notes on Shakespere*, 1818.
39. Samuel Taylor Coleridge, *Biographia Literaria*, 1817, Ch. 19.
40. George Gilfillan, "On the Life and Poetical Works of George Herbert," *The Poetical Works of George Herbert*, 1854, pp. xxi–xxvi.
41. Edwin P. Whipple, *The Literature of the Age of Elizabeth*, 1869, pp. 247–48.
42. G. A. Simcox, "Sandys, Herbert, Crashaw, Vaughan," *The English Poets*, ed. Thomas Humphry Ward, 1880, Volume 2, p. 193.
43. John Brown, "The Parson of Bemerton," *Good Words*, 1890, p. 697.
44. Izaak Walton, *The Life of Mr. George Herbert*, 1670.
45. Daniel Baker, "On Mr. George Herbert's Sacred Poems, Called, *The Temple*," *Poems upon Several Occassions*, 1697, pp. 83–89.
46. Margaret Fuller, "The Two Herberts," *Papers on Literature and Art*, 1846, pp. 15–34.
47. Robert Aris Willmott, "Introduction" to *The Works of George Herbert*, 1854, pp. xxi–xxx.
48. John Nichol, "Introduction" to *The Poetical Works of George Herbert*, 1863, pp. vi–vii, xix–xxvi.

JOHN WEBSTER

1. Henry Fitzjeffrey, "Notes from Blackfriars," *Certain Elegies by Sundry Excellent Wits*, 1617.
2. Samuel Sheppard, "The Fairy King," 1651.
3. Gerard Langbaine, *An Account of the English Dramatick Poets*, 1691, pp. 508–10.
4. Nathan Drake, *Shakspeare and His Times*, 1817, Volume 2, p. 565.
5. John Wilson (as "H.M."), *Blackwood's Edinburgh Magazine*, March 1818, pp. 657–58.
6. Thomas Campbell, *An Essay on English Poetry*, 1819.
7. William Hazlitt, *Lectures on the Literature of the Age of Elizabeth*, 1820.
8. Charles Knight, *William Shakspere: A Biography*, 1842.
9. Thomas B. Shaw, *Outlines of English Literature*, 1847, p. 130.
10. James Russell Lowell, "Library of Old Authors" (1858–64), *Works*, Riverside ed., Volume 1, pp. 279–81.
11. Edwin P. Whipple, *The Literature of the Age of Elizabeth*, 1869, pp. 139–41.
12. William Minto, *Characteristics of English Poets*, 1874.
13. Adolphus William Ward, *A History of English Dramatic Literature* (1875), 1899, Volume 3, pp. 51–65.
14. Algernon Charles Swinburne, "John Webster," 1882.
15. James Baldwin, "English Poetry," *English Literature and Literary Criticism*, 1882, p. 238.
16. George Saintsbury, *A History of Elizabethan Literature*, 1887, p. 274.
17. John Addington Symonds, "Introduction" to *Webster and Tourneur*, 1888, pp. xi–xxii.
18. Donald G. Mitchell, *English Lands, Letters, and Kings: From Elizabeth to Anne*, 1890, p. 90.
19. Frederic Ives Carpenter, *Metaphor and Simile in the Minor Elizabethan Drama*, 1895, pp. 75–77.
20. Edmund Gosse, A *Short History of Modern English Literature*, 1897, pp. 118–19.
21. John Webster, "Preface" to *The White Devil*, 1612.
22. Charles Lamb, *Specimens of English Dramatic Poets*, 1808.
23. John Wilson (as "H.M."), *Blackwood's Edinburgh Magazine*, August 1818, pp. 556–62.
24. Adolphus William Ward, *A History of English Dramatic Literature* (1875), 1899, Volume 3, pp. 56–59.
25. George Saintsbury, *A History of Elizabethan Literature*, 1887, p. 275.
26. Algernon Charles Swinburne, *Studies in Prose and Poetry*, 1894, p. 50.
27. John Ford, "To the Reader of the Author, and His *Dutchess of Malfi*," 1623.
28. William Rowley, "To His Friend, Mr. John Webster, upon His *Dutchess of Malfi*," 1623.
29. Charles Lamb, *Specimens of English Dramatic Poets*, 1808.
30. William Hazlitt, *Lectures on the Literature of the Age of Elizabeth*, 1820.
31. Abraham Mills, *The Literature of the Literary Men of Great Britain and Ireland*, 1851, Volume 1, p. 345.
32. Edmund Clarence Stedman, *The Nature and Elements of Poetry*, 1892, p. 249.
33. Algernon Charles Swinburne, *Studies in Prose and Poetry*, 1894, p. 51.
34. Adolphus William Ward, *A History of English Dramatic Literature* (1875), 1899 Volume 3, p. 62.
35. John Addington Symonds, "Introduction" to *Webster and Tourneur*, 1888, pp. xvii–xix.
36. Frederic Ives Carpenter, *Metaphor and Simile in the Minor Elizabethan Drama*, 1895, p. 80.
37. Alexander Dyce, "Some Account of John Webster and His Writings," *The Works of John Webster*, 1830, Volume 1, pp. v–xiv.
38. Charles Kingsley, "Plays and Puritans" (1859), *Plays and Puritans and Other Historical Essays*, 1873, pp. 50–56.
39. Algernon Charles Swinburne, "John Webster" (1886), *The Age of Shakespeare*, 1908, pp. 15–19.
40. Edmund Gosse, *The Jacobean Poets*, 1894, pp. 166–73.

BEN JONSON

1. Ben Jonson, *Conversations with William Drummond*, 1619.
2. Sir John Suckling, "The Wits," 1637.
3. Thomas Fuller, *The History of the Worthies of England*, 1662.
4. John Aubrey, "Ben Johnson," *Brief Lives*, 1669–96.
5. Peter Whalley, "Life of Jonson," *Jonson's Works*, 1756, p. lv.
6. George Walter Thornbury, *Shakspere's England*, 1856, Volume 2, p. 13.
7. Edwin P. Whipple, *The Literature of the Age of Elizabeth*, 1869, p. 85.
8. Arthur Penrhyn Stanley, *Historical Memorials of Westminster Abbey*, 1896, pp. 288–89.
9. William Minto, *Characteristics of English Poets*, 1874, p. 338.
10. Adolphus William Ward, *A History of English Dramatic Literature* (1875), 1899, Volume 2, pp. 297–314.
11. George Saintsbury, *Social England*, ed. H. D. Traill, 1895, Volume 4, p. 113.
12. George Brandes, *William Shakespeare: A Critical Study*, 1898, Volume 1, pp. 385–88.
13. Chettle Henry, *England's Mourning Garment*, 1603.
14. William Browne, *Britannia's Pastorals*, 1613, Book 2, Song 2.

15. Edmund Bolton, *Hypercritica*, 1624.
16. Francis Lenton, "The Young Gallant's Whirligig," 1629.
17. H. Ramsay, "Upon the Death of Benjamin Jonson," 1638.
18. Owen Feltham, "To the Memory of Immortal Ben," 1638.
19. Sir John Beaumont, "To the Memory of Him Who Can Never Be Forgotten, Master Benjamin Jonson," 1638.
20. Richard Flecknoe, "A Short Discourse of the English Stage," *Love's Kingdom*, 1664.
21. Thomas Fuller, *The History of the Worthies of England*, 1662.
22. John Dryden, "Preface" to *An Evening's Love; or, The Mock Astrologer*, 1671.
23. Thomas Shadwell, "Preface" to *The Humorists*, 1671.
24. Edward Phillips, *Theatrum Poetarum Anglicanorum*, 1675.
25. Samuel Butler, *Characters and Passages from Note-Books*, c. 1680.
26. Gerard Langbaine, *An Account of the English Dramatick Poets*, 1691, pp. 145–50.
27. William Congreve, "Mr. Congreve to Mr. Dennis, concerning Humour in Comedy," *Letters upon Several Occasions*, 1696, pp. 80–96.
28. William Collins, "An Epistle Address to Sir Thomas Hanmer on His Edition of Shakespear's Works," 1743.
29. Corbyn Morris, *An Essay towards Fixing the True Standards of Wit, Humour, Raillery, Satire, and Ridicule*, 1744, pp. 29–36.
30. Samuel Johnson, "Prologue, Spoken by Mr. Garrick at the Opening of the Theatre Royal, Drury Lane," 1747.
31. David Hume, *History of England*, 1754–62.
32. Edward Young, *Conjectures on Original Composition*, 1759.
33. Charles Churchill, *The Rosciad*, 1761.
34. James Granger, *Biographical History of England*, 1769–1824.
35. Sir Walter Scott, *Life of John Dryden*, 1808.
36. August Wilhelm Schlegel, *Lectures on Dramatic Art and Literature*, 1809, tr. John Black.
37. Samuel Taylor Coleridge, "Lecture VII: Ben Jonson, Beaumont and Fletcher, and Massinger" (1818), *Literary Remains*, ed. Henry Nelson Coleridge, 1836, Volume 1, p. 92.
38. Thomas Campbell, *An Essay on English Poetry*, 1819.
39. Henry Neele, *Lectures on English Poetry*, 1827.
40. Hermann Ulrici, *Shakespeare's Dramatic Art*, 1839, pp. 81–82.
41. Isaac Disraeli, "The 'Humours' of Jonson," *Amenities of Literature*, 1841.
42. Elizabeth Barrett Browning, *The Book of the Poets* (1842), *Life, Letters and Essays of Elizabeth Barrett Browning*, 1863.
43. Edwin P. Whipple, "Old English Dramatists" (1846), *Essays and Reviews*, 1850, Volume 2, p. 26.
44. Victor Hugo, *William Shakespeare*, tr. F. T. Marzials, 1864, p. 23.
45. Charles Cowden Clarke, "On the Comic Writers of England," *Gentleman's Magazine*, May 1871, p. 633.
46. William Minto, *Characteristics of English Poets*, 1874, p. 337.
47. Ralph Waldo Emerson, "Preface" to *Parnassus*, 1875, p. vi.
48. George Meredith, "On the Idea of Comedy and of the Uses of the Comic Spirit," 1877.
49. Algernon Charles Swinburne, "Ben Jonson," *Sonnets on English Dramatic Poets*, 1882.

50. Oswald Crawfurd, *English Comic Dramatists*, 1883, p. 12.
51. Donald G. Mitchell, *English Lands, Letters, and Kings: From Elizabeth to Anne*, 1890, p. 26.
52. Edmund Gosse, *The Jacobean Poets*, 1894, pp. 37–38.
53. Walter Raleigh, *Style*, 1897, pp. 68–71.
54. Herbert Arthur Evans, "Introduction" to *English Masques*, 1897, p. xi.
55. John Dryden, "Defence of the Epilogue," *The Conquest of Granada*, 1672.
56. Thomas Davies, *Dramatic Miscellanies*, 1783, Volume 2, p. 53.
57. Henry Hallam, *Introduction to the Literature of Europe*, 1839, Pt. 2, Ch. 6, Par. 53.
58. Richard Hurd, *A Dissertation on the Several Provinces of the Drama*, 1757, Volume 1, p. 266.
59. T. E. Browne, "Ben Jonson," *New Review*, May 1896, p. 522.
60. John Addington Symonds, *Ben Jonson*, 1886, p. 35.
61. Charles Lamb, *Specimens of the English Dramatic Poets*, 1808.
62. Josiah H. Penniman, *The War of the Theatres*, 1897, p. 118.
63. Samuel Taylor Coleridge, "Notes on Ben Jonson" (1818), *Literary Remains*, ed. Henry Nelson Coleridge, 1836, Volume 2, p. 274.
64. Edwin P. Whipple, *The Literature of the Age of Elizabeth*, 1869, p. 102.
65. Henry Morley and W. Hall Griffin, *English Writers*, 1895, Volume 11, p. 219.
66. Francis Beaumont, "To My Dear Friend, Master Ben Jonson, upon His *Fox*," 1607.
67. Thomas Davies, *Dramatic Miscellanies*, 1783, Volume 2, p. 97.
68. Samuel Taylor Coleridge, "Notes on Ben Jonson" (1818), *Literary Remains*, ed. Henry Nelson Coleridge, 1836, Volume 2, p. 276.
69. Adolphus William Ward, *A History of English Dramatic Literature* (1875), 1899, Volume 2, p. 363.
70. Ben Jonson, *Conversations with William Drummond*, 1619.
71. Samuel Taylor Coleridge, "Notes on Ben Jonson" (1818), *Literary Remains*, ed. Henry Nelson Coleridge, 1836, Volume 2, p. 277.
72. Charles Cowden Clarke, "On the Comic Writers of England," *Gentleman's Magazine*, May 1871, p. 643.
73. John Dryden, "Prologue" to *Albumazar*, 1668.
74. Charles Dibdin, *A Complete History of the Stage*, 1795, Volume 3, p. 295.
75. Charles Lamb, *Specimens of English Dramatic Poets*, 1808.
76. Edmund Gosse, *The Jacobean Poets*, 1894, p 28.
77. R. Baron, *Pocula Castalia*, 1650, p. 113.
78. Adolphus William Ward, *A History of English Dramatic Literature* (1875), 1899, Volume 2, p. 341.
79. John Dryden, *A Defence of An Essay of Dramatick Poesy*, 1668.
80. Charles Dibdin, *A Complete History of the Stage*, 1795, Volume 3, p. 297.
81. Adolphus William Ward, *A History of English Dramatic Literature* (1875), 1899, Volume 2, p. 37.
82. Edmund Gosse, *The Jacobean Poets*, 1894, p. 32.
83. George L. Craik, *A Compendious History of English Literature and of the English Language*, 1861, Volume 1, p. 605.
84. Charles Cowden Clarke, "On the Comic Writers of England," *Gentleman's Magazine*, May 1871, p. 649.

85. William Minto, *Characteristics of English Poets*, 1874, p. 343.
86. John Dryden, *An Essay of Dramatick Poesie*, 1668.
87. William Hazlitt, *Lectures on the Dramatic Literature of the Age of Elizabeth*, 1820.
88. John Addington Symonds, *Ben Jonson*, 1886, pp. 50–121.
89. Algernon Charles Swinburne, *A Study of Ben Jonson*, 1889, pp. 9–89.
90. Elisabeth Woodbridge, *Studies of Jonson's Comedy*, 1898, pp. 28–79.
91. George Saintsbury, "Elizabethan Criticism" (1900), *A History of English Criticism*, 1911, pp. 80–92.

RICHARD CRASHAW

1. Abraham Cowley, "On the Death of Mr. *Crashaw*," 1650.
2. George Gilfillan, "The Life and Poetry of Richard Crashaw," *The Poetical Works of Richard Crashaw*, 1857, p. vii.
3. Unsigned, "The Preface to the Reader," *The Delights of the Muses*, 1648.
4. Alexander Pope, Letter to H. Cromwell (December 17, 1710).
5. Nathan Drake, *Literary Hours*, 1798–1820, No. 28.
6. Thomas Campbell, *Specimens of the British Poets*, 1819, p. 357.
7. William Hazlitt, *Lectures on the Literature of the Age of Elizabeth*, 1820, p. 192.
8. Samuel Taylor Coleridge, cited in Thomas Allsop, *Letters, Conversations, and Recollections of S. T. Coleridge*, 1836, p. 606.
9. Sara Coleridge, Letter to Mrs. Richard Townsend (September 1847), *Memoir and Letters of Sara Coleridge*, ed. Edith Coleridge, 1873.
10. David Masson, *The Life of John Milton*, 1859, Volume 1, Ch. 6.
11. William B. Turnbull, "Preliminary Observations," *Complete Works of Richard Crashaw*, 1858, p. x.
12. D. F. M'Carthy, "Crashaw and Shelley," *Notes and Queries*, June 5, 1858, p. 419.
13. George L. Craik, *A Compendious History of English Literature and of the English Language*, 1861, Volume 2, p. 20.
14. Maurice F. Egan, "Three Catholic Poets," *Catholic World*, October 1880, pp. 138–40.
15. G. A. Simcox, "Sandys, Herbert, Crashaw, Vaughan," *The English Poets*, ed. Thomas Humphry Ward, 1880, pp. 195–96.
16. J. R. Tutin, "Preface" to *Poems of Richard Crashaw*, 1887, p. viii.
17. Sidney Lee, *Dictionary of National Biography*, 1888, Volume 13, pp. 35–36.
18. Francis Turner Palgrave, *The Treasury of Sacred Song*, 1889, Note, p. 342.
19. J. Howard B. Masterman, *The Age of Milton*, 1897.
20. Frederic Ives Carpenter, "Introduction" to *English Lyric Poetry, 1500–1700*, 1897, p. lix.
21. Francis Thompson, "Excursions in Criticism: VI.—Richard Crashaw," *Academy*, November 20, 1897, p. 427.
22. Herbert J. C. Grierson, "English Poetry," *The First Half of the Seventeenth Century*, 1906, pp. 169–71.
23. George Gilfillan, "The Life and Poetry of Richard Crashaw," *Poetical Works of Richard Crashaw*, 1857, pp. viii–xviii.
24. George MacDonald, "Crashaw and Marvell," *England's Antiphon*, 1868, pp. 238–46.
25. Alexander B. Grosart, "Essay on the Life and Poetry of Crashaw," *Complete Works of Richard Crashaw*, Volume 2, 1873, pp. lxii–lxxv.
26. Edmund Gosse, "Richard Crashaw" (1882/1913), *Seventeenth Century Studies*, 1913, Volume 1, pp. 157–82.
27. George Saintsbury, *A History of Elizabethan Literature*, 1887, pp. 364–69.
28. Francis Thompson, "Excursions in Criticism: VI.—Crashaw," *Academy*, November 20, 1897, pp. 427–28.
29. Felix E. Schelling, "Introduction" to *A Book of Seventeenth Century Lyrics*, 1899, pp. xxx–xxxiii, li–liii.
30. H. C. Beeching, "Introduction" to *Poems of Richard Crashaw*, ed. J. R. Tutin, 1905, pp. xxxvi–lv.

ROBERT HERRICK

1. Barron Field, *Quarterly Review*, August 1810, pp. 171–72.
2. William Carew Hazlitt, "Preface" to *Hesperides*, 1869, Volume 1, p. viii.
3. Justin S. Morrill, *Self-Consciousness of Noted Persons*, 1887, p. 90.
4. Donald G. Mitchell, *English Lands, Letters, and Kings: From Elizabeth to Anne*, 1890, p. 124.
5. Agnes Repplier, "English Love-Songs," *Points of View*, 1891, p. 33.
6. H. M. Sanders, "Robert Herrick," *Gentleman's Magazine*, June 1896, p. 604.
7. Thomas Bailey Aldrich, "Introduction" to *Poems of Robert Herrick*, 1900, pp. xxvi–xxx.
8. Edward Phillips, *Theatrum Poetarum Anglicanorum*, 1675.
9. William Winstanley, *The Lives of the Most Famous English Poets*, 1687.
10. Anthony à Wood, *Athenae Oxonienses*, 1691–1721.
11. James Granger, *Biographical History of England*, 1769–1824.
12. Nathan Drake, "On the Life, Writings and Genius of Robert Herrick," *Literary Hours*, 1804, Volume 2, pp. 368–71.
13. William Hazlitt, *Lectures on the Literature of the Age of Elizabeth*, 1820.
14. Robert Southey, *Lives of Uneducated Poets*, 1831, p. 85.
15. Ralph Waldo Emerson, "Ben Jonson, Herrick, Herbert, Wotton" (1835), *The Early Lectures of Ralph Waldo Emerson*, eds. Stephen E. Whicher, Robert E. Spiller, 1959, Volume 1, pp. 346–49.
16. Henry Hallam, *Introduction to the Literature of Europe*, 1837–39, Pt. 3, Ch. 5, Par. 57.
17. S. W. Singer, "Biographical Notice" to *Hesperides*, 1846, Volume 1, p. xxv.
18. Mary Russell Mitford, *Recollections of a Literary Life*, 1851, pp. 143–44.
19. David Masson, *The Life of John Milton*, 1859, Volume 1, Ch. 6.
20. George MacDonald, *England's Antiphon*, 1868, p. 163.
21. A. Bronson Alcott, *Concord Days*, 1872, p. 136.
22. William Michael Rossetti, Note to *Humorous Poems*, 1872, p. 98.
23. George Barnett Smith, "English Fugitive Poets," *Poets and Novelists*, 1875, pp. 381–82.
24. Edmund Gosse, "Robert Herrick," *The English Poets*, ed. Thomas Humphry Ward, 1880, Volume 2, p. 124.
25. W. Baptiste Scoones, *Four Centuries of English Letters*, 1880, p. 67.
26. John Dennis, *Heroes of Literature*, 1883, p. 97.
27. Ernest Rhys, "Introduction" to *Hesperides: Poems by Robert Herrick*, 1887, pp. xxxi–xxxiii.
28. Austin Dobson, "In a Copy of the Lyrical Poems of Robert Herrick," *Scribner's Magazine*, January 1887, p. 66.

29. George Saintsbury, A *History of Elizabethan Literature*, 1887, p. 355.
30. Andrew Lang, *Letters on Literature*, 1889, p. 149.
31. Donald G. Mitchell, *English Lands, Letters, and Kings: From Elizabeth to Anne*, 1890, p. 125.
32. W. E. Henley, "Herrick," *Views and Reviews*, 1890.
33. Richard Le Gallienne, "Robert Herrick" (1891), *Retrospective Reviews*, 1896, Volume 1, pp. 1–3.
34. Edward Everett Hale, Jr., "Introduction" to *Selections from the Poetry of Robert Herrick*, 1895, p. lxiii.
35. Frederic Ives Carpenter, "Introduction" to *English Lyric Poetry, 1500–1700*, 1897, p. liii.
36. J. Howard B. Masterman, *The Age of Milton*, 1897, pp. 101–5.
37. Robert Herrick, "The Argument of His Book," *Hesperides*, 1648.
38. Unsigned, "To Parson Weeks, an Invitation to London," *Musarum Deliciae*, 1656.
39. Unsigned, *Naps upon Parnassus*, 1658.
40. William Carew Hazlitt, "Preface" to *Hesperides*, 1869, Volume 1, p. viii.
41. W. J. Linton, *Rare Poems of the Sixteenth and Seventeenth Centuries*, 1882, p. 242.
42. Henry Morley, "Introduction" to *Hesperides*, 1884, p. 7.
43. George Saintsbury, *Social England*, ed. H. D. Traill, 1895, Volume 4, p. 300.
44. T. Ashe, "Robert Herrick," *Temple Bar*, May 1883, p. 132.
45. George Saintsbury, A *History of Elizabethan Literature*, 1887, p. 356.
46. Thomas Bailey Aldrich, "Introduction" to *Poems of Robert Herrick*, 1900, p. xxv.
47. Edmund Gosse, "Robert Herrick" (1875), *Seventeenth Century Studies* (1883), 1913, pp. 125–56.
48. F. T. Palgrave, "Robert Herrick," *Macmillan's Magazine*, April 1877, pp. 475–81.
49. Algernon Charles Swinburne, "Robert Herrick" (1891), *Studies in Prose and Poetry*, 1894.
50. Alfred W. Pollard, "Herrick and His Friends," *Macmillan's Magazine*, December 1892, pp. 142–48.
51. George Saintsbury, "Introduction" to *The Poetical Works of Robert Herrick*, Volume 1, 1893, pp. xxv–liii.
52. Thomas Bailey Aldrich, "Introduction" to *Poems of Robert Herrick*, 1900, pp. xxxviii–l.
53. F. Cornish Warre, "Robert Herrick," *Edinburgh Review*, January 1904, pp. 109–27.

JOHN MILTON

1. John Milton, A *Second Defence of the English People*, 1654, tr. Helen North.
2. John Milton, *Paradise Lost*, 1667, Book 7.
3. Gerard Langbaine, *An Account of the English Dramatick Poets*, 1691, p. 375.
4. Edward Phillips, "The Life of Mr. John Milton," *Letters of State*, English ed., 1694.
5. Thomas Ellwood, *The History of the Life of Thomas Ellwood*, 1714.
6. Jonathan Richardson, *Explanatory Notes and Remarks on Milton's Paradise Lost*, 1734.
7. Thomas Newton, "Life of Milton," *Milton's Poetical Works*, 1749–52.
8. Thomas Birch, *An Historical and Critical Account of the Life and Writings of Mr. John Milton*, 1753.
9. Samuel Johnson, "John Milton," *Lives of the English Poets*, 1779–81.
10. William Wordsworth, *The Prelude*, 1799–1805, Book 2.
11. François René, Vicomte de Chateaubriand, *Sketches of English Literature*, 1837, Volume 2, p. 80.
12. William H. Prescott, "Chateaubriand's English Literature" (1839), *Biographical and Critical Miscellanies*, 1845.
13. William Howitt, *Homes and Haunts of the Most Eminent British Poets*, 1847, Volume 1, pp. 75–115.
14. Alphonse de Lamartine, "Milton," *Memoirs of Celebrated Characters*, 1854.
15. Thomas Keightley, *An Account of the Life, Opinions, and Writings of John Milton*, 1855, p. 75.
16. Peter Bayne, *The Chief Actors in the Puritan Revolution*, 1878, p. 345.
17. Mark Pattison, *Milton*, 1879, p. 148.
18. Matthew Arnold, "A French Critic on Milton" (1877), *Mixed Essays*, 1879, p. 269.
19. C. M. Ingleby, *Shakespeare's Bones*, 1883.
20. George Saintsbury, A *History of Elizabethan Literature*, 1887, p. 317.
21. Augustine Birrell, "John Milton," *Obiter Dicta: Second Series*, 1887, p. 14.
22. Sir Leslie Stephen, *Dictionary of National Biography*, 1894 Volume 38, p. 25.
23. Edward Dowden, "The Teaching of English Literature," *New Studies in Literature*, 1895, p. 442.
24. William Vaughn Moody, "Life of Milton," *Poetical Works of Milton*, 1899, Cambridge ed., p. xiii.
25. William P. Trent, *John Milton: A Short Study of His Life, and Works*, 1899, p. 55.
26. Humphrey Moseley, "The Stationer to the Reader," *Milton's Poems*, 1645.
27. William Winstanley, *The Lives of the Most Famous English Poets*, 1687.
28. John Dryden, "Lines on Milton," 1688.
29. Joseph Addison, "An Account of the Greatest English Poets," 1694.
30. Laurence Echard, *The History of England*, 1718, Volume 3, p. 369.
31. James Thomson, "Summer," *The Seasons*, 1727.
32. Alexander Pope (1737–39), cited in Joseph Spence, *Anecdotes, Observations and Characters of Books and Men*, ed. S. W. Singer, 1820.
33. Thomas Gray, "Observations on English Metre" (c. 1761), *Works*, ed. Edmund Gosse, Volume 1, pp. 332–33.
34. David Hume, *History of England*, 1754–62.
35. Horace Walpole, Letter to John Pinkerton (June 26, 1785).
36. Robert Burns, "Poem on Pastoral Poetry," c. 1796.
37. Samuel Taylor Coleridge, "Notes on Milton" (1796), *Literary Remains*, ed. Henry Nelson Coleridge, 1836, Volume 1, p. 184.
38. William Godwin, "Milton and Clarendon," *The Enquirer*, 1797, p. 405.
39. William Wordsworth, "London, 1802," 1802.
40. George Gordon, Lord Byron, "Dedication" to *Don Juan*, 1818, Stanza 10.
41. John Keats, "On a Lock of Milton's Hair," 1818.
42. Thomas Campbell, *An Essay on English Poetry*, 1819.
43. Percy Bysshe Shelley, *Adonais*, 1821, Stanza 4.
44. Robert Southey, A *Vision of Judgment*, 1821, Sec. 9.
45. William Ellery Channing, *Remarks on the Character and Writings of John Milton*, 1826.
46. John Sterling, "Shades of the Dead" (1829), *Essays and Tales*, 1848, Volume 1, ed. Julius Charles Hare, p. 76.
47. James Montgomery, *Lectures on General Literature*, 1833, p. 92.
48. Thomas De Quincey, *Autobiography*, 1835.
49. Edwin Guest, A *History of English Rhythms*, 1838, Volume 2, pp. 240–42.

50. Thomas Carlyle, *Lectures on the History of Literature*, 1838, p. 165.
51. William Smyth, *Lectures on Modern History*, 1840.
52. Leigh Hunt, "Milton," *Imagination and Fancy*, 1844.
53. Thomas B. Shaw, *Outlines of English Literature*, 1847, p. 162.
54. Edwin P. Whipple, "Authors in Their Relations to Life," *Lectures on Subjects Connected with Literature and Life*, 1850, pp. 24–25.
55. George Meredith, "The Poetry of Milton," 1851.
56. Frederick Denison Maurice, "The Friendship of Books" (1856), *The Friendship of Books and Other Lectures*, ed. Thomas Hughes, 1874, p. 14.
57. George William Curtis, "The Duty of the American Scholar" (1856), *Orations and Addresses*, 1893, Volume 1, p. 12.
58. Charles Kingsley, "Plays and Puritans" (1859), *Plays and Puritans and Other Historical Essays*, 1873.
59. Samuel Leigh Sotheby, *Ramblings in the Elucidation of the Autograph of Milton*, 1861, p. 12.
60. Alfred, Lord Tennyson, "Milton," 1863.
61. Henry Morley, "Introduction" to *The King and the Commons*, 1868, p. xx.
62. George MacDonald, *England's Antiphon*, 1868, pp. 194–95.
63. John Robert Seeley, "Milton's Political Opinions," *Macmillan's Magazine*, February 1868, p. 302.
64. Hippolyte Taine, *History of English Literature*, tr. H. Van Laun, 1871, Bk. 2, Ch. 6.
65. Henry Wadsworth Longfellow, "Milton," *A Book of Sonnets*, 1873.
66. J. C. Shairp, *On Poetic Interpretation of Nature*, 1877, p. 186.
67. William Michael Rossetti, "John Milton," *Lives of Famous Poets*, 1878, p. 76.
68. James Anthony Froude, *Bunyan*, 1880, p. 116.
69. John Dennis, *Heroes of Literature*, 1883, p. 127.
70. Richard Henry Stoddard, "Introduction" to *English Verse: Chaucer to Burns*, 1883, p. xxxviii.
71. Hutcheson Macaulay Posnett, *Comparative Literature*, 1886, p. 384.
72. Harry Lyman Koopman, "Milton," *Orestes and Other Poems*, 1888, p. 148.
73. Frederick Pollock, "John Milton," *Fortnightly Review*, October 1890, p. 519.
74. Donald G. Mitchell, *English Lands, Letters, and Kings: From Elizabeth to Anne*, 1890, p. 179.
75. James Russell Lowell, "Fragments," *Century Magazine*, May 1894, pp. 24–25.
76. John Amphlett Evans, "Dryden and Ben Jonson," *Temple Bar*, May 1892, p. 109.
77. William Watson, "The Mystery of Style," *Excursions in Criticism*, 1893, pp. 105–10.
78. George Saintsbury, *Social England*, ed. H. D. Traill, 1895, Volume 4, p. 425.
79. Francis Turner Palgrave, *Landscape in Poetry*, 1896, pp. 158–59.
80. Augustus Hopkins Strong, *The Great Poets and Their Theology*, 1897, pp. 246–56.
81. Frederic Ives Carpenter, "Introduction" to *English Lyric Poetry, 1500–1700*, 1897, p. liv.
82. Walter Raleigh, *Style*, 1897, p. 35.
83. Henry A. Beers, *A History of English Romanticism in the Eighteenth Century*, 1898, p. 146.
84. John A. Hines, "Preface" to *Paradise Lost*, 1898, p. iii.
85. William P. Trent, *John Milton: A Short Study of His Life and Works*, 1899, p. 53.

86. Henry Lawes, "To Lord-Viscount Brackly," *Comus*, 1637.
87. Sir Henry Wotton, Letter to John Milton (April 13, 1638).
88. Thomas Warton, *Milton's Poems on Several Occasions*, 1785, p. 263.
89. Sir Walter Scott, *Life of John Dryden*, 1808.
90. Nathan Drake, *Shakspeare and His Times*, 1817, Volume 2, p. 579.
91. Robert Southey, "Todd's Edition of Milton," *Quarterly Review*, June 1827, p. 45.
92. Edgar Allan Poe, *Marginalia* (1844), *Complete Works*, ed. James A. Harrison, Volume 16, pp. 26–27.
93. Henry Reed, *Lectures on English Literature, from Chaucer to Tennyson*, 1855, pp. 189–90.
94. David Masson, *The Life of John Milton*, 1859, Volume 1, Ch. 7.
95. Adolphus William Ward, *A History of English Dramatic Literature* (1875), 1899, Volume 3, p. 200.
96. Peter Bayne, *The Chief Actors in the Puritan Revolution*, 1878, p. 309.
97. Stopford A. Brooke, *Milton*, 1879, p. 24.
98. Samuel R. Gardiner, *History of England*, 1883, Volume 7, p. 337.
99. George Saintsbury, *A History of Elizabethan Literature*, 1887, pp. 318–21.
100. J. Howard B. Masterman, *The Age of Milton*, 1897, p. 16.
101. Thomas Warton, *Milton's Poems on Several Occasions*, 1785, p. 36.
102. Thomas Green, *Extracts from the Diary of a Lover of Literature*, 1810.
103. Robert Southey, "Todd's Edition of Milton," *Quarterly Review*, June 1827, p. 46.
104. Edwin Guest, *A History of English Rhythms*, 1838, Volume 1, p. 274.
105. Stopford A. Brooke, *Milton*, 1879, p. 26.
106. Mark Pattison, *Milton*, 1879, pp. 27–28.
107. Sir Francis Hastings Doyle, *Reminiscences and Opinions*, 1886, p. 184.
108. George Saintsbury, *A History of Elizabethan Literature*, 1887, p. 322.
109. Eugene Lee-Hamilton, "Lycidas to Milton (1637)," *Imaginary Sonnets*, 1888.
110. J. Howard B. Masterman, *The Age of Milton*, 1897, p. 24.
111. William P. Trent, *John Milton: A Short Study of His Life and Works*, 1899, p. 140.
112. Andrew Marvell, "On Mr. *Milton's* Paradise Lost," 1674.
113. Thomas Rymer, *The Tragedies of the Last Age*, 1678.
114. John Oldham, "A Pastoral on the Death of the Earl of Rochester," 1680.
115. John Dryden, "Preface" to *Sylvae*, 1685.
116. John Dryden, *Discourse concerning the Original and Progress of Satire*, 1693.
117. Sir Richard Blackmore, *Essays on Several Subjects*, 1716.
118. Jonathan Swift, Letter to Charles Wogan (August 2, 1732).
119. Alexander Pope (1734–36), cited in Joseph Spence, *Anecdotes, Observations and Characters of Books and Men*, ed. S. W. Singer, 1820.
120. Theophilus Cibber, *Lives of the Poets*, 1753, Volume 2, p. 108.
121. Thomas Gray, *The Progress of Poesy*, 1757.
122. François Marie Arouet de Voltaire, *Candide*, 1759, Ch. 25.
123. James Beattie, "An Essay on Poetry and Music," 1776.

124. William Cowper, Letter to William Unwin (October 31, 1779).
125. William Godwin, "Of Choice in Reading," *The Enquirer*, 1797, p. 135.
126. Friedrich Schlegel, *Lectures on the History of Literature*, 1815.
127. John Keats, "Notes on Milton's *Paradise Lost*," 1818.
128. George Gordon, Lord Byron, "Some Observations upon an Article in *Blackwood's Magazine*," 1820.
129. Percy Bysshe Shelley, *A Defence of Poetry*, 1821.
130. Henry Neele, *Lectures on English Poetry*, 1827, Lecture 2.
131. Samuel Taylor Coleridge, *Table Talk*, August 18, 1833.
132. François René, Vicomte de Chateaubriand, *Sketches of English Literature*, 1837, Volume 2, pp. 118–30.
133. Henry Hallam, *Introduction to the Literature of Europe*, 1837–39, Pt. 4, Ch. 5, Par. 34.
134. Thomas Carlyle, *Lectures on the History of Literature*, 1838, p. 166.
135. William H. Prescott, "Chateaubriand's English Literature" (1839), *Biographical and Critical Miscellanies*, 1845.
136. Edward Everett, *Orations and Speeches*, 1850, Volume 2, p. 222.
137. Alphonse de Lamartine, *Memoirs of Celebrated Characters*, 1854.
138. Matthew Arnold, *On Translating Homer*, 1861.
139. Hippolyte Taine, *History of English Literature*, tr. H. Van Laun, 1871, Book 2, Ch. 6.
140. David Masson, *The Poetical Works of John Milton*, 1874, Volume 1, p. 101.
141. Edward FitzGerald, Letter to Charles Eliot Norton (February 7, 1876).
142. E. S. Nadel, "The Cosmogony of *Paradise Lost*," *Harper's New Monthly Magazine*, December 1877, p. 137.
143. Peter Bayne, *The Chief Actors in the Puritan Revolution*, 1878, pp. 335–36.
144. Stopford A. Brooke, *Milton*, 1879, p. 83.
145. Mark Pattison, *Milton*, 1879, p. 210.
146. Frederic Harrison, "The Choice of Books" (1879), *The Choice of Books and Other Literary Pieces*, 1886, p. 13.
147. Wilhelm Scherer, *A History of German Literature*, tr. Mary Emily Conybeare, 1883–86, Volume 2, pp. 31–33.
148. Aubrey De Vere, *Essays, Chiefly on Poetry*, 1887, Volume 2, p. 112.
149. Donald G. Mitchell, *English Lands, Letters, and Kings: From Elizabeth to Anne*, 1890, p. 171.
150. Edmund Clarence Stedman, *The Nature and Elements of Poetry*, 1892, p. 245.
151. William Dean Howells, *My Literary Passions*, 1895, p. 239.
152. Vida D. Scudder, *The Life of the Spirit in the Modern English Poets*, 1895, p. 19.
153. J. Howard B. Masterman, *The Age of Milton*, 1897, p. 54.
154. Thomas Ellwood, *The History of the Life of Thomas Ellwood*, 1714.
155. Samuel Taylor Coleridge, "Notes on Milton" (1807), *Literary Remains*, ed. Henry Nelson Coleridge, 1836, Volume 1, p. 179.
156. John Wilson, "Wordsworth" (c. 1826), *Essays Critical and Imaginary*, 1856.
157. Henry Hallam, *Introduction to the Literature of Europe*, 1837–39, Pt. 4, Ch. 5, Par. 35.
158. Mark Pattison, *Milton*, 1879, p. 187.
159. Edmund Gosse, *A Short History of Modern English Literature*, 1897, p. 167.
160. Augustus Hopkins Strong, *The Great Poets and Their Theology*, 1897, p. 252.
161. William Vaughn Moody, "Life of Milton," *Poetical Works of Milton*, 1899, Cambridge ed., p. xxxi.
162. Johann Wolfgang von Goethe, cited in Johann Peter Eckermann, *Conversations with Goethe*, 1830, tr. John Oxenford.
163. François René, Vicomte de Chateaubriand, *Sketches of English Literature*, 1837, Volume 2, p. 106.
164. Edwin Guest, *A History of English Rhythms*, 1838, Volume 2, p. 259.
165. James Russell Lowell, "Swinburne's Tragedies" (1866), *My Study Windows*, 1871, p. 220.
166. Adolphus William Ward, *A History of English Dramatic Literature* (1875), 1899, Volume 3, p. 204.
167. George Edmundson, *Milton and Vondel*, 1885, p. 170.
168. Frederic William Farrar, "Three Portraits of Milton," *English Illustrated Magazine*, November 1891, p. 120.
169. Robert Bridges, *Milton's Prosody*, 1893, p. 32.
170. Nathan Drake, *Literary Hours*, 1798–1820, Volume 1, p. 80.
171. William Wordsworth, "Sonnet," 1827.
172. Walter Savage Landor, "To the President of the French Republic," 1848.
173. James Ashcroft Noble, "The Sonnet in England," (1880), *The Sonnet in England and Other Essays*, 1893, p. 33
174. Richard Henry Stoddard, "The Sonnet in English Poetry," *Scribner's Monthly*, 1881, p. 915.
175. Hall Caine, *Sonnets of Three Centuries*, 1882, p. 280.
176. Thomas R. Lounsbury, *Studies in Chaucer*, 1891, Volume 1, p. 232.
177. A. T. Quiller-Couch, "Introduction" to *English Sonnets*, 1897, p. xvi.
178. Henry Hallam, *Introduction to the Literature of Europe*, 1837–39, Pt. 3, Ch. 5, Par. 63.
179. Henry Reed, *Lectures on English Literature, from Chaucer to Tennyson*, 1855, p. 193.
180. George MacDonald, *England's Antiphon*, 1868, p. 200.
181. Edmund Gosse, *A Short History of Modern English Literature*, 1897, p. 143.
182. Albert Perry Walker, *Selections from the Poetical Works of John Milton*, 1900, p. 257.
183. Oliver Goldsmith, "Introductory Criticism" to *The Beauties of English Poesy*, 1767.
184. Hugh Blair, *Lectures on Rhetoric and Belles Lettres*, 1783, Lecture 40.
185. William Ellery Channing, *Remarks on the Character and Writings of John Milton*, 1826.
186. John W. Hales, *Longer English Poems*, 1872, p. 231.
187. George Saintsbury, *A History of Elizabethan Literature*, 1887, p. 320.
188. A. C. Benson, "Andrew Marvell" (1892), *Essays*, 1896, p. 71.
189. William Vaughn Moody, *Poetical Works of Milton*, 1899, Cambridge ed., p. 26.
190. Thomas Keightley, *An Account of the Life, Opinions, and Writings of John Milton*, 1855, p. 388.
191. George Saintsbury, *A History of Elizabethan Literature*, 1887, p. 318.
192. J. Howard B. Masterman, *The Age of Milton*, 1897, p. 28.
193. William Vaughn Moody, *Poetical Works of Milton*, 1899, Cambridge ed., p. 320.
194. David Hume, *History of England*, 1754–62.
195. William Hazlitt, "On the Prose Style of Poets" (1822), *The Plain Speaker*, 1826.

196. James Montgomery, "Memoir," *The Poetical Works of John Milton*, 1843, Volume 1, p. xv.
197. Edgar Allan Poe, Review of *The Prose Works of John Milton* (1845), *Complete Works*, ed. James A. Harrison, Volume 12, p. 245.
198. Edmond Scherer, "Milton" (1868), *Essays on English Literature*, tr. George Saintsbury, 1891.
199. William Minto, *Manual of English Prose Literature*, 1872, p. 308.
200. Mark Pattison, *Milton*, 1879, p. 68.
201. Thomas Sergeant Perry, *English Literature in the Eighteenth Century*, 1883, p. 7.
202. George Saintsbury, *A History of Elizabethan Literature*, 1887, p. 325.
203. John Addington Symonds, "Notes on Style," *Essays Speculative and Suggestive*, 1890, Volume 1, p. 324.
204. Henry Craik, "Introduction" to *English Prose*, 1893, Volume 2, p. 6.
205. Adolphus William Ward, "John Milton," *English Prose*, ed. Henry Craik, 1893, Volume 2, p. 462.
206. Richard Garnett, "Introduction" to *Prose of Milton*, 1894, p. viii.
207. Hiram Corson, *An Introduction to the Prose and Poetical Works of John Milton*, 1899, p. xiii.
208. Mark Pattison, *Milton*, 1879, p. 55.
209. Augustine Birrell, "John Milton," *Obiter Dicta: Second Series*, 1887, pp. 22–23.
210. Henry Van Dyke, "Milton and Tennyson," *The Poetry of Tennyson*, 1889–98, p. 80.
211. William Godwin, *History of the Commonwealth of England*, 1824, Volume 1, p. 352.
212. W. E. H. Lecky, *Spirit of Rationalism in Europe*, 1865.
213. Stopford A. Brooke, *Milton*, 1879, p. 45.
214. Sir Leslie Stephen, *Dictionary of National Biography*, 1894, Volume 38, p. 29.
215. Order-Book of the Council of State, January 8, 1649/50.
216. Andrew Marvell, Letter to John Milton (June 2, 1654).
217. Thomas Hobbes, *Behemoth*, 1660, Pt. 4.
218. John Hacket, *The Life of Archbishop Williams*, 1693.
219. John Toland, *The Life of John Milton*, 1698.
220. Samuel Johnson, "John Milton," *Lives of the English Poets*, 1779–81.
221. Isaac Disraeli, "Milton," *Curiosities of Literature*, 1791.

222. William Francis Collier, *A History of English Literature*, 1861, p. 201.
223. Augustine Birrell, "John Milton," *Obiter Dicta: Second Series*, 1887, p. 34.
224. William Holden Hutton, *Social England*, ed. H. D. Traill, 1895, Volume 4, p. 289.
225. John Aubrey, "John Milton," *Brief Lives*, 1669–96.
226. Anthony à Wood, *Fasti Oxonienses*, 1691.
227. Joseph Addison, *The Spectator*, No. 267 (January 5, 1712); No. 273 (January 12, 1712); No. 279 (January 19, 1712); No. 285 (January 26, 1712).
228. François Marie Arouet de Voltaire, *An Essay upon Epick Poetry*, 1727.
229. Samuel Johnson, "John Milton," *Lives of the English Poets*, 1779–81.
230. Samuel Taylor Coleridge, "Milton" (1818), *Literary Remains*, ed. Henry Nelson Coleridge, 1836, Volume 1, pp. 166–78.
231. William Hazlitt, "On Shakspeare and Milton," *Lectures on the English Poets*, 1818.
232. William Hazlitt, "On Milton's Sonnets," *Table-Talk*, 1821–22.
233. Thomas Babington Macaulay, "Milton" (1825), *Critical, Historical, and Miscellaneous Essays*, Volume 1, 1860, pp. 204–66.
234. François René, Vicomte de Chateaubriand, "Milton in *Paradise Lost*," *Sketches of English Literature*, 1837, Volume 2, pp. 145–54.
235. Ralph Waldo Emerson, "Milton" (1838), *Complete Works*, Volume 12, 1904, pp. 247–79.
236. Thomas De Quincey, "On Milton" (1839), *Collected Writings*, ed. David Masson, 1890, Volume 10, pp. 398–406.
237. David Masson, "The Three Devils: Luther's Milton's, and Goethe's" (1844), *The Three Devils*, 1874, pp. 9–32.
238. Walter Bagehot, "John Milton" (1859), *Collected Works*, ed. Norman St. John-Stevas, 1965, Volume 2, pp. 134–48.
239. Edmond Scherer, "Milton and *Paradise Lost*" (1868), *Essays on English Literature*, tr. George Saintsbury, 1891, pp. 134–49.
240. Matthew Arnold, "Milton," *Essays in Criticism: Second Series*, 1888.
241. Edward Dowden, "The Idealism of Milton," *Transcripts and Studies*, 1888, pp. 454–73.

Volume 2
William Shakespeare

PERSONAL

1. Robert Greene, *Groats-worth of Wit*, 1592.
2. John Davies, *The Scourge of Folly*, c. 1611.
3. Incription on the tablet over Shakespeare's grave, April 25, 1616.
4. William Basse, "On Mr. Wm. Shakespeare," 1622.
5. Ben Jonson, "To the Reader," *Mr. William Shakespeares Comedies, Histories, & Tragedies*, 1623.
6. I. M., "To the Memorie of M. W. Shakespeare," *Mr. William Shakespeares Comedies, Histories, & Tragedies*, 1623.
7. John Ward, *Diary*, 1648–79.
8. Thomas Fuller, *The History of the Worthies of England*, 1662.
9. John Aubrey, *Brief Lives*, 1669–96.
10. Nicholas Rowe, "Some Account of the Life, &c. of Mr. William Shakespear," *The Works of Mr. William Shakespear*, 1709, Volume 1, pp. i–xxxvii.
11. Washington Irving, "Stratford-on-Avon," *The Sketch Book of Geoffrey Crayon, Gent.*, 1819–20.
12. Walter Bagehot, "Shakespeare—the Individual" (1853), *Collected Works*, ed. Norman St. John-Stevas, 1965, Volume 1, pp. 173–214.
13. Nathaniel Hawthorne, "Recollections of a Gifted Woman," *Our Old Home*, 1863.
14. John Richard Green, "The England of Shakspere," *History of the English People*, 1877–80, Volume 2, pp. 472–85.
15. A. C. Bradley, "Shakespeare the Man" (1904), *Oxford Lectures on Poetry*, 1909, pp. 311–57.

GENERAL

1. Francis Meres, *Palladis Tamia*, 1598.
2. John Weever, "Ad Gulielmum Shakespeare," *Epigrammes in the Oldest Cut and Newest Fashion*, 1599.

3. Leonard Digges, "To the Memorie of the Deceased Authour Maister W. Shakespeare," *Mr. William Shakespeares Comedies, Histories, & Tragedies*, 1623.

4. John Heminge, Henry Condell, "To the Great Variety of Readers," *Mr. William Shakespeares Comedies, Histories, & Tragedies*, 1623.

5. Hugh Holland, "Upon the Lines and Life of the Famous Scenicke Poet, Master William Shakespeare," *Mr. William Shakespeares Comedies, Histories, & Tragedies*, 1623.

6. Ben Jonson, "To the Memory of My Beloued, the Author Mr. William Shakespeare," *Mr. William Shakespeares Comedies, Histories, & Tragedies*, 1623.

7. Michael Drayton, "To My Most Dearely-Loved Friend Henery Reynolds, Esquire, of Poets and Poesie," *Elegies*, 1627.

8. John Milton, "Of Shakespear," 1630.

9. I. M. S., "On Worthy Master Shakespeare and His Poems," 1632.

10. Leonard Digges, "Upon Master William Shakespeare, the Deceased Authour, and His Poems," *Shakespeare's Poems*, 1640.

11. Ben Jonson, *Timber; or, Discoveries*, 1640.

12. Richard Flecknoe, "A Short Discourse of the English Stage," *Love's Kingdom*, 1664.

13. John Dryden, *An Essay of Dramatick Poesie*, 1668.

14. John Dryden, "Defence of the Epilogue," *The Conquest of Granada*, 1672.

15. Edward Phillips, *Theatrum Poetarum Anglicanorum*, 1675.

16. John Dryden, "Preface" to *Troilus and Cressida*, 1679.

17. Nahum Tate, "Preface" to *The Loyal General*, 1680.

18. Thomas Purney, "Preface" to *Pastorals; viz., The Bashful Swain*, 1717.

19. William Collins, "An Epistle Addrest to Sir Thomas Hanmer on His Edition of Shakespear's Works," 1743.

20. Thomas Gray, *The Progress of Poesy*, 1757.

21. David Hume, "Appendix to the Reign of James I," *History of England*, 1754–62.

22. Edward Young, *Conjectures on Original Composition*, 1759.

23. Henry Home, Lord Kames, *Elements of Criticism*, 1763, Ch. 17.

24. Hugh Blair, *Lectures on Rhetoric and Belles Lettres*, 1783, Lecture 3.

25. William Godwin, "Of English Style," *The Enquirer*, 1797, pp. 388–93.

26. Sir Walter Scott, "An Essay on the Drama," 1819.

27. Royall Tyler, *The Bay Boy*, c. 1815, Ch. 14.

28. Thomas Campbell, *An Essay on English Poetry*, 1819.

29. Johann Wolfgang von Goethe (1825), cited in Johann Peter Eckermann, *Conversations with Goethe*, 1830, tr. John Oxenford.

30. Thomas Babington Macaulay, "Madame D'Arblay" (1843), *Critical, Historical, and Miscellaneous Essays*, 1860, Volume 5, pp. 306–7.

31. Matthew Arnold, "Shakespeare" (1844), *Works*, 1903, Volume 2, p. 5.

32. Leigh Hunt, "Shakespeare," *Imagination and Fancy*, 1845.

33. James Anthony Froude, "England's Forgotten Worthies" (1852), *Short Studies on Great Subjects*, 1867, Volume 1, pp. 445–46.

34. William Cullen Bryant, "Shakespeare" (1870), *Prose Writings*, ed. Parke Godwin, 1884, Volume 2, pp. 305–6.

35. Havelock Ellis, "William Shakespeare" (1878), *From Marlowe to Shaw*, ed. John Gawsworth, 1950, pp. 30–31.

36. Algernon Charles Swinburne, "William Shakespeare," *Sonnets on English Dramatic Poets*, 1882.

37. John Addington Symonds, "Introductory" to *Shakspere's Predecessors in the English Drama*, 1884, pp. 16–19.

38. Walt Whitman, "A Thought on Shakspere" (1886), *Prose Works*, ed. Floyd Stovall, 1963, Volume 2, pp. 556–58.

39. W. E. Henley, "Shakespeare," *Views and Reviews*, 1890, pp. 101–3.

40. William Dean Howells, "Shakespeare," *My Literary Passions*, 1895, pp. 58–60.

41. Edmond Scherer, "Shakespeare," *Essays on English Literature*, tr. George Saintsbury, 1891, pp. 47–50.

42. Hallam Tennyson, *Alfred Lord Tennyson: A Memoir*, 1897, Volume 2, pp. 289–92.

43. Ambrose Bierce, "The Ravages of Shakspearitis" (1903), *Collected Works*, 1911, Volume 10, pp. 109–12.

44. Margaret Cavendish, Duchess of Newcastle, "Letter 123," *CCXI Sociable Letters*, 1664.

45. Nicholas Rowe, "Some Account of the Life, &c. of Mr. William Shakespear," *The Works of Mr. William Shakespear*, 1709, Volume 1, pp. xxvi-xxxv.

46. Alexander Pope, "The Preface of the Editor," *The Works of Mr. William Shakespear*, 1725, Volume 1, pp. i–xiii.

47. Samuel Johnson, *Preface to Shakespeare*, 1765.

48. Elizabeth Montagu, "On the Præternatural Beings," *An Essay on the Writings and Genius of Shakspeare*, 1769.

49. Edward Taylor (?), "On Shakespear," *Cursory Remarks on Tragedy*, 1774, pp. 31–51.

50. Richard Cumberland, *The Observer*, Nos. 69–72 (1786).

51. Charles Dibdin, "Shakespear," *A Complete History of the Stage*, 1795, Volume 3, pp. 14–28.

52. August Wilhelm Schlegel, "Lecture XXIII," *Lectures on Dramatic Art and Literature*, 1809, tr. John Black.

53. Nathan Drake, *Shakspeare and His Times*, 1817, pp. 596–601.

54. Samuel Taylor Coleridge, *Shakspeare, with Introductory Remarks on Poetry, the Drama, and the Stage* (1818), *Literary Remains*, ed. Henry Nelson Coleridge, 1836, Volume 2, pp. 53–83.

55. William Hazlitt, "Shakspeare and Milton," *Lectures on the English Poets*, 1818.

56. Thomas De Quincey, "Shakspeare" (1838), *Collected Writings*, ed. David Masson, 1889, Volume 4, pp. 70–79.

57. Thomas Carlyle, "The Hero as Poet," *On Heroes, Hero-Worship and the Heroic in History*, 1841.

58. H. N. Hudson, *Lectures on Shakspeare*, 1848, Volume 1, pp. 64–87.

59. Ralph Waldo Emerson, "Shakspeare; or, the Poet," *Representative Men*, 1850.

60. Victor Hugo, *William Shakespeare*, 1864, tr. F. T. Marzials.

61. James Russell Lowell, "Shakespeare Once More" (1868), *Works*, Riverside ed., Volume 3, pp. 151–227.

62. Edwin P. Whipple, "Shakespeare: I," *The Literature of the Age of Elizabeth*, 1869, pp. 32–56.

63. Karl Elze, "Shakespeare's Character and Conception of Human Nature," *William Shakespeare: A Literary Biography*, 1876, tr. L. Dora Schmitz.

64. George Bernard Shaw, "Better Than Shakespear?" (1897), *Plays and Players*, ed. A. C. Ward, 1952, pp. 152–57.

65. George Saintsbury, "Shakespeare," *A Short History of English Literature*, 1898, pp. 320–29.

66. George Santayana, "The Absence of Religion in Shakespeare," *Interpretations of Poetry and Religion*, 1900, pp. 147–65.

67. W. B. Yeats, "At Stratford-on-Avon" (1901), *Ideas of Good and Evil*, 1903, pp. 152–64.

68. Lytton Strachey, "Shakespeare's Final Period" (1904), *Literary Essays*, 1949, pp. 1–15.

69. Leo Tolstoy, *On Shakespeare*, trs. V. Tchertkoff, I. F. M., 1906, pp. 78–124.
70. George Edward Woodberry, "Shakspere," *Great Writers*, 1907, pp. 183–216.
71. George Saintsbury, "Shakespeare and the Grand Style," *Essays and Studies*, 1910, pp. 113–35.
72. J. J. Jusserand, "What to Expect of Shakespeare" (1911), *The School for Ambassadors and Other Essays*, 1925, pp. 293–322.
73. Alexander Pope, "The Preface of the Editor," *The Works of Mr. William Shakespear*, 1725, Volume 1, pp. xiv–xxiv.
74. Lewis Theobald, "Introduction" to *Shakespeare Restored*, 1726, pp. i–viii.
75. William Warburton, "Preface," *The Works of Shakespear*, 1747, Volume 1, pp. vii–xix.
76. Henry Fielding, *The Covent-Garden Journal*, No. 31 (April 18, 1752).
77. Samuel Johnson, *Proposals for Printing, by Subscription, the Dramatick Works of William Shakespeare*, 1756.
78. James Russell Lowell, "Shakespeare Once More" (1868), *Works*, 1890, Volume 3, pp. 166–73.
79. Thomas Spencer Baynes, "New Shakespearian Interpretations" (1872), *Shakespeare Studies*, 1894, pp. 300–357.
80. C. M. Ingleby, "The Still Lion Discovered," *Shakespeare Hermeneutics*, 1875, pp. 1–12.
81. Edmund Gosse, "The Age of Elizabeth," *Modern English Literature: A Short History*, 1897, pp. 104–7.
82. John Dennis, *Essay on the Genius and Writings of Shakespear*, 1712.
83. Lewis Theobald, "Preface" to *The Works of Shakespeare*, 1734, Volume 1, pp. xxvii–xxxiii.
84. Peter Whalley, *An Enquiry into the Learning of Shakespeare*, 1748, pp. 12–84.
85. J. Payne Collier, "On the Six Old Plays to Which Shakespeare Was, or Is Supposed to Have Been, Indebted," *The History of English Dramatic Poetry*, 1831, Volume 3, pp. 61–83.
86. Paul Stapfer, "Shakespeare's Classical Knowledge," *Shakespeare and Classical Antiquity*, tr. Emily J. Carey, 1880, pp. 73–106.
87. Delia Bacon, "William Shakespeare and His Plays: An Inquiry concerning Them," *Putnam's Monthly*, January 1856, pp. 1–19.
88. Nathaniel Hawthorne, "Recollections of a Gifted Woman," *Our Old Home*, 1863.
89. Nathaniel Holmes, "Philosopher and Poet," *The Authorship of Shakespeare*, 1866, pp. 589–601.
90. James Spedding, "On the Authorship of the Plays Attributed to Shakespeare" (1867), *Reviews and Discussions*, 1879, pp. 369–75.
91. James Freeman Clarke, "Did Shakespeare Write Bacon's Works?," *North American Review*, February 1881, pp. 163–75.
92. Ignatius Donnelly, "A Word Personal," *The Great Cryptogram: Francis Bacon's Cipher in the So-Called Shakespeare Plays*, 1888, Volume 2, pp. 889–94.
93. G. K. Chesterton, "Sensationalism and a Cipher" (1902), *Chesterton on Shakespeare*, ed. Dorothy Collins, 1971, pp. 179–86.
94. Mark Twain, "Is Shakespeare Dead?" (1909), *The Complete Essays of Mark Twain*, ed. Charles Neider, 1963, pp. 407–49.

COMEDIES

1. Sir William Temple, "Of Poetry," 1690.
2. George Meredith, "Essay on the Idea of Comedy and the Uses of the Comic Spirit," 1877.

3. J. J. Jusserand, "Shakespeare, His Dramatic Work," *A Literary History of the English People*, 1904, Volume 3, pp. 328–37.
4. Adolphus William Ward, "Shakespere's Dramatic Genius," *A History of English Dramatic Literature* 1875, 1899, Volume 2, pp. 272–82.
5. August Wilhelm Schlegel, *Lectures on Dramatic Art and Literature*, 1809, tr. John Black.
6. William Hazlitt, "The Comedy of Errors," *Characters of Shakespear's Plays*, 1817.
7. Samuel Taylor Coleridge, "Comedy of Errors," *Shakspeare, with Introductory Remarks on Poetry, the Drama, and the Stage*, 1818.
8. Richard Grant White, "Introduction" to *The Comedy of Errors, The Works of William Shakspeare*, 1865, Volume 3, pp. 135–39.
9. August Wilhelm Schlegel, *Lectures on Dramatic Art and Literature*, 1809, tr. John Black.
10. William Hazlitt, "The Taming of the Shrew," *Characters of Shakespear's Plays*, 1817.
11. Charlotte Carmichael Stopes, "The Taming of the Shrew," *Athenaeum*, June 11, 1904, pp. 762–64.
12. Samuel Johnson, *Notes on Shakespeare's Plays*, 1768.
13. August Wilhelm Schlegel, *Lectures on Dramatic Art and Literature*, 1809, tr. John Black.
14. Mary Preston, "Two Gentlemen of Verona," *Studies in Shakspeare*, 1869, pp. 84–102.
15. John Milton, "L'Allegro," 1633.
16. Samuel Pepys, *Diary*, September 29, 1662.
17. August Wilhelm Schlegel, *Lectures on Dramatic Art and Literature*, 1809, tr. John Black.
18. William Hazlitt, "The Midsummer Night's Dream," *Characters of Shakespear's Plays*, 1817.
19. G. G. Gervinus, "Midsummer-Night's Dream," *Shakespeare Commentaries*, tr. F. E. Bunnètt, 1845.
20. Robert Tofte, *The Months Minde of a Melancholy Lover*, 1598.
21. Walter Cope, Letter to Lord Viscount Cranborne, 1604.
22. August Wilhelm Schlegel, *Lectures on Dramatic Art and Literature*, 1809, tr. John Black.
23. William Hazlitt, "Love's Labour's Lost," *Characters of Shakespear's Plays*, 1817.
24. Samuel Taylor Coleridge, "Love's Labour's Lost," *Shakspeare, with Introductory Remarks on Poetry, the Drama, and the Stage*, 1818.
25. Walter Pater, "Love's Labours Lost" (1878), *Appreciations*, 1889.
26. August Wilhelm Schlegel, *Lectures on Dramatic Art and Literature*, 1809, tr. John Black.
27. William Hazlitt, "The Merchant of Venice," *Characters of Shakespear's Plays*, 1817.
28. G. H. Radford, "Shylock," *Shylock and Others*, 1894, pp. 9–26.
29. Samuel Johnson, *Notes on Shakespeare's Plays*, 1768.
30. August Wilhelm Schlegel, *Lectures on Dramatic Art and Literature*, 1809, tr. John Black.
31. William Hazlitt, "As You Like It," *Characters of Shakespear's Plays*, 1817.
32. William Maginn, "Jaques," *Shakespeare Papers*, 1856, pp. 46–65.
33. August Wilhelm Schlegel, *Lectures on Dramatic Art and Literature*, 1809, tr. John Black.
34. H. N. Hudson, "Much Ado about Nothing," *Shakespeare: His Life, Art, and Characters*, 1872, Volume 1, pp. 314–29.
35. John Manningham, *Diary*, February 2, 1601.
36. Samuel Pepys, *Diary*, January 6, 1663.

37. August Wilhelm Schlegel, *Lectures on Dramatic Art and Literature*, 1809, tr. John Black.
38. William Hazlitt, "*Twelfth Night; or, What You Will*," *Characters of Shakespear's Plays*, 1817.
39. Frank Harris, "Shakespeare as Lyric Poet: *Twelfth Night*," *The Man Shakespeare*, 1909, pp. 129–38.
40. Samuel Johnson, *Notes on Shakespeare's Plays*, 1768.
41. August Wilhelm Schlegel, *Lectures on Dramatic Art and Literature*, 1809, tr. John Black.
42. William Hazlitt, "*The Merry Wives of Windsor*," *Characters of Shakespear's Plays*, 1817.
43. Denton J. Snider, "*Merry Wives of Windsor*," *The Shakespearian Drama*, 1887, Volume 1, pp. 144–71.
44. August Wilhelm Schlegel, *Lectures on Dramatic Art and Literature*, 1809, tr. John Black.
45. William Hazlitt, "*All's Well That Ends Well*," *Characters of Shakespear's Plays*, 1817.
46. Frank Harris, "*All's Well That Ends Well*," *The Women Of Shakespeare*, 1912, pp. 134–60.
47. Samuel Johnson, *Notes on Shakespeare's Plays*, 1768.
48. August Wilhelm Schlegel, *Lectures on Dramatic Art and Literature*, 1809, tr. John Black.
49. William Hazlitt, "*Measure for Measure*," *Characters of Shakespear's Plays*, 1817.
50. Samuel Taylor Coleridge, "*Measure for Measure*," *Shakspeare, with Introductory Remarks on Poetry, the Drama, and the Stage*, 1818.
51. Walter Pater, "*Measure for Measure*" (1874), *Appreciations*, 1889.

HISTORIES

1. John Keats, "On Kean in *Richard Duke of York*" (1817), *Poetical Works and Other Writings*, ed. H. Buxton Forman, 1939, Volume 5, pp. 234–39.
2. Samuel Taylor Coleridge, "Shakspeare's English Historical Plays," *Shakspeare, with Introductory Remarks on Poetry, the Drama, and the Stage*, 1818.
3. Heinrich Heine, "Introduction" to *Notes on Shakespeare Heroines* (1838), tr. Ida Benecke, 1895, pp. 7–11.
4. Walt Whitman, "What Lurks behind Shakspere's Historical Plays?" (1884), *Prose Works*, 1963, Volume 2, ed. Floyd Stovall, pp. 554–56.
5. August Wilhelm Schlegel, *Lectures on Dramatic Art and Literature*, 1809, tr. John Black.
6. Walter Pater, "Shakespeare's English Kings," *Appreciations*, 1889.
7. Samuel Johnson, *Notes on Shakespeare's Plays*, 1768.
8. August Wilhelm Schlegel, *Lectures on Dramatic Art and Literature*, 1809, tr. John Black.
9. William Hazlitt, "*Henry VI*," *Characters of Shakespear's Plays*, 1817.
10. Ernest Rhys, "Shakespeare's *King Henry VI*," *Harper's New Monthly Magazine*, October–November 1905, pp. 720–27, 882–89.
11. Adolphus William Ward, "Part of Introduction to Shakespeare's *Henry VI*" (1907), *Collected Papers*, 1921, Volume 3, pp. 249–60.
12. Christopher Brooke, *The Ghost of Richard the Third*, 1614.
13. Richard Steele, *The Tatler*, No. 90 (November 5, 1709).
14. François Marie Arouet de Voltaire, Letter to Marie Vichy de Chamrond, Marquise du Deffand (December 9, 1760), *Selected Letters*, tr. Richard A. Brooks, 1973, p. 216.
15. August Wilhelm Schlegel, *Lectures on Dramatic Art and Literature*, 1809, tr. John Black.
16. Samuel Taylor Coleridge, "*Richard III*," *Shakspeare, with Introductory Remarks on Poetry, the Drama, and the Stage*, 1818.
17. Edward Dowden, "The English Historical Plays," *Shakspere: A Critical Study of His Mind and Art*, 1875, pp. 180–93.
18. August Wilhelm Schlegel, *Lectures on Dramatic Art and Literature*, 1809, tr. John Black.
19. William Hazlitt, "*King John*," *Characters of Shakespear's Plays*, 1817.
20. Edward Rose, "Shakespeare as an Adapter," *Macmillan's Magazine*, November 1878, pp. 69–77.
21. Samuel Johnson, *Notes on Shakespeare's Plays*, 1768.
22. August Wilhelm Schlegel, *Lectures on Dramatic Art and Literature*, 1809, tr. John Black.
23. William Hazlitt, "*Richard II*," *Characters of Shakespear's Plays*, 1817.
24. Samuel Taylor Coleridge, "*Richard II*," *Shakspeare, with Introductory Remarks on Poetry, the Drama, and the Stage*, 1818.
25. John W. Hales, "*Richard II*" (1875), *Notes and Essays on Shakespeare*, 1884, pp. 205–8.
26. Samuel Pepys, *Diary*, November 2, 1667.
27. Jeremy Collier, *A Short View of the Immorality and Profaneness of the English Stage*, 1698.
28. Richard Steele, *The Tatler*, No. 47 (July 28, 1709).
29. Edmund Burke, "Magnificence," *A Philosophical Enquiry into the Origin of Our Ideas of the Sublime and Beautiful*, 1757.
30. Samuel Johnson, *Notes on Shakespeare's Plays*, 1768.
31. August Wilhelm Schlegel, *Lectures on Dramatic Art and Literature*, 1809, tr. John Black.
32. Walter de la Mare, "Falstaff," *Characters from Shakespeare*, 1902.
33. Corbyn Morris, *An Essay towards Fixing the True Standards of Wit, Humour, Raillery, Satire, and Ridicule*, 1744, pp. 23–29.
34. Henry Mackenzie, *The Lounger*, 1786.
35. William Hazlitt, "*Henry IV*," *Characters of Shakespear's Plays*, 1817.
36. Henry Giles, "Falstaff: A Type of Epicurean Life," *Lectures and Essays*, 1850, Volume 1, pp. 29–44.
37. Samuel Johnson, *Notes on Shakespeare's Plays*, 1768.
38. William Hazlitt, "*Henry V*," *Characters of Shakespear's Plays*, 1817.
39. August Wilhelm Schlegel, *Lectures on Dramatic Art and Literature*, 1809, tr. John Black.
40. Denton J. Snider, "*Henry the Fifth*," *The Shakespearian Drama*, 1889, Volume 3, pp. 407–30.
41. Henry Wotton, Letter to Edmund Bacon (July 2, 1613), *Reliquiae Wottoniae*, 1685, pp. 425–26.
42. Samuel Johnson, *Notes on Shakespeare's Plays*, 1768.
43. August Wilhelm Schlegel, *Lectures on Dramatic Art and Literature*, 1809, tr. John Black.
44. William Hazlitt, "*Henry VIII*," *Characters on Shakespear's Plays*, 1817.
45. G. G. Gervinus, "*Henry VIII*," *Shakespeare Commentaries*, 1845, tr. F. E. Bunnètt.

TRAGEDIES

1. François Marie Arouet de Voltaire, "Letter 12: On Tragedy," *Letters on the English* (*Lettres philosophiques*), 1734, tr. Leonard Tancock.
2. Hugh Blair, *Lectures on Rhetoric and Belles Lettres*, 1783, Lecture 46.
3. Charles Lamb, "On the Tragedies of Shakspeare, Considered with Reference to Their Fitness for Stage Representation" (1812), *Works*, ed. E. V. Lucas, 1903, Volume 1, pp. 97–111.
4. John Wilson, "A Few Words on Shakespeare" (1819),

Essays, Critical and Imaginative, 1856, Volume 3, pp. 420–31.

5. Victor Hugo, *William Shakespeare,* 1864, tr. F. T. Marzials.

6. Algernon Charles Swinburne, *A Study on Shakespeare,* 1880, pp. 170–92.

7. Ben Jonson, "Induction" to *Bartholomew Fayre,* 1614.

8. Edward Ravenscroft, "To the Reader," *Titus Andronicus; or, The Rape of Lavinia,* 1687.

9. Samuel Johnson, *Notes on Shakespeare's Plays,* 1768.

10. August Wilhelm Schlegel, *Lectures on Dramatic Art and Literature,* 1809, tr. John Black.

11. G. G. Gervinus, "Titus Andronicus and Pericles," *Shakespeare Commentaries,* 1845, tr. F. E. Bunnètt.

12. Samuel Pepys, *Diary,* March 1, 1662.

13. Samuel Johnson, *Notes on Shakespeare's Plays,* 1768.

14. August Wilhelm Schlegel, *Lectures on Dramatic Art and Literature,* 1809, tr. John Black.

15. Walter de la Mare, "Juliet's Nurse," *Characters from Shakespeare,* 1902.

16. William Hazlitt, "Romeo and Juliet," *Characters of Shakespear's Plays,* 1817.

17. Samuel Taylor Coleridge, "Romeo and Juliet," *Shakspeare, with Introductory Remarks on Poetry, the Drama, and the Stage,* 1818.

18. Edward Dowden, "Romeo and Juliet," *Transcripts and Studies,* 1888, pp. 378–405.

19. John Weever, *The Mirror of Martyrs,* 1601.

20. John Dryden, "Prologue to *Iulius Caesar,*" 1672.

21. August Wilhelm Schlegel, *Lectures on Dramatic Art and Literature,* 1809, tr. John Black.

22. William Hazlitt, "Julius Cæsar," *Characters of Shakespear's Plays,* 1817.

23. Thomas Rymer, *A Short View of Tragedy,* 1693.

24. Richard G. Moulton, "Julius Caesar beside His Murderers and His Avenger: A Study in Character-Grouping," *Shakespeare as a Dramatic Artist,* 1888, pp. 168–84.

25. Anthony Scoloker, "Epistle to the Reader," *Daiphantus; or, The Passions of Love,* 1604.

26. Jeremy Collier, *A Short View of the Immorality and Profaneness of the English Stage,* 1698.

27. François Marie Arouet de Voltaire, "Ancient and Modern Tragedy" (1749), *Works,* tr. William F. Fleming, 1901, Volume 19, pp. 136–38.

28. Samuel Johnson, *Notes on Shakespeare's Plays,* 1768.

29. August Wilhelm Schlegel, *Lectures on Dramatic Art and Literature,* 1809, tr. John Black.

30. Edgar Allan Poe, "William Hazlitt" (1845), *Essays and Reviews,* ed. G. R. Thompson, 1984, pp. 272–73.

31. Matthew Arnold, "Hamlet Once More" (1884), *Works,* 1903, Volume 4, pp. 273–74.

32. Oscar Wilde, Letter to Lord Alfred Douglas (January–March 1897), *Selected Letters of Oscar Wilde,* ed. Rupert Hart-Davis, 1979, pp. 232–33.

33. G. K. Chesterton, "The True Hamlet" (1901), *Chesterton on Shakespeare,* 1971, ed. Dorothy Collins, pp. 41–43.

34. Walter de la Mare, "Polonius," *Characters from Shakespeare,* 1902.

35. Walter de la Mare, "Ophelia," *Characters from Shakespeare,* 1902.

36. Walter de la Mare, "Hamlet," *Characters from Shakespeare,* 1902.

37. James Drake, *The Antient and Modern Stages Survey'd,* 1699, pp. 201–6, 293–97.

38. William Popple, *The Prompter,* No. 57 (May 27, 1735).

39. Thomas Hanmer, *Some Remarks on the Tragedy of Hamlet Prince of Denmark,* 1736.

40. Henry Mackenzie, *The Mirror,* 1780.

41. Johann Wolfgang von Goethe, *Wilhelm Meister's Apprenticeship,* 1783, tr. Thomas Carlyle.

42. William Hazlitt, "Hamlet," *Characters of Shakespear's Plays,* 1817.

43. Samuel Taylor Coleridge, "Hamlet," *Shakspeare, with Introductory Remarks on Poetry, the Drama, and the Stage,* 1818.

44. Victor Hugo, *William Shakespeare,* 1864, tr. F. T. Marzials.

45. James Russell Lowell, "Shakespeare Once More" (1868), *Works,* Riverside ed., Volume 3, pp. 207–25.

46. George MacDonald, "The Elder Hamlet" (1875), *The Imagination and Other Essays,* 1893, pp. 170–81.

47. Anatole France, "Hamlet at the Comédie-Française" (1886), *On Life and Letters: First Series,* tr. A. W. Evans, 1924, pp. 1–7.

48. William Shakespeare, "A Never Writer, to an Ever Reader: News," *Troilus and Cressida,* 1609.

49. John Dryden, "Preface" to *Troilus and Cressida,* 1679.

50. Samuel Johnson, *Notes on Shakespeare's Plays,* 1768.

51. August Wilhelm Schlegel, *Lectures on Dramatic Art and Literature,* 1809, tr. John Black.

52. William Hazlitt, "Troilus and Cressida," *Characters of Shakespear's Plays,* 1817.

53. Samuel Taylor Coleridge, "Troilus and Cressida," *Shakspeare, with Introductory Remarks on Poetry, the Drama, and the Stage,* 1818.

54. William Godwin, *Life of Geoffrey Chaucer,* 1803–04, Volume 1, pp. 496–515.

55. Samuel Pepys, *Diary,* August 20, 1666.

56. Christopher Smart, "An Occasional Prologue to *Othello,*" 1751.

57. Samuel Johnson, *Notes on Shakespeare's Plays,* 1768.

58. August Wilhelm Schlegel, *Lectures on Dramatic Art and Literature,* 1809, tr. John Black.

59. Samuel Taylor Coleridge, "Notes to *Othello,*" *Shakspeare, with Introductory Remarks on Poetry, the Drama, and the Stage,* 1818.

60. Walter de la Mare, "Iago," *Characters from Shakespeare,* 1902.

61. Thomas Rymer, *A Short View of Tragedy,* 1693.

62. John Hughes, *The Guardian,* No. 37 (April 23, 1713).

63. William Hazlitt, "Othello," *Characters of Shakespear's Plays,* 1817.

64. John Quincy Adams, "The Character of Desdemona," *The American Monthly Magazine,* March 1836, pp. 209–17.

65. Nahum Tate, "To My Esteemed Friend Thomas Boteler, Esq.," *The History of King Lear,* 1681.

66. Nahum Tate, "Prologue" to *The History of King Lear,* 1681.

67. Samuel Johnson, *Notes on Shakespeare's Plays,* 1768.

68. August Wilhelm Schlegel, *Lectures on Dramatic Art and Literature,* 1809, tr. John Black.

69. John Keats, "On Sitting Down to Read *King Lear,* Once Again," 1818.

70. Percy Bysshe Shelley, *A Defence of Poetry,* 1821.

71. Aaron Hill, *The Prompter,* No. 95 (October 7, 1735).

72. Joseph Warton, *The Adventurer,* No. 113 (December 4, 1753); No. 116 (December 15, 1753).

73. William Hazlitt, "Lear," *Characters of Shakespear's Plays,* 1817.

74. Samuel Taylor Coleridge, "Lear," *Shakspeare, with Introductory Remarks on Poetry, the Drama, and the Stage,* 1818.

75. Charles Dickens, "The Restoration of Shakespeare's *Lear* to the Stage" (1838), *Works,* Centenary ed., 1911, Volume 34, pp. 77–81.

76. Leo Tolstoy, *On Shakespeare*, trs. V. Tchertkoff, I. F. M., 1906, pp. 46–63.
77. Samuel Pepys, *Diary*, January 7, 1667.
78. Samuel Johnson, *Notes on Shakespeare's Plays*, 1768.
79. August Wilhelm Schlegel, *Lectures on Dramatic Art and Literature*, 1809, tr. John Black.
80. Thomas De Quincey, "On the Knocking at the Gate in *Macbeth*" (1823), *Collected Writings*, ed. David Masson, Volume 10, pp. 392–94.
81. Johann Wolfgang von Goethe (1825), cited in Johann Peter Eckermann, *Conversations with Goethe*, 1830, tr. John Oxenford.
82. Walter de la Mare, "Macbeth," *Characters from Shakespeare*, 1902.
83. Walter de la Mare, "Banquo," *Characters from Shakespeare*, 1902.
84. William Hazlitt, "*Macbeth*," *Characters of Shakespear's Plays*, 1817.
85. Samuel Taylor Coleridge, "Notes on *Macbeth*," *Shakspeare, with Introductory Remarks on Poetry, the Drama, and the Stage*, 1818.
86. P. W. Clayden, "Macbeth and Lady Macbeth," *Fortnightly Review*, August 1867, pp. 156–68.
87. Henry Irving, "The Third Murderer in *Macbeth*," *Nineteenth Century*, April 1877, pp. 327–30.
88. August Wilhelm Schlegel, *Lectures on Dramatic Art and Literature*, 1809, tr. John Black.
89. William Hazlitt, "*Timon of Athens*," *Characters of Shakespear's Plays*, 1817.
90. John Charles Bucknill, "Timon of Athens," *The Mad Folk of Shakespeare*, 1867, pp. 236–67.
91. Samuel Johnson, *Notes on Shakespeare's Plays*, 1768.
92. August Wilhelm Schlegel, *Lectures on Dramatic Art and Literature*, 1809, tr. John Black.
93. Samuel Taylor Coleridge, "*Antony and Cleopatra*," *Shakspeare, with Introductory Remarks on Poetry, the Drama, and the the Stage*, 1818.
94. William Hazlitt, "*Antony and Cleopatra*," *Characters of Shakespear's Plays*, 1817.
95. George Brandes, "The Dark Lady as a Model—The Fall of the Republic a World-Catastrophe," *William Shakespeare: A Critical Study*, trs. William Archer, Mary Morison, 1898, pp. 152–59.
96. M. W. MacCallum, "Antony and Cleopatra," *Shakespeare's Roman Plays and Their Background*, 1910, pp. 300–317.
97. William Hazlitt, "*Coriolanus*," *Characters of Shakespear's Plays*, 1817.
98. A. C. Bradley, "*Coriolanus*" (1912), *A Miscellany*, 1929, pp. 73–104.

ROMANCES

1. G. G. Gervinus, "*Titus Andronicus and Pericles*," *Shakespeare Commentaries*, 1845, tr. F. E. Bunnètt.
2. Charles Knight, "*Pericles*," *Studies of Shakespeare*, 1849, pp. 52–56.
3. August Wilhelm Schlegel, *Lectures on Dramatic Art and Literature*, 1809, tr. John Black.
4. Walter de la Mare, "Imogen," *Characters from Shakespeare*, 1902.
5. William Richardson, "On the Characters of Imogen," *A Philosophical Analysis and Illustration of Some of Shakespeare's Remarkable Characters*, 1780, pp. 177–207.
6. William Hazlitt, "*Cymbeline*," *Characters of Shakespeare's Plays*, 1817.
7. Ben Jonson, *Conversations with William Drummond*, 1619.

8. Horace Walpole, *Historic Doubts on the Life and Reign of King Richard the Third*, 1767.
9. August Wilhelm Schlegel, *Lectures on Dramatic Art and Literature*, 1809, tr. John Black.
10. William Hazlitt, "*The Winter's Tale*," *Characters of Shakespear's Plays*, 1817.
11. Samuel Taylor Coleridge, "Notes on *The Winter's Tale*," *Shakspeare, with Introductory Remarks on Poetry, the Drama, and the Stage*, 1818.
12. William Archer, "*The Winter's Tale*," *Nineteenth Century*, October 1887, pp. 511–21.
13. Samuel Pepys, *Diary*, November 7, 1667.
14. Samuel Pepys, *Diary*, February 3, 1668.
15. John Dryden, "Preface" to *The Tempest*; or, *The Enchanted Island*, 1670.
16. John Dryden, "Prologue" to *The Tempest*; or, *The Enchanted Island*, 1670.
17. John Holt, *Remarks on* The Tempest, 1749, pp. 13–18.
18. Samuel Johnson, *Notes on Shakespeare's Plays*, 1768.
19. August Wilhelm Schlegel, *Lectures on Dramatic Art and Literature*, 1809, tr. John Black.
20. William Hazlitt, "*The Tempest*," *Characters of Shakespear's Plays*, 1817.
21. James Russell Lowell, "Shakespeare Once More" (1868), *Works*, Riverside ed., Volume 3, pp. 199–201.
22. Edmund Clarence Stedman, "Creation and Self-Expression," *The Nature and Elements of Poetry*, 1892.
23. Joseph Warton, *The Adventurer*, No. 93 (September 25, 1753). No. 97 (October 9, 1753).
24. Samuel Taylor Coleridge, "Notes on *The Tempest*," *Shakspeare, with Introductory Remarks on Poetry, the Drama, and the Stage*, 1818.

POEMS

1. Richard Barnfield, "A Remembrance of Some English Poets," *Poems in Divers Humors*, 1598.
2. John Benson, "To the Reader," *Shakespeare's Poems*, 1640.
3. William Hazlitt, "Poems and Sonnets," *Characters of Shakespear's Plays*, 1817.
4. George Saintsbury, *A Short History of English Literature*, 1898, pp. 317–19.
5. Sidney Lee, "The First Appeal to the Reading Public," *A Life of William Shakespeare*, 1898, pp. 74–81.
6. Thomas Thorpe, Dedication to Shakespeare's *Sonnets*, 1609.
7. John Addington Symonds, "On Some Principles of Criticism," *Essays Speculative and Suggestive*, 1890, Volume 1, pp. 117–19.
8. George Saintsbury, *A Short History of English Literature*, 1898, pp. 319–20.
9. Oscar Wilde, "The Portrait of Mr. W. H." (1889), *The Complete Shorter Fiction of Oscar Wilde*, ed. Isobel Murray, 1979, pp. 139–69.
10. George Brandes, "Platonism in Shakespeare's and Michael Angelo's Sonnets," *William Shakespeare: A Critical Study*, tr. William Archer, 1898, Volume 1, pp. 341–53.
11. H. C. Beeching, "The Sonnets of Shakespeare," *Cornhill Magazine*, February 1902, pp. 244–63.
12. Paul Elmer More, "Shakespeare's Sonnets," *Shelburne Essays: Second Series*, 1905, pp. 20–45.
13. William Shakespeare, "To the Right Honorable Henry Wriothesley, Earl of Southampton, and Baron of Titchfield," *Venus and Adonis*, 1593.
14. Unsigned, *The Return from Pernassus*, 1606, Pt. 1, Act 4, Sc. 1.
15. William Barkstead, *Mirra, the Mother of Adonis*, 1607.
16. Samuel Taylor Coleridge, *Biographia Literaria*, 1817.

17. William Shakespeare, "To the Right Honorable Henry Wriothesley, Earl of Southampton, and Baron of Titchfield," *The Rape of Lucrece*, 1594.
18. G. G. Gervinus, *Shakespeare's Commentaries*, 1845, tr. F. E. Bunnètt.

19. Thomas Heywood, "Epistle to Mr. Nicholas Okes," *An Apology for Actors*, 1612.
20. Sir A. T. Quiller-Couch, *"The Passionate Pilgrim"* (1895), *Adventures in Criticism*, 1896, pp. 29–38.

Volume 3

ANDREW MARVELL

1. John Norton, Letter to Reverend Marvell (c. January 1640).
2. John Milton, Letter to Lord Bradshaw (February 21, 1652/3).
3. John Aubrey, "Andrew Marvell," *Brief Lives*, 1669–96.
4. Richard Morton, *Pyretologia*, 1692.
5. Samuel Parker, *History of His Own Time*, 1727.
6. Charles Churchill, "The Author," 1763.
7. James Granger, *Biographical History of England*, 1769–1824.
8. John Aikin, *General Biography; or, Lives of the Most Eminent Persons*, 1799–1815.
9. William Lisle Bowles, "Introduction" to *The Works of Alexander Pope, Esq.*, 1806.
10. Thomas Campbell, *Specimens of the British Poets*, 1819.
11. Mary Russell Mitford, *Recollections of a Literary Life*, 1851, pp. 532–33.
12. Alexander B. Grosart, "Memorial-Introduction" to *The Complete Poems of Andrew Marvell*, 1872, p. lxvi.
13. Edmund K. Chambers, *Academy*, September 17, 1892, pp. 230–31.
14. Francis Turner Palgrave, *Landscape in Poetry*, 1896, p. 154.
15. Edgar Allan Poe, "Old English Poetry" (1845), *Complete Works*, ed. James A. Harrison, Volume 12, pp. 143–46.
16. Leigh Hunt, *Wit and Humour*, 1846.
17. James Russell Lowell, "Dryden" (1868), *Among My Books*, 1870, p. 19.
18. Edward FitzGerald, Letter to W. A. Wright (January 20, 1872).
19. Goldwin Smith, "Andrew Marvell," *The English Poets*, ed. Thomas Humphry Ward, 1880, Volume 2, pp. 382–84.
20. Alice Meynell, "Andrew Marvell," *Pall Mall Gazette*, July 14, 1897.
21. Henry Rogers, "Andrew Marvell," *Edinburgh Review*, January 1844, pp. 90–104.
22. John Ormsby, "Andrew Marvell," *Cornhill Magazine*, July 1869, pp. 21–40.
23. Edmund Gosse, "The Reaction," *From Shakespeare to Pope*, 1885, pp. 211–21.
24. A. C. Benson, "Andrew Marvell" (1892), *Essays*, 1896, pp. 68–95.
25. H. C. Beeching, "The Lyrical Poems of Andrew Marvell," *National Review*, July 1901, pp. 747–59.

JOHN BUNYAN

1. Charles Doe, *The Struggler: Life and Actions of John Bunyan*, 1692.
2. John Wilson, "Epistle to the Reader," *Bunyan's Works*, 1692.
3. Thomas Hearne, *Reliquiae Hearnianae*, April 7, 1723.
4. Edwin P. Whipple, "Wordsworth" (1844), *Essays and Reviews*, 1850, Volume 1, p. 229.
5. John Tulloch, *English Puritanism and Its Leaders*, 1861, pp. 477–88.
6. Alexander Smith, "Preface" to *Divine Emblems*, c. 1867, pp. viii–xi.

7. James Russell Lowell, "Spenser" (1875), *Works*, Riverside ed., Volume 4, pp. 322–23.
8. Walter Raleigh, *The English Novel*, 1894, pp. 115–18.
9. H. C. Beeching, "John Bunyan," *English Prose*, ed. Henry Craik, 1894, Volume 3, pp. 73–77.
10. Samuel Taylor Coleridge, *Table Talk*, June 10, 1830.
11. John Greenleaf Whittier, "John Bunyan," *Old Portraits and Modern Sketches*, 1849.
12. Benjamin Jowett, "John Bunyan and Benedict Spinoza" (1871), *Sermons Biographical and Miscellaneous*, ed. W. H. Fremantle, 1899, pp. 48–49.
13. John Bunyan, "The Author's Apology for His Book," *The Pilgrim's Progress*, 1678.
14. Jonathan Swift, "Letter to a Young Clergyman," 1720.
15. Laurence Sterne, *The Life and Opinions of Tristram Shandy*, 1759, Volume 1, Ch. 4.
16. William Cowper, *Tirocinium; or, A Review of Schools*, 1784.
17. James Boswell, *Life of Johnson*, 1791.
18. Charles Lamb, Letter to Bernard Barton (October 11, 1828).
19. Samuel Taylor Coleridge, "Notes on the *Pilgrim's Progress*" (1830), *Literary Remains*, ed. Henry Nelson Coleridge, 1836, Volume 3, pp. 391–92.
20. Robert Southey, "Preface" to *The Pilgrim's Progress*, 1830.
21. Sir Walter Scott, "Southey's Life of John Bunyan," *Quarterly Review*, October 1830, pp. 485–86.
22. Henry Hallam, *Introduction to the Literature of Europe*, 1837–39, Pt. 4, Ch. 7, Par. 57.
23. Thomas Carlyle, "The Hero as Divinity," *On Heroes, Hero-Worship and the Heroic in History*, 1841.
24. Thomas Babington Macaulay, "John Bunyan" (1854), *Critical, Historical, and Miscellaneous Essays*, 1860, Volume 6, pp. 148–50.
25. David Masson, *British Novelists and Their Styles*, 1859, p. 74.
26. A. P. Stanley, "John Bunyan," *Macmillan's Magazine*, July 1874, pp. 276–77.
27. John Richard Green, *History of the English People*, 1877–80, Bk. 8, Ch. 2.
28. Andrew Lang, "John Bunyan," *Essays in Little*, 1891, p. 188.
29. George Bernard Shaw, "Epistle Dedicatory" to *Man and Superman*, 1903.
30. Edmund Gosse, *A History of Eighteenth Century Literature*, 1888, p. 85.
31. Richard Garnett, *The Age of Dryden*, 1895, p. 239.
32. Richard Heath, "The Archetype of *The Holy War*," *Contemporary Review*, July 1897, pp. 111–18.
33. Thomas Babington Macaulay, "John Bunyan" (1830), *Critical, Historical and Miscellaneous Essays*, 1860, Volume 2, pp. 252–67.
34. George Barrell Cheever, "Southey's Life of Bunyan," *North American Review*, April 1833, pp. 453–65.
35. Hippolyte Taine, *History of English Literature*, tr. H. Van Laun, 1871, Bk. 2, Ch. 5.
36. George Edward Woodberry, "Three Men of Piety: I. Bunyan," *Studies in Letters and Life*, 1890, pp. 209–19.
37. Edward Dowden, "John Bunyan," *Puritan and Anglican*, 1901, pp. 232–36, 253–69.

JOHN DRYDEN

1. Sir George Etherege, Letter to John Dryden (c. March 1686/7).
2. John Dryden, A *Defence of* An Essay of Dramatick Poesy, 1668.
3. Earl of Chesterfield, Letter to John Dryden (August 10, 1697).
4. Unsigned, *Epigrams on the Paintings of the Most Eminent Masters*, 1700.
5. George Farquhar, Letter (1700), *Love and Business in a Collection of Occasionary Verse and Epistolary Prose*, 1701.
6. Thomas Hearne, "Epitaph upon Mr. John Dryden," *Reliquiae Hearnianae*, November 5, 1707.
7. William Congreve, Dedication to *The Dramatick Works of John Dryden, Esq.*, 1717.
8. Thomas Hearne, *Reliquiae Hearnianae*, November 6, 1726.
9. Colley Cibber, *An Apology for the Life of Mr. Colley Cibber*, 1739.
10. Alexander Pope (1742–43), cited in Joseph Spence, *Anecdotes, Observations and Characters of Books and Men*, ed. S. W. Singer, 1820.
11. Thomas Gray, Letter to William Mason (December 19, 1757).
12. Samuel Johnson, "Dryden," *Lives of the English Poets*, 1779–81.
13. Andrew Marvell, "On Mr. *Milton*'s Paradise Lost," 1674.
14. Edward Phillips, *Theatrum Poetarum Anglicanorum*, 1675.
15. John Wilmot, Earl of Rochester, "An Allusion to Horace: The 10th Satyr of the 1st Book," 1678.
16. Tom Brown, "Last Letter from Seignior Giusippe Hanesio," *Letters from the Living Dead*, 1687.
17. Joseph Addison, "To Mr. Dryden," 1693.
18. Sir Richard Blackmore, *A Satyr against Wit*, 1700.
19. John Dennis, Letter to Jacob Tonson (June 4, 1715).
20. William Congreve, Dedication to *The Dramatick Works of John Dryden, Esq.*, 1717.
21. Sir Samuel Garth, "Preface" to *Ovid's Metamorphoses*, 1717.
22. Jonathan Swift, Letter to Thomas Beach (April 12, 1735).
23. Alexander Pope, *Imitations of Horace*, 1737, *Ep.* II. i.263–81.
24. Colley Cibber, *An Apology for the Life of Mr. Colley Cibber*, 1739.
25. Alexander Pope (1742–43), cited in Joseph Spence, *Anecdotes, Observations and Characters of Books and Men*, ed. S. W. Singer, 1820.
26. David Hume, *History of England*, 1754–62.
27. Thomas Gray, *The Progress of Poesy*, 1757.
28. Edward Young, *Conjectures on Original Composition*, 1759.
29. Oliver Goldsmith, "An Account of the Augustan Age in England," *The Bee*, No. 8 (November 24, 1759).
30. Charles Churchill, *The Apology*, 1761, ll. 376–87.
31. Charles Churchill, *An Epistle to William Hogarth*, 1763, ll. 487–506.
32. James Granger, *Biographical History of England*, 1769–1824.
33. Horace Walpole, Letter to Robert Jephson (c. February 1775).
34. James Beattie, "An Essay on Poetry and Music," 1776.
35. William Cowper, Letter to William Unwin (January 5, 1782).
36. James Hurdis, *The Village Curate*, 1788.
37. William Wordsworth, Letter to Sir Walter Scott (November 7, 1805).
38. William Wordsworth, Letter to Sir Walter Scott (January 18, 1808).
39. William Hazlitt, *Lectures on the English Poets*, 1818.
40. Thomas Campbell, *An Essay on English Poetry*, 1819.
41. Samuel Taylor Coleridge, *Table Talk*, November 1, 1833.
42. Walter Savage Landor, "To Wordsworth," 1834.
43. Henry Hallam, *Introduction to the Literature of Europe*, 1837–39, Pt. 4, Ch. 5, Par. 38.
44. Elizabeth Barrett Browning, *The Book of the Poets* (1842), *Life, Letters and Essays of Elizabeth Barrett Browning*, 1863.
45. Leigh Hunt, *Wit and Humour*, 1846.
46. Hartley Coleridge, "Dryden," *Sketches of the English Poets*, 1849.
47. Arthur Hugh Clough, "On the Formulation of Classical English" (c. 1852), *Prose Remains*, 1888, pp. 325–29.
48. Hippolyte Taine, *History of English Literature*, tr. H. Van Laun, 1871, Bk. 3, Ch. 2.
49. Austin Dobson, *Handbook of English Literature*, 1874.
50. John Churton Collins, "John Dryden" (1878), *Essays and Studies*, 1895, pp. 85–90.
51. William Michael Rossetti, "John Dryden," *Lives of Famous Poets*, 1878, pp. 106–7.
52. Matthew Arnold, "Introduction" to *The English Poets*, ed. Thomas Humphry Ward, 1880, Volume 1, pp. xxxvii–xxxviii.
53. George Saintsbury, *Dryden*, 1881, pp. 187–92.
54. Gerard Manley Hopkins, Letter to Robert Bridges (November 6, 1887).
55. Edmund Gosse, "What Is a Great Poet?" (1889), *Questions at Issue*, 1893, pp. 101–3.
56. Alexander Pope (1734–36), cited in Joseph Spence, *Anecdotes, Observations and Characters of Books and Men*, ed. S. W. Singer, 1820.
57. August Wilhelm Schlegel, *Lectures on Dramatic Art and Literature*, 1809, tr. John Black.
58. William Hazlitt, *Lectures on the English Comic Writers*, 1819.
59. William Hazlitt, *Lectures on the Dramatic Literature of the Age of Elizabeth*, 1820.
60. Adolphus William Ward, *A History of English Dramatic Literature* (1875), 1899, Volume 3, pp. 387–90.
61. Edmund Gosse, *A Short History of Modern English Literature*, 1897, pp. 177–78.
62. Gerard Langbaine, *An Account of the English Dramatick Poets*, 1691.
63. Sir Walter Scott, *The Works of John Dryden*, 1808.
64. Henry Hallam, *Introduction to the Literature of Europe*, 1837–39, Pt. 4, Ch. 6, Par. 42.
65. Adolphus William Ward, *A History of English Dramatic Literature* (1875), 1899, Volume 3, pp. 360–61.
66. Thomas Davies, *Dramatic Miscellanies*, 1784, Volume 3, p. 93.
67. Adolphus William Ward, *A History of English Dramatic Literature* (1875), 1899, Volume 3, pp. 370–72.
68. George Saintsbury, *Dryden*, 1881, pp. 56–57.
69. Charles Dibdin, *A Complete History of the Stage*, 1795, Volume 4, pp. 169–70.
70. Sir Walter Scott, *The Works of John Dryden*, 1808.
71. Adolphus William Ward, *A History of English Dramatic Literature* (1875), 1899, Volume 3, pp. 372–73.
72. George Saintsbury, *Dryden*, 1881, pp. 58–59.
73. John Dryden, Dedication to *The Spanish Friar*, 1681.
74. Henry Hallam, *Introduction to the Literature of Europe*, 1837–39, Pt. 4, Ch. 6, Par. 44.

75. Adolphus William Ward, A *History of English Dramatic Literature* (1875), 1899, Volume 3, pp. 376–77.
76. Samuel Johnson, *The Rambler*, No. 125 (May 28, 1751).
77. Sir Walter Scott, *The Works of John Dryden*, 1808.
78. Henry Hallam, *Introduction to the Literature of Europe*, 1837–39, Pt. 4, Ch. 5, Par. 43.
79. Adolphus William Ward, A *History of English Dramatic Literature* (1875), 1899, Volume 3, p. 383.
80. Horace Walpole, Letter to Henry Seymour Conway (December 25, 1770).
81. Charles Burney, A *General History of Music*, 1776–89, Bk. 4, Ch. 5.
82. Sir Walter Scott, "Introduction" to *Marmion*, 1808.
83. Adolphus William Ward, A *History of English Dramatic Literature* (1875), 1899, Volume 3, pp. 382–83.
84. Sir George Etherege, Letter to Lord Middleton (June 23/July 3, 1687).
85. Sir Walter Scott, *The Works of John Dryden*, 1808.
86. Henry Hallam, *Introduction to the Literature of Europe*, 1837–39, Pt. 4, Ch. 5, Pars. 41–43.
87. Thomas Babington Macaulay, *History of England*, 1848–59.
88. John Dryden, Letter to His Sons (September 3, 1697).
89. Oliver Goldsmith, *The Beauties of English Poesy*, 1767.
90. John Pinkerton (as "Robert Heron"), "Letter V: On the Spirit of Lyric Poetry," *Letters of Literature*, 1785, p. 34.
91. John Henry Newman, "Poetry, with Reference to Aristotle's *Poetics*" (1828), *Essays Critical and Historical*, 1871.
92. Jonathan Swift, *The Battel of the Books*, 1704.
93. Alexander Pope, "Preface" to *The Iliad of Homer*, 1715.
94. Robert Burns, Letter to Mrs. Dunlop (May 4, 1788).
95. Henry Hallam, *Introduction to the Literature of Europe*, 1837–39, Pt. 4, Ch. 5, Par. 46.
96. John Conington, "Preface" to *The Aeneid of Virgil*, 1867.
97. Thomas James Mathias, *The Pursuits of Literature*, 1794.
98. James Russell Lowell, "Dryden" (1868), *Among My Books*, 1870, pp. 67–71.
99. John Dryden, "To the Reader," *Absalom and Achitophel*, 1681.
100. Joseph Addison, *The Spectator*, No. 512 (October 17, 1712).
101. Samuel Taylor Coleridge, *Table Talk*, August 6, 1832.
102. Thomas Babington Macaulay, *History of England*, 1848–59.
103. John Richard Green, *History of the English People*, 1877–80.
104. Oliver Goldsmith, *The Beauties of English Poesy*, 1767.
105. Sir Walter Scott, *The Works of John Dryden*, 1808.
106. Henry Hallam, *Introduction to the Literature of Europe*, 1837–39, Pt. 4, Ch. 5, Par. 40.
107. Jonathan Swift, "On Poetry: A Rhapsody," 1733.
108. Hugh Blair, *Lectures on Rhetoric and Belles Lettres*, 1783, Lecture 18.
109. Henry Hallam, "Scott's Edition of Dryden," *Edinburgh Review*, October 1808, pp. 133–34.
110. Edmund Gosse, A *History of Eighteenth Century Literature*, 1888, pp. 90–94.
111. Stopford A. Brooke, *English Literature*, 1896, pp. 177–78.
112. W. P. Ker, "Introduction" to *Essays of John Dryden*, 1900, pp. xxvii–xxx.
113. Thomas Shadwell, *The Medal of John Bayes: A Satyr against Folly and Knavery*, 1682.
114. Samuel Johnson, "Dryden," *Lives of the English Poets*, 1779–81.
115. Thomas Babington Macaulay, "John Dryden" (1828), *Critical, Historical, and Miscellaneous Essays*, 1860, Volume 1, pp. 351–75.
116. James Russell Lowell, "Dryden" (1868), *Among My Books*, 1870, pp. 4–24, 79–80.
117. George Saintsbury, "Later Dramas and Prose Works," *Dryden*, 1881, pp. 121–31.
118. John Amphlett Evans, "Dryden and Ben Jonson," *Temple Bar*, May 1892, pp. 101–12.

DANIEL DEFOE

1. Jonathan Swift, "Letter from a Member of the House of Commons in Ireland to a Member of the House of Commons in England concerning the Sacramental Test," 1708.
2. John Dunton, *The Life and Errors of John Dunton*, 1705.
3. Daniel Defoe, *Applebee's Journal*, 1720–26.
4. Alexander Pope, *The Dunciad*, 1728, Bk. 1, ll. 91–104; Bk. 2, ll. 139–40.
5. Walter Savage Landor, "Daniel Defoe," c. 1840.
6. John Oldmixon, *History of England*, 1739.
7. Alexander Pope (1742–43), cited in Joseph Spence, *Anecdotes, Observations and Characters of Books and Men*, ed. S. W. Singer, 1820.
8. Charles Lamb, Letter to Walter Wilson (December 16, 1822).
9. Thomas Frognall Dibdin, *The Library Companion*, 1824.
10. William Hazlitt, "Wilson's Life and Times of Daniel Defoe," 1830.
11. Charles Lamb, "Estimate of De Foe's Secondary Novels," 1830.
12. Edgar Allan Poe, "Daniel Defoe" (1836), *Essays and Reviews*, ed. G. R. Thompson, 1984, pp. 201–3.
13. Thomas De Quincey, "Homer and the Homeridae" (1841), *Collected Writings*, ed. David Masson, Volume 6, pp. 84–85.
14. John Forster, "Daniel De Foe," *Edinburgh Review*, October 1845, pp. 530–31.
15. Leigh Hunt, A *Book for a Corner*, 1849.
16. David Masson, *British Novelists and Their Styles*, 1859, pp. 95–98.
17. Hippolyte Taine, *History of English Literature*, tr. H. Van Laun, 1871, Bk. 3, Ch. 6.
18. William Minto, *Daniel Defoe*, 1879, pp. 152–54.
19. John W. Hales, "Defoe," *English Prose*, ed. Henry Craik, 1894, Volume 3, pp. 356–59.
20. Brander Matthews, "The Gift of Story-Telling," *Aspects of Fiction*, 1896, pp. 231–32.
21. Walter Sichel, *Bolingbroke and His Times*, 1901, Volume 1, pp. 120–21.
22. John Gay, "The Present State of Wit," 1711.
23. Walter Wilson, *Memoirs of the Life and Times of Daniel De Foe*, 1830, Volume 2, p. 201.
24. John Burton Hill, A *History of the Reign of Queen Anne*, 1880, Volume 3, pp. 95–96.
25. Daniel Defoe, "Preface" to *The Life and Strange Surprizing Adventures of Robinson Crusoe, of York, Mariner*, 1719.
26. Benjamin Hoadly, *London Journal*, September 4, 1725.
27. Jean Jacques Rousseau, *Émile*, 1762.
28. James Beattie, *Dissertations Moral and Critical*, 1783.
29. Hugh Blair, *Lectures on Rhetoric and Belles Lettres*, 1783, Lecture 37.
30. Hester Lynch Piozzi, *Anecdotes of the Late Samuel Johnson*, 1786.
31. Samuel Taylor Coleridge, A *Course of Lectures* (1818), *Literary Remains*, ed. Henry Nelson Coleridge, 1836, Volume 1, p. 189.
32. Thomas Babington Macaulay, "John Dryden" (1828),

Critical, Historical, and Miscellaneous Essays, 1860, Volume 1, pp. 331–32.

33. Samuel Taylor Coleridge, "Notes on *Robinson Crusoe*" (1830), *Literary Remains*, ed. Henry Nelson Coleridge, 1836, Volume 1, pp. 196–97.
34. George Borrow, *Lavengro*, 1851, Ch. 3.
35. Karl Marx, *Das Kapital*, 1867, Volume 1, Pt. 1, Ch. 1, Sec. 4.
36. H. Rider Haggard, *Books Which Have Influenced Me*, 1887, p. 66.
37. Julian Hawthorne, "Literature for Children," *Confessions and Criticisms*, 1887, pp. 122–24.
38. Frank R. Stockton, "My Favorite Novelist and His Best Book," *Munsey's Magazine*, June 1897, pp. 352–53.
39. Sir Walter Scott, "Daniel De Foe" (c. 1821), *Miscellaneous Works*, 1861, Volume 4, pp. 247–81.
40. Sir Leslie Stephen, "De Foe's Novels" (1868), *Hours in a Library* (1874–79), 1904, Volume 1, pp. 1–63.
41. George A. Aitken, "Defoe's 'Apparition of Mrs. Veal,'" *Nineteenth Century*, January 1895, pp. 95–100.
42. G. H. Maynadier, "Introduction" to *The Works of Daniel Defoe*, 1903, Volume 1, pp. xix–xxviii.

ALEXANDER POPE

1. Alexander Pope, *The Guardian*, No. 92 (June 26, 1713).
2. John Sheffield, Duke of Buckingham, "On Mr. Pope, and His Poems," 1717.
3. Thomas Hearne, *Reliquiae Hearnianae*, August 7, 1717.
4. Richard Savage, *The Wanderer*, 1729, Canto 1, ll. 353–78.
5. Thomas Hearne, *Reliquiae Hearnianae*, July 18, 1729.
6. Jonathan Swift, "A Libel on D—— D—— and a Certain Great Lord," 1730.
7. David Mallet, "Of Verbal Criticism," 1733.
8. Mrs. Blount (1737–39), cited in Joseph Spence, *Anecdotes, Observations and Characters of Books and Men*, ed. S. W. Singer, 1820.
9. Alexander Pope (1742–43), cited in Joseph Spence, *Anecdotes, Observations and Characters of Books and Men*, ed. S. W. Singer, 1820.
10. Thomas Gray, Letter to Horace Walpole (February 3, 1746).
11. William Warburton, "Advertisement" to *The Works of Alexander Pope*, 1751.
12. Oliver Goldsmith, *The Citizen of the World*, 1762, Letter 13.
13. Fanny Burney, *Diary*, December 8, 1771.
14. Edmond Malone, "Maloniana" (1783), cited in Sir James Prior, *The Life of Edmond Malone*, 1860, pp. 428–29.
15. Charles Lamb, Letter to B. W. Procter (April 13, 1823).
16. Thomas Babington Macaulay, "The Life and Writings of Addison" (1843), *Critical, Historical, and Miscellaneous Essays*, 1860, Volume 5, p. 408.
17. John Gay, "On a Miscellany of Poems," 1711.
18. Joseph Addison, *The Spectator*, No. 523 (October 30, 1712).
19. Thomas Parnell, "To Mr. Pope," 1717.
20. Jonathan Swift, *Verses on the Death of Dr. Swift*, 1731.
21. Chevalier Ramsay (1732–33), cited in Joseph Spence, *Anecdotes, Observations and Characters of Books and Men*, ed. S. W. Singer, 1820.
22. François Marie Arouet de Voltaire, *Letters on England (Lettres Philosophiques)*, 1734, tr. Leonard Tancock.
23. Lady Mary Wortley Montagu (1740–41), cited in Joseph Spence, *Anecdotes, Observations and Characters of Books and Men*, ed. S. W. Singer, 1820.
24. Joseph Warton, *An Essay on the Genius and Writings of Pope*, 1756–82, Volume 2, pp. 408–11.

25. Edward Young, *Conjectures on Original Composition*, 1759.
26. Charles Churchill, *The Apology*, 1761.
27. James Beattie, *Essays on Poetry and Music* (1776), 1779, pp. 18–19.
28. William Cowper, Letter to William Unwin (January 5, 1782).
29. Hugh Blair, *Lectures on Rhetoric and Belles Lettres*, 1783, Lecture 40.
30. Leigh Hunt, *The Feast of the Poets* (1811), 1814.
31. William Wordsworth, "Essay, Supplementary to the Preface" (1815), *Lyrical Ballads* (1798), 1815.
32. Samuel Taylor Coleridge, *Biographia Literaria*, 1817, Ch. 1.
33. George Gordon, Lord Byron "Letter to —— ——, Esqre, on the Rev. W. L. Bowles's Strictures on the Life and Writings of Pope," 1821.
34. Elizabeth Barrett Browning, *The Book of the Poets* (1842), *Life, Letters and Essays of Elizabeth Barrett Browning*, 1863.
35. Thomas De Quincey, "Alexander Pope" (c. 1842), *Collected Writings*, ed. David Masson, Volume 4, pp. 278–81.
36. William Makepeace Thackeray, *The English Humourists of the Eighteenth Century*, 1853, pp. 182–86.
37. Walter Bagehot, "William Cowper" (1855), *Works*, ed. Norman St. John-Stevas, Volume 1, pp. 289–91.
38. James Russell Lowell, "Pope" (1871), *Works*, Riverside ed., Volume 4, pp. 25–27, 56–57.
39. Hippolyte Taine, *History of English Literature*, tr. H. Van Laun, 1871, Bk. 3, Ch. 7.
40. Andrew Lang, "Epistle to Mr. Alexander Pope," *Letters to Dead Authors*, 1886, pp. 45–49.
41. Austin Dobson, "Alexander Pope," *Scribner's Magazine*, May 1888, p. 547.
42. Edmund Gosse, "What Is a Great Poet?" (1889), *Questions at Issue*, 1893, pp. 103–5.
43. Francis Thompson, "Pope," *Academy*, July 3, 1897, pp. 13–14.
44. George Granville, Lord Lansdowne, "A Letter with a Character of Mr. Wycherly" (c. 1706), *Genuine Works in Verse and Prose*, 1736, Volume 2, p. 113.
45. Jacob Tonson, Letter to Alexander Pope (April 20, 1706).
46. William Wycherley, "To My Friend, Mr. Pope, on His Pastorals," 1709.
47. Hugh Blair, *Lectures on Rhetoric and Belles Lettres*, 1783, Lecture 39.
48. Sir Leslie Stephen, *Alexander Pope*, 1880, pp. 23–24.
49. Joseph Addison, *The Spectator*, No. 253 (December 20, 1711).
50. John Dennis, *Reflections Critical and Satyrical, upon a Late Rhapsody, Call'd*, An Essay upon Criticism, 1711.
51. John Oldmixon, *An Essay on Criticism*, 1728, p. 2.
52. Henry St. John, Viscount Bolingbroke, *Letters on the Study and Use of History*, c. 1735, Letter 4.
53. Lady Mary Wortley Montagu (1740–41), cited in Joseph Spence, *Anecdotes, Observations and Characters of Books and Men*, ed. S. W. Singer, 1820.
54. William John Courthope, *The Works of Alexander Pope*, 1889, Volume 5, pp. 47–49, 68–70.
55. George Berkeley, Letter to Alexander Pope (May 1, 1714).
56. Alexander Pope (1737–39), cited in Joseph Spence, *Anecdotes, Observations and Characters of Books and Men*, ed. S. W. Singer, 1820.
57. Joseph Spence (1737–39), cited in Joseph Spence, *Anecdotes, Observations and Characters of Books and Men*, ed. S. W. Singer, 1820.
58. Oliver Goldsmith, *The Beauties of English Poesy*, 1767.

59. Oliver Goldsmith, *The Life of Dr. Parnell*, 1770.
60. Horace Walpole, Letter to John Pinkerton (June 26, 1785).
61. George Granville, Lord Lansdowne, Letter to Alexander Pope (October 21, 1713).
62. Jonathan Swift, Letter to Alexander Pope (June 28, 1715).
63. Lewis Theobald, *The Censor*, No. 33 (January 5, 1717).
64. John Gay, "Mr Popes Welcome from Greece a Copy of Verses Wrote by Mr Gay upon Mr Popes Having Finisht His Translations of Homers *Ilias*," 1720.
65. William Broome, Letter to Elijah Fenton (June 5, 1727).
66. Allan Ramsay, "To Mr. Pope," *Poems*, 1728.
67. Alexander Pope (1742–43), cited in Joseph Spence, *Anecdotes, Observations and Characters of Books and Men*, ed. S. W. Singer, 1820.
68. Hugh Blair, *Lectures on Rhetoric and Belles Lettres*, 1783, Lecture 43.
69. Edward Gibbon, *Memoirs of My Life*, 1792–93.
70. Matthew Arnold, *On Translating Homer*, 1861.
71. Richard Savage, *An Account of* The Dunciad, 1732.
72. Colley Cibber, *A Letter from Mr. Cibber to Mr. Pope*, 1742.
73. John, Lord Hervey, *The Difference between Verbal and Practical Virtue*, 1742.
74. Mrs. Racket (1742–43), cited in Joseph Spence, *Anecdotes, Observations and Characters of Books and Men*, ed. S. W. Singer, 1820.
75. Henry Fielding, *The Covent-Garden Journal*, No. 23 (March 21, 1752).
76. Adam Smith, *The Theory of Moral Sentiments*, 1759, Pt. 3, Ch. 2.
77. Horace Walpole, Letter to John Pinkerton (June 26, 1785).
78. William Somerville, "To the Author of the *Essay on Man*," c. 1732.
79. W. Belsham, "Remarks on Pope's *Essay on Man*," *Essays Philosophical and Moral, Historical and Literary*, 1799, Volume 1, p. 361.
80. Frederick Denison Maurice, *Moral and Metaphysical Philosophy*, 1862.
81. Sir Leslie Stephen, *History of English Thought in the Eighteenth Century*, 1876.
82. Augustine Birrell, "Pope," *Obiter Dicta: Second Series*, 1887.
83. Elijah Fenton, Letter to William Broome (September 1726).
84. Lady Mary Wortley Montagu, Letter to the Countess of Bute (June 23, 1754).
85. Oliver Goldsmith, *The Life of Richard Nash*, 1762.
86. Horace Walpole, Letter to William Mason (March 13, 1777).
87. William Cowper, Letter to William Unwin (June 8, 1780).
88. Hugh Blair, *Lectures on Rhetoric and Belles Lettres*, 1783, Lecture 37.
89. John Dennis, *A True Character of Mr. Pope, and His Writings*, 1716.
90. Alexander Pope, "Preface" to *The Works of Mr. Alexander Pope*, 1717.
91. Samuel Johnson, "Pope," *Lives of the English Poets*, 1779–81.
92. William Hazlitt, *Lectures on the English Poets*, 1818.
93. Sir Leslie Stephen, "Pope as a Moralist" (1873), *Hours in a Library* (1874–79), 1904, Volume 1, pp. 128–85.
94. H. D. Traill, "Pope," *National Review*, December 1889, pp. 493–503.
95. G. K. Chesterton, "Pope and the Art of Satire" (1902), *Varied Types*, 1908, pp. 43–55.

JONATHAN SWIFT

1. Sir William Temple, Letter to Sir Robert Southwell (May 29, 1690).
2. White Kennett, *Diary*, 1713.
3. Jonathan Swift, "Family of Swift," c. 1727.
4. Alexander Pope (1728–30), cited in Joseph Spence, *Anecdotes, Observations and Characters of Books and Men*, ed. S. W. Singer, 1820.
5. Alexander Pope (1742–43), cited in Joseph Spence, *Anecdotes, Observations and Characters of Books and Men*, ed. S. W. Singer, 1820.
6. John Boyle, Earl of Orrery, *Remarks on the Life and Writings of Dr. Jonathan Swift*, 1752, pp. 4–6.
7. Samuel Richardson, Letter to Lady Bradshaigh (April 22, 1752).
8. Patrick Delany, *Observations upon Lord Orrery's* Remarks on the Life and Writings of Dr. Jonathan Swift, 1754, pp. 288–91.
9. Thomas Amory, "The History of These Memoirs," *Memoirs of Several Ladies of Great Britain*, 1755, pp. xxviii–xxix.
10. Deane Swift, *An Essay upon the Life, Writings, and Character, of Dr. Jonathan Swift*, 1755, pp. 365–67.
11. Horace Walpole, Letter to Sir Horace Mann (January 13, 1780).
12. Edward Dowden, *Academy*, September 30, 1882, p. 233.
13. Thomas Parnell, "To Dr. Swift, on His Birthday, November 30th, 1713," 1713.
14. François Marie Arouet de Voltaire, "Letter 22: On Mr Pope and Some Other Famous Poets," *Letters on England* (*Lettres Philosophiques*), 1734, tr. Leonard Tancock.
15. Alexander Pope (1734–36), cited in Joseph Spence, *Anecdotes, Observations and Characters of Books and Men*, ed. S. W. Singer, 1820.
16. Lady Mary Wortley Montagu (1740–41), cited in Joseph Spence, *Anecdotes, Observations and Characters of Books and Men*, ed. S. W. Singer, 1820.
17. William Hayley, *The Triumphs of Temper*, 1781, Canto 3, ll. 587–648.
18. William Cowper, *Table Talk*, 1782, ll. 656–61.
19. Hugh Blair, *Lectures on Rhetoric and Belles Lettres*, 1783, Lecture 17.
20. James Boswell, *Life of Johnson*, 1791.
21. George Gordon, Lord Byron, *Hints from Horace*, 1811.
22. Samuel Taylor Coleridge, *A Course of Lectures* (1818), *Literary Remains*, ed. Henry Nelson Coleridge, 1836, Volume 1, p. 140.
23. William Hazlitt, *Lectures on the English Poets*, 1818.
24. Samuel Taylor Coleridge, *Table Talk*, June 15, 1830.
25. Thomas Carlyle, *Lectures on the History of Literature*, 1838.
26. Thomas Babington Macaulay, "Sir William Temple" (1838), *Critical, Historical, and Miscellaneous Essays*, 1860, Volume 4, pp. 102–3.
27. Thomas Babington Macaulay, "The Life and Writings of Addison" (1843), *Critical, Historical, and Miscellaneous Essays*, 1860, Volume 5, pp. 376–77.
28. Thomas De Quincey, "Schlosser's Literary History of the Eighteenth Century" (1847), *Collected Writings*, ed. David Masson, Volume 11, pp. 17–18.
29. William Makepeace Thackeray, *The History of Henry Esmond, Esq.*, 1852, Bk. 3, Ch. 5.
30. Ralph Waldo Emerson, "Literature," *English Traits*, 1856.
31. David Masson, *British Novelists and Their Styles*, 1859, pp. 90–94.

32. W. E. H. Lecky, "Jonathan Swift," *The Leaders of Public Opinion in Ireland*, 1861.
33. James Russell Lowell, "Forster's Life of Swift," *Nation*, April 20, 1876, p. 265.
34. James Thomson, "A Note on Forster's Life of Swift" (1876), *Essays and Phantasies*, 1881, pp. 287–88.
35. Sir Leslie Stephen, *Swift*, 1882, pp. 179–81.
36. F. C. Montague, "Political Pamphlets by Men of Genius," *Murray's Magazine*, November 1891, pp. 751–54.
37. Henry Craik, "Jonathan Swift," *English Prose*, ed. Henry Craik, 1894, Volume 3, pp. 387–90.
38. Edmund Gosse, *A Short History of Modern English Literature*, 1897, pp. 220–24.
39. Francis Atterbury, Letters to Bishop Trelawney (1704).
40. William Congreve, Letter to Joseph Keally (October 28, 1704).
41. Sir Richard Blackmore, "An Essay upon Wit," *Essays upon Several Subjects*, 1716, pp. 217–18.
42. William Godwin, "Of English Style," *The Enquirer*, 1797, p. 444.
43. Henry Hallam, *Introduction to the Literature of Europe*, 1837–39, Pt. 4, Ch. 7, Par. 61.
44. Edmund Gosse, *A History of Eighteenth Century Literature*, 1888, pp. 144–47.
45. Herbert Eveleth Greene, "The Allegory as Employed by Spenser, Bunyan, and Swift," *PMLA*, 1889, pp. 168–70.
46. Alexander Pope, *Imitations of Horace*, 1737, Ep. II.i.221–28.
47. John Wilson Croker, *A Sketch of the State of Ireland, Past and Present*, 1808.
48. Adams Sherman Hill, "The Character of Jonathan Swift," *North American Review*, January 1868, pp. 85–86.
49. Richard Ashe King, *Swift in Ireland*, 1895, pp. 108–9.
50. Lady Mary Wortley Montagu, Letter to the Countess of Mar (November 1726).
51. John Arbuthnot, Letter to Jonathan Swift (November 8, 1726).
52. John Gay, Alexander Pope, Letter to Jonathan Swift (November 17, 1726).
53. Edward Young, *Conjectures on Original Composition*, 1759.
54. Horace Walpole, "The Sequel to *Gulliver's Travels*" (Letter to the Countess of Upper Ossory, December 14, 1771).
55. Edmund Gosse, *A History of Eighteenth Century Literature*, 1888, pp. 160–62.
56. Alfred Ainger, "Swift—His Life and Genius" (1894), *Lectures and Essays*, 1905, Volume 1, pp. 252–56.
57. Walter Raleigh, *The English Novel*, 1894, pp. 136–38.
58. Joseph Warton, *An Essay on the Genius and Writings of Pope*, 1756–82.
59. Francis, Lord Jeffrey, "Scott's Edition of Swift," *Edinburgh Review*, September 1816, pp. 49–50.
60. Hippolyte Taine, *History of English Literature*, tr. H. Van Laun, 1871, Bk. 3, Ch. 5.
61. J. Nichol, "Jonathan Swift," *The English Poets*, ed. Thomas Humphry Ward, 1880, Volume 3, pp. 35–38.
62. Jonathan Swift, *Verses on the Death of Dr. Swift*, 1731.
63. Samuel Johnson, "Swift," *Lives of the English Poets*, 1779–81.
64. David Masson, "Dean Swift," *Essays Biographical and Critical*, 1856, pp. 169–77.
65. Charles Cowden Clarke, "On the Comic Writers of England: VI. Swift," *Gentleman's Magazine*, September 1871, pp. 436–56.
66. John Churton Collins, "Characteristics," *Jonathan Swift: A Biographical and Critical Study*, 1893, pp. 241–68.
67. Herbert Paul, "The Prince of Journalists," *Nineteenth Century*, January 1900, pp. 73–87.

HENRY FIELDING

1. Colley Cibber, *An Apology for the Life of Mr. Colley Cibber*, 1739.
2. Joseph Warton, Letter to Thomas Warton (October 29, 1746).
3. Horace Walpole, Letter to George Montagu (May 18, 1749).
4. Tobias Smollett, *The Adventures of Peregrine Pickle*, 1751.
5. Lady Mary Wortley Montagu, Letter to the Countess of Bute (September 22, 1755).
6. Lady Louisa Stuart, "Introductory Anecdotes," *The Letters and Works of Lady Mary Wortley Montagu*, ed. Lord Wharncliffe, 1837, Volume 1.
7. James P. Browne, "Preface" to *The Works of Henry Fielding, Esq.*, 1872, Volume 11, pp. 17–18.
8. Robert Louis Stevenson, *Virginibus Puerisque*, 1881.
9. James Russell Lowell, "Inscription for a Memorial Bust of Fielding," 1883.
10. Austin Dobson, "Henry Fielding (To James Russell Lowell)," 1883.
11. T. R. Lounsbury, "Letter on Fielding's Bust," *Century*, February 1884, p. 635.
12. Thomas Gray, Letter to Richard West (April 8, 1742).
13. Frances Thynne Hertford, Duchess of Somerset, Letter to Lady Luxborough (November 20, 1748).
14. Samuel Richardson, Letter to Anne Donnellan (February 22, 1752).
15. Christopher Smart, Prefatory Letter to *The Hilliad*, 1752.
16. James Beattie, *An Essay on Poetry and Music*, 1762, Pt. 1, Ch. 5, Note.
17. Vicesimus Knox, *Essays, Moral and Literary* (1777), 1782, Essay 14.
18. Hannah More (1780), *Memoirs of the Life and Correspondence of Mrs. Hannah More*, ed. William Roberts, 1835, Volume 1.
19. Hugh Blair, *Lectures on Rhetoric and Belles Lettres*, 1783, Lecture 37.
20. James Boswell, *Life of Johnson*, 1791.
21. James Boswell, *Life of Johnson*, 1791.
22. Anna Laetitia Barbauld, "Introduction" to *The Correspondence of Samuel Richardson*, 1804, Volume 1, p. 79.
23. Sir James Mackintosh, "Godwin's Lives of Edward and John Philips, Nephews of Milton," *Edinburgh Review*, October 1815, p. 485.
24. Sir Nathaniel William Wraxall, *Historical Memoirs of My Time*, 1815.
25. George Gordon, Lord Byron, *Journal*, January 4, 1821.
26. Thomas Carlyle, Letter to John A. Carlyle (November 11, 1823).
27. William Hazlitt, "Why the Heroes of Romances Are Insipid," 1827.
28. Robert Southey, Letter to Caroline Bowles (February 15, 1830).
29. Samuel Taylor Coleridge, "Notes on *Jonathan Wild*" (1832), *Literary Remains*, ed. Henry Nelson Coleridge, 1836, Volume 2.
30. Samuel Taylor Coleridge, *Table Talk*, July 5, 1834.
31. T. Noon Talfourd, "On the British Novels and Romances," *Critical and Miscellaneous Writings*, 1842.
32. Charlotte Brontë, Letter to W. S. Williams (December 23, 1847).
33. John Forster, *The Life and Times of Oliver Goldsmith*, 1848, Bk. 3, Ch. 13.
34. Thomas Keightley, "On the Life and Writings of Henry Fielding," *Fraser's Magazine*, February 1858, p. 217.

35. William Forsyth, *The Novels and Novelists of the Eighteenth Century*, 1871, p. 274.

36. G. P. Lathrop, "The Growth of the Novel," *Atlantic*, June 1874, pp. 686–87.

37. Bayard Tuckerman, *A History of English Prose Fiction*, 1882, p. 204.

38. Austin Dobson, *Fielding* (1883), 1889, pp. 121–23.

39. James Russell Lowell, "Address on Unveiling the Bust of Fielding (1883)," *Works*, Riverside ed., Volume 6, pp. 63–64.

40. Edmund Gosse, A *History of Eighteenth Century Literature*, 1888, pp. 256–57.

41. Robert Louis Stevenson, "Some Gentlemen in Fiction," *Scribner's Magazine*, June 1888, p. 766.

42. Andrew Lang, *Letters on Literature*, 1889, pp. 38–39.

43. Walter Lewin, "The Abuse of Fiction," *Forum*, August 1889, pp. 667–68.

44. W. E. Henley, "Fielding," *Views and Reviews*, 1890, pp. 229–32.

45. W. H. S. Aubrey, *The Rise and Growth of the English Nation*, 1895, Volume 3, p. 121.

46. Henry Craik, "Introduction" to *English Prose*, ed. Henry Craik, 1895, Volume 4, pp. 10–11.

47. George Saintsbury, "Fielding," *English Prose*, ed. Henry Craik, 1895, Volume 4, pp. 114–15.

48. Edmund Gosse, A *Short History of Modern English Literature*, 1897, pp. 243–44.

49. James Bramston, *Seasonable Reproof*, 1736.

50. James Harris, *Philological Inquiries*, c. 1750, Pt. 2, Ch. 7.

51. William Hazlitt, *Lectures on the English Comic Writers*, 1819.

52. Thomas Roscoe, "Life and Works of Henry Fielding," *The Works of Henry Fielding*, 1840.

53. Edwin P. Whipple, "The Life and Works of Henry Fielding," *North American Review*, January 1849, p. 51.

54. Henry Fielding, Dedication to George, Lord Lyttelton, *Tom Jones*, 1749.

55. Astraea and Minerva Hill, Letter to Samuel Richardson (July 27, 1749).

56. Samuel Richardson, Letter to Astraea and Minerva Hill (August 4, 1749).

57. Aaron Hill, Letter to Samuel Richardson (August 11, 1749).

58. Thomas Cawthorn, "To Henry Fielding, Esq.; on Reading His Inimitable *History of Tom Jones*," *Gentleman's Magazine*, September 1749, p. 371.

59. James Burnett, Lord Monboddo, *Of the Origin and Progress of Language*, 1773–92, Pt. 2, Bk. 4, Ch. 8.

60. Sir John Hawkins, *The Life of Samuel Johnson, LL.D.*, 1787.

61. Edward Gibbon, *Memoirs of My Life*, 1792–93.

62. Madame de Staël, *The Influence of Literature upon Society*, 1800, Ch. 15.

63. John Dunlop, *The History of Fiction* (1814), 1842, Ch. 14.

64. William Beloe, *The Sexagenarian*, 1817, Volume 1, p. 13.

65. Samuel Taylor Coleridge, "Notes on *Tom Jones*," *Literary Remains*, ed. Henry Nelson Coleridge, 1836, Volume 2, pp. 374–75.

66. William Carleton (c. 1869), *The Life of William Carleton: Being His Autobiography and Letters*, ed. David J. O'Donoghue, 1896, Volume 1, p. 74.

67. Frederic Harrison, "The Choice of Books" (1879), *The Choice of Books and Other Literary Pieces*, 1886, p. 63.

68. Anthony Trollope, *An Autobiography*, 1883, Ch. 17.

69. Wilbur L. Cross, *The Development of the English Novel*, 1899, pp. 45–46.

70. G. K. Chesterton, "Tom Jones and Morality," *All Things Considered*, 1907, pp. 193–99.

71. Arthur Murphy, "An Essay on the Life and Genius of Henry Fielding, Esq.," *Collected Works of Henry Fielding, Esq.*, 1762.

72. William Hazlitt, *Lectures on the English Comic Writers*, 1819.

73. Sir Walter Scott, "Fielding" (1820), *Lives of the Novelists*, 1825.

74. William Makepeace Thackeray, "Hogarth, Smollett, and Fielding," *The English Humourists of the Eighteenth Century*, 1853.

75. Hippolyte Taine, "Fielding," *History of English Literature*, tr. H. Van Laun, 1871, Bk. 3, Ch. 6.

76. Charles Cowden Clarke, "On the Comic Writers of England: XIV. Fielding, Smollett and Sterne," *Gentleman's Magazine*, May 1872, pp. 556–65.

77. Sir Leslie Stephen, "Fielding's Novels" (1877), *Hours in a Library* (1874–79), 1904, Volume 3, pp. 1–43.

78. Clara Thomson, "A Note on Fielding's *Amelia*," *Westminster Review*, November 1899, pp. 579–88.

LAURENCE STERNE

1. Lady Mary Coke, *Journal*, March 14, 1768.

2. David Garrick, "Epitaph on Laurence Sterne," c. 1768.

3. Edmond Malone, "Maloniana" (1787), cited in Sir James Prior, *Life of Edmond Malone*, 1860, pp. 373–74.

4. James Boswell, *Life of Johnson*, 1791.

5. George Gordon, Lord Byron, *Journal*, December 1, 1813.

6. Thomas Carlyle, *Lectures on the History of Literature*, 1838.

7. James P. Browne, "Preface" to *The Works of Laurence Sterne*, 1873, Volume 1, pp. 26–27.

8. Thomas Gray, Letter to Thomas Wharton (April 22, 1760).

9. Charles Churchill, *The Ghost*, 1762, Bk. 3, ll. 967–78.

10. Anna Seward, Letter to George Gregory (December 5, 1787).

11. Thomas James Mathias, *The Pursuits of Literature* (1794), 1798, p. 59, Note.

12. Anna Laetitia Barbauld, "On the Origin and Progress of Novel-Writing," *The British Novelists*, 1810, Volume 1, pp. 40–42.

13. Sir James Mackintosh (May 31, 1811), cited in Robert James Mackintosh, *Memoirs of the Life of Sir James Mackintosh*, 1853, Volume 2, p. 102.

14. William Hazlitt, *Lectures on the English Comic Writers*, 1819.

15. Alexander Pushkin, "Fragments from Letters, Thoughts, and Notes" (1827), *The Critical Prose of Alexander Pushkin*, ed. and tr. Carl R. Proffer, 1969, p. 49.

16. Samuel Taylor Coleridge, *Table Talk*, August 18, 1833.

17. T. Noon Talfourd, "Mackenzie," *Critical and Miscellaneous Writings*, 1842, p. 7.

18. William Makepeace Thackeray, *The English Humourists of the Eighteenth Century*, 1853.

19. R. Shelton Mackenzie, Note to John Wilson, *Noctes Ambrosianae*, 1854, Volume 4, p. 214.

20. David Masson, *British Novelists and Their Styles*, 1859, pp. 145–48.

21. James Russell Lowell, "Lessing" (1866), *Works*, Riverside ed., Volume 2, p. 170.

22. Edmond Scherer, "Laurence Sterne; or, The Humorist" (1870), *Essays on English Literature*, tr. George Saintsbury, 1891, pp. 161, 172–73.

23. Hall Caine, *Academy*, November 4, 1882, pp. 321–22.

24. Sir Arthur Quiller-Couch, "Laurence Sterne" (1891), *Adventures in Criticism*, 1896, pp. 43–44.

25. Henry Childs Merwin, "The Philosophy of Sterne," *Atlantic*, October 1894, p. 523.
26. William Edward Simonds, *An Introduction to the Study of English Fiction*, 1894, pp. 51–52.
27. Joseph Texte, *Jean-Jacques Rousseau and the Cosmopolitan Spirit in Literature* (1895), tr. J. W. Matthews, 1899, p. 288.
28. Edmund Gosse, *A Short History of Modern English Literature*, 1897, pp. 244–45.
29. Laurence Sterne, Letter (Summer 1759).
30. Laurence Sterne, "Dedication to Mr. Pitt," *The Life and Opinions of Tristram Shandy, Gent.*, 1760.
31. Horace Walpole, Letter to David Dalrymple (April 4, 1760).
32. William Warburton, Letter to David Garrick (May 13, 1760).
33. Thomas Gray, Letter to Thomas Wharton (c. June 20, 1760).
34. William Warburton, Letter to Richard Hurd (December 27, 1761).
35. Oliver Goldsmith, *The Citizen of the World*, 1762, Letter 53.
36. David Hume, Letter to William Strahan (January 30, 1773).
37. James Boswell, *Life of Johnson*, 1791.
38. Sidney Lanier, *The English Novel*, 1883, pp. 186–87.
39. Augustine Birrell, *Essays about Men, Women, and Books*, 1894, pp. 36–37.
40. Walter Raleigh, *The English Novel*, 1894, pp. 195–98.
41. Anthony Hope, "My Favorite Novelist and His Best Book," *Munsey's Magazine*, December 1897, pp. 351–53.
42. Horace Walpole, Letter to Sir George Montagu (March 12, 1768).
43. Fanny Burney, *Diary*, Spring 1769.
44. Thomas Jefferson, Letter to Robert Skipwith (August 3, 1771).
45. John Wesley, *Journal*, February 11, 1772.
46. Vicesimus Knox, "On the Manner of Writing Voyages and Travels," *Essays, Moral and Literary* (1777), 1782, No. 24.
47. George Whitfield (or Whitefield), *A Letter from the Rev. George Whitfield, B.A., to the Rev. Laurence Sterne, M.A.*, 1760.
48. Sir Walter Scott, "Sterne" (1821), *Lives of the Novelists*, 1825.
49. Whitwell Elwin, "Sterne," *Quarterly Review*, March 1854, pp. 334–40.
50. Henry T. Tuckerman, "The Sentimentalist: Laurence Sterne," *Essays, Biographical and Critical*, 1857, pp. 327–41.
51. Walter Bagehot, "Sterne and Thackeray" (1864), *Collected Works*, ed. Norman St. John-Stevas, 1965, Volume 2, pp. 288–98.
52. Hippolyte Taine, *History of English Literature*, tr. H. Van Laun, 1871, Bk. 2, Ch. 6.
53. Charles Cowden Clarke, "On the Comic Writers of England: XIV. Fielding, Smollett and Sterne," *Gentleman's Magazine*, May 1872, pp. 575–80.
54. Sir Leslie Stephen, "Sterne" (1880), *Hours in a Library* (1874–79), 1904, Volume 4, pp. 57–101.
55. H. D. Traill, "Laurence Sterne," *English Prose*, ed. Henry Craik, 1895, Volume 4, pp. 207–10.
56. Herbert Paul, "Sterne," *Nineteenth Century*, December 1896, pp. 997–1000.
57. Wilbur L. Cross, "Laurence Sterne," *The Development of the English Novel*, 1899, pp. 70–76.

THOMAS GRAY

1. Horace Walpole, Letter to George Montagu (September 3, 1748).
2. John Sharp, Letter (March 12, 1756).
3. James Beattie, Letter to Sir William Forbes (1765).
4. William Temple, Letter to James Boswell (1772).
5. William Michael Rossetti, "Thomas Gray," *Lives of Famous Poets*, 1878, pp. 154–56.
6. Robert Lloyd, *An Epistle to C. Churchill, Author of* The Rosciad, 1762.
7. William Cowper, Letter to Joseph Hill (April 20, 1777).
8. Thomas Warton, "To Mr. Gray," 1777.
9. James Boswell, *Life of Johnson*, 1791.
10. William Wordsworth, "Preface" (1800) to *Lyrical Ballads* (1798), 1800.
11. William Wordsworth, Letter to R. P. Gillies (April 15, 1816).
12. William Hazlitt, *Lectures on the English Poets*, 1818.
13. Thomas Campbell, *Specimens of the British Poets*, 1819.
14. Henry Francis Cary, "Notices of Miscellaneous English Poets" (1823), cited in Henry Cary, *Memoirs of the Rev. Henry Francis Cary*, 1847, Volume 2, p. 293.
15. Thomas Carlyle, "Goethe" (1828), *Critical and Miscellaneous Essays*, 1839–69.
16. Samuel Taylor Coleridge, *Table Talk*, October 23, 1833.
17. Hartley Coleridge, "Young and His Contemporaries," *Sketches of English Poets*, 1849.
18. Whitwell Elwin, "Life and Works of Gray," *Quarterly Review*, January 1854, pp. 25–26.
19. James Russell Lowell, "Carlyle" (1866), *Works*, Riverside ed., Volume 2, pp. 80–81.
20. W. J. Courthope, "Wordsworth and Gray," *Quarterly Review*, January 1876, pp. 58–59.
21. J. C. Shairp, *On Poetic Interpretation of Nature*, 1877, pp. 209–10.
22. Edward FitzGerald, Letter to James Russell Lowell (June 13, 1879).
23. Edward Dowden, *Academy*, July 22, 1882, pp. 58–59.
24. Thomas R. Lounsbury, "Gray's Works," *Nation*, March 5, 1885, pp. 205–6.
25. James Russell Lowell, "Gray," *New Princeton Review*, March 1886, pp. 175–76.
26. Edmund Gosse, *A History of Eighteenth Century Literature*, 1888, pp. 235–41.
27. Duncan C. Tovey, "Introductory Essay" to *Gray and His Friends: Letters and Relics*, 1890, pp. 32–33.
28. John W. Hales, "Thomas Gray," *English Prose*, ed. Henry Craik, 1895, Volume 4, pp. 221–24.
29. Thomas Gray, Letter to Horace Walpole (February 11, 1751).
30. Horace Walpole, "Advertisement" to *Elegy Written in a Country Church-Yard*, 1751.
31. Oliver Goldsmith, *The Beauties of English Poesy*, 1767.
32. George Gordon, Lord Byron, "Letter to —— ——, Esqre, on the Rev. W. L. Bowles's Strictures on the Life and Writings of Pope," 1821.
33. Walter Savage Landor, "The *Elegy in a Country Church-yard*" (1843), cited in John Forster, *Walter Savage Landor: A Biography*, 1869, p. 570.
34. Walter Bagehot, "Wordsworth, Tennyson, and Browning; or, Pure, Ornate, and Grotesque Art in English Poetry," 1864.
35. Thomas Gray, Letter to Richard Hurd (August 25, 1757).
36. Oliver Goldsmith, "*Odes*, by Mr. Gray," *Monthly Review*, September 1757.
37. Adam Smith, *The Theory of Moral Sentiments* (1759), 1790, Sec. 3, Ch. 2.

38. Bennet Langton (1780), cited in James Boswell, *Life of Johnson*, 1791.

39. Thomas Wharton, Letter to William Mason (May 29, 1781).

40. Henry Wadsworth Longfellow, Letter to Zilpah Longfellow (April 1823).

41. Edward Bulwer-Lytton, "Gray's Works" (1837), *Miscellaneous Works*, 1868, Volume 1, p. 153.

42. Leigh Hunt, *A Book for a Corner*, 1849.

43. Stopford A. Brooke, *Theology in the English Poets*, 1874.

44. H. C. Beeching, *Academy*, January 24, 1885, p. 53.

45. Samuel Johnson, "Gray," *Lives of the English Poets*, 1779–81.

46. Sir Leslie Stephen, "Gray and His School" (1879), *Hours in a Library* (1874–79), 1904, Volume 4, pp. 13–33.

47. Matthew Arnold, "Thomas Gray," *The English Poets*, ed. Thomas Humphry Ward, 1880, Volume 3, pp. 303–16.

48. A. C. Benson, "Thomas Gray" (1888), *Essays* (1896), 1907, pp. 119–46.

TOBIAS SMOLLETT

1. Charles Churchill, *The Apology*, 1761, ll. 298–313.

2. Cuthbert Shaw, *The Race*, 1766.

3. Horace Walpole, Letter to Sir Horace Mann (March 15, 1770).

4. Andrew Henderson, *A Second Letter to Dr. Samuel Johnson*, 1775.

5. Alexander Carlyle, *Anecdotes and Characters of the Times*, 1800–05.

6. Leigh Hunt, "Memorandum" (March 17, 1813), *The Correspondence of Leigh Hunt*, 1862, Volume 1, p. 80.

7. Thomas Roscoe, "Life and Works of Tobias Smollett" (1840), *Miscellaneous Works of Tobias Smollett*, 1856, Volume 1, pp. 32–33.

8. Thomas Carlyle, *History of Friedrich II. of Prussia*, 1858–65, Bk. 12, Ch. 12.

9. W. Sargent, "Some Inedited Memorials of Smollett," *Atlantic*, June 1859, p. 702.

10. Alexander Fraser Tytler, Lord Woodhouselee, *Essay on the Principles of Translation*, 1791.

11. Thomas James Mathias, *The Pursuits of Literature* (1794), 1798, p. 59, Note.

12. William Godwin, "Of English Style," *The Enquirer*, 1797, p. 467.

13. George Gregory, *Letters on Literature, Taste, and Composition*, 1808, Volume 2, pp. 72–73.

14. Edward Mangin, *An Essay on Light Reading*, 1808, pp. 50–51.

15. Alexander Chalmers, "The Life of Tobias Smollett, M.D.," *The Works of the English Poets*, 1810, Volume 15, pp. 551–53.

16. John Dunlop, *The History of Fiction* (1814), 1842, Volume 2, p. 408.

17. William Hazlitt, *Lectures on the English Comic Writers*, 1819.

18. John Keats, Letter to George and Thomas Keats (January 5, 1818).

19. George Eliot, "The Progress of Fiction as an Art," *Westminster Review*, October 1853, p. 355.

20. William Makepeace Thackeray, *The English Humourists of the Eighteenth Century*, 1853.

21. George Gilfillan, "Thackeray," *A Third Gallery of Portraits*, 1854, p. 230.

22. Charles Dickens, Letter to Frank Stone (May 30, 1854).

23. David Masson, *British Novelists and Their Styles*, 1859, pp. 133–45.

24. James Russell Lowell, Letter to Charles Eliot Norton (July 8, 1867).

25. William Forsyth, *The Novels and Novelists of the Eighteenth Century*, 1871, p. 278.

26. Sidney Lanier, *The English Novel*, 1883, p. 185.

27. William Stebbing, *Some Verdicts of History Reviewed*, 1887, pp. 6–7.

28. J. Logie Robertson, *A History of English Literature*, 1894, pp. 234–35.

29. George Eyre-Todd, *Scottish Poetry of the Eighteenth Century*, 1896, Volume 1, p. 151.

30. Edmund Gosse, *A Short History of Modern English Literature*, 1897, pp. 245–47.

31. George Saintsbury, *A Short History of English Literature*, 1898, pp. 606–7.

32. W. E. Henley, "Introduction" to *The Works of Tobias Smollett*, 1899, Volume 1, pp. 44–48.

33. Richard Burton, "The Vigorous Dr. Smollett," *Dial*, February 1, 1902, p. 83.

34. T. Noon Talfourd, "On British Novels and Romances," *Critical and Miscellaneous Writings*, 1842, pp. 14–15.

35. Charles Cowden Clarke, "On the Comic Writers of England: XIV. Fielding, Smollett and Sterne," *Gentleman's Magazine*, May 1872, pp. 565–67.

36. Mark Pattison, "Pope and His Editors" (1872), *Essays*, ed. Henry Nettleship, 1889, Volume 2, p. 356.

37. James Hannay, "Sea Novels—Captain Marryat," *Cornhill Magazine*, February 1873, pp. 173–75.

38. G. H. Maynadier, "Introduction" to *The Adventures of Roderick Random*, 1902, Volume 1, pp. 26–27.

39. John Cleland, *Monthly Review*, March 1751, pp. 357–58.

40. Mary Delany, Letter to Mrs. Dewes (1752).

41. Lady Anne Hamilton, *The Epics of the Ton*, 1807.

42. Robert Dwer Joyce, "Reflections," *Scribner's Monthly Magazine*, August 1877, p. 446.

43. David Herbert, "Life of Tobias George Smollett," *The Works of Tobias Smollett*, 1870.

44. Oliver Goldsmith, "Smollett's *History of England*," *Monthly Review*, June 1757, pp. 531–32.

45. Lady Mary Wortley Montagu, Letter to the Countess of Bute (October 3, 1758).

46. William Warburton, Letter to Richard Hurd (January 30, 1759), *Letters from a Late Eminent Prelate*, 1808.

47. Fanny Burney, *Diary*, April 1770.

48. William Smyth, *Lectures on Modern History*, 1840, Lecture 26.

49. Francis Garden, Lord Gardenstone, *Travelling Memoranda*, 1792–95.

50. George Stillman Hillard, *Six Months in Italy*, 1853, Volume 2, pp. 375–77.

51. W. J. Prowse, "Smollett at Nice," *Macmillan's Magazine*, April 1870, pp. 529–30.

52. Horace Walpole, *Memoirs of the Reign of King George the Third*, 1771.

53. Sir Walter Scott, "Tobias Smollett" (1821), *Lives of the Novelists*, 1825.

54. David Herbert, "Life of Tobias George Smollett," *The Works of Tobias Smollett*, 1870.

55. Eugene Schuyler, "Smollett in Search of Health" (1889), *Italian Influences*, 1901, p. 242.

56. Austin Dobson, "The Topography of *Humphry Clinker*," *Eighteenth Century Vignettes: Second Series*, 1894.

57. Oliver Goldsmith, *The Beauties of English Poesy*, 1767.

58. Thomas Campbell, *Specimens of the British Poets*, 1819.

59. James Grant Wilson, *The Poets and Poetry of Scotland*, 1876, Volume 1, p. 203.

60. Robert Anderson, "The Life of Tobias Smollett, M.D.," *The History of England* by Tobias Smollett, 1805, Volume 1, pp. 107–13, 123–25.

61. Sir Walter Scott, "Tobias Smollett" (1821), *Lives of the Novelists*, 1825.
62. Hippolyte Taine, *History of English Literature*, tr. H. Van Laun, 1871, Bk. 3, Ch. 6.
63. George Barnett Smith, "Tobias Smollett," *Gentleman's Magazine*, June 1875, pp. 729–37.
64. Edmund Gosse, "The Novelists," A *History of Eighteenth Century Literature*, 1888, pp. 258–64.
65. Walter Raleigh, "The Novels of the Eighteenth Century," *The English Novel*, 1894, pp. 185–90.
66. George Saintsbury, "Tobias Smollett," *English Prose*, ed. Henry Craik, 1895, Volume 4, pp. 257–60.
67. Oliphant Smeaton, *Tobias Smollett*, 1897, pp. 122–46.
68. Wilbur L. Cross, "Tobias Smollett," *The Development of the English Novel*, 1899, pp. 63–69.

OLIVER GOLDSMITH

1. David Garrick, "Jupiter and Mercury: A Fable," n.d.
2. Thomas Warton, Letter to Joseph Warton (January 22, 1765).
3. Hester Lynch Piozzi, "The Streatham Portraits" (1773), *Autobiography, Letters and Literary Remains*, ed. A. Hayward, 1861, Volume 2, pp. 12–13.
4. Sir John Hawkins, *The Life of Samuel Johnson, LL.D.*, 1787.
5. James Boswell, *Life of Johnson*, 1791.
6. Thomas Percy, "Life of Dr. Oliver Goldsmith," *The Miscellaneous Works of Oliver Goldsmith*, 1801.
7. James Northcote, *Memoirs of Sir Joshua Reynolds, Knt.*, 1813, pp. 210–12.
8. Joseph Cradock, *Literary and Miscellaneous Memoirs*, 1828, Volume 1, pp. 230–32.
9. George Colman the Younger, *Random Records*, 1830, Volume 1, pp. 110–12.
10. Washington Irving, *Oliver Goldsmith: A Biography*, 1849.
11. Walter Savage Landor, "Erin," *Heroic Idyls*, 1863.
12. William Kenrick, *Monthly Review*, June 1760, p. 39.
13. Thomas Chatterton, "The Art of Puffing by a Bookseller's Journeyman," 1770.
14. James Boswell, *Life of Johnson*, 1791.
15. Richard Cumberland, *Memoirs of Richard Cumberland*, 1807, Volume 1, pp. 351–53.
16. Edward Bulwer-Lytton, "Goldsmith," *Edinburgh Review*, July 1848, pp. 206–8.
17. Hartley Coleridge, "Young and His Contemporaries," *Sketches of English Poets*, 1849.
18. William Makepeace Thackeray, *The English Humourists of the Eighteenth Century*, 1853.
19. William Black, *Goldsmith*, 1878, pp. 150–52.
20. C. R. L. Fletcher, *The Development of English Prose Style*, 1881, pp. 22–23.
21. Edmund Gosse, A *Short History of Modern English Literature*, 1897, pp. 253–54.
22. Oliver Goldsmith, "Advertisement" to *The Vicar of Wakefield*, 1766.
23. Fanny Burney, *Diary*, 1768.
24. Anne Grant, *Letters from the Mountains*, June 20, 1773.
25. James Boswell, *Life of Johnson*, 1791.
26. Edward Mangin, *An Essay on Light Reading*, 1808, pp. 123–28.
27. Johann Wolfgang von Goethe, *Autobiography*, 1811, tr. R. O. Moon.
28. William Hazlitt, *Lectures on the English Poets*, 1818.
29. Sir Walter Scott, "Oliver Goldsmith" (1823), *Lives of the Novelists*, 1825.
30. Hippolyte Taine, *History of English Literature*, tr. H. Van Laun, 1871, Bk. 3, Ch. 6.

31. Edmund Burke, Letter to Richard Shackleton (May 6, 1780).
32. James Boswell, *Life of Johnson*, 1791.
33. George Gilfillan, "The Life of Oliver Goldsmith," *The Poetical Works of Goldsmith, Collins, and T. Warton*, 1854, pp. xxiv–xxvi.
34. Thomas Babington Macaulay, "Oliver Goldsmith" (1856), *Critical, Historical, and Miscellaneous Essays*, 1860, Volume 6, pp. 162–63.
35. J. C. Shairp, *On Poetic Interpretation of Nature*, 1877, pp. 211–13.
36. William Michael Rossetti, "Oliver Goldsmith," *Lives of Famous Poets*, 1878, pp. 174–75.
37. Horace Walpole, Letter to William Mason (May 27, 1773).
38. Thomas Davies, *Memoirs of the Life of David Garrick*, 1780.
39. Charles Dibdin, A *Complete History of the Stage*, 1795, Volume 5, pp. 282–84.
40. Sir Walter Scott, "An Essay on the Drama," 1819.
41. Percy Fitzgerald, *Principles of Comedy and Dramatic Effect*, 1870, pp. 91–93.
42. John Aikin, "On the Poetry of Dr. Goldsmith," *The Poetical Works of Oliver Goldsmith*, 1796.
43. E. T. Channing, "Prior's Life of Goldsmith," *North American Review*, July 1837, pp. 106–16.
44. Leigh Hunt, *Wit and Humour*, 1846.
45. Henry Giles, "Oliver Goldsmith," *Lectures and Essays*, 1850, Volume 1, pp. 235–57.
46. Edward Dowden, "Oliver Goldsmith," *The English Poets*, ed. Thomas Humphry Ward, 1880, Volume 3, pp. 368–72.
47. Austin Dobson, *"The Citizen of the World," Eighteenth Century Vignettes: First Series*, 1892.
48. Henry James, "Introduction" to *The Vicar of Wakefield*, 1900.

DAVID HUME

1. Dr. Campbell, Letter to David Hume (June 25, 1762).
2. Tobias Smollett, Letter to David Hume (August 31, 1768).
3. Joseph Black, Letter to Adam Smith (August 26, 1776).
4. Adam Smith, Letter to William Strahan (November 9, 1776).
5. James Boswell, *Journal of a Tour to the Hebrides*, 1785.
6. Edmond Malone, "Maloniana" (1787), cited in Sir James Prior, *Life of Edmond Malone*, 1860, p. 368.
7. Alexander Carlyle, *Anecdotes and Characters of the Times*, 1800–05.
8. William Mason, "An Heroic Epistle to Sir William Chambers, Knight," 1773.
9. James Boswell, *Life of Johnson*, 1791.
10. Ralph Waldo Emerson, Letter to Mary Moody Emerson (October 16, 1823).
11. Thomas Carlyle, "Boswell's Life of Johnson" (1832), *Critical and Miscellaneous Essays*, 1839–69.
12. Walter Bagehot, "Adam Smith as a Person," 1864.
13. Edmund Gosse, A *History of Eighteenth Century Literature*, 1888, pp. 299–300.
14. J. H. Millar, "David Hume," *English Prose*, ed. Henry Craik, 1895, Volume 4, pp. 187–88.
15. George Saintsbury, A *Short History of English Literature*, 1898, pp. 623–24.
16. William Warburton, Letter to Richard Hurd (September 28, 1749), *Letters from a Late Eminent Prelate*, 1808.
17. William Cowper, Letter to William Unwin (July 12, 1784).

18. Thomas Carlyle, Letter to Thomas Mitchell (May 24, 1815).
19. William Warburton, Letter to Richard Hurd (March 3, 1759), *Letters from a Late Eminent Prelate*, 1808.
20. Edmond Malone, "Maloniana" (1787), cited in Sir James Prior, *Life of Edmond Malone*, 1860, pp. 369–70.
21. Joseph Priestley, *Lectures on History and General Policy*, 1788, Lecture 27.
22. Edward Gibbon, *Memoirs of My Life*, 1792–93.
23. Friedrich Schlegel, *Lectures on the History of Literature*, 1815.
24. Thomas Babington Macaulay, "History" (1828), *Critical, Historical, and Miscellaneous Essays*, 1860, Volume 1, p. 420.
25. Thomas Arnold, *Introductory Lectures on Modern History*, 1842, Lecture 5.
26. Edmund Gosse, *A Short History of Modern English Literature*, 1897, pp. 256–57.
27. John Leland, *A View of the Principal Deistical Writers*, 1754–56.
28. Thomas Reid, Letter to David Hume (March 18, 1763).
29. James Boswell, *Life of Johnson*, 1791.
30. Robert Hall, "The Sentiments Proper to the Present Crisis" (1803), *Miscellaneous Works and Remains*, 1846, pp. 357–58.
31. William Hamilton, "Fragments on the Scottish Philosophy" (1836), *Lectures on Metaphysics and Logic*, 1859.
32. John Stuart Mill, "Bentham" (1838), *Dissertations and Discussions*, 1859, Volume 1.
33. Ralph Waldo Emerson, "Literature," *English Traits*, 1856.
34. John Hunt, "David Hume," *Contemporary Review*, May 1869, pp. 99–100.
35. Friedrich Überweg, *History of Philosophy*, 1871, tr. George S. Morris.
36. James McCosh, *The Scottish Philosophy*, 1874, pp. 145–47.
37. Thomas Henry Huxley, *Hume*, 1879, pp. 207–8.
38. William Knight, *Hume*, 1886, pp. 231–33.
39. Henry Calderwood, *David Hume*, 1888, p. 32.
40. Henry Craik, *A Century of Scottish History*, 1901, pp. 440–41.
41. David Hume, "My Own Life" (1776), *The Life of David Hume, Esq.*, 1777.
42. Walter Savage Landor, "David Hume and John Home," *Imaginary Conversations: Second Series*, 1824.
43. Eugene Lawrence, "David Hume," *The Lives of the British Historians*, 1855, Volume 2, pp. 194–215.
44. Sir Leslie Stephen, *History of English Thought in the Eighteenth Century*, 1876.
45. Josiah Royce, *The Spirit of Modern Philosophy*, 1892, pp. 93–98.

SAMUEL JOHNSON

1. Tobias Smollett, Letter to John Wilkes (March 16, 1759).
2. Ozias Humphrey, Letter to William Humphrey (September 19, 1764).
3. Cuthbert Shaw, *The Race*, 1766.
4. Horace Walpole, *Memoirs of the Reign of King George the Third*, 1771.
5. Samuel Johnson, *Diaries, Prayers, and Annals*, April 7, 1776.
6. Fanny Burney, Letter to Samuel Crisp (March 28, 1777).
7. Hannah More (c. April 1782), *Memoirs of the Life and Correspondence of Mrs. Hannah More*, ed. William Roberts, 1835, Volume 1, p. 249.
8. Anna Seward, Letter to Miss Weston (October 29, 1784).
9. John Hoole, *Journal Narrative Relative to Doctor John-son's Last Illness Three Weeks before His Death*, November 28, 1784.
10. William Windham, *Diary*, December 13, 1784.
11. Charles Burney, Letter to Samuel Parr (December 21, 1784), cited in *The Works of Samuel Parr*, ed. John Johnstone, 1828, Volume 1, p. 535.
12. James Boswell, *Journal of a Tour to the Hebrides with Samuel Johnson, LL.D.*, 1785.
13. George Steevens, "Johnsoniana," *Gentleman's Magazine*, January 1785.
14. Hester Lynch Piozzi, *Anecdotes of the Late Samuel Johnson, LL.D.*, 1786.
15. Soame Jenyns, "Epitaph on Dr. Samuel Johnson," c. 1787.
16. Sir John Hawkins, *The Life of Samuel Johnson, LL.D.*, 1787.
17. John Wolcot (as "Peter Pindar"), *A Poetical and Congratulatory Epistle to James Boswell, Esq., on His Journal of a Tour to the Hebrides with the Celebrated Doctor Johnson*, 1787.
18. George Horne, *The Olla Podrida*, No. 13 (June 9, 1787).
19. Sir Joshua Reynolds (c. 1792), cited in C. R. Leslie, Tom Taylor, *Life and Times of Sir Joshua Reynolds*, 1865.
20. Thomas Carlyle, "Boswell's *Life of Johnson*" (1832), *Critical and Miscellaneous Essays*, 1839–69.
21. Samuel Taylor Coleridge, *Table Talk*, July 4, 1833.
22. Nathaniel Hawthorne, "Lichfield and Uttoxeter," *Our Old Home*, 1863.
23. Ralph Waldo Emerson, "Clubs," *Society and Solitude*, 1870.
24. Horace Walpole, "General Criticism on Dr. Johnson's Writings" (c. 1779), *Works*, 1798, Volume 4, pp. 361–62.
25. William Cowper, "Epitaph on Dr. Johnson," 1785.
26. John Courtenay, *A Poetical Review of the Literary and Moral Character of the Late Samuel Johnson, LL.D.*, 1786.
27. Anna Laetitia Barbauld, Letter to John Aikin (May 1791), *Works*, 1825, Volume 2, p. 158.
28. George Mason, *Gentleman's Magazine*, 1796, pp. 758–59.
29. Samuel Taylor Coleridge, *A Course of Lectures* (1818), *Literary Remains*, ed. Henry Nelson Coleridge, 1836, Volume 1, p. 239.
30. William Hazlitt, *Lectures on the English Comic Writers*, 1819.
31. George Gordon, Lord Byron, *Don Juan*, 1823, Canto 13, Stanza 7.
32. W. B. O. Peabody, "Croker's Boswell," *North American Review*, January 1832, pp. 100–104.
33. Hippolyte Taine, *History of English Literature*, tr. H. Van Laun, 1871, Bk. 3, Ch. 6.
34. Sir Leslie Stephen, *History of English Thought in the Eighteenth Century*, 1876.
35. Richard Holt Hutton, "Mr. Leslie Stephen on Johnson" (1878), *Criticisms of Contemporary Thought and Thinkers*, 1894, Volume 1, pp. 164–70.
36. C. R. L. Fletcher, *The Development of English Prose Style*, 1881, p. 19.
37. John Ruskin, *Praeterita*, 1885, Volume 1, p. 416.
38. Henry Craik, "Samuel Johnson," *English Prose*, ed. Henry Craik, 1895, Volume 4, pp. 135–40.
39. George Saintsbury, *A Short History of English Literature*, 1898, pp. 615–17.
40. Thomas Gray, Letter to Horace Walpole (c. January 1748).
41. Oliver Goldsmith, *The Beauties of English Poesy*, 1767.
42. James Boswell, *Life of Johnson*, 1791.
43. George Gordon, Lord Byron, *Journals*, January 9, 1821.

44. W. J. Courthope, "Samuel Johnson," *The English Poets*, ed. Thomas Humphry Ward, 1880, Volume 3, pp. 245–47.
45. Samuel Richardson, Letter to Edward Cave (August 9, 1750).
46. Lady Mary Wortley Montagu, Letter to the Countess of Bute (July 23, 1754).
47. William Shenstone, Letter to Richard Graves (February 9, 1760).
48. Samuel Taylor Coleridge, *Table Talk*, November 1, 1833.
49. Henry, Lord Brougham, "Johnson," *Lives of Men of Letters and Science Who Flourished in the Time of George III*, 1846, Volume 2, pp. 32–34.
50. Philip Dormer Stanhope, Earl of Chesterfield, *The World*, No. 100 (November 28, 1754).
51. David Garrick, "On Johnson's Dictionary," 1755.
52. Adam Smith, *Edinburgh Review*, May 1755.
53. James Beattie, "Remarks on the Usefulness of Classical Learning" (1769), *Essays on Poetry and Music* (1776), 1779, pp. 511–12.
54. James Boswell, *Life of Johnson*, 1791.
55. Noah Webster, Letter to David Ramsay (October 1807).
56. Charles Mackay, *Through the Long Day*, 1887, Volume 2, pp. 395–96.
57. Fanny Burney, *Diary*, July 17, 1768.
58. James Boswell, *Life of Johnson*, 1791.
59. Sir Walter Scott, "Samuel Johnson" (1821), *Lives of the Novelists*, 1825.
60. John Wilson (as "Christopher North"), *Noctes Ambrosianae* (April 1829), 1854.
61. Thomas Babington Macaulay, "Samuel Johnson" (1856), *Critical, Historical, and Miscellaneous Essays*, 1860, Volume 6, pp. 197–98.
62. Walter Raleigh, *The English Novel*, 1894, pp. 203–6.
63. William Cowper, Letter to William Unwin (January 17, 1782).
64. Sir James Mackintosh (December 1811), cited in Robert James Mackintosh, *Memoirs of the Life of Sir James Mackintosh*, 1835, Volume 2, pp. 170–71.
65. Thomas De Quincey, "Postscript Respecting Johnson's Life of Milton" (1859), *Collected Writings*, ed. David Masson, Volume 4, pp. 113–17.
66. Sir Leslie Stephen, *Samuel Johnson*, 1878, pp. 186–87.
67. Lytton Strachey, "The Lives of the Poets" (1906), *Literary Essays*, 1949, pp. 94–97.
68. Thomas Babington Macaulay, "Samuel Johnson" (1831), *Critical, Historical, and Miscellaneous Essays*, 1860, Volume 2, pp. 398–426.
69. Thomas Carlyle, "The Hero as Man of Letters," *On Heroes, Hero-Worship and the Heroic in History*, 1841.
70. Sir Leslie Stephen, "Dr. Johnson's Writings," *Hours in a Library* (1874–79), 1904, Volume 2, pp. 146–88.
71. Matthew Arnold, "Johnson's Lives," *Macmillan's Magazine*, June 1878, pp. 153–60.
72. Augustine Birrell, "Dr. Johnson" (1885), *Obiter Dicta: Second Series*, 1887, pp. 126–48.
73. George Birkbeck Hill, "Dr. Johnson as a Radical," *Contemporary Review*, June 1889, pp. 888–89.
74. Walter Raleigh, "Samuel Johnson" (1907), *Six Essays on Johnson*, 1910, pp. 9–31.

EDWARD GIBBON

1. John Byrom, Letter to Mrs. Byrom (May 15, 1737), *The Private Journal and Literary Remains of John Byrom*, ed. Richard Parkinson, 1856, Volume 2, Pt. 1, p. 158.
2. James Boswell, Letter to William Temple (May 3, 1779).
3. Fanny Burney, Letter to Samuel Crisp (1782).
4. Edmond Malone, "Maloniana" (1787), cited in Sir James Prior, *Life of Edmond Malone*, 1860, p. 382.
5. Edward Gibbon, *Memoirs of My Life*, 1792–93.
6. Mary Berry, *Journal*, July 6, 1803.
7. George Gordon, Lord Byron, Letter to John Murray (June 27, 1816).
8. Sir James Bland Burges (1818), cited in *Selections from the Letters and Correspondence of Sir James Bland Burges*, ed. James Hutton, 1885, pp. 59–61.
9. George Colman the Younger, *Random Records*, 1830, Volume 1, pp. 121–22.
10. Thomas De Quincey, "The Lake Poets: Southey, Wordsworth, and Coleridge," *Literary and Lake Reminiscences*, 1839.
11. Samuel Rogers, *Table Talk*, c. 1855.
12. William Cowper, Letter to John Newton (July 27, 1783).
13. Hannah More, *Diary* (January 19, 1784), *Memoirs of the Life and Correspondence of Mrs. Hannah More*, ed. William Roberts, 1835, Volume 2, p. 413.
14. Walter Savage Landor, "Gibbon," 1854.
15. Ralph Waldo Emerson, "Books," *Society and Solitude*, 1870.
16. George Saintsbury, "Edward Gibbon," *English Prose*, ed. Henry Craik, 1895, Volume 4, pp. 455–59.
17. Edward Gibbon, "Preface" to the First Edition of *The History of the Decline and Fall of the Roman Empire*, 1776.
18. Horace Walpole, Letter to Edward Gibbon (February 14, 1776).
19. David Hume, Letter to Edward Gibbon (March 18, 1776).
20. William Robertson, Letter to Edward Gibbon (May 12, 1781).
21. Horace Walpole, Letter to William Mason (January 27, 1781).
22. Edward Gibbon, "Preface" to the Fourth Volume of the Quarto Edition of *The History of the Decline and Fall of the Roman Empire*, 1788.
23. Horace Walpole, Letter to Thomas Barret (June 5, 1788).
24. James Beattie, Letter to the Duchess of Gordon (November 20, 1788), cited in Sir William Forbes, *An Account of the Life and Writings of James Beattie, LL.D.* (1806), 1824, Volume 2, pp. 225–26.
25. Adam Smith, Letter to Edward Gibbon (December 10, 1788).
26. Richard Porson, "Preface" to *Letters to Mr. Archdeacon Travis*, 1790, pp. xxviii–xxxi.
27. John Foster, Letter to John Fawcett (May 23, 1805), *The Life and Correspondence of John Foster*, ed. J. E. Ryland, 1846, Volume 1, p. 262.
28. Friedrich Schlegel, *Lectures on the History of Literature*, 1815.
29. Thomas Carlyle, Letter to Robert Mitchell (February 16, 1818).
30. Henry Crabb Robinson, *Diary*, April 7, 1820.
31. F. P. G. Guizot, "Preface" to *The History of the Decline and Fall of the Roman Empire*, 1828.
32. Samuel Taylor Coleridge, *Table Talk*, August 15, 1833.
33. John Stuart Mill, "Carlyle's French Revolution," 1837.
34. Thomas Babington Macaulay, *Diary* (December 22, 1838), cited in G. Otto Trevelyan, *The Life and Letters of Lord Macaulay*, 1876, Volume 2, p. 40.
35. Edgar Allan Poe, *Marginalia* (1844), *Essays and Reviews*, ed. G. R. Thompson, 1984, pp. 1320–21.
36. C. A. Sainte-Beuve, "Gibbon," 1853.
37. Samuel Rogers, *Table Talk*, c. 1855.
38. Henry Thomas Buckle, *History of Civilization in England*, 1857–61.

39. Frederick Denison Maurice, *Moral and Metaphysical Philosophy*, 1862.
40. John Burroughs, "Ruskin's Judgment of Gibbon and Darwin," *Critic*, May 1, 1886, p. 213.
41. Edward A. Freeman, Letter to Goldwin Smith (April 25, 1888), cited in W. R. W. Stephens, *The Life and Letters of Edward A. Freeman*, 1895, Volume 2, p. 380.
42. Woodrow Wilson, "Mere Literature," *Mere Literature and Other Essays*, 1896, p. 22.
43. Edmund Gosse, *A Short History of Modern English Literature*, 1897, pp. 258–60.
44. Herbert Paul, "Gibbon's Life and Letters," *Nineteenth Century*, February 1897, pp. 306–7.
45. Maria Josepha Holroyd, Letter (1793), cited in *The Girlhood of Maria Josepha Holroyd*, ed. J. H. Adeane, 1896, p. 273.
46. John, Lord Sheffield, "Preface" to *Miscellaneous Works of Edward Gibbon, Esquire*, 1796, Volume 1, pp. iii–vii.
47. Arthur Young, *Autobiography* (entry for May 1, 1796), ed. M. Bentham-Edwards, 1898, pp. 258–59.
48. Earl of Sheffield, "Introduction" to *The Autobiographies of Edward Gibbon*, ed. John Murray, 1896, pp. v–ix.
49. Frederic Harrison, "The New Memoirs of Edward Gibbon," *Forum*, February 1897, pp. 754–55.
50. H. H. Milman, "Guizot's Edition of Gibbon," *Quarterly Review*, January 1834, pp. 286–307.
51. Walter Bagehot, "Edward Gibbon" (1856), *Collected Works*, ed. Norman St. John-Stevas, 1965, Volume 1, pp. 378–91.
52. Sir Leslie Stephen, "Gibbon's Autobiography," *Studies of a Biographer*, 1898, Volume 1, pp. 172–87.
53. J. B. Bury, "Introduction" (1896) to *The History of the Decline and Fall of the Roman Empire*, 1909, pp. vii–xxii.

ROBERT BURNS

1. Robert Burns, Letter to Frances Dunlop (July 10, 1796).
2. Robert Burns, Letter to George Thomson (July 12, 1796).
3. Maria Riddell, Letter to *Dumfries Journal* (August 7, 1796), cited in James Currie, *The Life of Robert Burns*, 1800.
4. Dugald Stewart, Letter to James Currie (c. 1800), cited in James Currie, *The Life of Robert Burns*, 1800.
5. Dorothy Wordsworth, *Journal*, August 18, 1803.
6. William Wordsworth, "At the Grave of Burns," 1803.
7. John Keats, "On Visiting the Tomb of Burns," 1818.
8. Sir Walter Scott, Letter to John Gibson Lockhart (1827), cited in John Gibson Lockhart, *Memoirs of the Life of Sir Walter Scott*, 1837–38.
9. Thomas De Quincey, "A Liverpool Literary Coterie" (1837), *Collected Writings*, ed. David Masson, Volume 2, p. 134.
10. George Gilfillan, "Life of Robert Burns," *The Poetical Works of Robert Burns*, 1856, Volume 1, pp. 29–30.
11. Nathaniel Hawthorne, "Some of the Haunts of Burns" (1860), *Old Our Home*, 1863.
12. Dante Gabriel Rossetti, Letter to William Bell Scott (August 25, 1871).
13. L. M. Roberts, "The Burns and Dunlop Correspondence," *Fortnightly Review*, November 1895, p. 669.
14. Henry Mackenzie, *The Lounger*, No. 97 (December 9, 1786).
15. William Cowper, Letter to Samuel Rose (July 24, 1787).
16. William Cowper, Letter to Samuel Rose (August 27, 1787).
17. Joseph Ritson, "A Historical Essay on Scotish Song," *Scotish Song*, 1794, Volume 1, pp. 74–75.
18. James Currie, *The Life of Robert Burns*, 1800.

19. David Irving, "The Life of Robert Burns," *The Lives of the Scottish Poets*, 1804, Volume 2, pp. 487–90.
20. Mary Russell Mitford, Letter to Sir William Elford (November 10, 1813).
21. George Gordon, Lord Byron, *Journal*, December 13, 1813.
22. Gilbert Burns, Letter to Alexander Peterkin (September 29, 1814), cited in Alexander Peterkin, *Life and Works of Robert Burns*, 1814.
23. William Wordsworth, *Letter to a Friend of Robert Burns*, 1816.
24. William Hazlitt, *Lectures on the English Poets*, 1818.
25. John Keats, Letter to J. H. Reynolds (July 13, 1818).
26. Thomas Campbell, *Specimens of the British Poets*, 1819.
27. William H. Prescott, "Scottish Song" (1826), *Biographical and Critical Miscellanies*, 1845, pp. 547–48.
28. Walter Savage Landor, "Southey and Porson: Second Conversation," *Imaginary Conversations: Third Series*, 1828.
29. John Gibson Lockhart, *Life of Robert Burns*, 1828, pp. 225–26.
30. Allan Cunningham, *The Life of Robert Burns*, *The Works of Robert Burns*, 1834, Volume 1, pp. 365–66.
31. Elizabeth Barrett Browning, *A Vision of Poets*, 1844, ll. 403–5.
32. David Macbeth Moir, "Stanzas for the Burns Festival," 1844.
33. Aubrey De Vere, "To Burns's Highland Mary," 1847.
34. Arthur Hugh Clough, "Lecture on the Development of English Literature" (1852), *Prose Remains*, 1888, p. 350.
35. John Greenleaf Whittier, "Burns: On Receiving a Sprig of Heather in Blossom," 1854.
36. Ralph Waldo Emerson, "Robert Burns" (1859), *Works*, 1904, Volume 11, pp. 439–43.
37. Oliver Wendell Holmes, "For the Burns Centennial Celebration," 1859.
38. James Russell Lowell, "At the Burns Centennial," 1859.
39. William Cullen Bryant, "An Address on Burns" (1871), *Prose Writings*, ed. Parke Godwin, 1884, Volume 2, p. 320.
40. Joaquin Miller, "Burns and Byron" (1870), *Songs of the Sierras*, 1871, pp. 259–60.
41. Hippolyte Taine, *History of English Literature*, tr. H. Van Laun, 1871, Bk. 4, Ch. 1.
42. John Bascom, *Philosophy of English Literature*, 1874, pp. 220–22.
43. William Michael Rossetti, "Robert Burns," *Lives of Famous Poets*, 1878, p. 189.
44. George William Curtis, "Robert Burns" (1880), *Orations and Addresses*, ed. Charles Eliot Norton, 1894, Volume 3, pp. 317–19.
45. Henry Wadsworth Longfellow, "Robert Burns," *Harper's New Monthly Magazine*, August 1880, pp. 321–23.
46. William Jolly, *Robert Burns at Mossgiel*, 1881, pp. 125–27.
47. Agnes Maule Machar, "An Evening with Burns," *Century Magazine*, January 1884, p. 479.
48. Andrew Lang, "To Robert Burns," *Letters to Dead Authors*, 1886.
49. Aubrey De Vere, "The Two Chief Schools of English Poetry," *Essays Chiefly on Poetry*, 1887, Volume 2, pp. 120–22.
50. Charles Mackay, *Through the Long Day*, 1887, Volume 1, pp. 147–48.
51. John Stuart Blackie, *Life of Robert Burns*, 1888, pp. 157–61.
52. James Whitcomb Riley, "To Robert Burns," 1888.

53. Hugh Walker, *Three Centuries of Scottish Literature*, 1893, Volume 2, pp. 147–50.
54. Ernest Rhys, "Introduction" to *The Lyric Poems of Robert Burns*, 1895, pp. 9–10.
55. Algernon Charles Swinburne, "Robert Burns," *Nineteenth Century*, February 1896, pp. 181–84.
56. Edward Dowden, *The French Revolution and English Literature*, 1897, p. 146.
57. Andrew J. George, *Carlyle's Essay on Burns*, 1897, pp. 114–15.
58. W. E. Henley, "Robert Burns: Life, Genius, Achievement," *The Complete Poetical Works of Robert Burns*, 1897, Volume 1, pp. 13–14.
59. Walter Raleigh, *Style*, 1897, pp. 76–77.
60. Francis Thompson, "Mr. Henley's *Burns*," *Academy*, March 6, 1897, p. 274.
61. Henry Grey Graham, "Robert Burns," *Scottish Men of Letters in the Eighteenth Century*, 1901, pp. 382–83.
62. Robert Burns, "Preface" to *Poems, Chiefly in the Scottish Dialect*, 1786.
63. Anna Laetitia Barbauld, Letter to Dr. Aikin (January 31, 1787), *The Works of Anna Laetitia Barbauld*, 1825, Volume 2, p. 151.
64. John Moore, Letter to Robert Burns (May 23, 1787).
65. Frances Dunlop, Letter to Robert Burns (September 23, 1789).
66. James Currie, *The Life of Robert Burns*, 1800.
67. Charlotte Brontë, Letter to W. S. Williams (April 2, 1849).
68. J. C. Shairp, *On Poetic Interpretation of Nature*, 1877, pp. 224–30.
69. J. C. Shairp, *Robert Burns*, 1879, pp. 201–5.
70. Alexander Bain, *English Composition and Rhetoric*, 1888, Pt. 2, pp. 157–58.
71. W. E. Henley, Thomas F. Henderson, *The Poetry of Robert Burns*, 1896, Volume 1, pp. 361–62, Note.
72. Sir Archibald Geikie, *Types of Scenery and Their Influence on Literature*, 1898, pp. 26–31.
73. Charles Whibley, "Burns," *Macmillan's Magazine*, January 1898, pp. 182–83.
74. Robert Burns, Letter to Dr. John Moore (August 2, 1787).
75. Thomas Carlyle, "Burns" (1828), *Critical and Miscellaneous Essays*, 1839–69.
76. Matthew Arnold, "Introduction" to *The English Poets*, ed. Thomas Humphry Ward, 1880, Volume 1, pp. xli–xlvi.
77. John Service, "Robert Burns," *The English Poets*, ed. Thomas Humphry Ward, 1880, Volume 3, pp. 515–23.
78. Robert Louis Stevenson, "Some Aspects of Robert Burns," *Familiar Studies of Men and Books*, 1882, pp. 95–103.
79. Walt Whitman, "Robert Burns as Poet and Person" (1882/1886), *Prose Works*, ed. Floyd Stovall, 1963, Volume 2, pp. 558–68.
80. Gabriel Setoun, "Summary and Estimate," *Robert Burns*, 1896, pp. 148–60.

RICHARD BRINSLEY SHERIDAN

1. Fanny Burney, *Diary*, 1779.
2. Samuel Taylor Coleridge, "To Richard Brinsley Sheridan, Esq.," 1795.
3. Francis Horner, *Journal* (January 29, 1806), *Memoirs and Correspondence of Francis Horner*, ed. Leonard Horner, 1843, Volume 1, p. 357.
4. Richard Brinsley Sheridan, Letter to Samuel Rogers (May 15, 1816).
5. George Gordon, Lord Byron, "Monody on the Death of the Right Hon. R. B. Sheridan," 1816, ll. 47–118.
6. Thomas Moore, "Lines on the Death of Sheridan," 1816.
7. Caroline Norton, "Books of Gossip: Sheridan and His Biographers," *Macmillan's Magazine*, January 1861, p. 177.
8. Hall Caine, *Academy*, September 15, 1883, pp. 171–72.
9. Marquess of Dufferin and Ava, "Introduction" to *Sheridan: A Biography* by W. Fraser Rae, 1896, Volume 1, pp. viii–ix.
10. W. Fraser Rae, *Sheridan: A Biography*, 1896, Volume 1, pp. 346–47.
11. William Ewart Gladstone, "Sheridan," *Nineteenth Century*, June 1896, p. 1037.
12. Sir Nathaniel Wraxall (1784), *Posthumous Memoirs of His Own Time*, 1836, Volume 1, pp. 39–41.
13. Sir James Mackintosh, *Journal* (February 7, 1812), cited in Robert James Mackintosh, *Memoirs of the Life of Sir James Mackintosh*, 1853, Volume 2, pp. 203–4.
14. George Gordon, Lord Byron, *Journal*, December 17–18, 1813.
15. William Hazlitt, *Lectures on the English Comic Writers*, 1819.
16. Sir Walter Scott, "An Essay on the Drama," 1819.
17. Benjamin Robert Haydon, Letter to Mary Russell Mitford (December 10, 1825).
18. John Wilson Croker, "Memoirs of Sheridan by Dr. Watkins and Mr. Moore," *Quarterly Review*, March 1826, pp. 592–93.
19. Francis, Lord Jeffrey, "Moore's Life of Sheridan," *Edinburgh Review*, December 1826, pp. 7–8.
20. Thomas Babington Macaulay, "Machiavelli" (1827), *Critical, Historical, and Miscellaneous Essays*, 1860, Volume 1, p. 295.
21. Oswald Crawfurd, *English Comic Dramatists*, 1883, p. 262.
22. Edmund Gosse, *A History of Eighteenth Century Literature*, 1888, pp. 337–38.
23. William Winter, "Sheridan and *The School for Scandal*," *Old Shrines and Ivy*, 1892, pp. 225–30.
24. F. Marion Crawford, *The Novel: What It Is*, 1893, p. 100.
25. Sir Henry Irving, cited in W. Fraser Rae, *Sheridan: A Biography*, 1896, Volume 2, p. 322.
26. George Saintsbury, *A Short History of English Literature*, 1898, p. 641.
27. John Watkins, *Memoirs of Richard Brinsley Sheridan*, 1817, Volume 1, pp. 145–46.
28. Samuel Rogers, *Table Talk*, c. 1855.
29. H. Barton Baker, "Richard Brinsley Sheridan," *Gentleman's Magazine*, September 1878, pp. 307–8.
30. Sir Squire Bancroft, cited in W. Fraser Rae, *Sheridan: A Biography*, 1896, Volume 2, p. 321.
31. John Watkins, *Memoirs of Richard Brinsley Sheridan*, 1817, Volume 1, pp. 147–48.
32. William Bodham Donne, "Songs from the Dramatists" (1854), *Essays on the Drama*, 1858, p. 117.
33. Brander Matthews, "Pinafore's Predecessor," *Harper's New Monthly Magazine*, March 1880, pp. 504–8.
34. David Garrick, Letter to Richard Brinsley Sheridan (May 12, 1777).
35. Horace Walpole, Letter to William Mason (May 16, 1777).
36. Charles Lamb, "On the Artificial Comedy of the Last Century" (1822), *Essays of Elia*, 1823.
37. Brander Matthews, "Introduction to *The School for Scandal*," *Sheridan's Comedies*, 1891, pp. 196–99.
38. Horace Walpole, Letter to the Countess of Upper Ossory (February 9, 1787).
39. Gilbert Elliot, First Earl of Minto, Letter to Lady Elliot (June 5, 1788), cited in the Countess of Minto, *Life and Letters of Sir Gilbert Elliot*, 1874, Volume 1, pp. 208–9.
40. Horace Walpole, Letter to Thomas Barret (June 5, 1788).

41. Edward Gibbon, Letter to Lord Sheffield (June 14, 1788).
42. Thomas Babington Macaulay, "Warren Hastings" (1841), *Critical, Historical, and Miscellaneous Essays*, 1860, Volume 5, pp. 121–22.
43. A. V. Dicey, "Sheridan," *Nation*, August 14, 1884, p. 137.
44. Lorenzo Sears, *The History of Oratory*, 1895, pp. 295–96.
45. Thomas Moore, *Memoirs of the Life of Richard Brinsley Sheridan*, 1825, Volume 1, pp. 245–56.
46. William Cullen Bryant, "The Character of Sheridan" (1826), *Prose Writings*, ed. Parke Godwin, 1884, Volume 2, pp. 366–69.
47. Leigh Hunt, "Biographical and Critical Sketch of Richard Brinsley Sheridan," *The Dramatic Works of Richard Brinsley Sheridan*, 1841.

48. George Gabriel Sigmond, "The Life of the Right Honourable Richard Brinsley Sheridan," *The Dramatic Works of Richard Brinsley Sheridan*, 1848.
49. Edwin P. Whipple, "Richard Brinsley Sheridan" (1848), *Essays and Reviews*, 1850, Volume 2, pp. 262–74.
50. Hippolyte Taine, *History of English Literature*, tr. H. Van Laun, 1871, Bk. 3, Ch. 1.
51. Margaret Oliphant, "His First Dramatic Works," *Sheridan*, 1883, pp. 49–55.
52. Richard Grant White, "Introduction" to *The Dramatic Works of Richard Brinsley Sheridan*, 1883, pp. xxxii–xlii.
53. Augustine Birrell, "Introduction" to *The School for Scandal and The Rivals*, 1896, pp. xvii–xxii.
54. G. S. Street, "Sheridan and Mr. Shaw," *Blackwood's Magazine*, June 1900, pp. 832–36.

Volume 4

JANE AUSTEN

1. Mary Russell Mitford, Letter to Sir William Elford (April 3, 1815).
2. Sir Samuel Egerton Brydges, *Autobiography*, 1834, Volume 2, p. 41.
3. James Edward Austen-Leigh, *A Memoir of Jane Austen*, 1870, Ch. 5.
4. Sir Walter Scott, Letter to Joanna Baillie (February 10, 1822).
5. Unsigned, "Mrs. Gore's *Women as They Are; or, The Manners of the Day*," *Edinburgh Review*, July 1830, pp. 449–50.
6. Frances Ann Kemble, *Record of a Girlhood*, July 31, 1831.
7. Sara Coleridge, Letter to Emily Trevenen (August 1834), *Memoirs and Letters of Sara Coleridge*, ed. Edith Coleridge, 1873, Volume 1, p. 75.
8. Henry Wadsworth Longfellow, *Journal*, May 23, 1839.
9. Thomas Babington Macaulay, "Madame D'Arblay" (1843), *Critical, Historical, and Miscellaneous Essays*, 1860, Volume 5, pp. 307–8.
10. George Henry Lewes, "Recent Novels: French and English," *Fraser's Magazine*, December 1847, p. 687.
11. Charlotte Brontë, Letter to George Henry Lewes (January 18, 1848).
12. George Eliot (?), "The Progress of Fiction as an Art," *Westminster Review*, October 1853, p. 358.
13. Elizabeth Barrett Browning, Letter to John Ruskin (November 5, 1855).
14. David Masson, *British Novelists and Their Styles*, 1859, pp. 188–89.
15. G. F. Chorley, "Miss Austen and Miss Mitford," *Quarterly Review*, January 1870, pp. 200–203.
16. T. E. Kebbel, "Jane Austen," *Fortnightly Review*, February 1870, pp. 190–93.
17. Edward FitzGerald, Letter to W. F. Pollock (December 24, 1870).
18. John W. Hales, *Notes and Essays on Shakespeare*, 1873, p. 72.
19. George William Curtis, "Editor's Easy Chair," *Harper's New Monthly Magazine*, January 1881, pp. 308–9.
20. Henry Morley, *Of English Literature in the Reign of Victoria*, 1881, pp. 111–12.
21. George Barnett Smith, "More Views of Jane Austen," *Gentleman's Magazine*, January 1885, pp. 44–45.
22. Thomas Wentworth Higginson, *Women and Men*, 1887, pp. 156–57.
23. James Ashcroft Noble, *Academy*, August 11, 1889, pp. 96–97.

24. William Dean Howells, *Criticism and Fiction*, 1891, Sec. 15.
25. George Saintsbury, *A History of Nineteenth Century Literature*, 1896, pp. 128–31.
26. Edmund Gosse, *A Short History of Modern English Literature*, 1897, pp. 295–97.
27. Vida D. Scudder, *Social Ideals in English Letters*, 1898, pp. 129–30.
28. Janet Harper, "The Renascence of Jane Austen," *Westminster Review*, April 1900, p. 445.
29. Mary Russell Mitford, Letter to Sir William Elford (December 20, 1814).
30. Henry Crabb Robinson, *Diary*, January 12, 1819.
31. Sir Walter Scott, *Journal*, March 14, 1826.
32. Henry Crabb Robinson, *Diary*, September 22, 1839.
33. Charlotte Brontë, Letter to George Henry Lewes (January 12, 1848).
34. Julia Kavanagh, "Miss Austen's Six Novels," *English Women of Letters*, 1863, Volume 2, pp. 195–96.
35. William C. Macready, *Diary*, February 15, 1834.
36. William C. Macready, *Diary*, July 10, 1836.
37. Charlotte Brontë, Letter to W. S. Williams (April 12, 1850).
38. Margaret Oliphant, *The Literary History of England, 1790–1825*, 1882, Volume 3, pp. 231–33.
39. Adolphus Alfred Jack, "Miss Austen," *Essays on the Novel*, 1897, pp. 263–67.
40. Maria Edgeworth, Letter to Mrs. Ruxton (February 21, 1818).
41. Henry Crabb Robinson, *Diary*, September 23, 1842.
42. Thomas Babington Macaulay, *Journal* (May 1, 1851), cited in G. Otto Trevelyan, *The Life and Letters of Lord Macaulay*, 1876, Volume 2, p. 249.
43. Thomas Babington Macaulay, *Journal* (August 12, 1854), cited in G. Otto Trevelyan, *The Life and Letters of Lord Macaulay*, 1876, Volume 2, p. 320.
44. Margaret Oliphant, *The Literary History of England, 1790–1825*, 1882, Volume 3, pp. 228–29.
45. Sir Francis Hastings Doyle, *Reminiscences*, 1886, pp. 353–57.
46. Sir Walter Scott, "*Emma*," *Quarterly Review*, October 1815, pp. 192–200.
47. Henry Austen, "Biographical Notice of the Author," *Northanger Abbey and Persuasion*, 1818.
48. Unsigned, "*Northanger Abbey* and *Persuasion*," *British Critic*, March 1818, pp. 296–301.
49. Archbishop Whately, "Modern Novels," *Quarterly Review*, January 1821, pp. 359–63, 375–76.
50. George Henry Lewes, "The Novels of Jane Austen,"

Blackwood's Edinburgh Magazine, July 1859, pp. 104–13.

51. W. F. Pollock, "British Novelists," *Fraser's Magazine*, January 1860, pp. 30–35.
52. Andrew Lang, "Letter to Jane Austen," *Letters to Dead Authors*, 1886.
53. Goldwin Smith, *Life of Jane Austen*, 1890, pp. 185–91.
54. W. B. Shubrick Clymer, "A Note on Jane Austen," *Scribner's Magazine*, March 1891, pp. 377–84.
55. Walter Raleigh, "Jane Austen," *The English Novel*, 1894, pp. 261–66.
56. Hiram M. Stanley, "*Mansfield Park*," *Essays on Literary Art*, 1897, pp. 47–53.
57. Wilbur L. Cross, "Jane Austen: The Critic of Romance and of Manners," *The Development of the English Novel*, 1899, pp. 115–24.
58. James Oliphant, "Scott and Jane Austen," *Victorian Novelists*, 1899, pp. 25–30.
59. Earl of Iddesleigh, "A Chat about Jane Austen's Novels," *Nineteenth Century*, May 1900, pp. 812–18.
60. Francis Hovey Stoddard, "Growth of Personality in Fiction," *The Evolution of the English Novel*, 1900, pp. 52–58.

JOHN KEATS

1. William Wordsworth, Letter to Benjamin Robert Haydon (January 16, 1820).
2. Joseph Severn, *Journal*, February 27, 1821.
3. William Maginn, Letter to William Blackwood (April 10, 1821), cited in Margaret Oliphant, *William Blackwood and His Sons*, 1897, Volume 1, p. 375.
4. Benjamin Robert Haydon, Letter to Mary Russell Mitford (April 21, 1821), *The Life, Letters and Table Talk of Benjamin Robert Haydon*, ed. Richard Henry Stoddard, 1876, pp. 207–9.
5. Percy Bysshe Shelley, "Fragment on Keats," 1821.
6. James Russell Lowell, "To the Spirit of Keats," 1841.
7. Aubrey De Vere, "To Keats," c. 1842.
8. Elizabeth Barrett Browning, A *Vision of Poets*, 1844, ll. 407–11.
9. Christina Rossetti, "On Keats," 1849.
10. Henry Wadsworth Longfellow, "Keats," A *Book of Sonnets*, 1873.
11. Charles Cowden Clarke, "Recollections of John Keats," *Recollections of Writers*, 1878, pp. 144, 155–56.
12. Dante Gabriel Rossetti, "John Keats," *Five English Poets*, 1880–81.
13. Andrew Lang, *Letters on Literature*, 1889, pp. 197–98.
14. David Masson, "The Story of Gifford and Keats," *Nineteenth Century*, April 1892, pp. 603–5.
15. William Watson, "The Punishment of Genius," *Excursions in Criticism*, 1893, pp. 23–27.
16. C. and J. Ollier, Letter to George Keats (April 29, 1817).
17. George Gordon, Lord Byron, Letter to John Murray (October 12, 1820).
18. George Gordon, Lord Byron, "A Second Letter to John Murray, Esq., on the Rev. W. L. Bowles's Strictures on the Life and Writings of Pope," 1821.
19. George Gordon, Lord Byron, Letter to Percy Bysshe Shelley (April 26, 1821).
20. George Gordon, Lord Byron, "Reply to Blackwood's *Edinburgh Magazine*," 1821, Note.
21. William Hazlitt, "On Effeminacy of Character," *Table-Talk*, 1821–22.
22. George Gordon, Lord Byron, *Don Juan*, 1823, Canto 11, Stanza 60.
23. William Hazlitt, "A Critical List of Authors Contained in This Volume," *Select British Poets*, 1824.

24. Edwin P. Whipple, "English Poets of the Nineteenth Century" (1845), *Essays and Reviews*, 1849, Volume 1, pp. 350–54.
25. Thomas De Quincey, "Gilfillan's Literary Portraits" (1845–46), *Collected Writings*, ed. David Masson, Volume 11, pp. 388–93.
26. Aubrey De Vere, *Edinburgh Review*, October 1849, pp. 424–26.
27. Walter Savage Landor, Letter to John Forster (March 24, 1850).
28. Walter Savage Landor, "English Hexameters" (1850), 1853.
29. George Meredith, "The Poetry of Keats," 1851.
30. Elizabeth Barrett Browning, *Aurora Leigh*, 1856, Bk. 1, ll. 1003–15.
31. John Ruskin, *Modern Painters*, 1856, Pt. 4, Ch. 16.
32. Matthew Arnold, *On Translating Homer*, 1861.
33. William Michael Rossetti, "John Keats," *Lives of Famous Poets*, 1878, pp. 359–61.
34. Matthew Arnold, "John Keats," *The English Poets*, ed. Thomas Humphry Ward, 1880, Volume 4, pp. 435–37.
35. Edmond Scherer, "Wordsworth and Modern Poetry" (1882), *Essays on English Literature*, tr. George Saintsbury, 1891, pp. 191–93.
36. John Campbell Shairp, "Poetic Style in Modern English Poetry," *Aspects of Poetry* (1881), 1882, pp. 126–28.
37. H. Buxton Forman, "Preface" to *The Poetical Works and Other Writings of John Keats*, 1883, Volume 1, pp. xviii–xxi.
38. Richard Henry Stoddard, "Introduction" to *The Poems of Algernon Charles Swinburne*, 1884, p. xi.
39. James Ashcroft Noble, "Leigh Hunt: The Man and the Writer" (1886), *The Sonnet in England and Other Essays*, 1893, p. 107.
40. Sidney Colvin, *Keats*, 1887, pp. 214–18.
41. William Michael Rossetti, *Life of Keats*, 1887, pp. 205–9.
42. Coventry Patmore, "Keats," *Principle in Art*, 1889, pp. 81–83.
43. John Addington Symonds, "A Comparison of Elizabethan with Victorian Poetry," *Essays Speculative and Suggestive*, 1890.
44. John Davidson, *Sentences and Paragraphs*, 1893, p. 12.
45. Hallam Tennyson, *Alfred Lord Tennyson: A Memoir*, 1897, Volume 2, p. 286.
46. John Keats, "Preface" to *Endymion*, 1818.
47. John Gibson Lockhart, "Cockney School of Poetry," *Blackwood's Magazine*, August 1818, pp. 519–22.
48. Percy Bysshe Shelley, Letter to John Keats (July 27, 1820).
49. Richard Monckton Milnes, Lord Houghton, *Life, Letters, and Literary Remains of John Keats*, 1848, Volume 2, pp. 103–8.
50. Hall Caine, "Keats," *Cobwebs of Criticism*, 1883, pp. 175–76.
51. Percy Bysshe Shelley, Letter to Marianne Hunt (November 11, 1820).
52. Percy Bysshe Shelley, Letter to Lord Byron (May 4, 1821).
53. George H. Calvert, *Brief Essays and Brevities*, 1874, p. 217.
54. Leigh Hunt, "On 'La Belle Dame sans Mercy,'" *Indicator*, May 10, 1820.
55. Rufus W. Griswold, "John Keats," *The Poets and Poetry of England in the Nineteenth Century*, 1844, p. 302.
56. Hugh Miller, "The Poesy of Intellect and Fancy" (1856), *Essays*, 1862, p. 452.
57. John Ruskin, *Modern Painters*, 1860, Pt. 6, Ch. 9.
58. Sidney Lanier, *The English Novel*, 1883, p. 95.
59. Margaret J. Preston, "Keats's Greek Urn," *Century Magazine*, February 1887, p. 586.

60. Joseph Severn, Letter to Harry Buxton Forman (February 5, 1878).
61. John Addington Symonds, Letter to Edmund Gosse (February 16, 1878).
62. Richard Henry Stoddard, "John Keats and Fanny Brawne," *Appleton's Journal*, April 1878, pp. 381–82.
63. John Wilson Croker, "Keats's *Endymion*," *Quarterly Review*, April 1818, pp. 204–8.
64. John Hamilton Reynolds, "Keats and the *Quarterly Review*," *Alfred, West of England Journal and General Advertiser*, October 6, 1818.
65. Peter George Patmore, "*Endymion, a Poetic Romance*," *London Magazine*, April 1820, pp. 381–89.
66. Leigh Hunt, *The Indicator*, No. 43 (August 2, 1820); No. 44 (August 9, 1820).
67. Francis, Lord Jeffrey, "Keats's *Poems*," *Edinburgh Review*, August 1820, pp. 203–7.
68. Percy Bysshe Shelley, *Adonais: An Elegy on the Death of John Keats*, 1821.
69. James Russell Lowell, "Keats" (1854), *Works*, Riverside ed., 1890, Volume 1, pp. 241–46.
70. Algernon Charles Swinburne, "Keats" (1882), *Miscellanies*, 1886, pp. 210–18.
71. Edmund C. Stedman, "Keats," *Century Magazine*, February 1884, pp. 600–602.
72. William John Courthope, "Keats' Place in English Poetry," *National Review*, September 1887, pp. 19–24.
73. Robert Bridges, "Critical Introduction" to *Poems of John Keats*, ed. G. Thorn Drury, 1894, Volume 1, pp. xl–lv, c–ciii.
74. Leon H. Vincent, "A Reading in the Letters of John Keats," *Atlantic*, September 1894, pp. 399–408.
75. Henry Van Dyke, "The Influence of Keats," *Century Magazine*, October 1895, pp. 910–13.
76. Montgomery Schuyler, "The Centenary of Keats," *Forum*, November 1895, pp. 359–63.
77. George Saintsbury, "The New Poetry," A *History of Nineteenth Century Literature*, 1896, pp. 86–91.
78. Frederic Harrison, "Lamb and Keats," *Contemporary Review*, July 1899, pp. 62–68.

PERCY BYSSHE SHELLEY

1. Henry Crabb Robinson, *Diary*, November 6, 1817.
2. William Hazlitt, "On Paradox and Commonplace," *Table-Talk*, 1821–22.
3. Mary Shelley, "Preface" to *Posthumous Poems*, 1824.
4. Marguerite, Countess of Blessington, *Conversations of Lord Byron*, 1834.
5. Thomas De Quincey, "Notes on Gilfillan's Literary Portraits" (1845–46), *Collected Writings*, ed. David Masson, Volume 11, pp. 375–77.
6. Leigh Hunt, *Autobiography*, 1850, Ch. 15.
7. Walter Savage Landor, "To Shelley," 1853.
8. Samuel Rogers, *Table Talk*, c. 1855.
9. Thomas Jefferson Hogg, *The Life of Percy Bysshe Shelley*, 1858.
10. Edward John Trelawny, *Recollections of the Last Days of Shelley and Byron*, 1858.
11. Thomas Love Peacock, "Memoirs of Percy Bysshe Shelley (II)," *Fraser's Magazine*, January 1860.
12. William Graham, *Last Links with Byron, Shelley, and Keats*, 1898, pp. 56–57.
13. Charles Lamb, Letter to Bernard Barton (August 17, 1824).
14. Thomas Lovell Beddoes, Letter to Thomas Forbes Kelsall (August 25, 1824).
15. John Wilson, "Preface" to *Blackwood's Edinburgh Magazine*, January–June 1826, p. xxix.

16. Thomas Babington Macaulay, "John Bunyan" (1830), *Critical, Historical, and Miscellaneous Essays*, 1860, Volume 2, p. 257.
17. Robert Browning, *Pauline*, 1833, ll. 151–71.
18. Leigh Hunt, *Imagination and Fancy*, 1844.
19. Edgar Allan Poe, "Elizabeth Barrett Browning" (1845), *Essays and Reviews*, ed. G. R. Thompson, 1984, pp. 139–40.
20. George Meredith, "The Poetry of Shelley," 1851.
21. David Macbeth Moir, *Sketches of the Poetical Literature of the Past Half-Century*, 1851, pp. 227–29.
22. Walter Bagehot, "Percy Bysshe Shelley" (1856), *Collected Works*, ed. Norman St. John-Stevas, Volume 1, pp. 466–68.
23. Hippolyte Taine, *History of English Literature*, tr. H. Van Laun, 1871, Bk. 4, Ch. 1.
24. John Addington Symonds, *Shelley*, 1878, pp. 183–84.
25. Dante Gabriel Rossetti, "Percy Bysshe Shelley," *Five English Poets*, 1880–81.
26. Harriet Monroe, "With a Copy of Shelley," *Century Magazine*, December 1889, p. 313.
27. Edmund Gosse, "Shelley in 1892" (1892), *Questions at Issue*, 1893, pp. 208–15.
28. Algernon Charles Swinburne, "The Centenary of Shelley," 1892.
29. George Saintsbury, A *History of Nineteenth Century Literature*, 1896, p. 86.
30. John Cordy Jeaffreson, *The Real Shelley*, 1885, Volume 1, pp. 117–19.
31. Walter Raleigh, *The English Novel*, 1894, pp. 251–52.
32. Unsigned, *Blackwood's Edinburgh Magazine*, September 1820, p. 680.
33. Unsigned, *Quarterly Review*, October 1821, pp. 175–76.
34. William P. Trent, "Apropos of Shelley," *The Authority of Criticism and Other Essays*, 1899, pp. 86–87.
35. William Godwin, Letter to Mary Shelley (March 30, 1820), cited in C. Kegan Paul, *William Godwin: His Friends and Contemporaries*, 1876, Volume 2, p. 272.
36. R. Pickett Scott, *The Place of Shelley among the Poets of His Time*, 1878, pp. 32–36.
37. William Hazlitt, "Shelley's Posthumous Poems," *Edinburgh Review*, July 1824, pp. 494–98.
38. Mary Shelley, "Preface" to *The Poetical Works of Percy Bysshe Shelley*, 1839.
39. Edwin P. Whipple, "English Poets of the Nineteenth Century" (1845), *Essays and Reviews*, 1850, Volume 1, pp. 308–17.
40. Robert Browning, "Introduction" to *Letters of Percy Bysshe Shelley*, 1852.
41. Algernon Charles Swinburne, "Notes on the Text of Shelley," *Fortnightly Review*, May 1869, pp. 555–59.
42. Sir Leslie Stephen, "Godwin and Shelley" (1879), *Hours in a Library* (1874–79), 1904, Volume 3, pp. 377–406.
43. Stopford A. Brooke, "Some Thoughts on Shelley," *Macmillan's Magazine*, June 1880, pp. 124–35.
44. Edward Dowden, "Last Words on Shelley" (1887), *Transcripts and Studies*, 1888, pp. 93–111.
45. W. B. Yeats, "The Philosophy of Shelley's Poetry" (1900), *Ideas of Good and Evil*, 1903, pp. 128–41.
46. A. C. Bradley, "Shelley's View of Poetry" (1904), *Oxford Lectures on Poetry*, 1909, pp. 151–74.

GEORGE GORDON, LORD BYRON

1. Maria Edgeworth, Letter to Sophy Ruxton (May 16, 1813).
2. George Ticknor, *Journal* (June 20, 1815), *Life, Letters, and Journals of George Ticknor*, ed. Anna Ticknor, 1876, Volume 1, pp. 58–60.

3. Sydney Smith, Letter to Francis, Lord Jeffrey (March 1816).
4. Samuel Taylor Coleridge, Letter (c. May 1816).
5. Thomas Carlyle, Letter to Jane Welsh (May 19, 1824).
6. Thomas Medwin, *Conversations of Lord Byron*, 1824.
7. Sir Walter Scott, "Death of Lord Byron" (1824), *Prose Works*, 1861, Volume 4, pp. 344–49.
8. Leigh Hunt, *Lord Byron and Some of His Contemporaries*, 1828, pp. 82–86.
9. Marguerite, Countess of Blessington, *Conversations of Lord Byron*, 1834.
10. Matthew Arnold, "Stanzas from the Grande Chartreuse," 1855, ll. 133–38.
11. Samuel Rogers, *Table Talk*, c. 1855.
12. Edward John Trelawny, *Recollections of the Last Days of Shelley and Byron*, 1858.
13. Joaquin Miller, "At Lord Byron's Tomb" (1870), *Poetical Works*, ed. Stuart P. Sherman, 1923, pp. 410–11.
14. William Graham, *Last Links with Byron, Shelley, and Keats*, 1898, pp. 31–32.
15. Henry, Lord Brougham, "Lord Byron's Poems," *Edinburgh Review*, January 1808, pp. 285–89.
16. Leigh Hunt, *The Feast of the Poets* (1811), 1814, ll. 222–42.
17. Friedrich Schlegel, *Lectures on the History of Literature*, 1815.
18. William Hazlitt, *Lectures on the English Poets*, 1818.
19. Robert Southey, "Preface" to *The Vision of Judgment*, 1821.
20. Percy Bysshe Shelley, *Adonais*, 1821, Stanza 30.
21. William Maginn, "Odoherty on Werner," *Blackwood's Edinburgh Magazine*, December 1822, pp. 711–12.
22. Samuel Taylor Coleridge, *Table Talk*, December 29, 1822.
23. Thomas Lovell Beddoes, Letter to Thomas Kelsall (March 25, 1825).
24. Thomas Carlyle, *Journal* (December 3, 1826), cited in James Anthony Froude, *Thomas Carlyle*, 1882, Volume 1, p. 304.
25. John Quincy Adams, *Memoirs* (entry for April 1830), 1874–77, Volume 8, p. 218.
26. John Galt, *The Life of Lord Byron*, 1830, Ch. 49.
27. Johann Wolfgang von Goethe (1827), cited in Johann Peter Eckermann, *Conversations with Goethe*, 1830, tr. John Oxenford.
28. William H. Prescott, "English Literature of the Nineteenth Century," *North American Review*, July 1832, pp. 176–78.
29. Walter Savage Landor, *A Satire on Satirists*, 1836, ll. 167–74.
30. Elizabeth Barrett Browning, *A Vision of Poets*, 1844, ll. 412–14.
31. Robert Browning, Letter to Elizabeth Barrett Browning (August 22, 1846).
32. William Michael Rossetti, "Lord Byron," *Lives of Famous Poets*, 1878, p. 307.
33. W. E. Henley, "Byron," *Views and Reviews*, 1890.
34. George Saintsbury, *A History of Nineteenth Century Literature*, 1896, pp. 78–81.
35. Edward Dowden, *The French Revolution and English Literature*, 1897, pp. 261–65.
36. Lionel Johnson, "Byron," *Academy*, May 7, 1898, pp. 489–90.
37. Johann Wolfgang von Goethe, "Byron's *Manfred*" (1820), *Literary Essays*, tr. J. E. Spingarn, 1921, pp. 202–4.
38. George Gordon, Lord Byron, Letter to John Murray (June 7, 1820).

39. Margaret Oliphant, *The Literary History of England, 1790–1825*, 1882, Volume 3, pp. 72–73.
40. Josiah Royce, *The Religious Aspect of Philosophy*, 1885, pp. 120–21.
41. Leigh Hunt, *Examiner*, October 31, 1819, pp. 700–702.
42. Robert Southey, Letter to Walter Savage Landor (February 20, 1820).
43. Johann Wolfgang von Goethe, "Byron's *Don Juan*" (1821), *Literary Essays*, tr. J. E. Spingarn, 1921, pp. 205–7.
44. Samuel Taylor Coleridge, *Table Talk*, June 7, 1824.
45. William Hazlitt, *Conversations of James Northcote, Esq.*, 1830.
46. Thomas Babington Macaulay, *Journal* (August 3, 1849), cited in G. Otto Trevelyan, *The Life and Letters of Lord Macaulay*, 1876, Volume 2, p. 227.
47. J. A. Symonds, "Lord Byron," *The English Poets*, ed. Thomas Humphry Ward, 1880, Volume 4, p. 250.
48. William Hazlitt, "Lord Byron's Tragedy of *Marino Faliero*," *London Magazine*, May 1821.
49. John Nichol, *Byron*, 1880, pp. 138–39.
50. William Hazlitt, "Lord Byron," *The Spirit of the Age*, 1825.
51. Thomas Babington Macaulay, "Moore's Life of Lord Byron" (1831), *Critical, Historical, and Miscellaneous Essays*, 1860, Volume 2, pp. 352–67.
52. Giuseppe Mazzini, "Byron and Goethe" (1839), *Essays*, ed. William Clarke, 1887, pp. 86–93.
53. Algernon Charles Swinburne, "Byron" (1866), *Essays and Studies*, 1875.
54. Matthew Arnold, "Byron" (1881), *Essays in Criticism: Second Series*, 1888.
55. G. K. Chesterton, "The Optimism of Byron" (1901), *Varied Types*, 1908, pp. 29–39.
56. John Churton Collins, "The Collected Works of Lord Byron," *Studies in Poetry and Criticism*, 1905, pp. 107–23.

WILLIAM BLAKE

1. Charles Lamb, Letter to Bernard Barton (May 15, 1824).
2. Frederick Tatham, "The Life of William Blake" (1832), *The Letters of William Blake*, ed. A. G. B. Russell, 1906, pp. 37–41.
3. Seymour Kirkup, Letter to Lord Houghton (March 25, 1870), cited in T. Wemyss Reid, *The Life, Letters, and Friendships of Richard Monckton Milnes, First Lord Houghton*, 1891, Volume 2, pp. 222–23.
4. Dante Gabriel Rossetti, "William Blake," *Five English Poets*, 1880–81.
5. Allan Cunningham, "William Blake," *The Lives of the Most Eminent British Painters and Sculptors*, 1830, Volume 2.
6. Anna Jameson, *Sacred and Legendary Art*, 1848, Volume 1, p. 85.
7. Walter Thornbury, *British Artists from Hogarth to Turner*, 1861, Volume 2, p. 27.
8. Dante Gabriel Rossetti, "Supplementary" to *The Life of William Blake* by Alexander Gilchrist, 1863, Volume 1, pp. 381–82.
9. Mary Abigail Dodge, "Pictor Ignotus," *Atlantic*, April 1864, pp. 436–37.
10. James Smetham, "William Blake" (1869), *Literary Works*, ed. William Davies, 1893, pp. 193–94.
11. Charles Eliot Norton, "Blake's Songs and Poetical Sketches," *North American Review*, April 1869, pp. 641–43.
12. Margaret Oliphant, *The Literary History of England, 1790–1825*, 1882, Volume 2, pp. 287–94.

13. Richard Henry Stoddard, *Under the Evening Lamp*, 1892, pp. 174–75.
14. J. J. Jusserand, *Piers Plowman: A Contribution to the History of English Mysticism*, trs. Marion Richards, Elise Richards, 1894, pp. 218–19.
15. John Vance Cheney, "William Blake," *That Dome in Air: Thoughts on Poetry and the Poets*, 1895, pp. 170–76.
16. A. C. Benson, "William Blake," *Essays*, 1896, pp. 150–62.
17. Stopford A. Brooke, *English Literature*, 1896, p. 223.
18. Benjamin Heath Malkin, "Letter to Thomas Johnes," *A Father's Memoirs of His Child*, 1806, pp. xviii–xxv.
19. Henry Crabb Robinson, *Diary*, 1825–26.
20. Samuel Palmer, Letter to Alexander Gilchrist (August 23, 1855), *Life of William Blake* by Alexander Gilchrist, 1863, Volume 1, pp. 301–4.
21. James Thomson, "The Poems of William Blake" (1864), *Biographical and Critical Studies*, 1896, pp. 240–69.
22. Algernon Charles Swinburne, "The Prophetic Books," *William Blake: A Critical Essay*, 1866, pp. 298–304.
23. Moncure D. Conway, *Fortnightly Review*, February 1868, pp. 216–20.
24. Henry G. Hewlett, "Imperfect Genius: William Blake," *Contemporary Review*, October 1876, pp. 763–67.
25. J. Comyns Carr, "William Blake," *The English Poets*, ed. Thomas Humphry Ward, 1880, Volume 3, pp. 596–600.
26. Coventry Patmore, "Blake," *Principle in Art*, 1889, pp. 97–102.
27. W. B. Yeats, Edwin J. Ellis, *The Works of William Blake*, 1893, Volume 1, pp. vii–xiii, 235–45.
28. Lionel Johnson, *Academy*, August 26, 1893, pp. 163–65.
29. Lucy Allen Paton, "A Phase of William Blake's Romanticism," *Poet-Lore*, October 1893, pp. 481–88.
30. Alfred T. Story, *William Blake: His Life, Character and Genius*, 1893, pp. 153–60.
31. George Saintsbury, *A History of Nineteenth Century Literature*, 1896, pp. 9–13.
32. W. B. Yeats, "Academy Portraits: XXXII. William Blake," *Academy*, June 19, 1897, pp. 634–35.
33. Henry Justin Smith, "The Poetry of William Blake," *Century Magazine*, June 1900, pp. 284–91.

WILLIAM HAZLITT

1. Henry Crabb Robinson, *Diary*, January 14–15, 1812.
2. George Ticknor, *Journal* (1819), *Life, Letters, and Journals of George Ticknor*, ed. Anna Ticknor, 1876, Volume 1, pp. 293–94.
3. Leigh Hunt, Letter to Percy Bysshe and Mary Shelley (July 11, 1821).
4. Benjamin Robert Haydon, Letter to Mary Russell Mitford (September 8, 1822), cited in *The Life, Letters and Table Talk of Benjamin Robert Haydon*, ed. Richard Henry Stoddard, 1876, pp. 210–12.
5. Thomas Carlyle, Letter to Anna D. B. Montagu (October 27, 1830).
6. T. Noon Talfourd, "Thoughts upon the Intellectual Character of the Late William Hazlitt," *Literary Remains of the Late William Hazlitt*, 1836, pp. xlvi–xlvii.
7. Peter George Patmore, "William Hazlitt," *My Friends and Acquaintance*, 1854, Volume 2, pp. 270–75.
8. S. C. Hall, *Retrospect of a Long Life*, 1883, p. 318.
9. John Keats, Letter to Benjamin Robert Haydon (March 14, 1818).
10. John Wilson, "Notice of Hazlitt's *Lectures on English Poetry*," *Blackwood's Edinburgh Magazine*, April 1818, p. 75.
11. George Gordon, Lord Byron, *Journal*, January 28, 1821.

12. J. H. Merivale, "Hazlitt's *Literary Remains*," *Edinburgh Review*, January 1837, pp. 214–15.
13. Heinrich Heine, *Notes on Shakespeare Heroines* (1838), tr. Ida Benecke, 1895, pp. 25–26.
14. Henry T. Tuckerman, "William Hazlitt," *Atlantic*, June 1870, pp. 678–79.
15. Margaret Oliphant, *The Literary History of England, 1790–1825*, 1882, Volume 2, pp. 298–99.
16. Louise Imogen Guiney, "William Hazlitt," *A Little English Gallery*, 1894, pp. 278–84.
17. W. E. Henley, "Introduction" to *The Collected Works of William Hazlitt*, eds. A. R. Waller, Arnold Glover, 1902, Volume 1, pp. xxii–xxv.
18. Leigh Hunt, "Mr. Hazlitt and the Utilitarians," *Tatler*, September 28, 1830.
19. Thomas De Quincey, "Notes on Gilfillan's Literary Portraits" (1845–46), *Collected Writings*, ed. David Masson, Volume 11, pp. 341–54.
20. Sir Leslie Stephen, "William Hazlitt" (1875), *Hours in a Library* (1874–79), 1904, Volume 2, pp. 235–86.
21. George Saintsbury, "Hazlitt" (1887), *Collected Essays and Papers*, 1923, Volume 1, pp. 106–33.
22. Augustine Birrell, "William Hazlitt," *Res Judicatae*, 1892, pp. 224–31.
23. Paul Elmer More, "The First Complete Edition of Hazlitt," *Shelburne Essays: Second Series*, 1905, pp. 73–86.

SIR WALTER SCOTT

1. Dorothy Wordsworth, *Journal*, September 18, 1803.
2. Anna Seward, Letter to Henry Francis Cary (May 10, 1807).
3. George Crabbe, Letter to Sir Walter Scott (October 13, 1812).
4. George Ticknor, *Journal* (March 14, 1819), *Life, Letters, and Journals of George Ticknor*, ed. Anna Ticknor, 1876, Volume 1, p. 280.
5. Charles Robert Leslie, Letter to Miss Leslie (June 28, 1820), *Autobiographical Recollections*, ed. Tom Taylor, 1860, pp. 218–19.
6. Maria Edgeworth, Letter to Sophy Ruxton (June 8, 1823).
7. Felicia Dorothea Hemans, Letter (July 13, 1829), *Memorials of Mrs. Hemans*, ed. Henry F. Chorley, 1835, Volume 2, p. 33.
8. William Wordsworth, "On the Departure of Sir Walter Scott from Abbotsford, for Naples," 1831.
9. Maria Edgeworth, Letter to John Bannatyne (November 12, 1832).
10. Washington Irving, "Abbotsford," *The Crayon Miscellany*, 1835.
11. John Gibson Lockhart, *Memoirs of the Life of Sir Walter Scott*, 1837–38, Ch. 84.
12. Thomas Babington Macaulay, Letter to Macvey Napier (June 26, 1838), cited in G. Otto Trevelyan, *The Life and Letters of Lord Macaulay*, 1876, Volume 2, p. 16.
13. William Makepeace Thackeray, "George the Fourth" (1854), *The Four Georges*, 1861.
14. Nathaniel Hawthorne, *The English Note-Books*, 1856.
15. Sir Arthur Quiller-Couch, "Scott and Burns" (1893), *Adventures in Criticism*, 1895.
16. T. T. Munger, "The Head of Sir Walter Scott," *Century Magazine*, April 1894, p. 955.
17. James Hogg, *The Queen's Wake*, 1813.
18. John Scott, "The Author of the Scotch Novels," *London Magazine*, January 1820, p. 12.
19. George Gordon, Lord Byron, *Journal*, January 12, 1821.
20. Henry Francis Cary, "Notices of Miscellaneous English Poets," *Memoir of the Rev. Henry Francis Cary*, 1823, Volume 2, pp. 300–301.

21. Johann Wolfgang von Goethe, cited in Johann Peter Eckermann, *Conversations with Goethe*, 1830, tr. John Oxenford.
22. William Wordsworth, "Yarrow Revisited," 1831.
23. William Maginn, "The Death of Sir Walter Scott," *Fraser's Magazine*, October 1832, p. 381.
24. Donald MacLeod, *Life of Sir Walter Scott*, 1852, pp. 278–80.
25. Sir Archibald Alison, *History of Europe from 1815 to 1852*, 1852–59, Ch. 5.
26. Henry James, "Senior's *Essays on Fiction*," *North American Review*, October 1864, pp. 584–87.
27. Frederic Harrison, "The Choice of Books" (1879), *The Choice of Books and Other Literary Pieces*, 1886, pp. 64–65.
28. William Cullen Bryant, "Sir Walter Scott" (1872), *Prose Writings*, ed. Parke Godwin, 1884, Volume 2, pp. 310–12.
29. Mark Twain, *Life on the Mississippi*, 1883, Ch. 46.
30. Robert Buchanan, *The Outcast*, 1891, Canto 2.
31. W. H. Mallock, "Are Scott, Dickens, and Thackeray Obsolete?," *Forum*, December 1892, pp. 508–9.
32. Robert Louis Stevenson, "A Gossip on Romance," *Memories and Portraits*, 1895.
33. George Gordon, Lord Byron, *English Bards and Scotch Reviewers*, 1809, ll. 165–88.
34. Francis, Lord Jeffrey, "Scott's *Lady of the Lake*," *Edinburgh Review*, August 1810, p. 293.
35. Friedrich Schlegel, *Lectures on the History of Literature*, 1815.
36. Heinrich Heine, *Politische Annalen*, 1828, p. 181.
37. Margaret Fuller, "Modern British Poets," *Papers on Literature and Art*, 1846.
38. Ralph Waldo Emerson, "Literature," *English Traits*, 1856.
39. Matthew Arnold, *On Translating Homer*, 1861.
40. Francis Turner Palgrave, "Sir Walter Scott," *Poetical Works of Sir Walter Scott*, 1866, p. xxvii.
41. M. D. Conway, "The Scott Centenary at Edinburgh," *Harper's New Monthly Magazine*, February 1872, p. 337.
42. William Michael Rossetti, "Walter Scott," *Lives of Famous Poets*, 1878, pp. 233–34.
43. John Tulloch, *Movements of Religious Thought in Britain during the Nineteenth Century*, 1885, p. 82.
44. William Dean Howells, "Scott," *My Literary Passions*, 1895, pp. 33–34.
45. J. Gale Pedrick, "The Heraldic Aspect of Scott's Poetical Works," *Gentleman's Magazine*, November 1898, pp. 470–71.
46. Joanna Baillie, Letter to George Thomson (February 18, 1805), cited in James Cuthbert Hadden, *George Thomson: The Friend of Burns*, 1898, p. 153.
47. Francis, Lord Jeffrey, "Scott's *Lay of the Last Minstrel*," *Edinburgh Review*, April 1805, p. 20.
48. Sir James Mackintosh, Letter to George Philips (September 25, 1805), *Memoirs of the Life of Sir James Mackintosh*, ed. Robert James Mackintosh, 1853, Volume 1, p. 254.
49. R. P. Gillies, *Memoirs of a Literary Veteran*, 1851, Ch. 19.
50. William John Courthope, "The Revival of Romance: Scott, Byron, Shelley," *The Liberal Movement in English Literature*, 1885, p. 130.
51. George Gordon, Lord Byron, Letter to Francis Hodgson (October 3, 1810).
52. Samuel Taylor Coleridge, Letter to William Wordsworth (October 1810).
53. Stendhal (Henri Beyle), *Le National*, February 19, 1830.
54. William H. Prescott, "English Literature of the Nineteenth Century," *North American Review*, July 1832, pp. 187–90.
55. Samuel Taylor Coleridge, *Table Talk*, November 1, 1833.
56. Honoré de Balzac, Letter to Mme. Hanska (January 20, 1838).
57. William H. Prescott, "Sir Walter Scott" (1838), *Biographical and Critical Miscellanies*, 1845.
58. John W. Hales, *Notes and Essays on Shakespeare*, 1873, pp. 72–73.
59. James Freeman Clarke, "Culture by Reading Books," *Self-Culture*, 1880, p. 316.
60. Sidney Lanier, *The English Novel*, 1883, p. 193.
61. Andrew D. White, "Walter Scott at Work," *Scribner's Magazine*, February 1889, p. 132.
62. William Dean Howells, *Criticism and Fiction*, 1891, pp. 21–22.
63. Edmund Gosse, *A Short History of Modern English Literature*, 1897, pp. 299–302.
64. Brander Matthews, "The Historical Novel," *Forum*, September 1897, p. 84.
65. Francis Hovey Stoddard, *The Evolution of the English Novel*, 1900, pp. 104–5.
66. Jane Austen, Letter to Anna Austen (September 28, 1814).
67. Thomas Carlyle, Letter to Robert Mitchell (October 18, 1814).
68. Maria Edgeworth, Letter to James Ballantyne (October 23, 1814).
69. Mary Russell Mitford, Letter to Sir William Elford (October 31, 1814).
70. Johann Wolfgang von Goethe (1828), cited in Johann Peter Eckermann, *Conversations with Goethe*, 1830, tr. John Oxenford.
71. R. H. Barham, *Journal* (February 11, 1833), *The Life and Letters of the Rev. Richard Harris Barham*, ed. R. H. Dalton Barham, 1870, Volume 1, p. 214.
72. William C. Macready, Letter to Mrs. Pollock (March 26, 1855).
73. Alfred, Lord Tennyson (1890), cited in Hallam Tennyson, *Alfred Lord Tennyson: A Memoir*, 1897, Volume 2, p. 372.
74. John Wilson, "Ivanhoe," *Blackwood's Edinburgh Magazine*, December 1819, pp. 262–63.
75. Johann Wolfgang von Goethe, cited in Johann Peter Eckermann, *Conversations with Goethe*, 1830, tr. John Oxenford.
76. Sir Leslie Stephen, "Sir Walter Scott" (1871), *Hours in a Library* (1874–79), 1904, Volume 1, p. 215.
77. Frances Ann Kemble, Letter (May 1827), *Record of a Girlhood*, 1878.
78. Charlotte Brontë, Letter to Ellen Nussey (January 1, 1833).
79. Edward FitzGerald, Letter to Fanny Kemble (April 25, 1879).
80. William Wilberforce, Letter to J. Stephen (August 13, 1822), cited in Robert Isaac Wilberforce, Samuel Wilberforce, *The Life of William Wilberforce*, 1838, Volume 5, p. 133.
81. Edward FitzGerald, Letter to Frances Ann Kemble (December 1881).
82. Anne Grant, Letter to Mrs. Smith (February 6, 1824), *Memoirs and Correspondence of Mrs. Grant of Laggan*, ed. J. P. Grant, 1844, Volume 3, pp. 20–21.
83. John Ruskin, "Fiction—Fair and Foul," *Nineteenth Century*, June 1880, p. 955.
84. Sydney Smith, Letter to Lord Holland (July 1828).

85. William Francis Collier, A *History of English Literature*, 1861, pp. 411–12.
86. Johann Wolfgang von Goethe, cited in Johann Peter Eckermann, *Conversations with Goethe*, 1830, tr. John Oxenford.
87. William Wetmore Story, *Conversations in a Studio*, 1890, Volume 1, pp. 273–74.
88. William Hazlitt, "Sir Walter Scott," *The Spirit of the Age*, 1825.
89. Thomas Carlyle, "Sir Walter Scott" (1837), *Critical and Miscellaneous Essays*, 1839–69.
90. Walter Bagehot, "The Waverley Novels" (1858), *Collected Works*, ed. Norman St. John-Stevas, 1965, Volume 2, pp. 47–48, 62–75.
91. George Gilfillan, "The Master of the Novel," *Life of Sir Walter Scott*, 1871, pp. 367–75.
92. Sir Leslie Stephen, "Sir Walter Scott" (1871), *Hours in a Library* (1874–79), 1904, Volume 1, pp. 186–93, 200–10.
93. George Saintsbury, "Conclusion," *Sir Walter Scott*, 1897, pp. 147–56.
94. William Henry Hudson, "Scott as a Poet," *Sir Walter Scott*, 1901, pp. 236–57.

SAMUEL TAYLOR COLERIDGE

1. Samuel Taylor Coleridge, Letter to Thomas Poole (October 9, 1797).
2. Dorothy Wordsworth, *Journal*, November 10, 1801.
3. William Wordsworth, *The Prelude*, 1805, Bk. 14, ll. 275–82.
4. George Gordon, Lord Byron, Letter to William Harness (December 8, 1811).
5. John Gibson Lockhart, *Peter's Letters to His Kinsfolk*, 1819, Letter 54.
6. William Hazlitt, "My First Acquaintance with Poets," *Liberal*, April 1823.
7. Samuel Taylor Coleridge, "Epitaph," 1833.
8. Sara Coleridge, Letter to Mrs. Plummer (October 1834).
9. Charles Lamb, "The Death of Coleridge" (1834), *Works*, ed. E. V. Lucas, 1903, Volume 1, pp. 351–52.
10. Thomas De Quincey, "Samuel Taylor Coleridge" (1834–35), *Collected Writings*, ed. David Masson, Volume 2, pp. 163–64.
11. Caroline Fox, *Journal* (December 18, 1836), *Memories of Old Friends*, ed. Horace W. Pym, 1882, p. 14.
12. Joseph Cottle, *Early Recollections, Chiefly Relating to the Late Samuel Taylor Coleridge*, 1837, Volume 2, pp. 169–72.
13. Thomas Hood, *Literary Reminiscences*, c. 1845, No. 4.
14. Leigh Hunt, *Autobiography*, 1850, Ch. 16.
15. Thomas Carlyle, *Life of John Sterling*, 1851, Pt. 1, Ch. 8.
16. George Gordon, Lord Byron, *English Bards and Scotch Reviewers*, 1809, ll. 255–64.
17. John Wilson, "Observations on Coleridge's *Biographia Literaria*," *Blackwood's Edinburgh Magazine*, October 1817, pp. 5–6.
18. William Hazlitt, *Lectures on the English Poets*, 1818.
19. George Gordon, Lord Byron, "Dedication" to *Don Juan*, 1819.
20. Percy Bysshe Shelley, *Peter Bell the Third*, 1819, Pt. 5, Stanzas 1–5.
21. Percy Bysshe Shelley, *Letter to Maria Gisborne*, 1820, ll. 202–8.
22. John Sterling, "Coleridge," *Poems*, 1839, pp. 153–55.
23. Elizabeth Barrett Browning, *A Vision of Poets*, 1844, ll. 415–17.
24. Leigh Hunt, *Imagination and Fancy*, 1844.

25. Margaret Fuller, "Modern British Poets," *Papers on Literature and Art*, 1846.
26. George Meredith, "The Poetry of Coleridge," 1851.
27. Ralph Waldo Emerson, "Literature," *English Traits*, 1856.
28. Frederick Denison Maurice, *Moral and Metaphysical Philosophy*, 1862.
29. Matthew Arnold, "Joubert" (1864), *Essays in Criticism*, 1865.
30. Dante Gabriel Rossetti, "Samuel Taylor Coleridge," *Five English Poets*, 1880–81.
31. W. P. Ker, "Samuel Taylor Coleridge," *English Prose*, ed. Henry Craik, 1896, Volume 5, pp. 76–80.
32. Francis Thompson, "Academy Portraits: XIII. S. T. Coleridge," *Academy*, February 6, 1897, pp. 179–80.
33. Richard Garnett, "The Poetry of Coleridge" (1898), *Essays of an Ex-Librarian*, 1901, pp. 88–91.
34. Thomas B. Shaw, *Outlines of English Literature*, 1847.
35. Peter Bayne, "Samuel Taylor Coleridge," *Essays in Biography and Criticism: Second Series*, 1858, p. 142.
36. Hall Caine, *Cobwebs of Criticism*, 1883, p. 59.
37. H. D. Traill, *Coleridge*, 1884, pp. 46–53.
38. William Watson, "Coleridge's Supernaturalism," *Excursions in Criticism*, 1893, pp. 98–101.
39. Thomas Love Peacock, *Nightmare Abbey*, 1818, Ch. 8.
40. George H. Calvert, *Coleridge, Shelley, Goethe: Biographic Aesthetic Studies*, 1880, pp. 12–16.
41. George Gordon, Lord Byron, Letter to John Murray (September 30, 1816).
42. John Gibson Lockhart, "On the Lake School of Poetry: III. Coleridge," *Blackwood's Edinburgh Magazine*, October 1819, pp. 8–9.
43. John Sterling, "On Coleridge's *Christabel*" (1828), *Essays and Tales*, ed. Julius Charles Hare, 1848, Volume 1, pp. 101–2.
44. Edgar Allan Poe, "The Rationale of Verse," 1848.
45. William Watson, "Lines in a Flyleaf of *Christabel*," 1893.
46. Charles Knight, *Studies of Shakspere*, 1849, p. 560.
47. George Gilfillan, "Jeffrey and Coleridge," A *Third Gallery of Portraits*, 1854, pp. 223–26.
48. Laura Johnson Wylie, *Studies in the Evolution of English Criticism*, 1894, pp. 199–200.
49. William Hazlitt, "Mr. Coleridge," *The Spirit of the Age*, 1825.
50. Walter Pater, "Coleridge" (1865), *Appreciations*, 1889.
51. Algernon Charles Swinburne, "Coleridge" (1869), *Essays and Studies*, 1875, pp. 259–75.
52. Gertrude Garrigues, "Coleridge's *Ancient Mariner*," *Journal of a Speculative Philosophy*, July 1880, pp. 327–38.
53. James Russell Lowell, "Coleridge" (1885), *Works*, Riverside ed., 1890, Volume 6, pp. 69–77.
54. Edward Dowden, "Coleridge as a Poet" (1889), *New Studies in Literature*, 1895, pp. 313–54.

CHARLES LAMB

1. Samuel Taylor Coleridge, "To a Friend Who Had Declared His Intention of Writing No More Poetry," 1796.
2. Samuel Taylor Coleridge, Letter to William Godwin (May 21, 1800).
3. Henry Crabb Robinson, *Diary*, July 3, 1814.
4. John Keats, Letter to George and Thomas Keats (January 5, 1818).
5. William Hazlitt, "On the Conversation of Authors: Part II" (1820), *The Plain Speaker*, 1826.
6. Charles Lamb, "An Autobiographical Sketch" (1827), *Works*, ed. E. V. Lucas, 1903, Volume 1, pp. 320–21.
7. Thomas Carlyle, *Journal* (1831), cited in James Anthony Froude, *Thomas Carlyle*, 1882, Volume 2, p. 170.

8. William Maginn, "Charles Lamb, Esq.," *Fraser's Magazine*, February 1835, p. 136.
9. William Wordsworth, "Written after the Death of Charles Lamb," 1835.
10. George Daniel, *Recollections of Charles Lamb* (c. 1835), 1927, pp. 48–51.
11. Robert Southey, Letter to Edward Moxon (February 2, 1836).
12. Edward Moxon, *Sonnets*, 1837, Pt. 2, Sonnet 12.
13. Benjamin Robert Haydon, Letter to William Wordsworth (October 16, 1842), *Life, Letters and Table Talk of Benjamin Robert Haydon*, ed. Richard Henry Stoddard, 1876, p. 201.
14. Thomas De Quincey, "Charles Lamb" (1848), *Collected Writings*, ed. David Masson, Volume 5, pp. 257–58.
15. Leigh Hunt, *Autobiography*, 1850, Ch. 16.
16. Peter George Patmore, *My Friends and Acquaintance*, 1854, Volume 1, pp. 21–28.
17. William Watson, "At the Grave of Charles Lamb, in Edmonton," *Lachrymae Musarum and Other Poems*, 1893, pp. 44–45.
18. John Wilson, "The Works of Charles Lamb," *Blackwood's Edinburgh Magazine*, August 1818, p. 599.
19. Robert Southey, Letter to C. W. W. Wynn (January 25, 1823).
20. Henry Nelson Coleridge, "*The Last Essays of Elia*," *Quarterly Review*, July 1835, pp. 58–64.
21. Henry F. Chorley, "Charles Lamb," *The Authors of England*, 1838, pp. 75–76.
22. Henry T. Tuckerman, "The Humorist: Charles Lamb," *Characteristics of Literature*, 1849.
23. Edward Bulwer-Lytton, "Charles Lamb and Some of His Companions," *Quarterly Review*, January 1867, pp. 9–11.
24. Edward Dowden, "Charles Lamb," *The English Poets*, ed. Thomas Humphry Ward, 1880, Volume 4, pp. 326–27.
25. John Dennis, "Charles Lamb and His Friends," *Fraser's Magazine*, May 1882, pp. 613–14.
26. Margaret Oliphant, *The Literary History of England, 1790–1825*, 1882, Volume 2, pp. 11–13.
27. Algernon Charles Swinburne, "On Lamb's *Specimens of Dramatic Poets*," 1882.
28. Algernon Charles Swinburne, "Charles Lamb and George Wither" (1885), *Miscellanies*, 1886, pp. 194–200.
29. Augustine Birrell, "Charles Lamb," *Obiter Dicta: Second Series*, 1887, pp. 226–31.
30. William Tirebuck, "Introduction" to *The Poetical Works of Bowles, Lamb, and Hartley Coleridge*, 1887, pp. xx–xxiii.
31. William Hazlitt, "Elia, and Geoffrey Crayon," *The Spirit of the Age*, 1825.
32. John Forster, "Charles Lamb," *New Monthly Magazine*, February 1835, pp. 200–206.
33. Walter Pater, "Charles Lamb" (1878), *Appreciations*, 1889.
34. Brander Matthews, "Charles Lamb's Dramatic Attempts," *Lippincott's Magazine*, May 1883, pp. 493–99.
35. Edmund Gosse, "Charles Lamb," *Quarterly Review*, October 1900, pp. 312–35.
36. Paul Elmer More, "Charles Lamb," *Shelburne Essays: Second Series*, 1905, pp. 90–99.

EMILY BRONTË

1. Emily Brontë, Untitled Poem, 1846.
2. Matthew Arnold, "Haworth Churchyard," 1855.
3. Elizabeth Gaskell, *The Life of Charlotte Brontë*, 1857, Ch. 12.

4. James Ashcroft Noble, "Emily Brontë," *Academy*, May 19, 1883, p. 340.
5. Richard Garnett, "Emily Brontë," *The Poets and the Poetry of the Century*, ed. Alfred H. Miles, 1892, Volume 8, pp. 283–85.
6. Angus M. MacKay, *The Brontës: Fact and Fiction*, 1897, pp. 21–23.
7. Margaret Oliphant, *Women Novelists of Queen Victoria's Reign*, 1897, p. 28.
8. Charlotte M. Mew, "The Poems of Emily Brontë," *Temple Bar*, August 1904, pp. 153–54.
9. Catharine M. Sedgwick, Letter to Mrs. K. S. Minot (May 27, 1848), cited in Mary E. Dewey, *Life and Letters of Catharine M. Sedgwick*, 1871, p. 307.
10. Edwin P. Whipple, "Novels of the Season," *North American Review*, October 1848, pp. 357–59.
11. Sydney Dobell, "Currer Bell" (1850), *The Life and Letters of Sydney Dobell*, ed. Emily Jolly, 1878, Volume 1, pp. 169–71.
12. George Henry Lewes, *Leader*, December 28, 1850, p. 953.
13. Dante Gabriel Rossetti, Letter to William Allingham (September 19, 1854).
14. W. Clark Russell, *The Book of Authors*, 1871, p. 499, Note.
15. T. Wemyss Reid, *Charlotte Bontë: A Monograph*, 1877, pp. 201–2.
16. J. F., "*Wuthering Heights*," *Temple Bar*, December 1887, p. 562.
17. Frederic Harrison, "Charlotte Brontë's Place in Literature," *Forum*, March 1895, p. 32.
18. Clement K. Shorter, *Charlotte Brontë and Her Circle*, 1896, p. 158.
19. Richard D. Graham, *The Masters of Victorian Literature*, 1897, p. 45.
20. Hugh Walker, *The Age of Tennyson*, 1897, p. 103.
21. Wilbur L. Cross, *The Development of the English Novel*, 1899, pp. 166–67.
22. William Dean Howells, "Heroines of Nineteenth-Century Fiction: XIX. The Two Catharines of Emily Brontë," *Harper's Bazaar*, December 29, 1900, pp. 2224–30.
23. Alice Meynell, "Charlotte and Emily Brontë" (1911), *Hearts of Controversy*, 1917, pp. 96–99.
24. Edmund Gosse, "Emily Brontë," *The English Poets*, ed. Thomas Humphry Ward, 1880, Volume 4, pp. 581–82.
25. Clement K. Shorter, *Victorian Literature: Sixty Years of Books and Bookmen*, 1897, p. 47.
26. Charlotte Brontë, "Preface" to *Wuthering Heights*, 1850.
27. George Barnett Smith, "The Brontës" (1873), *Poets and Novelists*, 1876, pp. 236–42.
28. A. Mary F. Robinson, "*Wuthering Heights*: Its Origin," *Emily Brontë*, 1883, pp. 206–24.
29. Algernon Charles Swinburne, "Emily Brontë" (1883), *Miscellanies*, 1886, pp. 260–70.
30. Arthur L. Salmon, "A Modern Stoic: Emily Brontë," *Poet-Lore*, January 1892, pp. 64–70.
31. A. M. Williams, "Emily Brontë," *Temple Bar*, July 1893, pp. 434–39.
32. Angus M. MacKay, "On the Interpretation of Emily Brontë," *Westminster Review*, August 1898, pp. 203–6, 217–18.
33. Mary A. Ward, "Introduction" to *Wuthering Heights*, 1900, pp. xxiii–xxxviii.

EDGAR ALLAN POE

1. Edgar Allan Poe, "Alone," 1829.
2. L. A. Wilmer, Letter to Mr. Tomlin (May 20, 1843), cited in *Passages from the Correspondence and Other*

Papers of Rufus W. Griswold, ed. W. M. Griswold, 1898, p. 143.

3. Edgar Allan Poe, Letter to Virginia Poe (June 12, 1846).

4. Rufus Wilmot Griswold, *New York Tribune*, October 9, 1849.

5. Maria Clemm, Letter to "Annie" (October 13, 1849), cited in John H. Ingram, *Edgar Allan Poe: His Life, Letters, and Opinions*, 1880, Volume 2, pp. 239–40.

6. N. P. Willis, "Death of Edgar A. Poe" (1849), cited in *The Complete Works of Edgar Allan Poe*, ed. James A. Harrison, 1902, Volume 1, pp. 360–62.

7. George R. Graham, "The Late Edgar Allan Poe" (letter to N. P. Willis, February 2, 1850), *Graham's Magazine*, March 1850, pp. 225–26.

8. Thomas Powell, "Edgar Allan Poe," *The Living Authors of America*, 1850, pp. 123–24.

9. Sarah Helen Whitman, *Edgar Poe and His Critics*, 1860, pp. 82–85.

10. Horace Greeley, *Recollections of a Busy Life*, 1868, pp. 196–97.

11. Maunsell B. Field, *Memories of Many Men and of Some Women*, 1873, pp. 224–25.

12. John H. B. Latrobe, "Reminiscences of Poe," *Edgar Allan Poe: A Memorial Volume*, ed. Sara Sigourney Rice, 1877, pp. 60–61.

13. Susan T. Weiss, "Last Days of Edgar A. Poe," *Scribner's Monthly*, March 1878, pp. 711–12.

14. James Russell Lowell, *A Fable for Critics*, 1848.

15. John R. Thompson, "The Late Edgar A. Poe," *Southern Literary Messenger*, November 1849, p. 694.

16. James Hannay, "The Life and Genius of Edgar Allan Poe," *The Poetical Works of Edgar Allan Poe*, 1852, pp. xxv–xxvi.

17. Thomas Holley Chivers, *New Life of Edgar Allan Poe*, c. 1857.

18. Stéphane Mallarmé, "Le Tombeau d'Edgar Poe," 1876.

19. Richard Henry Horne (April 8, 1876), *Edgar Allan Poe: A Memorial Volume*, ed. Sara Sigourney Rice, 1877, pp. 81–84.

20. Thomas Wentworth Higginson, "Poe" (1879), *Short Studies of American Authors*, 1888, pp. 16–20.

21. Joris-Karl Huysmans, *À Rebours*, tr. Robert Baldick, 1884, Ch. 14.

22. Hallam Tennyson, *Alfred Lord Tennyson: A Memoir*, 1897, Volume 2, pp. 292–93.

23. William Gilmore Simms, "Poe's Poetry," *Charleston Southern Patriot*, November 10, 1845.

24. Algernon Charles Swinburne, *Under the Microscope*, 1872.

25. Walt Whitman, "Edgar Poe's Significance," *Critic*, June 3, 1882, p. 147.

26. Edmund Gosse, "Has America Produced a Poet?" (1889), *Questions at Issue*, 1893, pp. 88–90.

27. John Burroughs, "Mr. Gosse's Puzzle over Poe," *Dial*, October 16, 1893, pp. 214–15.

28. Joel Benton, "Poe's Opinion of 'The Raven'" (1897), *In the Poe Circle*, 1899, pp. 57–60.

29. Henry Wadsworth Longfellow, Letter to Edgar Allan Poe (May 19, 1841).

30. Margaret Fuller, "Poe's Tales," *New York Daily Tribune*, July 11, 1845.

31. Robert Louis Stevenson, *Academy*, January 2, 1875, pp. 1–2.

32. Brander Matthews, *The Philosophy of the Short-Story* (1885), 1901, pp. 44–48.

33. Francis Thompson, "A Dreamer of Things Impossible" (1901), *Literary Criticism*, ed. Terence L. Connolly, 1948, pp. 317–22.

34. Nathaniel Hawthorne, Letter to Edgar Allan Poe (June 17, 1846), cited in George E. Woodberry, "Poe in New York," *Century Magazine*, October 1894, p. 860.

35. Eugene Benson, "Poe and Hawthorne," *Galaxy*, December 1868, pp. 747–48.

36. Henry James, *Hawthorne*, 1879, p. 62.

37. Barrett Wendell, *A Literary History of America*, 1900, pp. 208–9.

38. James Russell Lowell, "Edgar Allan Poe," *Graham's Magazine*, February 1845, pp. 49–53.

39. Charles Baudelaire, "Edgar Allan Poe: His Life and Works," tr. Jean Alexander, *Revue de Paris*, March–April 1852, pp. 90–110.

40. George Gilfillan, "Edgar Poe," *A Third Gallery of Portraits*, 1854, pp. 380–88.

41. John Mackinnon Robertson, "Poe" (1885), *New Essays towards a Critical Method*, 1897, pp. 92–104.

42. Edmund Clarence Stedman, "Edgar Allan Poe," *Poets of America*, 1885, pp. 225–28, 248–64.

43. George E. Woodberry, "The End of the Play," *Edgar Allan Poe*, 1885, pp. 286–301.

44. Charles Whibley, "Edgar Allan Poe," *New Review*, January 1896, pp. 617–25.

45. Lewis E. Gates, "Edgar Allan Poe," *Studies and Appreciations*, 1900, pp. 110–28.

WILLIAM WORDSWORTH

1. Dorothy Wordsworth, *Journal*, January 29, 1802.

2. Henry Crabb Robinson, *Diary*, May 8, 1812.

3. Robert Southey, Letter to Bernard Barton (December 19, 1814).

4. John Gibson Lockhart, "Letters from the Lakes," *Blackwood's Edinburgh Magazine*, March 1819, pp. 739–40.

5. George Ticknor, *Journal* (March 21, 1819), *Life, Letters and Journals of George Ticknor*, ed. Anna Ticknor, 1876, Volume 1, p. 287.

6. Charles Mayne Young, *Journal* (July 6, 1828), cited in Julian Charles Young, *A Memoir of Charles Mayne Young*, 1871, pp. 112–15.

7. John Wilson (as "Christopher North"), *Noctes Ambrosianae* (November 1832), 1854.

8. Thomas De Quincey, "The Lake Poets: William Wordsworth" (1839), *Collected Writings*, ed. David Masson, Volume 2, pp. 242–43.

9. Robert Browning, "The Lost Leader," *Dramatic Romances and Lyrics*, 1845.

10. Leigh Hunt, *Autobiography*, 1850, Ch. 15.

11. Ralph Waldo Emerson, "First Visit to England," *English Traits*, 1856.

12. Thomas Carlyle, "Appendix" (1867), *Reminiscences*, ed. James Anthony Froude, 1881, Volume 2, pp. 338–41.

13. Charles Burney, *Monthly Review*, June 1799, p. 210.

14. Robert Southey, Letter to John Rickman (March 30, 1804).

15. George Gordon, Lord Byron, *English Bards and Scotch Reviewers*, 1809, ll. 235–54.

16. Charles Lamb, William Gifford, "Wordsworth's *Excursion*," *Quarterly Review*, October 1814, pp. 110–11.

17. Sydney Smith, Letter to Francis, Lord Jeffrey (December 30, 1814).

18. John Keats, "Addressed to Haydon," 1816.

19. William Hazlitt, *Lectures on the English Poets*, 1818.

20. Percy Bysshe Shelley, *Peter Bell the Third*, 1819, Pt. 4, Stanzas 7–10.

21. Thomas Love Peacock, "The Four Ages of Poetry," 1820.

22. Sir Walter Scott, Letter to Allan Cunningham (c. December 1820).

23. Henry Wadsworth Longfellow, *Notebook* (1829), cited in

Samuel Longfellow, *Life of Henry Wadsworth Longfellow*, 1891, Volume 1, p. 172.

24. Thomas Babington Macaulay, "Moore's Life of Lord Byron" (1831), *Critical, Historical, and Miscellaneous Essays*, 1860, Volume 2, p. 356.
25. Sir Henry Taylor, "Wordsworth's *Poetical Works*," *Quarterly Review*, November 1834, pp. 325–29.
26. George Eliot, Letter to Maria Lewis (November 22, 1839).
27. Elizabeth Barrett Browning, *The Book of the Poets* (1842), *Life, Letters and Essays of Elizabeth Barrett Browning*, 1863.
28. Margaret Fuller, "Modern British Poets," *Papers on Literature and Art*, 1846.
29. Leigh Hunt, Letter to "J. F." (July 8, 1848).
30. Matthew Arnold, "Memorial Verses," 1850.
31. George Meredith, "The Poetry of Wordsworth," 1851.
32. John Stuart Mill, *Autobiography*, 1873, Ch. 5.
33. Harriet Martineau, *Autobiography*, ed. Maria Weston Chapman, 1877, Volume 1, pp. 507–8.
34. Matthew Arnold, "Preface" to *The Poems of Wordsworth*, 1879.
35. Edmond Scherer, "Wordsworth and Modern Poetry in England" (1882), *Essays on English Literature*, tr. George Saintsbury, 1891, pp. 199–201.
36. Aubrey De Vere, "Remarks on the Personal Character of Wordsworth's Poetry" (1883), *Wordsworthiana*, ed. William Knight, 1889, pp. 148–50.
37. William Watson, "Wordsworth's Grave," 1890.
38. Edward Dowden, *The French Revolution and English Literature*, 1897, pp. 197–200.
39. William Wordsworth, "Preface" to *Lyrical Ballads* (1798), 1800.
40. Vida D. Scudder, "Wordsworth and New Democracy," *The Life of the Spirit in the Modern English Poets*, 1895, pp. 60–64.
41. John Wilson, Letter to James Hogg (1815), cited in Mary Gordon, *"Christopher North": A Memoir of John Wilson*, 1863, p. 130.
42. Francis, Lord Jeffrey, "Wordsworth's *White Doe*," *Edinburgh Review*, October 1815, pp. 355–56.
43. John Campbell Shairp, *"The White Doe of Rylstone,"* *Aspects of Poetry*, 1881, pp. 319–21.
44. William Hazlitt, "Observations on Mr. Wordsworth's Poem the *Excursion*" (1814), *The Round Table*, 1817.
45. Henry Crabb Robinson, *Diary*, November 21–23, 1814.
46. Robert Southey, Letter to Sir Walter Scott (December 24, 1814).
47. George Gordon, Lord Byron, "Dedication" to *Don Juan*, 1819.
48. John Wilson, "An Hour's Talk about Poetry," *Blackwood's Edinburgh Magazine*, September 1831, pp. 477–78.
49. T. E. Brown, Letter to S. T. Irwin (December 11, 1894).
50. Samuel Taylor Coleridge, "To William Wordsworth, Composed on the Night after His Recitation of a Poem on the Growth of an Individual Mind," 1807.
51. Thomas Babington Macaulay, *Journal* (July 28, 1850), cited in G. Otto Trevelyan, *The Life and Letters of Lord Macaulay*, 1876, Volume 2, pp. 238–39.
52. F. W. H. Myers, *Wordsworth*, 1881, pp. 36–37.
53. William Wordsworth, Letter to Lady Beaumont (May 21, 1807).
54. Francis, Lord Jeffrey, "Wordsworth's *Excursion*," *Edinburgh Review*, November 1814, pp. 1–6, 29–30.
55. Samuel Taylor Coleridge, *Biographia Literaria*, 1817, Ch. 22.
56. William Hazlitt, "Mr. Wordsworth," *The Spirit of the Age*, 1825.

57. Walter Pater, "Wordsworth" (1874), *Appreciations*, 1889.
58. Sir Leslie Stephen, "Wordsworth's Ethics" (1876), *Hours in a Library* (1874–79), 1904, Volume 3, pp. 139–78.
59. Arthur Symons, "Wordsworth," *Fortnightly Review*, January 1902, pp. 39–52.

JAMES FENIMORE COOPER

1. Sir Walter Scott, *Journal*, November 3, 1826.
2. Edgar Allan Poe, "Autography" (1841), *Complete Works*, ed. James A. Harrison, 1902, Volume 15, p. 205.
3. Samuel Griswold Goodrich, *Recollections of a Lifetime*, 1856, Letter 36.
4. Horace Greeley, *Recollections of a Busy Life*, 1868, p. 261.
5. Maunsell B. Field, *Memories of Many Men and of Some Women*, 1873, p. 178.
6. S. C. Hall, *Retrospect of a Long Life*, 1883, pp. 227–28.
7. William Hazlitt, "American Literature—Dr. Channing," *Edinburgh Review*, October 1829, pp. 128–29.
8. John Gibson Lockhart, "Cooper's *England*," *Quarterly Review*, October 1837, p. 330.
9. Thomas Carlyle, Letter to Ralph Waldo Emerson (December 8, 1837).
10. Honoré de Balzac (1840), *The Personal Opinions of Honoré de Balzac*, tr. Katharine Prescott Wormeley, 1899, pp. 117–20.
11. Edgar Allan Poe, *Graham's Magazine*, November 1843, p. 262.
12. Margaret Fuller, "American Literature," *Papers on Literature and Art*, 1846.
13. James Russell Lowell, *A Fable for Critics*, 1848.
14. Fitz-Greene Halleck (c. 1850), cited in James Grant Wilson, *Bryant and His Friends*, 1885, pp. 238–39.
15. William Cullen Bryant, "James Fenimore Cooper" (1852), *Prose Writings*, ed. Parke Godwin, 1884, Volume 1, pp. 328–29.
16. Herman Melville, Letter to the Cooper Memorial Committee (1852), cited in *Memorial of James Fenimore Cooper*, ed. George Palmer Putnam, 1852.
17. James Herbert Morse, "The Native Element in American Fiction," *Century Magazine*, June 1883, pp. 290–91.
18. Edwin P. Whipple, "American Literature" (1886), *American Literature and Other Papers*, 1887, pp. 47–50.
19. Brander Matthews, *An Introduction to the Study of American Literature*, 1896, pp. 66–67.
20. Thomas Wentworth Higginson, "James Fenimore Cooper," *American Prose*, ed. George Rice Carpenter, 1898, p. 150.
21. W. B. Shubrick Clymer, *James Fenimore Cooper*, 1900, pp. 58–61.
22. Maria Edgeworth, Letter to Sophy Ruxton (July 8, 1821).
23. W. Phillip, "*The Pilot, a Tale of the Sea*," *North American Review*, April 1824, p. 328.
24. Sir Walter Scott, *Journal*, January 14, 1828.
25. Henry Cabot Lodge, *Studies in History*, 1884, pp. 353–54.
26. Joseph Conrad, "Tales of the Sea" (1898), *Notes on Life and Letters*, 1921, pp. 55–56.
27. Sir Walter Scott, *Journal*, January 28, 1828.
28. Thomas Powell, "James Fenimore Cooper," *The Living Authors of America*, 1850, pp. 12–13, 47–48.
29. Henry S. Pancoast, *An Introduction to American Literature*, 1898, pp. 136–38.
30. Barrett Wendell, *A Literary History of America*, 1900, p. 186.
31. William Gilmore Simms, "The Writings of James Fenimore Cooper" (1842), *Views and Reviews in American Literature, History, and Fiction*, 1845.

32. Francis Parkman, "James Fenimore Cooper," *North American Review*, January 1852, pp. 147–58.

33. Thomas R. Lounsbury, *James Fenimore Cooper*, 1882, pp. 269–84.

34. Mark Twain, "Fenimore Cooper's Literary Offenses," *North American Review*, July 1895, pp. 1–12.

35. T. E. Kebbel, "Leather-Stocking," *Macmillan's Magazine*, January 1899, pp. 195–97.

MARY SHELLEY

1. Sir Timothy Shelley, Letter to Lord Byron (February 6, 1823), cited in Florence Ashton Marshall, *The Life and Letters of Mary Wollstonecraft Shelley*, 1889, Volume 2, p. 66.

2. Mary Shelley, Letter to Lord Byron (February 1823), cited in Florence Ashton Marshall, *The Life and Letters of Mary Wollstonecraft Shelley*, 1889, Volume 2, p. 67.

3. William Godwin, Letter to Mary Shelley (February 18, 1823), cited in Florence Ashton Marshall, *The Life and Letters of Mary Wollstonecraft Shelley*, 1889, Volume 2, pp. 68–69.

4. Edward John Trelawny, *Recollections of the Last Days of Shelley and Byron*, 1858.

5. Robert Dale Owen, *Threading My Way: An Autobiography*, 1874, pp. 322–23.

6. Mary Cowden Clarke, *Recollections of Writers*, 1878, pp. 37–38.

7. Florence Ashton Marshall, *The Life and Letters of Mary Wollstonecraft Shelley*, 1889, Volume 2, pp. 322–25.

8. Robert Browning, Letter to Elizabeth Barrett Browning (September 11, 1845).

9. Thornton Hunt, "Shelley," *Atlantic*, February 1863, pp. 198–99.

10. Florence Ashton Marshall, *The Life and Letters of Mary Wollstonecraft Shelley*, 1889, Volume 2, p. 264.

11. C. H. Herford, *The Age of Wordsworth*, 1897, pp. 97–98.

12. Hester Lynch Piozzi, Letter to Fanny Burney (October 20, 1820).

13. Richard Henry Horne, "Mrs. Shelley," *A New Spirit of the Age*, 1844, pp. 317–21.

14. Margaret Oliphant, *The Literary History of England, 1790–1825*, 1882, Volume 3, pp. 69–70.

15. Percy Bysshe Shelley, "Dedication: to Mary —— ——," *The Revolt of Islam*, 1817.

16. John Wilson Croker, "*Frankenstein, or the Modern Prometheus*," *Quarterly Review*, January 1818, pp. 379–85.

17. Sir Walter Scott, "Remarks on Frankenstein," *Blackwood's Edinburgh Magazine*, March 1818, pp. 613–20.

18. Unsigned, "*Valperga*," *Blackwood's Edinburgh Magazine*, March 1823, pp. 283–85.

19. George Gilfillan, "Mrs. Shelley" (1848), *A Second Gallery of Literary Portraits*, 1850.

20. Helen Moore, "*Frankenstein*, and Other Writings," *Mary Wollstonecraft Shelley*, 1886, pp. 244–64.

21. Lucy Madox Rossetti, "Literary Work," *Mrs. Shelley*, 1890, pp. 186–204.

22. Richard Garnett, "Introduction" to *Tales and Stories of Mary Wollstonecraft Shelley*, 1891, pp. v–xii.

CHARLOTTE BRONTË

1. Robert Southey, Letter to Caroline Bowles (1837), *The Correspondence of Robert Southey with Caroline Bowles*, ed. Edward Dowden, 1881, p. 348.

2. Charlotte Brontë (as "Currer Bell"), "Biographical Notice of Ellis and Acton Bell," *Wuthering Heights and Agnes Grey*, 1850.

3. George Eliot, Letter to Mr. and Mrs. Charles Bray (March 5, 1853).

4. Matthew Arnold, "Haworth Churchyard," 1855.

5. Caroline Fox, *Journal* (July 9, 1857), *Memories of Old Friends*, ed. Horace N. Pym, 1881, p. 336.

6. Harriet Martineau, *Autobiography*, ed. Maria Weston Chapman, 1877, Volume 2, p. 24.

7. Millicent Garrett Fawcett, *Some Eminent Women of Our Times*, 1889, p. 109.

8. Anne Thackeray Ritchie, "My Witches Caldron," *Macmillan's Magazine*, February 1891, pp. 251–52.

9. William Wright, *The Brontës in Ireland*, 1893, pp. 15–16.

10. Clement K. Shorter, *The Brontës and Their Circle*, 1896, p. 21.

11. Peter Bayne, "Currer Bell," *Essays in Biography*, 1857, pp. 409–15.

12. Celia Thaxter, Letter to Elizabeth Hoxie (March 28, 1857).

13. A. Mary F. Robinson, *Emily Brontë*, 1883, pp. 5–6.

14. Anthony Trollope, *An Autobiography*, 1883, Ch. 13.

15. Andrew Lang, "Charlotte Brontë," *Good Words*, 1889, p. 239.

16. Frederic Harrison, "Charlotte Brontë's Place in Literature," *Forum*, March 1895, pp. 30–40.

17. George Saintsbury, "Three Mid-Century Novelists," *Corrected Impressions*, 1895, pp. 157–62.

18. Angus M. MacKay, *The Brontës: Fact and Fiction*, 1897, pp. 40–42.

19. Hugh Walker, *The Age of Tennyson*, 1897, pp. 103–6.

20. Francis Hovey Stoddard, *The Evolution of the English Novel*, 1900, pp. 62–65.

21. Charlotte Brontë (as "Currer Bell"), Letter to Messrs. Smith, Elder, & Co. (August 24, 1847).

22. Sir George Murray Smith, "In the Early Forties," *Critic*, January 1901, p. 52.

23. Henry F. Chorley, *Athenaeum*, October 23, 1847, pp. 1100–1101.

24. John Gibson Lockhart, Letter to Mrs. Hope (December 29, 1847), cited in Andrew Lang, *The Life and Letters of John Gibson Lockhart*, 1897, Volume 2, p. 310.

25. George Eliot, Letter to Charles Bray (June 11, 1848).

26. Edwin P. Whipple, "Novels of the Season," *North American Review*, October 1848, pp. 355–57.

27. William Makepeace Thackeray, "The Last Sketch," *Cornhill Magazine*, April 1860, p. 487.

28. James Russell Lowell, Letter to Charles Eliot Norton (July 8, 1867).

29. Algernon Charles Swinburne, *A Note on Charlotte Brontë*, 1877, pp. 26–28.

30. Queen Victoria, *Journal*, November 23, 1880.

31. Augustine Birrell, *Life of Charlotte Brontë*, 1887, pp. 105–8.

32. Elizabeth Barrett Browning, Letter to Mrs. Jameson (April 2, 1850).

33. Charles Kingsley, Letter to Elizabeth Gaskell (May 14, 1857).

34. Wilbur L. Cross, *The Development of the English Novel*, 1899, pp. 231–32.

35. Harriet Martineau, *Daily News*, February 3, 1853, p. 2.

36. George Eliot, Letter to Mrs. Charles Bray (February 15, 1853).

37. Bryan Waller Procter, Letter to James T. Fields (February 1853), cited in James T. Fields, "'Barry Cornwall' and Some of His Friends," *Harper's New Monthly Magazine*, December 1875, p. 60.

38. Matthew Arnold, Letter to Mrs. Forster (April 14, 1853).

39. George Henry Lewes, "*Ruth* and *Villette*," *Westminster Review*, April 1853, pp. 485–90.

40. Catharine M. Sedgwick, Letter to Dr. Dewey (April

1853), cited in Mary E. Dewey, *Life and Letters of Catharine M. Sedgwick*, 1871, p. 349.
41. Margaret Oliphant, *The Victorian Age of English Literature*, 1892, Volume 1, pp. 307–8.
42. Elizabeth Rigby, "*Vanity Fair* and *Jane Eyre*," *Quarterly Review*, December 1848, pp. 165–76.
43. George Henry Lewes, "Currer Bell's *Shirley*," *Edinburgh Review*, January 1850, pp. 158–61.
44. Sydney Dobell, "Currer Bell" (1850), *The Life and Letters of Sydney Dobell*, ed. Emily Jolly, 1878, Volume 1, pp. 176–86.
45. John Skelton, "Charlotte Brontë," *Fraser's Magazine*, May 1857, pp. 579–82.
46. T. Wemyss Reid, *Charlotte Brontë: A Monograph*, 1877, pp. 7–13, 219–25.
47. Sir Leslie Stephen, "Charlotte Brontë" (1877), *Hours in a Library* (1874–79), 1904, Volume 3, pp. 301–11.
48. James Oliphant, *Victorian Novelists*, 1899, pp. 72–77.
49. Lewis E. Gates, "Charlotte Brontë," *Studies and Appreciations*, 1900, pp. 129–62.

WASHINGTON IRVING

1. Frances Ann Kemble, Letter (April 10, 1833), *Record of a Girlhood*, 1878, p. 572.
2. Charles Dickens, Letter to Washington Irving (1841), cited in Pierre M. Irving, *The Life and Letters of Washington Irving*, 1862–64, Volume 3, pp. 164–65.
3. Oliver Wendell Holmes, *Proceedings of the Massachusetts Historical Society*, December 1859, p. 420.
4. William Makepeace Thackeray, "Nil Nisi Bonum" (1860), *Roundabout Papers*, 1863.
5. S. C. Hall, *Retrospect of a Long Life*, 1883, p. 421.
6. William Hazlitt, "Elia, and Geoffrey Crayon," *The Spirit of the Age*, 1825.
7. Alexander Hill Everett, "Irving's *Life of Columbus*," *North American Review*, January 1829, pp. 113–15.
8. James Kent, Speech (1832), cited in William Kent, *Memoirs and Letters of James Kent*, 1898, pp. 231–34.
9. Edgar Allan Poe, "A Chapter on Autography" (1841), *Complete Works*, ed. James A. Harrison, 1902, Volume 15, p. 182.
10. Charles Dickens, Speech at Banquet in His Honour, New York (February 18, 1842).
11. Edgar Allan Poe, "Nathaniel Hawthorne" (1842), *Essays and Reviews*, ed. G. R. Thompson, 1984, pp. 570–71.
12. James Russell Lowell, *A Fable for Critics*, 1848.
13. Mary Russell Mitford, *Recollections of a Literary Life*, 1851, p. 516.
14. Henry Wadsworth Longfellow, *Proceedings of the Massachusetts Historical Society*, December 1859, pp. 393–94.
15. Edward Everett, *Proceedings of the Massachusetts Historical Society*, December 1859, pp. 399–400.
16. William Cullen Bryant, "Washington Irving" (1860), *Prose Writings*, ed. Parke Godwin, 1884, Volume 1, pp. 364–66.
17. Walter Savage Landor, "*On the Widow's Ordeal* by Washington Irving," 1863.
18. Walter Savage Landor, Letter to Rose Graves Sawle (January 19, 1863).
19. Edward Dowden, "The Poetry of Democracy: Walt Whitman," *Studies in Literature*, 1878, p. 470.
20. John Nichol, *American Literature*, 1882, pp. 173–74.
21. Edmund Gosse, "Irving's *Sketch-Book*," *Critic*, March 31, 1883, pp. 140–41.
22. A. G. Sedgwick, "Washington Irving," *Nation*, April 5, 1883, pp. 291–92.
23. Edwin P. Whipple, "American Literature" (1886), *American Literature and Other Papers*, 1887, pp. 42–45.

24. William Dean Howells, "Irving," *My Literary Passions*, 1895.
25. J. H. Millar, "Washington Irving," *English Prose*, ed. Henry Craik, 1896, Volume 5, pp. 233–35.
26. Brander Matthews, "Washington Irving," *American Prose*, ed. George Rice Carpenter, 1898, pp. 120–23.
27. Sir Walter Scott, Letter to Henry Brevoort (April 23, 1813).
28. Washington Irving, "The Author's Apology," *A History of New York*, 1848.
29. J. Franklin Jameson, *The History of Historical Writing in America*, 1891, pp. 97–98.
30. Gulian C. Verplanck, "*Sketch Book of Geoffrey Crayon*," *Analectic Magazine*, July 1819, pp. 78–79.
31. William Godwin, Letter to James Ogilvie (September 15, 1819), cited in Pierre M. Irving, *The Life and Letters of Washington Irving*, 1862–64, Volume 1, p. 422.
32. Francis, Lord Jeffrey, "*The Sketch Book*," *Edinburgh Review*, August 1820, pp. 160–62.
33. Edward Everett, "*Bracebridge Hall*," *North American Review*, July 1822, pp. 209–10.
34. Francis, Lord Jeffrey, "*Bracebridge Hall*," *Edinburgh Review*, November 1822, pp. 338–39.
35. Francis, Lord Jeffrey, "*Life and Voyages of Christopher Columbus*," *Edinburgh Review*, September 1828, p. 1.
36. James W. Alexander, Letter (February 17, 1829), *Forty Years' Familiar Letters*, ed. John Hall, 1860, Volume 1, p. 122.
37. Joseph Story, Letter to William W. Story (February 21, 1836), cited in William W. Story, *Life and Letters of Joseph Story*, 1851, Volume 2, p. 229.
38. William Cullen Bryant, "Washington Irving" (1860), *Prose Writings*, ed. Parke Godwin, 1884, Volume 1, pp. 352–54.
39. William H. Prescott, "Irving's *Conquest of Granada*" (1829), *Biographical and Critical Miscellanies*, 1845.
40. Edward Everett, "Irving's *Alhambra*," *North American Review*, October 1832, p. 281.
41. George Bancroft, Letter to Washington Irving (May 30, 1855), cited in Pierre M. Irving, *The Life and Letters of Washington Irving*, 1862–63, Volume 4, p. 194.
42. Cornelius Conway Felton, *Proceedings of the Massachusetts Historical Society*, December 1859, pp. 413–14.
43. William Cullen Bryant, "Washington Irving" (1860), *Prose Writings*, ed. Parke Godwin, 1884, Volume 1, pp. 360–63.
44. Donald G. Mitchell, "Washington Irving," *Atlantic*, June 1864, pp. 700–701.
45. Richard Henry Dana, "*The Sketch Book*," *North American Review*, September 1819, pp. 334–37.
46. George Washington Greene, "Irving's Works," *Biographical Studies*, 1860, pp. 163–76.
47. George Parsons Lathrop, "Poe, Irving, Hawthorne," *A Study of Hawthorne*, 1876, pp. 300–306.
48. Charles Dudley Warner, *Washington Irving*, 1881, pp, 285–303.
49. Barrett Wendell, *A Literary History of America*, 1900, pp. 171–80.

THOMAS BABINGTON MACAULAY

1. Hannah More, Letter to Zachary Macaulay (June 28, 1808), *Letters of Hannah More to Zachary Macaulay*, ed. Arthur Roberts, 1860, pp. 26–27.
2. Henry Crabb Robinson, *Diary*, November 29, 1826.
3. Thomas Carlyle, *Journal* (January 13, 1832), cited in James Anthony Froude, *Thomas Carlyle*, 1882, Volume 2, pp. 186–87.

4. Charles Cavendish Fulke Greville, *Diary*, February 6, 1832.
5. Thomas Moore, *Journal*, October 21, 1840.
6. Henry, Lord Brougham, Letter to Macvey Napier (August 14, 1842), *Selection from the Correspondence of the Late Macvey Napier*, ed. Macvey Napier, 1879, p. 403.
7. Nathaniel Hawthorne, *The English Note-Books*, July 13, 1856.
8. John Lothrop Motley, Letter to His Wife (May 30, 1858), *Correspondence*, ed. George William Curtis, 1889, Volume 1, pp. 236–37.
9. Alfred, Lord Tennyson, Letter to the Duke of Argyll (1860), cited in Hallam Tennyson, *Alfred Lord Tennyson: A Memoir*, 1897, Volume 1, p. 458.
10. Harriet Martineau, *Autobiography*, ed. Maria Weston Chapman, 1877, Volume 1, pp. 261–62.
11. Edgar Allan Poe, "Thomas Babington Macaulay" (1841), *Essays and Reviews*, ed. G. R. Thompson, 1984, pp. 321–24.
12. Ralph Waldo Emerson, "Literature," *English Traits*, 1856.
13. Harriet Martineau, *Autobiography*, ed. Maria Weston Chapman, 1877, Volume 1, pp. 262–64.
14. Augustine Birrell, "Carlyle," *Obiter Dicta*, 1885, pp. 29–32.
15. George Saintsbury, "Macaulay," *Corrected Impressions*, 1895.
16. W. P. Ker, "Thomas Babington Macaulay," *English Prose*, ed. Henry Craik, 1896, Volume 5, pp. 411–18.
17. John Wilson (as "Christopher North"), *Noctes Ambrosianae* (August 1831), 1854.
18. John Wilson Croker, Speech in the House of Commons on the Reform Bill (September 22, 1831), *The Croker Papers*, ed. Louis J. Jennings, 1885, Volume 2, pp. 130–31.
19. James Grant, *Random Recollections of the House of Commons*, 1836, pp. 176–78.
20. H. H. Milman, *Proceedings of the Royal Society of London*, 1860–62, Volume 11, pp. xix–xx.
21. Thomas Carlyle, *Journal* (November 1, 1833), cited in James Anthony Froude, *Thomas Carlyle*, 1882, Volume 2, p. 301.
22. Thomas Babington Macaulay, Letter to Macvey Napier (November 26, 1836), *Selection from the Correspondence of Macvey Napier*, ed. Macvey Napier, 1879, pp. 180–81.
23. Henry, Lord Brougham, Letter to Macvey Napier (July 28, 1837), *Selection from the Correspondence of Macvey Napier*, ed. Macvey Napier, 1879, pp. 196–97.
24. Matthew Arnold, "A French Critic on Milton" (1877), *Mixed Essays*, 1879.
25. John Wilson, "*Lays of Ancient Rome*," *Blackwood's Edinburgh Magazine*, December 1842, pp. 805–7, 823–24.
26. John Stuart Mill, "Macaulay's *Lays of Ancient Rome*," *Westminster Review*, February 1843, pp. 105–6.
27. Walter Savage Landor, "To Macaulay," 1846.
28. Edward A. Freeman, "A Review of My Opinions," *Forum*, April 1892, pp. 152–53.
29. Francis, Lord Jeffrey, Letter to Thomas Babington Macaulay (1848), cited in G. Otto Trevelyan, *The Life and Letters of Lord Macaulay*, 1876, Volume 2, pp. 205–6.
30. John Gibson Lockhart, Letter to John Wilson Croker (January 12, 1849), *The Croker Papers*, ed. Louis J. Jennings, 1885, Volume 3, pp. 194–95.
31. Henry Greville, *Diary*, February 7, 1849.
32. Sir Archibald Alison, "Macaulay's *History of England*," *Blackwood's Edinburgh Magazine*, April 1849, pp. 387–90.
33. Maria Edgeworth, Letter to Dr. Holland (April 2, 1849), cited in Helen Zimmern, *Maria Edgeworth*, 1884, pp. 299–300.
34. Leopold von Ranke, *History of England*, 1875, Volume 6, p. 144.
35. Woodrow Wilson, *Mere Literature and Other Essays*, 1896, pp. 167–69.
36. John Wilson Croker, "Mr. Macaulay's *History of England*," *Quarterly Review*, October 1849, pp. 549–53, 629–30.
37. Walter Bagehot, "Mr. Macaulay" (1856), *Collected Works*, ed. Norman St. John-Stevas, 1965, Volume 1, pp. 421–28.
38. Sir Leslie Stephen, "Macaulay," *Hours in a Library* (1874–79), 1904, Volume 3, pp. 237–71.
39. William Ewart Gladstone, "Lord Macaulay," *Quarterly Review*, July 1876, pp. 15–24.
40. John Morley, "Macaulay" (1876), *Critical Miscellanies*, 1886, Volume 1, pp. 267–82.
41. A. V. Dicey, "Macaulay and His Critics," *Nation*, May 15, 1902, pp. 388–89.

HENRY DAVID THOREAU

1. Louisa May Alcott, "Thoreau's Flute," *Atlantic*, September 1863, pp. 280–81.
2. Moncure Daniel Conway, "Thoreau," *Fraser's Magazine*, April 1866, pp. 461–62.
3. Rose Hawthorne Lathrop, *Memories of Hawthorne*, 1897, p. 420.
4. Thomas Carlyle, Letter to Ralph Waldo Emerson (May 18, 1847).
5. A. Bronson Alcott, "Thoreau" (April 5, 1869), *Concord Days*, 1872, pp. 11–16.
6. William Ellery Channing, *Thoreau: The Poet-Naturalist* (1873), ed. F. B. Sanborn, 1902, pp. 229–34.
7. Alexander Hay Japp (as "H. A. Page"), *Thoreau: His Life and Aims*, 1878, pp. 257–64.
8. Thomas Wentworth Higginson, "Thoreau" (1879), *Short Studies of American Authors*, 1888, pp. 27–30.
9. Henry James, *Hawthorne*, 1880, pp. 93–94.
10. F. B. Sanborn, *Henry D. Thoreau*, 1882, pp. 284–87, 301–4.
11. Alfred H. Welsh, *Development of English Literature and Language*, 1883, Volume 2, p. 413.
12. Edwin P. Whipple, "American Literature" (1886), *American Literature and Other Papers*, 1887, pp. 111–12.
13. Charles F. Richardson, *American Literature, 1607–1885*, 1887, Volume 1, pp. 388–89.
14. Havelock Ellis, "Whitman," *The New Spirit*, 1890, pp. 93–99.
15. P. Anderson Graham, "The Philosophy of Idleness," *Nature in Books*, 1891, pp. 85–87.
16. Brander Matthews, *An Introduction to the Study of American Literature*, 1896, pp. 192–93.
17. Thomas Wentworth Higginson, "Henry David Thoreau," *American Prose*, ed. George Rice Carpenter, 1898, pp. 341–42.
18. Donald G. Mitchell, *American Lands and Letters: Leather-Stocking to Poe's "Raven"*, 1899, pp. 278–80.
19. Walter C. Bronson, *A Short History of American Literature*, 1900, p. 213.
20. Barrett Wendell, *A Literary History of America*, 1900, pp. 333–37.
21. Andrew Preston Peabody, *North American Review*, October 1854, p. 536.
22. George William Curtis, "Editor's Easy Chair," *Harper's New Monthly Magazine*, July 1862, p. 270.
23. William Dean Howells, "My First Visit to New England" (1894), *Literary Friends and Acquaintance*, 1900.

24. Theodore F. Wolfe, "The Concord Pilgrimage," *Literary Shrines*, 1895, p. 71.
25. Fred Lewis Pattee, *A History of American Literature*, 1896, pp. 224–25.
26. Ralph Waldo Emerson, "Thoreau," *Atlantic*, August 1862, pp. 239–49.
27. James Russell Lowell, "Thoreau" (1865), *Works*, Riverside ed., 1890, Volume 1, pp. 368–81.
28. Robert Louis Stevenson, "Henry David Thoreau: His Character and Opinions" (1880) and "Preface, By Way of

Criticism" (1882), *Familiar Studies of Men and Books*, 1882, pp. 137–73, 18–21.
29. Henry S. Salt, *Life of Henry David Thoreau*, 1890, pp. 170–76.
30. Bradford Torrey, "Thoreau's Attitude toward Nature," *Atlantic*, November 1899, pp. 706–10.
31. Frederick M. Smith, "Thoreau," *Critic*, July 1900, pp. 60–67.
32. Paul Elmer More, "A Hermit's Notes on Thoreau," *Atlantic*, June 1901, pp. 857–64.

Volume 5

WILLIAM MAKEPEACE THACKERAY

1. Thomas Carlyle, Letter to Ralph Waldo Emerson (September 9, 1853).
2. Lewis Carroll, *Diary*, May 9, 1857.
3. Charles Knight, *Passages of a Working Life*, 1863, Pt. 3, Ch. 2.
4. Charles Dickens, "In Memoriam," *Cornhill Magazine*, February 1864, p. 129.
5. Charlotte Brontë, "Preface" to *Jane Eyre*, 1847.
6. James Russell Lowell, Letter to C. F. Briggs (February 15, 1854).
7. Ralph Waldo Emerson, "Literature," *English Traits*, 1856.
8. Peter Bayne, "The Modern Novel: Dickens—Bulwer—Thackeray," *Essays in Biography and Criticism*, 1857, pp. 389–92.
9. David Masson, *British Novelists and Their Styles*, 1859, pp. 248–49.
10. George William Curtis, "The Easy Chair," *Harper's New Monthly Magazine*, August 1862, p. 423.
11. Walter Bagehot, "Sterne and Thackeray" (1864), *Collected Works*, ed. Norman St. John-Stevas, 1965, Volume 2, pp. 304–6.
12. Edward FitzGerald, Letter to George Crabbe (January 12, 1864).
13. James Hannay, *Studies on Thackeray*, 1864, pp. 8–14.
14. Bayard Taylor, "William Makepeace Thackeray" (1864), *Critical Essays and Literary Notes*, 1880, p. 134.
15. James T. Fields, "Thackeray," *Yesterdays with Authors*, 1871, p. 35.
16. George Lamb, "Recollections of Thackeray," *Harper's New Monthly Magazine*, January 1877, pp. 259–60.
17. Harriet Martineau, *Autobiography*, ed. Maria Weston Chapman, 1877, Volume 2, pp. 60–61.
18. Anthony Trollope, *An Autobiography*, 1883, Ch. 13.
19. Edward Dowden, "Victorian Literature," *Transcripts and Studies*, 1888, pp. 168–71.
20. Robert Louis Stevenson, "Some Gentlemen in Fiction," 1888.
21. Lionel Johnson, *Academy*, March 7, 1891, p. 227.
22. Algernon Charles Swinburne, "Social Verse" (1891), *Studies in Prose and Poetry*, 1894, pp. 106–7.
23. Margaret Oliphant, *The Victorian Age of English Literature*, 1892, Volume 1, pp. 290–93.
24. W. H. Mallock, "Are Scott, Dickens, and Thackeray Obsolete?," *Forum*, December 1892, pp. 512–13.
25. Walter Whyte, "William Makepeace Thackeray," *The Poets and the Poetry of the Century*, ed. Alfred H. Miles, 1894, Volume 10, pp. 319–22.
26. Hjalmar Hjorth Boyesen, "The Great Realists and the Empty Story-Tellers," *Forum*, February 1895. p. 727.
27. William Dean Howells, "Thackeray," *My Literary Passions*, 1895.
28. William Samuel Lilly, "The Humourist as Philosopher—

Thackeray," *Four English Humourists of the Nineteenth Century*, 1895, p. 51.
29. Frederick Locker-Lampson, *My Confidences*, 1895, p. 302.
30. George Saintsbury, "Thackeray," *Corrected Impressions*, 1895.
31. Edmund Gosse, *A Short History of Modern English Literature*, 1897, pp. 352–54.
32. Lewis Melville, *The Life of William Makepeace Thackeray*, 1899, Volume 2, p. 250.
33. Henry A. Beers, *A History of English Romanticism in the Nineteenth Century*, 1901, pp. 397–98.
34. Walter Frewen Lord, "The Apostle of Mediocrity," *Nineteenth Century*, March 1902, p. 410.
35. Charles Whibley, *William Makepeace Thackeray*, 1903, pp. 234–38.
36. Jane Welsh Carlyle, Letter to Thomas Carlyle (September 16, 1847).
37. Abraham Hayward, "Thackeray's Writings," *Edinburgh Review*, January 1848, p. 50.
38. Charlotte Brontë, Letter to W. S. Williams (March 29, 1848).
39. Edwin P. Whipple, "Novels of the Season," *North American Review*, October 1848, pp. 368–69.
40. Richard Malcolm Johnston, "The Extremity of Satire," *Catholic World*, February 1886, pp. 688–90.
41. Edward FitzGerald, Letter to Frederick Tennyson (June 8, 1852).
42. Anthony Trollope, "W. M. Thackeray," *Cornhill Magazine*, February 1864, pp. 136–37.
43. James T. Fields, "Thackeray," *Yesterdays with Authors*, 1871, p. 16.
44. Henry J. Nicoll, *Landmarks of Literature*, 1882, pp. 389–91.
45. Nathaniel Hawthorne, *The English Note-Books*, 1855.
46. Whitwell Elwin, "The Newcomes," *Quarterly Review*, September 1855, pp. 350–58.
47. Andrew Preston Peabody, *North American Review*, January 1856, p. 284.
48. Anne Thackeray Ritchie, "Introduction" to *The Newcomes*, 1898–99, p. xxii.
49. Caroline Fox, *Journal* (June 12, 1851), *Memories of Old Friends*, ed. Horace N. Pym, 1882, p. 292.
50. George Gilfillan, "Thackeray," *A Third Gallery of Portraits*, 1854, pp. 261–62.
51. George Ticknor, Letter to Sir Edmund Head (December 23, 1855), *Life, Letters, and Journals of George Ticknor*, ed. Anna Ticknor, 1876, Volume 2, p. 294.
52. M. E. W. Sherwood, *An Epistle to Posterity*, 1897, p. 79.
53. John Foster Kirk, "Thackeray, as a Novelist," *North American Review*, July 1853, pp. 212–19.
54. Margaret Oliphant, "Mr. Thackeray and His Novels," *Blackwood's Edinburgh Magazine*, January 1855, pp. 88–96.

55. David Masson, "Thackeray," *Macmillan's Magazine*, February 1864, pp. 363–68.
56. W. E. Henley, "Thackeray," *Views and Reviews*, 1890, pp. 10–22.
57. Henry D. Sedgwick, Jr., "Some Aspects of Thackeray," *Atlantic*, November 1898, pp. 707–19.

NATHANIEL HAWTHORNE

1. Nathaniel Hawthorne, Letter to His Mother (March 13, 1821), cited in Julian Hawthorne, *Nathaniel Hawthorne and His Wife*, 1884, Volume 1, pp. 107–8.
2. S. G. Goodrich, *Recollections of a Lifetime*, 1856, Volume 2, pp. 269–70.
3. Maria Mitchell, *Journal* (August 5, 1857), *Life, Letters, and Journals of Maria Mitchell*, ed. Phebe Mitchell Kendall, 1896, p. 89.
4. Franklin Pierce, Letter to Horatio Bridge (May 21, 1864), cited in Horatio Bridge, *Personal Recollections of Nathaniel Hawthorne*, 1893, pp. 176–79.
5. Henry Wadsworth Longfellow, "Hawthorne," 1864.
6. A. Bronson Alcott, "Hawthorne" (July 1869), *Concord Days*, 1872, pp. 193–97.
7. George S. Hillard, "The English Note-Books of Nathaniel Hawthorne," *Atlantic*, September 1870, pp. 258–59.
8. S. C. Hall, *Retrospect of a Long Life*, 1883, p. 420.
9. William Dean Howells, "My First Visit to New England" (1894), *Literary Friends and Acquaintance*, 1900.
10. Horatio Bridge (1836), *Personal Recollections of Nathaniel Hawthorne*, 1893, p. 71.
11. Edgar Allan Poe, "Nathaniel Hawthorne" (1847), *Essays and Reviews*, ed. G. R. Thompson, 1984, pp. 587–88.
12. James Russell Lowell, A *Fable for Critics*, 1848.
13. Rufus W. Griswold, Letter to James T. Fields (January 24, 1850), cited in *Passages from the Correspondence and Other Papers of Rufus W. Griswold*, ed. W. M. Griswold, 1898, p. 258.
14. Oliver Wendell Holmes, Letter to Nathaniel Hawthorne (April 9, 1851), cited in George Parsons Lathrop, A *Study of Hawthorne*, 1876, p. 232.
15. George Eliot, Letter to Mrs. Taylor (August 19, 1852).
16. Alexander Smith, "A Shelf in My Bookcase," *Dreamthorp*, 1863, pp. 190–94.
17. Charles Sumner, Letter to Henry Wadsworth Longfellow (May 21, 1864), cited in Edward L. Pierce, *Memoir and Letters of Charles Sumner*, 1893, Volume 4, p. 202.
18. Oliver Wendell Holmes, "Hawthorne," *Atlantic*, July 1864, pp. 100–101.
19. George William Curtis, "Editor's Easy Chair," *Harper's New Monthly Magazine*, August 1864, p. 405.
20. James Russell Lowell, "Thoreau" (1865), *Works*, Riverside ed., 1890, Volume 1, p. 365.
21. Noah Porter, *Books and Reading*, 1870, p. 230.
22. Edward FitzGerald, Letter to W. F. Pollock (November 1872).
23. George Parsons Lathrop, A *Study of Hawthorne*, 1876, pp. 326–31.
24. Edmund Clarence Stedman, "Hawthorne," 1877.
25. Emily Dickinson, Letter to Thomas Wentworth Higginson (1879).
26. Thomas Wentworth Higginson, "Hawthorne," *Short Studies of American Authors*, 1880, pp. 8–9.
27. James Herbert Morse, "The Native Element in American Fiction," *Century*, July 1883, pp. 293–94.
28. Alfred H. Welsh, *Development of English Literature and Language*, 1883, Volume 2, pp. 512–13.
29. Henry Cabot Lodge, *Studies in History*, 1884, pp. 21–22.
30. Andrew Lang, "To Edgar Allan Poe," *Letters to Dead Authors*, 1886, p. 149.
31. Edward P. Roe, "The Element of Life in Fiction," *Forum*, April 1888, p. 229.
32. John Vance Cheney, "Hawthorne," *The Golden Guess: Essays on Poetry and the Poets*, 1891, pp. 291–92.
33. Hamilton W. Mabie, "The Most Popular Novels in America," *Forum*, December 1893, p. 512.
34. Camilla Toulmin Crosland, *Landmarks of a Literary Life*, 1893, pp. 210–11.
35. Barrett Wendell, "American Literature," *Stelligeri and Other Essays concerning America*, 1893, p. 139.
36. Henry A. Beers, *Initial Studies in American Letters*, 1895, p. 123.
37. Charles F. Johnson, *Elements of Literary Criticism*, 1898, pp. 34–35.
38. Wilbur L. Cross, *The Development of the English Novel*, 1899, pp. 163–66.
39. Bradford Torrey, "Writers That Are Quotable," *Atlantic*, March 1899, p. 407.
40. Henry Wadsworth Longfellow, "Hawthorne's *Twice-Told Tales*," *North American Review*, July 1837, pp. 59, 63.
41. Edgar Allan Poe, "Nathaniel Hawthorne" (1842), *Essays and Reviews*, ed. G. R. Thompson, 1984, pp. 568–69.
42. Nathaniel Hawthorne, Letter to Richard Henry Stoddard (1853), cited in Julian Hawthorne, *Nathaniel Hawthorne and His Wife*, 1884, Volume 1, p. 98.
43. Arthur Cleveland Coxe, "The Writings of Hawthorne," *Church Review*, January 1851, p. 507.
44. Bryan Waller Procter, Letter to James T. Fields (February 1853), cited in James T. Fields, "'Barry Cornwall' and Some of His Friends," *Harper's New Monthly Magazine*, December 1875, pp. 59–60.
45. Nathaniel Hawthorne, *The English Note-Books*, 1855.
46. Berkeley Aikin, Letter to Nathaniel Hawthorne (1862), cited in Julian Hawthorne, *Nathaniel Hawthorne and His Wife*, 1884, Volume 2, p. 305.
47. Francis Hovey Stoddard, *The Evolution of the English Novel*, 1900, pp. 75–80.
48. Sophia Hawthorne, Letter (January 27, 1851), cited in Julian Hawthorne, *Nathaniel Hawthorne and His Wife*, 1884, Volume 1, p. 383.
49. Nathaniel Hawthorne, Letter to Horatio Bridge (March 15, 1851), cited in Horatio Bridge, *Personal Recollections of Nathaniel Hawthorne*, 1893, p. 125.
50. James Russell Lowell, Letter to Nathaniel Hawthorne (April 24, 1851), cited in Julian Hawthorne, *Nathaniel Hawthorne and His Wife*, 1884, Volume 1, pp. 390–91.
51. Herman Melville, Letter to Nathaniel Hawthorne (1851), cited in George Parsons Lathrop, A *Study of Hawthorne*, 1876, pp. 230–31.
52. Washington Irving, Letter to Nathaniel Hawthorne (1852), cited in Julian Hawthorne, *Nathaniel Hawthorne and His Wife*, 1884, Volume 1, p. 440.
53. George S. Hillard, Letter to Nathaniel Hawthorne (July 27, 1852), cited in Julian Hawthorne, *Nathaniel Hawthorne and His Wife*, 1884, Volume 1, p. 448.
54. John Nichol, *American Literature*, 1882, pp. 345–47.
55. John Lothrop Motley, Letter to Nathaniel Hawthorne (March 29, 1860), cited in George Parsons Lathrop, A *Study of Hawthorne*, 1876, pp. 262–63.
56. Henry Bright, Letter to Nathaniel Hawthorne (1860), cited in Julian Hawthorne, *Nathaniel Hawthorne and His Wife*, 1884, Volume 2, p. 240.
57. Nathaniel Hawthorne, Letter to Henry Bright (1860), cited in Julian Hawthorne, *Nathaniel Hawthorne and His Wife*, 1884, Volume 2, p. 241.
58. William Ellery Channing, Letter to Nathaniel Hawthorne (September 3, 1860), cited in Julian Hawthorne, *Nathaniel Hawthorne and His Wife*, 1884, Volume 2, p. 265.

59. James Russell Lowell, "Swinburne's Tragedies" (1866), *Works*, Riverside ed., Volume 2, pp. 125–26.
60. George Parsons Lathrop, A *Study of Hawthorne*, 1876, pp. 260–61.
61. Arthur Sherburne Hardy, "Hawthorne's Italian Romance," *Book Buyer*, November 1889, pp. 427–28.
62. Katharine Lee Bates, *American Literature*, 1897, pp. 314–15.
63. Andrew Preston Peabody, "Nathaniel Hawthorne," *North American Review*, January 1853, pp. 227–33.
64. Richard Holt Hutton, "Nathaniel Hawthorne," *Literary Essays*, 1871, pp. 437–58.
65. Sir Leslie Stephen, "Nathaniel Hawthorne" (1875), *Hours in a Library* (1874–79), 1904, Volume 1, pp. 244–70.
66. Henry James, *Hawthorne*, 1879, pp. 106–17.
67. Anthony Trollope, "The Genius of Nathaniel Hawthorne," *North American Review*, September 1879, pp. 204–22.
68. George E. Woodberry, *Nathaniel Hawthorne*, 1902, pp. 189–202.

CHARLES DICKENS

1. Thomas Carlyle, Letter to John A. Carlyle (March 17, 1840).
2. Philip Hone, *Diary*, January 24, 1842.
3. Richard Henry Dana, *Journal* (February 5, 1842), cited in Charles Francis Adams, *Richard Henry Dana: A Biography*, 1890, Volume 1, p. 33.
4. Frances Ann Kemble, Letter (April 22, 1842), *Records of Later Life*, 1882, p. 318.
5. Nathaniel Hawthorne, *The English Note-Books*, October 22, 1853.
6. Hans Christian Andersen, Letter to the Grand Duke of Weimar (August 9, 1857).
7. John Forster, *The Life of Charles Dickens*, 1872–74, Bk. 11, Ch. 3.
8. Mamie Dickens, Georgina Hogarth, "Preface" to *The Letters of Charles Dickens*, 1882, Volume 1, p. viii.
9. Percy Fitzgerald, "Charles Dickens as an Editor," *Recreations of a Literary Man*, 1882, pp. 31–32.
10. Thomas Adolphus Trollope, *What I Remember*, 1888.
11. William Cullen Bryant, *New York Evening Post* (February 18, 1842), cited in Parke Godwin, A *Biography of William Cullen Bryant*, 1883, Volume 1, pp. 396–97.
12. Elizabeth Barrett Browning, Letter to James Martin (February 6, 1843).
13. Edwin P. Whipple, "Novels and Novelists: Charles Dickens" (1844), *Literature and Life*, 1849, pp. 58–63.
14. Leigh Hunt, "To Charles Dickens," 1849.
15. Mary Russell Mitford, Letter to Mr. Starkey (January 31, 1853).
16. George Eliot, "Natural History of German Life: Riehl," 1856.
17. Ralph Waldo Emerson, "Literature," *English Traits*, 1856.
18. John Ruskin, *Modern Painters*, 1856, Volume 3, Pt. 4, App. 3.
19. Peter Bayne, "The Modern Novel: Dickens—Bulwer—Thackeray," *Essays in Biography and Criticism*, 1857, pp. 384–86.
20. David Masson, *British Novelists and Their Styles*, 1859, pp. 251–52.
21. Walter Savage Landor, "Dickens," 1863.
22. Alexander Smith, "On Vagabonds," *Dreamthorp*, 1863, pp. 287–88.
23. Charles Eliot Norton, "Charles Dickens," *North American Review*, April 1868, pp. 671–72.

24. F. B. Perkins, *Charles Dickens: A Sketch of His Life and Works*, 1870, p. 63.
25. Edward FitzGerald, Letter to Frances Ann Kemble (August 24, 1874).
26. Harriet Martineau, *Autobiography*, ed. Maria Weston Chapman, 1877, Volume 2, pp. 61–63.
27. Justin McCarthy, A *History of Our Own Times*, 1879–80, Ch. 29.
28. Algernon Charles Swinburne, "Dickens," 1882.
29. Adolphus William Ward, *Dickens*, 1882, pp. 197–200.
30. Anthony Trollope, *An Autobiography*, 1883, Ch. 13.
31. Edwin P. Whipple, "In Dickens-Land," *Scribner's Magazine*, December 1887, pp. 744–45.
32. Robert Louis Stevenson, "Some Gentlemen in Fiction," 1888.
33. W. E. Henley, "Dickens," *Views and Reviews*, 1890, pp. 3–9.
34. William Dean Howells, *Criticism and Fiction*, 1891, pp. 174–75.
35. W. H. Mallock, "Are Scott, Dickens, and Thackeray Obsolete?," *Forum*, December 1892, pp. 511–12.
36. William Samuel Lilly, "Dickens," *Four English Humourists of the Nineteenth Century*, 1895, pp. 14–15.
37. David Christie Murray, *My Contemporaries in Fiction*, 1897, pp. 9–14.
38. Herbert Paul, "The Apotheosis of the Novel," *Nineteenth Century*, May 1892, p. 773.
39. Laurence Hutton, "Charles Dickens," *Outlook*, October 1898, p. 321.
40. Wilbur L. Cross, *The Development of the English Novel*, 1899, pp. 192–93.
41. Richard Burton, "The Fundamentals of Fiction," *Forces in Fiction and Other Essays*, 1902, p. 7.
42. John Wilson Croker, "The Pickwick Papers," *Quarterly Review*, December 1837, p. 484.
43. Richard Grant White, "The Styles of Dickens and Disraeli," *Galaxy Magazine*, August 1870, p. 258.
44. S. C. Hall, *Retrospect of a Long Life*, 1883, p. 394.
45. Margaret Oliphant, *The Victorian Age of English Literature*, 1892, Volume 1, pp. 251–52.
46. Edgar Allan Poe, "Charles Dickens" (1841), *Essays and Reviews*, ed. G. R. Thompson, 1984, pp. 218–19.
47. Edgar Allan Poe, "Charles Dickens" (1841), *Essays and Reviews*, ed. G. R. Thompson, 1984, pp. 213–17.
48. Thomas De Quincey, Letter to His Daughter (September 19, 1847), cited in Alexander Hay Japp (as "H. A. Page"), *Thomas De Quincey: His Life and Writings*, 1877, Volume 1, pp. 348–49.
49. Sara Coleridge, Letter to Aubrey De Vere (October 2, 1849), *Memoir and Letters of Sara Coleridge*, ed. Edith Coleridge, 1873, Volume 2, p. 407.
50. Bret Harte, "Dickens in Camp," 1870.
51. George Gissing, "Dickens in Memory," *Critic*, January 1902, pp. 48–49.
52. Francis, Lord Jeffrey, Letter to Charles Dickens (October 16, 1842), cited in Lord Henry Cockburn, *Life of Lord Jeffrey*, 1852, Volume 2, p. 294.
53. Henry Wadsworth Longfellow, Letter to Charles Sumner (October 16, 1842), cited in Samuel Longfellow, *Life of Henry Wadsworth Longfellow*, 1891, Volume 1, p. 421.
54. Thomas Babington Macaulay, Letter to Macvey Napier (October 19, 1842), cited in G. Otto Trevelyan, *The Life and Letters of Lord Macaulay*, 1876, Volume 2, p. 109.
55. James Spedding, "Dickens's *American Notes*" (1843), *Reviews and Discussions*, 1849, pp. 247–48.
56. William Makepeace Thackeray, "A Box of Novels," *Fraser's Magazine*, February 1844, pp. 168–69.

57. Julia C. R. Dorr, "Christmas and Its Literature," *Book Buyer*, December 1868, pp. 284–85.
58. Philip Hone, *Diary*, July 29, 1843.
59. Sara Coleridge, Letter to Mrs. H. M. Jones (August 17, 1848), *Memoir and Letters of Sara Coleridge*, ed. Edith Coleridge, 1873, Volume 2, p. 346.
60. William Dean Howells, "Dickens," *My Literary Passions*, 1895.
61. Charlotte Brontë, Letter to W. S. Williams (September 13, 1849).
62. Charles Dickens, "Preface" to *David Copperfield*, 1850.
63. William Makepeace Thackeray, "Mr. Brown the Elder Takes Mr. Brown the Younger to a Club," *Sketches and Travels in London*, 1850.
64. Hans Christian Andersen, "A Visit to Charles Dickens," *Temple Bar*, December 1870, p. 29.
65. Mowbray Morris, "Charles Dickens," *Fortnightly Review*, December 1882, pp. 776–77.
66. James Russell Lowell, Letter to Charles Eliot Norton (April 8, 1887).
67. Walter Bagehot, "Charles Dickens" (1858), *Collected Works*, ed. Norman St. John-Stevas, 1965, Volume 2, pp. 81–107.
68. George Henry Lewes, "Dickens in Relation to Criticism," *Fortnightly Review*, February 1872, pp. 143–49.
69. Frederic Harrison, "Charles Dickens," *Studies in Early Victorian Literature*, 1895, pp. 133–44.
70. George Gissing, "Humour and Pathos," *Charles Dickens: A Critical Study*, 1898, pp. 197–215.
71. Algernon Charles Swinburne, "Charles Dickens," *Quarterly Review*, July 1902, pp. 20–32.

GEORGE ELIOT

1. Nathaniel Hawthorne, *The French and Italian Note-Books*, February 5, 1860.
2. Hallam Tennyson, *Journal* (July 22, 1871), cited in Hallam Tennyson, *Alfred Lord Tennyson: A Memoir*, 1897, Volume 2, p. 107.
3. Justin McCarthy, "'George Eliot' and George Lewes," *Modern Leaders*, 1872, p. 137.
4. Thomas Henry Huxley, Letter to Herbert Spencer (December 27, 1880), cited in Leonard Huxley, *Life and Letters of Thomas Henry Huxley*, 1900, Volume 2, p. 19.
5. C. Kegan Paul, "George Eliot," *Harper's New Monthly Magazine*, May 1881, p. 921.
6. Emily Dickinson, Letter to Thomas Niles (April 1883).
7. Sidney Lanier, *The English Novel*, 1883, p. 301.
8. John W. Cross, *George Eliot's Life as Related in Her Letters and Journals*, 1884, Volume 1, p. 310.
9. Charles Godfrey Leland, *Memoirs*, 1893, p. 390.
10. Edmond Scherer, "George Eliot" (1861), *Essays on English Literature*, tr. George Saintsbury, 1891, pp. 5–6.
11. Walter Bagehot, "Sterne and Thackeray" (1864), *Collected Works*, ed. Norman St. John-Stevas, 1965, Volume 2, pp. 289–90.
12. Henry James, "The Novels of George Eliot," *Atlantic*, October 1866, p. 488.
13. Arthur Sedgwick, "*Felix Holt, the Radical*," *North American Review*, October 1866, pp. 562–63.
14. George Parsons Lathrop, "Growth of the Novel," *Atlantic*, June 1874, pp. 688–89.
15. William Cleaver Wilkinson, "The Literary and Ethical Quality of George Eliot's Novels," *A Free Lance in the Field of Life and Letters*, 1874, p. 49.
16. Edmund Clarence Stedman, *Victorian Poets*, 1875, p. 254.
17. Justin McCarthy, *A History of Our Own Times*, 1879–80, Ch. 67.
18. F. W. H. Myers, "George Eliot," *Modern Essays*, 1883.
19. Anthony Trollope, *An Autobiography*, 1883, Ch. 13.
20. John Tulloch, *Movements of Religious Thought in Britain during the Nineteenth Century*, 1885.
21. Charles L. Reade, Compton Reade, *Charles Reade: A Memoir*, 1887, pp. 301–2.
22. Walter Lewin, "The Abuse of Fiction," *Forum*, August 1889, p. 665.
23. Oscar Browning, *Life of George Eliot*, 1890, pp. 140–44.
24. George Saintsbury, "Three Mid-Century Novelists," *Corrected Impressions*, 1895.
25. Henry Craik, "George Eliot," *English Prose*, ed. Henry Craik, 1896, Volume 5, pp. 663–66.
26. Edmund Gosse, *A Short History of Modern English Literature*, 1897, pp. 369–71.
27. Wilbur L. Cross, *The Development of the English Novel*, 1899, pp. 250–52.
28. George Eliot, *Journal* (November 16, 1858), cited in *George Eliot's Life as Related in Her Letters and Journals*, ed. John W. Cross, 1884, Volume 2, pp. 51–52.
29. Jane Welsh Carlyle, Letter to Thomas Carlyle (February 20, 1859).
30. Edward Bulwer-Lytton, Letter to John Blackwood (April 24, 1859), cited in *George Eliot's Life as Related in Her Letters and Journals*, ed. John W. Cross, 1884, Volume 2, pp. 74–75.
31. Charles Dickens, Letter to George Eliot (July 10, 1859).
32. Noah Porter, *Books and Reading*, 1870, p. 119.
33. L. Bulkley, "Dinah Morris and Mrs. Elizabeth Evans," *Century Magazine*, August 1882, p. 552.
34. William Dean Howells, "George Eliot, Hawthorne, Goethe, Heine," *My Literary Passions*, 1895.
35. John Blackwood, Letter to George Eliot (February 19, 1861).
36. Henry James, "The Novels of George Eliot," *Atlantic*, October 1866, p. 482.
37. Frederic Harrison, "George Eliot," *Studies in Early Victorian Literature*, 1895, pp. 211–13.
38. Connop Thirlwall, Letter (June 4, 1872), *Letters to a Friend*, ed. Arthur Penrhyn Stanley, 1881, p. 278.
39. Alfred H. Welsh, *Development of English Literature and Language*, 1883, Volume 2, p. 447.
40. Bessie Rayner Belloc, *In a Walled Garden*, 1894, p. 12.
41. Herbert Paul, "George Eliot," *Nineteenth Century*, June 1902, pp. 941–43.
42. Harriet Beecher Stowe, Letter to George Eliot (March 18, 1876), cited in Charles Edward Stowe, *Life of Harriet Beecher Stowe*, 1889, pp. 473–74.
43. R. E. Francillon, "George Eliot's First Romance," *Gentleman's Magazine*, October 1876, pp. 411–13.
44. Bayard Taylor, "George Eliot" (1876), *Critical Essays and Literary Notes*, 1880, p. 347.
45. Walter Besant, *The Art of Fiction*, 1884, p. 21.
46. Emily Dickinson, Letter to Maria Whitney (Spring 1885).
47. Henry James, *Galaxy*, March 1873, pp. 424–28.
48. Joseph Jacobs, "Mordecai: A Protest against the Critics" (1877), *Jewish Ideals and Other Essays*, 1896, pp. 61–83.
49. George Willis Cooke, "The Limitations of Her Thought," *George Eliot: A Critical Study of Her Life, Writings and Philosophy*, 1884, pp. 413–24.
50. Vida D. Scudder, "George Eliot and the Social Conscience," *Social Ideals in English Letters*, 1898, pp. 180–92.
51. W. C. Brownell, "George Eliot," *Scribner's Magazine*, December 1900, pp. 711–26.
52. Sir Leslie Stephen, *George Eliot*, 1902, pp. 200–206.

THOMAS CARLYLE

1. Henry Crabb Robinson, *Diary*, February 12, 1832.
2. Ralph Waldo Emerson, Letter to Alexander Ireland (August 30, 1833).
3. George Ticknor, *Journal* (June 1, 1838), *Life, Letters, and Journals of George Ticknor*, ed. Anna Ticknor, 1876, Volume 2, pp. 180–81.
4. Charles Sumner, Letter to George S. Hillard (December 4, 1838), cited in Edward L. Pierce, *Memoir and Letters of Charles Sumner*, 1877, Volume 2, p. 22.
5. Thomas Carlyle, *Journal* (October 10, 1843), cited in James Anthony Froude, *Thomas Carlyle: A History of His Life in London, 1834–1881*, 1884, Volume 1, p. 1.
6. Margaret Fuller, Letter (December 1846), *Memoirs*, 1852, Volume 2, pp. 188–90.
7. John Stuart Blackie, Letter to Augusta Wyld (1848), cited in Anna M. Stoddart, *John Stuart Blackie: A Biography*, 1895, Volume 1, pp. 241–42.
8. Sydney Dobell, Letter to George Gilfillan (December 12, 1849), *The Life and Letters of Sydney Dobell*, ed. Emily Jolly, 1878, Volume 1, pp. 112–13.
9. Leigh Hunt, *Autobiography*, 1850, Ch. 24.
10. Elizabeth Barrett Browning, Letter to Mrs. Jameson (October 22, 1851).
11. Harriet Martineau, *Autobiography*, ed. Maria Weston Chapman, 1877, Volume 1, pp. 287–88.
12. Henry James, Sr., "Some Personal Recollections of Carlyle" (1881), *Literary Remains*, 1884, pp. 423–26.
13. Johann Wolfgang von Goethe (1827), cited in Johann Peter Eckermann, *Conversations with Goethe*, 1830, tr. John Oxenford.
14. William Sewell, "Carlyle's Works," *Quarterly Review*, September 1840, pp. 451–52.
15. Thomas Babington Macaulay, Letter to Leigh Hunt (October 29, 1841).
16. Edgar Allan Poe, "William Ellery Channing" (1843), *Essays and Reviews*, ed. G. R. Thompson, 1984, pp. 460–61.
17. Edward A. Freeman, Letter to Eleanor Gutch (May 16, 1848), cited in W. R. W. Stephens, *The Life and Letters of Edward A. Freeman*, 1895, Volume 1, p. 93.
18. James Russell Lowell, *A Fable for Critics*, 1848.
19. Charlotte Brontë, Letter to W. S. Williams (April 16, 1849).
20. James Martineau, Letter to R. H. Hutton (May 19, 1852), cited in James Drummond, *The Life and Letters of James Martineau*, 1902, Volume 1, pp. 340–41.
21. Frederick Denison Maurice, Letter to J. M. Ludlow (May 30, 1862), *The Life of Frederick Denison Maurice*, ed. Frederick Maurice, 1884, Volume 2, pp. 404–5.
22. John Stuart Mill, *Autobiography*, 1873, Ch. 5.
23. Edward Dowden, "The Transcendental Movement and Literature" (1877), *Studies in Literature*, 1878, pp. 74–76.
24. Harriet Martineau, *Autobiography*, ed. Maria Weston Chapman, 1877, Volume 1, pp. 291–92.
25. Thomas Henry Huxley, Letter to Lord Stanley (March 9, 1881), cited in Leonard Huxley, *Life and Letters of Thomas Henry Huxley*, 1900, Volume 2, p. 34.
26. Matthew Arnold, Letter to M. Fontanès (March 25, 1881).
27. Edmond Scherer, "Thomas Carlyle" (1881), *Essays on English Literature*, tr. George Saintsbury, 1891, p. 235.
28. Walt Whitman, "Death of Thomas Carlyle" (1881), *Prose Works*, ed. Floyd Stovall, 1963, Volume 1, pp. 249–53.
29. John Tyndall, "On Unveiling the Statue of Thomas Carlyle" (1882), *New Fragments*, 1900, pp. 393–96.
30. Frederic Harrison, "Froude's Life of Carlyle" (1885), *The Choice of Books and Other Literary Pieces*, 1886, pp. 194–99.
31. Edward Caird, "The Genius of Carlyle," *Essays in Literature and Philosophy*, 1892, Volume 1, pp. 264–67.
32. John Nichol, *Thomas Carlyle*, 1892, pp. 241–45.
33. William Roscoe Thayer, "Carlyle" (1895), *Throne-Makers*, 1899, pp. 182–85.
34. Lewis E. Gates, "English Literature of the Nineteenth Century: A Retrospect: II. The Return to Conventional Life," *Critic*, March 1900, pp. 273–75.
35. Alexander H. Everett, "Thomas Carlyle," *North American Review*, October 1835, pp. 459–60.
36. George Eliot, Letter to Martha Jackson (December 16, 1841).
37. Francis Thompson, "*Sartor* Re-read," *Academy*, July 6, 1901, pp. 17–18.
38. John Stuart Mill, "The French Revolution," *London and Westminster Review*, July 1837, pp. 17–18.
39. Lucy Aikin, Letter to William Ellery Channing (April 18, 1838), *Correspondence of William Ellery Channing and Lucy Aikin*, ed. Anna Letitia Le Breton, 1874, p. 309.
40. Edward FitzGerald, Letter to Bernard Barton (April 1838).
41. John Henry Newman, Letter to Mrs. J. Mozley (April 23, 1839).
42. Herman Merivale, "Carlyle on the French Revolution," *Edinburgh Review*, July 1840, pp. 415–16.
43. John Campbell Shairp, "Prose Poets: Thomas Carlyle," *Aspects of Poetry* (1881), 1882, pp. 368–69.
44. George Saintsbury, "Thomas Carlyle," *Corrected Impressions*, 1895.
45. John Gibson Lockhart, Letter to Thomas Carlyle (April 27, 1843), cited in Andrew Lang, *The Life and Letters of John Gibson Lockhart*, 1897, Volume 2, pp. 238–39.
46. Ralph Waldo Emerson, *Dial*, July 1843, pp. 100–101.
47. Arnold Toynbee, *Lectures on the Industrial Revolution in the Eighteenth Century in England*, 1884, pp. 209–11.
48. John Sterling, "Carlyle's Works," *London and Westminster Review*, October 1839, pp. 8–23.
49. Henry David Thoreau, "Thomas Carlyle and His Works" (1847), *Writings*, 1906, Volume 4, pp. 323–33.
50. James Russell Lowell, "Carlyle" (1866), *Works*, Riverside ed., Volume 2, pp. 91–109.
51. Sir Leslie Stephen, "Carlyle's Ethics," *Hours in a Library* (1874–79), 1904, Volume 4, pp. 232–80.
52. G. K. Chesterton, "Thomas Carlyle" (1902), *Varied Types*, 1908, pp. 109–22.

RALPH WALDO EMERSON

1. Thomas Carlyle, Letter to His Mother (August 26, 1833), *The Correspondence of Thomas Carlyle and Ralph Waldo Emerson*, 1883, Volume 1, p. 4.
2. Theodore Parker, *Journal* (July 15, 1838), cited in John Weiss, *Life and Correspondence of Theodore Parker*, 1864, Volume 1, p. 113.
3. Ralph Waldo Emerson, Letter to Thomas Carlyle (May 10, 1838).
4. Charles Sumner, Letter to Lord Houghton (March 2, 1839), cited in T. Wemyss Reid, *The Life, Letters, and Friendships of Richard Monckton Milnes, First Lord Houghton*, 1891, Volume 1, pp. 237–39.
5. John Quincy Adams, *Diary*, August 2, 1840.
6. Rufus Dawes, "Boyhood Memories," *Boston Miscellany*, February 1843, p. 60.
7. Henry Crabb Robinson, Letter to Thomas Robinson (April 22, 1848).
8. Arthur Hugh Clough, Letter to Thomas Arnold (July 16, 1848).

9. Maria Mitchell, *Journal* (November 14, 1855), *Life, Letters, and Journals of Maria Mitchell*, ed. Phebe Mitchell Kendall, 1896, pp. 45–47.

10. Walt Whitman, "A Visit, at the Last, to R. W. Emerson" (1881), *Prose Works*, ed. Floyd Stovall, 1963, Volume 1, pp. 278–80.

11. James Martineau, Letter to Alexander Ireland (December 31, 1882), cited in James Drummond, *The Life and Letters of James Martineau*, 1902, Volume 2, pp. 312–13.

12. Louisa May Alcott, "Reminiscences of Ralph Waldo Emerson," *Some Noted Princes, Authors, and Statesmen of Our Time*, ed. James Parton, 1885, pp. 284–88.

13. Orestes Augustus Brownson, "Emerson's *Essays*," *Boston Quarterly Review*, July 1841, p. 292.

14. Caroline Fox, *Journal* (June 8, 1841), *Memories of Old Friends*, ed. Horace N. Pym, 1882, p. 140.

15. Thomas Carlyle, "Preface by the English Editor" to *Essays*, 1841, pp. v–xiii.

16. Edgar Allan Poe, "A Chapter on Autography" (1842), *Complete Works*, ed. James A. Harrison, 1902, Volume 15, p. 260.

17. Henry David Thoreau, *Journal* (1845–47), *Writings*, 1906, Volume 7, pp. 431–33.

18. Theodore Parker, "The Writings of Ralph Waldo Emerson," *Massachusetts Quarterly Review*, March 1850, p. 254.

19. Thomas Babington Macaulay, *Diary* (January 12, 1850), cited in G. Otto Trevelyan, *The Life and Letters of Lord Macaulay*, 1876, Volume 2, p. 234.

20. Thomas Powell, "Ralph Waldo Emerson," *The Living Authors of America*, 1850, pp. 66–67, 75–77.

21. James Russell Lowell, "Emerson the Lecturer" (1861–68), *Works*, Riverside ed., Volume 1, pp. 349–52.

22. George Ripley, *Journal* (1869), cited in Octavius Brooks Frothingham, *George Ripley*, 1882, pp. 266–68.

23. Walt Whitman, "Emerson's Books (The Shadows of Them)" (1880), *Prose Works*, ed. Floyd Stovall, 1963, Volume 2, pp. 515–18.

24. Joseph O'Connor, "Ralph Waldo Emerson," *Catholic World*, April 1878, pp. 92–95.

25. Coventry Patmore, "Emerson," *Principle in Art*, 1889, pp. 130–31.

26. Henry James, *Nathaniel Hawthorne*, 1879, pp. 82–83.

27. W. L. Courtnay, "Ralph Waldo Emerson," *Fortnightly Review*, September 1885, p. 331.

28. Edwin P. Whipple, "American Literature" (1886), *American Literature and Other Papers*, 1887, pp. 59–65.

29. Maurice Maeterlinck, "Emerson," trs. Charlotte Porter, Helen A. Clarke, *Poet-Lore*, 1898, pp. 82–84.

30. George Edward Woodberry, *Ralph Waldo Emerson*, 1907, pp. 186–87.

31. Margaret Fuller, "Emerson's Essays," *New York Daily Tribune*, December 7, 1844.

32. Charlotte Brontë, Letter to W. S. Williams (February 4, 1849).

33. Edward FitzGerald, Letter to John Allen (March 4, 1850).

34. Charles Eliot Norton, "Emerson's *Representative Men*," *North American Review*, April 1850, pp. 520–21.

35. William P. Trent, A *History of American Literature*, 1607–1865, 1903, pp. 333–36.

36. James Russell Lowell, Letter to James B. Thayer (December 24, 1883).

37. C. C. Everett, "The Poems of Emerson," *Andover Review*, March 1887, pp. 239–40.

38. Charles F. Richardson, *American Literature, 1607–1885*, 1887, Volume 2, pp. 169–71.

39. Edmund Gosse, "Has America Produced a Poet?" (1889), *Questions at Issue*, 1893, pp. 86–88.

40. C. P. Cranch, "Emerson's Limitations as a Poet," *Critic*, February 27, 1892, p. 129.

41. George Gilfillan, "Emerson," A *Third Gallery of Portraits*, 1854, pp. 328–36.

42. Matthew Arnold, "Emerson" (1884), *Discourses in America*, 1885, pp. 150–207.

43. Henry James, Sr., "Mr. Emerson," *Literary Remains*, 1884, pp. 293–302.

44. Edmund Clarence Stedman, "Ralph Waldo Emerson," *Poets of America*, 1885, pp. 133–79.

45. George Santayana, "Emerson," *Interpretations of Poetry and Religion*, 1900, pp. 217–33.

46. Sir Leslie Stephen, "Emerson," *National Review*, February 1901, pp. 882–98.

HENRY WADSWORTH LONGFELLOW

1. Samuel Kettell, *Specimens of American Poetry*, 1829, Volume 3, p. 238.

2. Charles Sumner, Letter to George Sumner (July 8, 1842), cited in Edward L. Pierce, *Memoir and Letters of Charles Sumner*, 1877, Volume 2, p. 215.

3. James Russell Lowell, "To H. W. L. (On His Birthday, 27th February, 1867)" (1867), cited in Samuel Longfellow, *Life of Henry Wadsworth Longfellow*, 1891, Volume 3, pp. 84–85.

4. Charles Dickens, Letter to Charles Dickens, Jr. (November 30, 1867).

5. George William Curtis, "Longfellow" (1882), *Literary and Social Essays*, 1894, pp. 202–4.

6. Austin Dobson, "H. W. Longfellow: In Memoriam," *Athenaeum*, April 1, 1882, p. 411.

7. Lord Ronald Gower, *My Reminiscences* (1883), 1895, pp. 454–56.

8. Oliver Wendell Holmes, "At the Saturday Club," 1884.

9. William James Stillman, *The Autobiography of a Journalist*, 1901, Volume 1, pp. 233–35.

10. Nathaniel Hawthorne, Letter to Henry Wadsworth Longfellow (December 26, 1839), cited in Samuel Longfellow, *Life of Henry Wadsworth Longfellow*, 1891, Volume 1, p. 349.

11. Edgar Allan Poe, "A Chapter on Autography" (1841), *Complete Works*, ed. James A. Harrison, 1902, Volume 15, pp. 191–92.

12. Edgar Allan Poe, "Henry Wadsworth Longfellow" (1842), *Essays and Reviews*, ed. G. R. Thompson, 1984, pp. 682–83, 690–92.

13. William Cullen Bryant, Letter to Henry Wadsworth Longfellow (January 31, 1846).

14. James Russell Lowell, A *Fable for Critics*, 1848.

15. George Gilfillan, "Henry Wadsworth Longfellow," A *Second Gallery of Literary Portraits*, 1850, pp. 374–77.

16. Thomas Powell, "Henry Wadsworth Longfellow," *The Living Authors of America*, 1850, p. 168.

17. Matthew Arnold, Letter to His Mother (April 14, 1862).

18. William Michael Rossetti, "Henry Wadsworth Longfellow," *Lives of Famous Poets*, 1878, pp. 388–91.

19. Anthony Trollope, "Henry Wadsworth Longfellow," *North American Review*, April 1881, pp. 384–85.

20. Walt Whitman, "Death of Longfellow" (1882), *Prose Works*, ed. Floyd Stovall, 1963, Volume 1, pp. 284–86.

21. Edmund Clarence Stedman, "Henry Wadsworth Longfellow," *Poets of America*, 1885, pp. 180–83.

22. Eric S. Robertson, *Life of Henry Wadsworth Longfellow*, 1887, pp. 174–77.

23. Edmund Gosse, "Has America Produced a Poet?" (1889), *Questions at Issue*, 1893, pp. 82–83.

24. W. E. Henley, "Longfellow," *Views and Reviews*, 1890, pp. 151–53.

25. James Whitcomb Riley, "Longfellow" (1892), *Complete Works*, 1916, Volume 6, p. 1561.
26. William Dean Howells, "Editor's Easy Chair," *Harper's New Monthly Magazine*, April 1902, pp. 834–35.
27. Nathaniel Hawthorne, *Salem Advertiser*, November 13, 1847.
28. G. W. Peck, "*Evangeline*," *American Review*, February 1848, pp. 162–63.
29. William Cullen Bryant, Letter to Richard Henry Dana (September 12, 1848).
30. Sara Coleridge, Letter to Aubrey De Vere (September 1848), *Memoir and Letters of Sara Coleridge*, ed. Edith Coleridge, 1873, Volume 2, pp. 183–85.
31. Matthew Arnold, *On Translating Homer*, 1861.
32. Ralph Waldo Emerson, Letter to Henry Wadsworth Longfellow (November 25, 1855), cited in Samuel Longfellow, *Life of Henry Wadsworth Longfellow*, 1891, Volume 2, pp. 294–95.
33. Arthur Hugh Clough, Letter to F. J. Child (January 16, 1856).
34. John Nichol, *American Literature*, 1882, pp. 202–4.
35. George Ticknor, Letter to Henry Wadsworth Longfellow (June 1, 1867), cited in Samuel Longfellow, *Life of Henry Wadsworth Longfellow*, 1891, Volume 3, pp. 90–91.
36. John Fiske, "Longfellow's Dante" (1867), *The Unseen World and Other Essays*, 1876, pp. 263–65.
37. Charles Eliot Norton, "Longfellow's Translation of the *Divine Comedy*," *North American Review*, July 1867, pp. 133–34.
38. James Russell Lowell, Letter to James B. Thayer (October 1867).
39. William Cullen Bryant, Letter to James T. Field (October 31, 1867), cited in Parke Godwin, *A Biography of William Cullen Bryant*, 1883, Volume 2, p. 265.
40. Edwin P. Whipple, "Poets and Poetry of America" (1844), *Essays and Reviews*, 1850, Volume 1, pp. 58–66.
41. Margaret Fuller, "American Literature," *Papers on Literature and Art*, 1846.
42. Henry Norman, "A Study of Longfellow," *Fortnightly Review*, January 1883, pp. 100–115.
43. H. E. Scudder, "Longfellow's Art," *Atlantic*, March 1887, pp. 399–409.
44. George Saintsbury, "Longfellow's Poems" (1907), *Prefaces and Essays*, 1933, pp. 324–44.

ANTHONY TROLLOPE

1. Walter Herries Pollock, "Anthony Trollope," *Harper's New Monthly Magazine*, May 1883, pp. 911–912.
2. Julian Hawthorne, "The Maker of Many Books," *Manhattan*, December 1883, pp. 573–74.
3. Thomas Adolphus Trollope, *What I Remember*, 1888.
4. Andrew K. H. Boyd, *Twenty-five Years of St. Andrews*, 1892, Volume 1, pp. 100–101.
5. Charles K. Tuckerman, *Personal Recollections of Notable People*, 1895, Volume 2, pp. 8–9.
6. Nathaniel Hawthorne, Letter to Joseph M. Field (February 11, 1860), cited in Anthony Trollope, *An Autobiography*, 1883, Ch. 8.
7. James Hain Friswell, "Anthony Trollope," *Modern Men of Letters Honestly Criticised*, 1870, pp. 143–44.
8. Edward FitzGerald, Letter to W. F. Pollock (November 30, 1873).
9. Justin McCarthy, *A History of Our Own Times*, 1879–80, Ch. 67.
10. Edward A. Freeman, "Anthony Trollope," *Macmillan's Magazine*, January 1883, p. 240.
11. Richard F. Littledale, *Academy*, October 27, 1883, p. 274.
12. Edwin P. Whipple, "In Dickens-Land," *Scribner's Magazine*, December 1887, p. 743.
13. Margaret Oliphant, The *Victorian Age of English Literature*, 1892, Volume 2, pp. 471–77.
14. William Dean Howells, "Valdés, Galdós, Verga, Zola, Trollope, Hardy," *My Literary Passions*, 1895.
15. Frederick Locker-Lampson, *My Confidences*, 1895, pp. 334–35.
16. George Saintsbury, A *History of Nineteenth Century Literature*, 1896, pp. 329–31.
17. H. D. Traill, *Social England*, 1897, Volume 6, p. 517.
18. Wilbur L. Cross, *The Development of the English Novel*, 1899, pp. 223–24.
19. Justin McCarthy, *Reminiscences*, 1899, Volume 1, pp. 374–75.
20. Walter Frewen Lord, "The Novels of Anthony Trollope," *Nineteenth Century*, May 1901, pp. 805–16.
21. James Bryce, "Anthony Trollope," *Studies in Contemporary Biography*, 1903, pp. 123–130.
22. Unsigned, "Orley Farm," *National Review*, January 1863, pp. 36–40.
23. A. V. Dicey, "Anthony Trollope," *Nation*, March 12, 1874, pp. 174–75.
24. Anthony Trollope, *An Autobiography*, 1883, Ch. 10, 20.
25. Henry James, "Anthony Trollope," *Century Magazine*, July 1883, pp. 385–95.
26. Frederic Harrison, "Anthony Trollope," *Studies in Early Victorian Literature*, 1895, pp. 183–204.
27. Sir Leslie Stephen, "Anthony Trollope," *National Review*, September 1901, pp. 69–84.
28. Gamaliel Bradford, Jr., "Anthony Trollope," *Atlantic*, March 1902, pp. 426–31.

EMILY DICKINSON

1. Unsigned, "Emily Dickinson's Personality," *Book Buyer*, May 1892, pp. 157–58.
2. Thomas Wentworth Higginson, "Preface" to *Poems by Emily Dickinson*, eds. Mabel Loomis Todd, T. W. Higginson, 1890, pp. iii–vi.
3. Unsigned, "Recent Poetry," *Nation*, November 27, 1890, p. 423.
4. William Dean Howells, "Editor's Study," *Harper's New Monthly Magazine*, January 1891, pp. 319–20.
5. Unsigned, "Talk about New Books," *Catholic World*, January 1891, pp. 603–4.
6. Unsigned, "A Poet and Some Others," *Saturday Review*, September 5, 1891, p. 279.
7. Thomas Bailey Aldrich, "In Re Emily Dickinson," *Atlantic*, January 1892, pp. 143–44.
8. Francis H. Stoddard, "Technique in Emily Dickinson's Poems," *Critic*, January 9, 1892, pp. 24–25.
9. Lucy Larcom, Letter to Miss Forbes (March 14, 1893), cited in Daniel Dulany Addison, *Lucy Larcom: Life, Letters, and Diary*, 1894, p. 285.
10. Mabel Loomis Todd, "Preface" to *Poems by Emily Dickinson*, 1896, pp. vii–viii.
11. Thomas Wentworth Higginson, "Recent Poetry," *Nation*, October 8, 1896, p. 275.
12. Katharine Lee Bates, *American Literature*, 1897, pp. 178–79.
13. Walter C. Bronson, A *Short History of American Literature*, 1900, p. 285.
14. John Churton Collins, "The Poetry and Poets of America," *Studies in Poetry and Criticism*, 1905, p. 75.
15. Warwick James Price, "Three Forgotten Poetesses," *Forum*, March 1912, pp. 361–63.
16. Unsigned, "Emily Dickinson's Letters," *Book Buyer*, November 1894, pp. 485–86.

17. Unsigned, "Emily Dickinson's Letters," *Nation*, December 13, 1894, p. 446.
18. Unsigned, "Letters of Emily Dickinson," *Critic*, February 16, 1895, p. 119.
19. Louis J. Block, "A New England Nun," *Dial*, March 1, 1895, pp. 146–47.
20. Thomas Wentworth Higginson, "Emily Dickinson's Letters," *Atlantic*, October 1891, pp. 444–53.
21. Hamilton Aïdé, "Poems by Emily Dickinson," *Nineteenth Century*, April 1892, pp. 703–6.
22. Mabel Loomis Todd, "Introduction" to *Letters of Emily Dickinson*, 1894.
23. James Fullarton Muirhead, "Some Literary Straws," *The Land of Contrasts: A Briton's View of His American Kin*, 1898, pp. 178–86.
24. Martha Hale Shackford, "The Poetry of Emily Dickinson," *Atlantic*, January 1913, pp. 93–97.

MATTHEW ARNOLD

1. Thomas Arnold, Letter to William Charles Lake (August 17, 1840), cited in Katharine Lake, *Memorials of William Charles Lake*, 1901, p. 161.
2. Charlotte Brontë, Letter to James Taylor (January 15, 1851).
3. John Tulloch, Letter (1874), cited in Margaret Oliphant, *A Memoir of the Life of John Tulloch*, 1889, p. 287.
4. Maria Mitchell, *Journal* (January 9, 1884), *Life, Letters, and Journals of Maria Mitchell*, ed. Phebe Mitchell Kendall, 1896, pp. 195–96.
5. Sir Edwin Arnold, "To Matthew Arnold," *Pall Mall Gazette*, April 15, 1888.
6. George Edward Woodberry, "Matthew Arnold" (1890), *Literary Essays*, 1920, pp. 75–76.
7. A. E. Housman (c. 1891), *Selected Prose*, ed. John Carter, 1961, pp. 196–98.
8. Augustine Birrell, "Matthew Arnold," *Res Judicatae*, 1892, pp. 185–89.
9. Hugh Walker, *Academy*, December 21, 1895, p. 538.
10. W. H. Johnson, "The 'Passing' of Matthew Arnold," *Dial*, November 16, 1899, pp. 352–53.
11. G. K. Chesterton, "Matthew Arnold," *Bookman* (New York), October 1902, pp. 118–20.
12. James Anthony Froude, "Arnold's Poems" (1854), *Essays in Literature and History*, 1906, pp. 4–5.
13. J. C. Shairp, "Poems by Matthew Arnold," *North British Review*, August 1854, pp. 502–4.
14. George Eliot, *Westminster Review*, July 1855, pp. 297–98.
15. Andrew Lang, "Matthew Arnold," *Century Magazine*, April 1882, pp. 863–64.
16. Edward Clodd, "Matthew Arnold's Poetry," *Gentleman's Magazine*, March 1886, p. 359.
17. Richard Le Gallienne, "Matthew Arnold" (1888), *English Poems*, 1892, p. 113.
18. Andrew Lang, "Introductory: Of Modern English Poetry," *Letters on Literature*, 1889, pp. 11–14.
19. W. E. Henley, "Matthew Arnold," *Views and Reviews*, 1890, pp. 83–86.
20. Lionel Johnson, *Academy*, January 10, 1891, pp. 31–32.
21. Edwin P. Whipple, "Matthew Arnold," *North American Review*, May 1884, pp. 439–42.
22. W. E. Henley, "Matthew Arnold," *Views and Reviews*, 1890, pp. 88–91.
23. George Saintsbury, "Matthew Arnold," *Corrected Impressions*, 1895.
24. Frederic Harrison, "Matthew Arnold," *Nineteenth Century*, March 1896, pp. 441–43.

25. J. Llewelyn Davies, "Mr. Arnold's New Religion," *Contemporary Review*, May 1873, pp. 845–46.
26. H. D. Traill, "Neo-Christianity and Mr. Matthew Arnold," *Contemporary Review*, April 1884, pp. 575–76.
27. Richard Holt Hutton, "Newman and Arnold: II. Matthew Arnold," *Contemporary Review*, April 1886, pp. 526–28.
28. Henry Sidgwick, "The Prophet of Culture," *Macmillan's Magazine*, August 1867, pp. 271–280.
29. Algernon Charles Swinburne, "Matthew Arnold's New Poems" (1867), *Essays and Studies*, 1875, pp. 152–83.
30. Henry James, "Matthew Arnold" (1884), *Literary Reviews and Essays*, ed. Albert Mordell, 1957, pp. 341–53.
31. Sir Leslie Stephen, "Matthew Arnold" (1893), *Studies of a Biographer*, 1899, Volume 2, pp. 76–122.

ROBERT BROWNING

1. William Charles Macready, *Diary*, December 31, 1835.
2. George Stillman Hillard, *Six Months in Italy*, 1853, p. 114.
3. Nathaniel Hawthorne, *The English Note-Books*, July 13, 1856.
4. Benjamin Jowett, Letter (June 12, 1865), cited in Evelyn Abbott, Lewis Campbell, *The Life and Letters of Benjamin Jowett*, 1897, Volume 1, pp. 400–401.
5. Alfred, Lord Tennyson, Dedication to *Tiresias and Other Poems*, 1885.
6. Thomas Adolphus Trollope, *What I Remember*, 1888.
7. George William Curtis, "Editor's Easy Chair," *Harper's New Monthly Magazine*, March 1890, p. 637.
8. James Fotheringham, *Studies of the Mind and Art of Robert Browning*, 1898, pp. 42–43.
9. Frederic Harrison, "Personal Reminiscences," *George Washington and Other American Addresses*, 1901, p. 207.
10. William James Stillman, *The Autobiography of a Journalist*, 1901, Volume 2, p. 627.
11. Elizabeth Barrett Browning, *Lady Geraldine's Courtship*, 1844, Stanza 41.
12. Walter Savage Landor, "To Robert Browning," 1845.
13. Margaret Fuller, "Browning's Poems" (1846), *Art, Literature, and the Drama*, 1860, p. 209.
14. George Eliot, *Westminster Review*, January 1856, pp. 290–91.
15. John Ruskin, *Modern Painters*, 1856, Pt. 5, Ch. 20.
16. James Thomson, "The Poems of William Blake" (1864), *Biographical and Critical Studies*, 1896, pp. 266–67.
17. Edward FitzGerald, Letter to Alfred, Lord Tennyson (April 1869).
18. Edmund Clarence Stedman, *Victorian Poets*, 1875, pp. 338–41.
19. Algernon Charles Swinburne, *George Chapman: A Critical Essay*, 1875, pp. 15–18.
20. Harriet Martineau, *Autobiography*, ed. Maria Weston Chapman, 1877, Volume 1, pp. 314–15.
21. Justin McCarthy, *A History of Our Own Times*, 1879–80, Ch. 29.
22. William John Alexander, *An Introduction to the Poetry of Robert Browning*, 1889, pp. 2, 210.
23. Andrew Lang, "Introductory: Of Modern English Poetry," *Letters on Literature*, 1889, pp. 8–11.
24. John T. Nettleship, "Robert Browning," *Academy*, December 21, 1889, p. 406.
25. Algernon Charles Swinburne, "A Sequence of Sonnets on the Death of Robert Browning: I," *Fortnightly Review*, January 1890, p. 1.
26. Aubrey De Vere, "Robert Browning," *Macmillan's Magazine*, February 1890, p. 258.
27. Annie E. Ireland, "Browning's Types of Womanhood," *The Woman's World*, 1890.

28. John Addington Symonds, "A Comparison of Elizabethan with Victorian Poetry," *Essays Speculative and Suggestive*, 1890, Volume 2, p. 246.
29. Barrett Wendell, *English Composition*, 1891, p. 208.
30. Oscar Wilde, *The Critic as Artist*, 1891.
31. Arthur Christopher Benson, "The Poetry of Edmund Gosse" (1894), *Essays*, 1896, p. 298.
32. George Saintsbury, *A History of Nineteenth Century Literature*, 1896, pp. 272–76.
33. Augustine Birrell, "Robert Browning" (1897), *Essays and Addresses*, 1901, pp. 185–94.
34. Thomas Wentworth Higginson, "The Biography of Browning's Fame," *The Boston Browning Society Papers*, 1897, p. 5.
35. Francis Thompson, "Academy Portraits: XXVI. Robert Browning," *Academy*, May 8, 1897, p. 499.
36. Arthur Waugh, *Robert Browning*, 1899, pp. 150–152.
37. W. J. Fox, *Monthly Repository*, November 1835, p. 716.
38. Leigh Hunt, *London Journal*, November 21, 1835, p. 405.
39. John Forster, "Evidences of a New Genius for Dramatic Poetry," *New Monthly Magazine*, March 1836, pp. 289–90.
40. R. H. Horne, "Robert Browning and J. W. Marston," *A New Spirit of the Age*, 1844, pp. 280–82.
41. Thomas Lovell Beddoes, Letter to Thomas Forbes Kelsall (November 13, 1844).
42. Harriet Waters Preston, "Robert and Elizabeth Browning," *Atlantic*, June 1899, p. 814.
43. William Charles Macready, *Diary*, March 19, 1837.
44. Herman Merivale, "Browning's *Strafford*: A Tragedy," *Edinburgh Review*, July 1837, pp. 147–48.
45. Charlotte Porter, "Dramatic Motive in Browning's *Strafford*" (1893), *The Boston Browning Society Papers*, 1897, pp. 190–91.
46. Charles Dickens, Letter to John Forster (November 25, 1842).
47. John Forster, *Examiner*, February 18, 1843, p. 101.
48. Helena Faucit Martin, "On Some of Shakespeare's Female Characters: III. Desdemona," *Blackwood's Edinburgh Magazine*, March 1881, p. 326.
49. Thomas R. Lounsbury, "A Philistine View," *Atlantic*, December 1899, p. 773.
50. Dante Gabriel Rossetti, Letter to William Allingham (November 25, 1855).
51. John Greenleaf Whittier, Letter to Lucy Larcom (1855), cited in Samuel T. Pickard, *Life and Letters of John Greenleaf Whittier*, 1895, Volume 1, p. 370.
52. Margaret Oliphant, "Modern Light Literature—Poetry," *Blackwood's Edinburgh Magazine*, February 1856, p. 137.
53. Andrew Lang, "Adventures among Books," *Scribner's Magazine*, November 1891, p. 652.
54. Dante Gabriel Rossetti, Letter to William Allingham (December 23, 1868).
55. John Morley, "On *The Ring and the Book*," *Fortnightly Review*, March 1869, pp. 341–42.
56. Robert Buchanan, *Athenaeum*, March 20, 1869, p. 399.
57. Gerard Manley Hopkins, Letter to R. W. Dixon (October 12, 1881).
58. Alexandra Orr, *A Handbook to the Works of Robert Browning*, 1885, pp. 75–76.
59. William Dean Howells, "Certain Preferences and Experiences," *My Literary Passions*, 1895.
60. Henry James, "Browning's *Inn Album*," *Nation*, January 20, 1876, p. 49.
61. A. C. Bradley, "Mr. Browning's *Inn Album*," *Macmillan's Magazine*, February 1876, p. 354.

62. Walter Bagehot, "Wordsworth, Tennyson, and Browning; or, Pure, Ornate, and Grotesque Art in English Poetry" (1864), *Collected Works*, ed. Norman St. John-Stevas, 1965, Volume 2, pp. 352–61.
63. Edward Dowden, "Mr. Browning's *Sordello*," *Fraser's Magazine*, October 1867, pp. 518–22.
64. Alfred Austin, "The Poetry of the Period," *Temple Bar*, June 1869, pp. 320–33.
65. Arthur Galton, "Mr. Browning," *Urbana Scripta*, 1885, pp. 59–76.
66. Henry James, "Browning in Westminster Abbey," *Speaker*, January 4, 1890, pp. 10–12.
67. George Edward Woodberry, "On Browning's Death," *Studies in Letters and Life*, 1890, pp. 276–96.
68. George Santayana, "The Poetry of Barbarism: III. Robert Browning," *Interpretations of Poetry and Religion*, 1900, pp. 188–214.
69. G. K. Chesterton, *Robert Browning*, 1903, pp. 177–202.

HERMAN MELVILLE

1. William Ellery Channing, "The Island Nukuheva," 1847.
2. Nathaniel Hawthorne, Letter to Horatio Bridge (August 7, 1850), cited in Horatio Bridge, *Personal Recollections of Nathaniel Hawthorne*, 1893, p. 123.
3. William T. Porter (?), "*Moby Dick, or the Whale*," *Spirit of the Times*, December 6, 1851.
4. Fitz-James O'Brien, "Our Young Authors—Melville," *Putnam's Monthly*, February 1853, p. 163.
5. W. Clark Russell, "Sea-Stories," *Contemporary Review*, September 1884, pp. 356–58.
6. Robert Buchanan, "Socrates in Camden, with a Look Round," *Academy*, August 15, 1885, p. 103.
7. Charles F. Richardson, *American Literature, 1607–1885*, 1887, Volume 2, pp. 403–4.
8. Edwin P. Whipple, "American Literature" (1886), *American Literature, and Other Papers*, 1887, p. 125.
9. Robert Louis Stevenson, Letter to Charles Baxter (September 6, 1888).
10. Unsigned, *New York Times*, October 2, 1891, p. 4.
11. Richard Henry Stoddard, *Critic*, November 14, 1891, p. 272.
12. John St. Loe Strachey, "Herman Melville," *Spectator*, June 24, 1893, pp. 858–59.
13. William P. Trent, *A History of American Literature, 1607–1865*, 1903, pp. 389–91.
14. Joseph Conrad, Letter to Humphrey Milford (January 15, 1907).
15. Nathaniel Hawthorne, *Salem Advertiser*, March 25, 1846.
16. Henry Wadsworth Longfellow, *Journal* (July 29, 1846), cited in Samuel Longfellow, *Life of Henry Wadsworth Longfellow*, 1891, Volume 2, p. 52.
17. James Russell Lowell, Letter to Sydney H. Gay (September 1848).
18. Thomas Low Nichols, *Forty Years of American Life, 1821–1861*, 1864, Ch. 25.
19. Katharine Lee Bates, *American Literature*, 1898, p. 276.
20. Jack London, "*Typee*" (1910), *The Cruise of the Snark*, 1911, pp. 154–55.
21. Horace Greeley, *New York Daily Tribune*, November 22, 1851.
22. George Ripley (?), "Literary Notices," *Harper's New Monthly Magazine*, December 1852, p. 137.
23. Unsigned, "Review of New Books," *Graham's Magazine*, October 1852, p. 445.
24. Unsigned, "New Novels," *Athenaeum*, November 20, 1852, pp. 1265–66.

25. Julian Hawthorne, "The American Element in Fiction," *North American Review*, August 1886, p. 175.
26. Evert A. Duyckinck, "Melville's *Moby Dick; or, The Whale*," *Literary World*, November 15, 1851, p. 381; November 22, 1851, pp. 403–4.
27. Unsigned, "*Pierre; or, The Ambiguities*," *Literary World*, August 21, 1852, pp. 118–20.
28. Unsigned, "*Pierre; or, The Ambiguities*," *American Whig Review*, November 1852, pp. 446–54.
29. "Sir Nathaniel," "American Authorship: IV. Herman Melville," *New Monthly Magazine*, July 1853, pp. 300–308.
30. Henry S. Salt, "Marquesan Melville," *Gentleman's Magazine*, March 1892, pp. 248–57.
31. Archibald MacMechan, "The Best Sea Story Ever Written," *Queen's Quarterly*, October 1899, pp. 120–30.

ALFRED, LORD TENNYSON

1. Frances Ann Kemble, *Journal* (March 16, 1832), *Record of a Girlhood*, 1878, Volume 3, p. 209.
2. Hartley Coleridge, "To Alfred Tennyson," 1835.
3. Jane Welsh Carlyle, Letter to Helen Welsh (March 1843), *Letters and Memorials of Jane Welsh Carlyle*, ed. James Anthony Froude, 1883, Volume 1, pp. 191–92.
4. Thomas Carlyle, Letter to Ralph Waldo Emerson (August 5, 1844).
5. Ralph Waldo Emerson, *Journal*, 1848.
6. Walter Savage Landor, Untitled poem, 1853.
7. Lewis Carroll, *Diary*, September 22, 1857.
8. Nathaniel Hawthorne (1857), cited in Julian Hawthorne, *Nathaniel Hawthorne and His Wife*, 1884, Volume 2, pp. 143–46.
9. Queen Victoria, *Journal*, August 7, 1883.
10. Richard Le Gallienne, "'Tennyson' at the Farm," *English Poems*, 1892, p. 102.
11. W. J. Fox, "Tennyson's Poems," *Westminster Review*, January 1831, p. 214.
12. Arthur Henry Hallam, "Extract from a Review of Tennyson's Poems" (1831), *Remains in Verse and Prose*, 1863, pp. 304–5.
13. Margaret Fuller, *Journal* (August 1842), *Memoirs*, 1852, Volume 2, p. 66.
14. Samuel Taylor Coleridge, *Table Talk*, April 24, 1833.
15. John Wilson, "Tennyson's Poems," *Blackwood's Edinburgh Magazine*, May 1832, pp. 728–29.
16. Ralph Waldo Emerson, *Dial*, April 1843.
17. Edwin P. Whipple, "English Poets of the Nineteenth Century" (1845), *Essays and Reviews*, 1850, Volume 1, pp. 339–42.
18. Thomas Powell, "Alfred Tennyson," *The Living Authors of England*, 1849, p. 48.
19. Edgar Allan Poe, "The Poetic Principle" (1850), *Essays and Reviews*, ed. G. R. Thompson, 1984, p. 92.
20. John Ruskin, Letter to Alfred, Lord Tennyson (1860), cited in Hallam Tennyson, *Alfred Lord Tennyson: A Memoir*, 1897, Volume 1, pp. 453–54.
21. Matthew Arnold, *On Translating Homer: Last Words*, 1862.
22. J. Hain Friswell, "Mr. Alfred Tennyson," *Modern Men of Letters Honestly Criticised*, 1870, pp. 155–56.
23. Hippolyte Taine, *History of English Literature*, tr. H. Van Laun, 1871, Bk. 5, Ch. 6.
24. Henry Wadsworth Longfellow, "Wapentake: T. Alfred Tennyson," *A Book of Sonnets*, 1873.
25. Walt Whitman, "A Word about Tennyson" (1887), *Prose Works*, ed. Floyd Stovall, 1964, Volume 2, pp. 570–72.
26. Andrew Lang, "Introductory: Of Modern English Poetry," *Letters on Literature*, 1889, pp. 4–8.

27. Edmund Gosse, "The Influence of Democracy" (1891), *Questions at Issue*, 1893, p. 40.
28. Aubrey De Vere, "To Alfred Tennyson," *Century Magazine*, May 1893, p. 37.
29. R. C. Jebb, "Alfred, Lord Tennyson," *The English Poets*, ed. Thomas Humphry Ward, 1880 (1894), Volume 4, pp. 755–57.
30. Max Nordau, *Degeneration*, 1895, p. 99.
31. George Saintsbury, "Tennyson," *Corrected Impressions*, 1895.
32. G. K. Chesterton, "Two Great Victorian Poets: I. Tennyson," *Bookman* (New York), October 1902, pp. 349–51.
33. Henry Wadsworth Longfellow, *Journal* (February 7, 1848), cited in Samuel Longfellow, *Life of Henry Wadsworth Longfellow*, 1891, Volume 2, p. 109.
34. Bayard Taylor, Letter to Mary Agnew (February 13, 1848), *Life and Letters of Bayard Taylor*, eds. Marie Hansen-Taylor, Horace E. Scudder, 1884, Volume 1, p. 119.
35. Edward FitzGerald, Letter to Frederick Tennyson (May 4, 1848).
36. Max Müller, Letter to F. Palgrave (June 18, 1850), *Life and Letters of Max Müller*, ed. Georgina Max Müller, 1902, Volume 1, p. 116.
37. Sara Coleridge, Letter to Aubrey De Vere (August 6, 1850), *Memoir and Letters of Sara Coleridge*, ed. Edith Coleridge, 1873, Volume 2, p. 287.
38. Sara Coleridge, Letter to Edward Quillinan (August 15, 1850), *Memoir and Letters of Sara Coleridge*, ed. Edith Coleridge, 1873, Volume 2, pp. 292–93.
39. Charlotte Brontë, Letter to Elizabeth Gaskell (August 27, 1850).
40. Henry Hallam, Letter to Alfred, Lord Tennyson (1850), cited in Hallam Tennyson, *Alfred Lord Tennyson: A Memoir*, 1897, Volume 1, p. 327.
41. Vida D. Scudder, *The Life of the Spirit in the Modern English Poets*, 1895, pp. 284–88.
42. George Brimley, "Tennyson's Poems" (1855), *Essays*, ed. George William Clark, 1868, pp. 75–84.
43. Edmund Clarence Stedman, "Alfred Tennyson," *Victorian Poets*, 1875, pp. 173–74.
44. Thomas Babington Macaulay, *Journal* (July 11, 1859), cited in G. Otto Trevelyan, *The Life and Letters of Lord Macaulay*, 1876, Volume 2, p. 398.
45. W. E. Gladstone, "Tennyson's Poems—*Idylls of the King*," *Quarterly Review*, October 1859, pp. 479–80.
46. Prince Albert, Letter to Alfred, Lord Tennyson (May 17, 1860).
47. Thomas Carlyle, Letter to Ralph Waldo Emerson (January 27, 1867).
48. James Russell Lowell, Letter to Charles Eliot Norton (December 4, 1872).
49. Algernon Charles Swinburne, "Tennyson and Musset" (1881), *Miscellanies*, 1886, pp. 249–51.
50. James Anthony Froude, Letter to Alfred, Lord Tennyson (May 7, 1875), cited in Hallam Tennyson, *Alfred Lord Tennyson: A Memoir*, 1897, Volume 2, pp. 180–81.
51. William Watson, *Academy*, April 9, 1892, p. 341.
52. Hugh Walker, *The Age of Tennyson*, 1897, pp. 224–27.
53. George Gilfillan, "Alfred Tennyson" (1847), *A Second Gallery of Literary Portraits*, 1850, pp. 214–31.
54. Charles Kingsley, "Tennyson" (1850), *Literary and General Essays*, 1880, pp. 103–24.
55. Walter Bagehot, "Tennyson's *Idylls*" (1859), *Collected Works*, ed. Norman St. John-Stevas, 1965, Volume 2, pp. 179–207.
56. Edward Dowden, "Mr Tennyson and Mr Browning" (1867), *Studies in Literature*, 1878, pp. 195–211.

57. Sir Leslie Stephen, "Life of Tennyson," *Studies of a Biographer*, 1899, Volume 2, pp. 196–240.
58. Lewis E. Gates, "Nature in Tennyson's Poetry," *Studies and Appreciations*, 1900, pp. 77–91.

WALT WHITMAN

1. A. Bronson Alcott, *Diary*, November 10, 1856.
2. Moncure D. Conway, "Walt Whitman," *Fortnightly Review*, October 15, 1866, pp. 544–45.
3. William Douglas O'Connor, "*The Good Gray Poet*: Supplement" (1866), *In Re Walt Whitman*, eds. Horace L. Traubel, Richard Maurice Bucke, Thomas B. Harned, 1893, p. 154.
4. Robert Buchanan, *A Look round Literature*, 1887, pp. 345–46.
5. Ernest Rhys, "To Walt Whitman on His Seventieth Birthday" (1889), *A London Rose and Other Rhymes*, 1894, p. 84.
6. Edmund Clarence Stedman, "W. W.," 1892.
7. Hamlin Garland, "Walt Whitman," *In Re Walt Whitman*, eds. Horace L. Traubel, Richard Maurice Bucke, Thomas B. Harned, 1893, p. 328.
8. Henry David Thoreau, Letter to Harrison Blake (December 7, 1856).
9. Henry James, "Mr. Walt Whitman," *Nation*, November 16, 1865, p. 626.
10. William Michael Rossetti, Letter to Anne Gilchrist (June 23, 1869).
11. Anne Gilchrist, Letter to William Michael Rossetti (July 11, 1869), *In Re Walt Whitman*, eds. Horace L. Traubel, Richard Maurice Bucke, Thomas B. Harned, 1893, pp. 42–43.
12. Peter Bayne, "Walt Whitman's Poems," *Contemporary Review*, December 1875, pp. 49–51, 68–69.
13. Arthur Clive, "Walt Whitman, the Poet of Joy," *Gentleman's Magazine*, December 1875, p. 716.
14. George Eliot, Letter to John Blackwood (April 18, 1876).
15. William Michael Rossetti, "Henry Wadsworth Longfellow," *Lives of Famous Poets*, 1878, p. 391.
16. John Ruskin, Letter to William Harrison Riley (1879), *In Re Walt Whitman*, eds. Horace L. Traubel, Richard Maurice Bucke, Thomas B. Harned, 1893, p. 352.
17. Gerard Manley Hopkins, Letter to Robert Bridges (October 18, 1882).
18. G. C. Macaulay, "Walt Whitman," *Nineteenth Century*, December 1882, pp. 905–9.
19. Sidney Lanier, *The English Novel*, 1883, pp. 45–47.
20. George Selwyn, "Walt Whitman at Camden," *Critic*, February 28, 1885, p. 98.
21. Charles F. Richardson, *American Literature, 1607–1885*, 1887, Volume 2, p. 269.
22. Edwin P. Whipple, "American Literature" (1886), *American Literature and Other Papers*, 1887, pp. 112–114.
23. Oliver Elton, *Academy*, April 5, 1890, p. 231.
24. Robert G. Ingersoll, "Liberty in Literature" (1890), *In Re Walt Whitman*, eds. Horace L. Traubel, Richard Maurice Bucke, Thomas B. Harned, 1893, p. 281.
25. John Addington Symonds, "Democratic Art," *Essays Speculative and Suggestive*, 1890, Volume 2, pp. 47–50.
26. William Clarke, *Walt Whitman*, 1892, pp. 50–52.
27. Harriet Monroe, "A Word about Walt Whitman," *Critic*, April 16, 1892, p. 231.
28. Richard Maurice Bucke, "The Man Walt Whitman," *In Re Walt Whitman*, eds. Horace L. Traubel, Richard Maurice Bucke, Thomas B. Harned, 1893, p. 59.
29. Barrett Wendell, "American Literature," *Stelligeri and Other Essays concerning America*, 1893, pp. 142–43.

30. William Morton Payne, "Whitmaniana," *Dial*, December 16, 1893, p. 390.
31. William Dean Howells, "First Impressions of Literary New York," *Harper's New Monthly Magazine*, June 1895, p. 65.
32. Max Nordau, *Degeneration*, 1895, pp. 230–32.
33. Willa Cather, "Whitman" (1896), *The Kingdom of Art*, ed. Bernice Slote, 1966, pp. 351–53.
34. Henry Childs Merwin, "Men and Letters," *Atlantic*, May 1897, p. 719.
35. Hallam Tennyson, *Alfred Lord Tennyson: A Memoir*, 1897, Volume 2, p. 424.
36. Jennette Barbour Perry, "Whitmania," *Critic*, February 26, 1898, pp. 137–38.
37. Thomas Wentworth Higginson, "Whitman," *Contemporaries*, 1899, pp. 79–84.
38. J. A. MacCulloch, "Walt Whitman: The Poet of Brotherhood," *Westminster Review*, November 1899, pp. 563–64.
39. William P. Trent, *A History of American Literature, 1607–1865*, 1903, pp. 493–94.
40. Ralph Waldo Emerson, Letter to Walt Whitman (July 21, 1855).
41. Charles A. Dana, *New York Tribune*, July 23, 1855, p. 3.
42. Walt Whitman, *Brooklyn Daily Times*, September 29, 1855.
43. Dante Gabriel Rossetti, Letter to William Allingham (April 1856).
44. William Allingham, Letter to Dante Gabriel Rossetti (April 10, 1857).
45. Sidney Lanier, Letter to Bayard Taylor (February 3, 1878).
46. Walter Lewin, "*Leaves of Grass*," *Murray's Magazine*, September 1887, pp. 327–28.
47. Walt Whitman, "An Old Man's Rejoinder" (1890), *Good-Bye My Fancy*, 1891.
48. C. D. Lanier, "Walt Whitman," *Chautauquan*, June 1902, p. 310.
49. George Saintsbury, *Academy*, October 10, 1874, pp. 398–400.
50. Edmund Clarence Stedman, "Walt Whitman," *Scribner's Monthly*, November 1880, pp. 54–63.
51. Robert Louis Stevenson, "Walt Whitman" (1882), *Familiar Studies of Men and Books*, 1886, pp. 104–12.
52. Walker Kennedy, "Walt Whitman," *North American Review*, June 1884, pp. 593–601.
53. Algernon Charles Swinburne, "Whitmania," *Fortnightly Review*, August 1887, pp. 170–76.
54. Pauline W. Roose, "A Child-Poet: Walt Whitman," *Gentleman's Magazine*, May 1892, pp. 473–80.
55. John Addington Symonds, *Walt Whitman: A Study*, 1893, pp. 67–76.
56. John Burroughs, "His Ruling Ideas and Aims," *Whitman: A Study*, 1896, pp. 73–80.
57. George Santayana, "The Poetry of Barbarism: II. Walt Whitman," *Interpretations of Poetry and Religion*, 1900, pp. 177–87.

WALTER PATER

1. Michael Field, "Walter Pater," *Academy*, August 11, 1894, p. 102.
2. Edmund Gosse, "Walter Pater" (1894), *Critical Kit-Kats*, 1896, pp. 261–65.
3. Henry James, Letter to Edmund Gosse (December 13, 1894).
4. George Saintsbury, "Walter H. Pater," *English Prose*, ed. Henry Craik, 1896, Volume 5, pp. 747–50.

5. Vernon Lee (Violet Paget), *Renaissance Fancies and Studies*, 1896, pp. 255–60.
6. Hamilton Wright Mabie, *Books and Culture*, 1896, pp. 100–102.
7. George Moore, "Avowals: VI. Walter Pater," *Pall Mall Magazine*, August 1904, pp. 528–31.
8. George Saintsbury, "Walter Pater" (1906), *Prefaces and Essays*, 1933, pp. 359–60.
9. John Buchan, "Walter Pater," *Spectator*, June 25, 1910, pp. 1075–76.
10. John Addington Symonds, "Art and Archaeology," *Academy*, March 15, 1873, pp. 104–5.
11. George Eliot, Letter to John Blackwood (November 5, 1873).
12. William Sharp, *Athenaeum*, February 28, 1885, pp. 272–73.
13. John Addington Symonds, Letter to Henry Sidgwick (April 5, 1885).
14. Mrs. Humphry Ward, "*Marius the Epicurean*," *Macmillan's Magazine*, May 1885, pp. 136–37.
15. Richard Le Gallienne, "Walter Pater: *Marius the Epicurean*" (1892), *Retrospective Reviews*, 1896, Volume 1, pp. 174–75.
16. Oscar Wilde, "Mr. Pater's Last Volume," *Speaker*, March 22, 1890.
17. John Morley, "Mr. Pater's Essays," *Fortnightly Review*, April 1873, pp. 471–77.
18. Arthur Symons, "Walter Pater" (1896), *Studies in Prose and Verse*, 1904, pp. 63–76.
19. Edward Dowden, "Walter Pater" (1902), *Essays Modern and Elizabethan*, 1910, pp. 1–25.
20. Richard Le Gallienne, "On Re-reading Walter Pater," *North American Review*, February 1912, pp. 214–24.

ROBERT LOUIS STEVENSON

1. W. E. Henley, "Apparition," *In Hospital*, 1888, p. 41.
2. J. M. Barrie, "Scotland's Lament," *McClure's Magazine*, February 1895, pp. 286–88.
3. Edmund Gosse, "Robert Louis Stevenson" (1895), *Critical Kit-Kats*, 1896, pp. 299–302.
4. Andrew Lang, "Recollections of Robert Louis Stevenson," *North American Review*, February 1895, pp. 191–93.
5. Austin Dobson, "R. L. S.: In Memoriam" (1901), *Poetical Works*, 1923, p. 398.
6. Isobel Strong, Lloyd Osbourne, *Memories of Vailima*, 1902, pp. 151–54.
7. Gerard Manley Hopkins, Letter to R. W. Dixon (August 15, 1883).
8. William Archer, "In Memoriam: R. L. S.," *New Review*, January 1895, p. 94.
9. Lord Rosebery, "Robert Louis Stevenson" (1896), *Miscellanies Literary and Historical*, 1921, Volume 2, pp. 24–26.
10. Walter Raleigh, "Robert Louis Stevenson," *English Prose*, ed. Henry Craik, 1896, Volume 5, pp. 761–64.
11. Arthur Wing Pinero, "Robert Louis Stevenson: The Dramatist," *Critic*, April 1903, p. 342.
12. G. K. Chesterton, "Stevenson" (1901), *Five Types*, 1910, pp. 39–43.
13. John Addington Symonds, Letter to Robert Louis Stevenson (March 1, 1886), cited in Horatio N. Brown, *John Addington Symonds: A Biography*, 1895, Volume 2, pp. 256–57.
14. Stephen Gwynn, "Mr. Robert Louis Stevenson," *Fortnightly Review*, December 1894, p. 787.
15. Arthur Machen, *Hieroglyphics: A Note upon Ecstasy in Literature* (1902), 1923, pp. 70–74.
16. George Moore, *Hawk*, November 5, 1889, pp. 489–90.

17. A. Conan Doyle, "Mr. Stevenson's Methods in Fiction," *National Review*, January 1890, pp. 653–54.
18. Henry James, "Robert Louis Stevenson," *Century Magazine*, April 1888, pp. 869–79.
19. J. M. Barrie, "Robert Louis Stevenson," *An Edinburgh Eleven*, 1889, pp. 118–28.
20. Andrew Lang, "Mr. Stevenson's Works," *Essays in Little*, 1891, pp. 24–35.
21. Arthur Symons, "Robert Louis Stevenson" (1894), *Studies in Prose and Verse*, 1904, pp. 77–82.
22. Sir Leslie Stephen, "Robert Louis Stevenson," *Studies of a Biographer*, 1902, Volume 4, pp. 206–46.

JOHN RUSKIN

1. John Ruskin, Letter to Dante Gabriel Rossetti (c. April 1855), *Ruskin: Rossetti: Preraphaelitism*, ed. William Michael Rossetti, 1899, pp. 71–73.
2. Matthew Arnold, Letter to His Mother (June 16, 1863).
3. M. H. Spielmann, "John Ruskin at Home," *McClure's Magazine*, March 1894, pp. 316–17.
4. H. D. Rawnsley, *Ruskin and the English Lakes*, 1901, pp. 189–90.
5. William James Stillman, *The Autobiography of a Journalist*, 1901, Volume 1, p. 320.
6. George Eliot, Letter to Sara Sophia Hennell (January 17, 1858).
7. Margaret Oliphant, Letter to William Blackwood (November 4, 1861), *Autobiography and Letters*, ed. Mrs. Harry Coghill, 1899, p. 180.
8. J. Hain Friswell, "The Ethics of Ruskin," *Modern Men of Letters Honestly Criticised*, 1870, pp. 115–16.
9. James McNeill Whistler (1878), *The Gentle Art of Making Enemies*, 1890, pp. 33–34.
10. Arthur George Sedgwick, "Ruskin's *Arrows of the Chace*," *Nation*, September 15, 1881, pp. 220–21.
11. Edward Dowden, "Victorian Literature," *Transcripts and Studies*, 1888, p. 233.
12. Walter Lewin, *Academy*, February 21, 1891, p. 177.
13. John M. Robertson, "John Ruskin," *Modern Humanists*, 1891, pp. 206–10.
14. Max Nordau, *Degeneration*, 1895, pp. 77–78.
15. George Saintsbury, "Mr. Ruskin," *Corrected Impressions*, 1895.
16. Edmund Gosse, *A Short History of Modern English Literature*, 1897, pp. 356–58.
17. W. C. Brownell, "John Ruskin," *Scribner's Magazine*, April 1900, pp. 505–6.
18. John La Farge, "Ruskin, Art and Truth," *International Monthly*, Volume 2 (1900), pp. 513–17.
19. H. H. Lancaster, "The Writings of John Ruskin," *North British Review*, February 1862, pp. 3–36.
20. Stopford A. Brooke, "Ruskin's Lectures on Art," *Macmillan's Magazine*, October 1870, pp. 423–34.
21. Frederic Harrison, "Past and Present" (1876), *The Choice of Books and Other Literary Pieces*, 1886, pp. 121–35.
22. Sir Leslie Stephen, "John Ruskin" (1900), *Studies of a Biographer*, 1902, Volume 3, pp. 83–118.

OSCAR WILDE

1. Thomas F. Plowman, "The Aesthetes: The Story of a Nineteenth-Century Cult," *Pall Mall Magazine*, January 1895, pp. 41–42.
2. Chris Healy, *Confessions of a Journalist*, 1904, pp. 131–38.
3. Wilfred Scawen Blunt, *My Diaries* (entry for November 16, 1905), 1920, Volume 2, pp. 125–26.
4. Ford Madox Ford, *Ancient Lights and Certain New Reflections*, 1911, pp. 150–53.

5. Katharine Tynan, *Twenty-five Years: Reminiscences*, 1913, pp. 149–50.
6. Ambrose Bierce, "Prattle," *Wasp*, March 31, 1882.
7. W. B. Yeats, "Oscar Wilde's Last Book" (1891), *Uncollected Prose*, ed. John P. Frayne, 1970, Volume 1, pp. 203–4.
8. Arthur Symons, "An Artist in Attitudes: Oscar Wilde" (1901), *Studies in Prose and Verse*, 1904, pp. 124–28.
9. Max Beerbohm, "'A Lord of Language,'" *Vanity Fair*, March 2, 1905, p. 309.
10. J. Comyns Carr, *Some Victorian Poets*, 1908, pp. 213–14.
11. St. John Hankin, "The Collected Plays of Oscar Wilde," *Fortnightly Review*, May 1908, pp. 801–2.
12. Lord Alfred Douglas, "The Genius of Oscar Wilde," *Academy*, July 11, 1908, p. 35.
13. G. K. Chesterton, "Oscar Wilde" (1909), *A Handful of Authors*, ed. Dorothy Collins, 1953, pp. 143–46.
14. James Joyce, "Oscar Wilde: The Poet of *Salomé*" (1909), *Critical Writings*, eds. Ellsworth Mason, Richard Ellmann, 1959, pp. 203–5.
15. Archibald Henderson, *Interpreters of Life and the Modern Spirit*, 1911, pp. 99–103.
16. Walter Pater, "A Novel by Mr. Wilde" (1891), *Sketches and Reviews*, 1919, pp. 126–33.
17. Richard Le Gallienne, *Academy*, July 4, 1891, pp. 7–8.
18. Agnes Repplier, "The Best Book of the Year," *North American Review*, January 1892, pp. 97–100.
19. Lord Alfred Douglas, *Spirit Lamp*, May 1893, pp. 21–27.
20. Edward E. Hale, Jr., "Signs of Life in Literature," *Dial*, July 1, 1894, pp. 12–13.
21. William Archer, "*A Woman of No Importance*" (1893), *The Theatrical "World" of 1893*, 1894, pp. 105–12.
22. George Bernard Shaw, "Two New Plays" (1895), *Works*, 1930–38, Volume 23, pp. 9–11.
23. J. T. Grein, "*The Importance of Being Earnest*" (1901), *Dramatic Criticism*, 1902, Volume 3, pp. 264–66.
24. Max Beerbohm, "A Classic Farce" (1909), *Last Theatres*, ed. Rupert Hart-Davis, 1970, pp. 508–11.
25. E. V. Lucas, *Times Literary Supplement*, February 24, 1905, pp. 64–65.
26. G. Lowes Dickinson, *Independent Review*, April 1905, pp. 375–77.
27. Robert H. Sherard, *Oscar Wilde: The Story of an Unhappy Friendship*, 1905, pp. 183–94.
28. Hugh Walker, "The Birth of a Soul: (Oscar Wilde: The Closing Phase)," *Hibbert Journal*, January 1905, pp. 756–68.
29. Wilfrid M. Leadman, "The Literary Position of Oscar Wilde," *Westminster Review*, August 1906, pp. 201–8.

30. Lewis Piaget Shanks, "Oscar Wilde's Place in Literature," *Dial*, April 16, 1910, pp. 261–63.
31. Arthur Ransome, "Afterthought," *Oscar Wilde: A Critical Study*, 1912, pp. 220–34.

STEPHEN CRANE

1. Harry Thurston Peck, "Stephen Crane," *Bookman* (New York), May 1895, pp. 229–30.
2. Joseph Conrad, Letter to Stephen Crane (December 1, 1897).
3. Joseph Conrad, Letter to Edward Garnett (December 5, 1897).
4. Unsigned, "Recent Short Stories," *Spectator*, July 23, 1898, pp. 120–21.
5. Edward Garnett, "Mr. Stephen Crane: An Appreciation," *Academy*, December 17, 1898, pp. 483–84.
6. William Dean Howells, "Frank Norris," *North American Review*, December 1902, pp. 770–71.
7. William Dean Howells, "An Appreciation," *Maggie: A Girl of the Streets*, 1896.
8. William Morton Payne, "Recent Fiction," *Dial*, February 1, 1896, p. 80.
9. A. C. McClurg, "The Red Badge of Hysteria," *Dial*, April 16, 1896, pp. 227–28.
10. D. Appleton & Company, "*The Red Badge of Courage*: A Correction," *Dial*, May 1, 1896, p. 263.
11. J. L. Onderdonk, "A Red Badge of Bad English," *Dial*, May 1, 1896, p. 263.
12. Unsigned, "The Rambler," *Book Buyer*, April 1896, pp. 140–41.
13. Charles Dudley Warner, "Editor's Study," *Harper's New Monthly Magazine*, May 1896, p. 962.
14. Unsigned, "*The Red Badge of Courage*," *Spectator*, June 27, 1896, p. 924.
15. Unsigned, "The Latest Fiction," *New York Times*, October 19, 1895, p. 3.
16. George Wyndham, "A Remarkable Book," *New Review*, January 1896, pp. 32–40.
17. Harold Frederic, "Stephen Crane's Triumph," *New York Times*, January 26, 1896, p. 22.
18. H. D. Traill, "The New Realism," *Fortnightly Review*, January 1897, pp. 63–66.
19. Stephen Gwynn, "Novels of American Life," *Edinburgh Review*, April 1898, pp. 411–14.
20. Willa Cather, "When I Knew Stephen Crane," *Library*, June 23, 1900.
21. Hamlin Garland, "Stephen Crane: A Soldier of Fortune," *Saturday Evening Post*, July 28, 1900.
22. H. G. Wells, "Stephen Crane: From an English Standpoint," *North American Review*, August 1900, pp. 233–42.

INDEX TO CRITICS

INDEX TO CRITICS

ABBOTT, EDWIN ABBOTT
Sir Francis Bacon 1:330, 334

ADAMS, CHARLES KENDALL
Sir Francis Bacon 1:339

ADAMS, JOHN QUINCY
Sir Francis Bacon 1:337
William Shakespeare 2:1135
George Gordon, Lord Byron 4:2022
Ralph Waldo Emerson 5:2724

ADDISON, JOSEPH
Geoffrey Chaucer 1:8
Edmund Spenser 1:221, 231
Sir Francis Bacon 1:327, 331
John Milton 1:581, 608
John Dryden 3:1309, 1332
Alexander Pope 3:1404, 1416

AÏDÉ, HAMILTON
Emily Dickinson 5:2847

AIKIN, BERKELEY
Nathaniel Hawthorne 5:2587

AIKIN, JOHN
Andrew Marvell 3:1254
Oliver Goldsmith 3:1659

AIKIN, LUCY
Sir Francis Bacon 1:337
Thomas Carlyle 5:2698

AINGER, ALFRED
Jonathan Swift 3:1476

AITKEN, GEORGE A.
Daniel Defoe 3:1395

ALBERT, PRINCE CONSORT OF
VICTORIA
Alfred, Lord Tennyson 5:2975

ALCOTT, A. BRONSON
Robert Herrick 1:544
Henry David Thoreau 4:2505
Nathaniel Hawthorne 5:2579
Walt Whitman 5:3009

ALCOTT, LOUISA MAY
Henry David Thoreau 4:2503
Ralph Waldo Emerson 5:2727

ALDRICH, THOMAS BAILEY
Robert Herrick 1:542, 548, 566
Emily Dickinson 5:2842

D'ALEMBERT, JEAN LE ROND
Sir Francis Bacon 1:340

ALEXANDER, JAMES W.
Washington Irving 4:2455

ALEXANDER, WILLIAM JOHN
Robert Browning 5:2898

ALFORD, HENRY
John Donne 1:385

ALISON, SIR ARCHIBALD
Sir Walter Scott 4:2135
Thomas Babington Macaulay
4:2480

ALLINGHAM, WILLIAM
Walt Whitman 5:3022

AMORY, THOMAS
Jonathan Swift 3:1461

ANDERSEN, HANS CHRISTIAN
Charles Dickens 5:2614, 2629

ANDERSON, ROBERT
Tobias Smollett 3:1625

APPLETON, D., & COMPANY
Stephen Crane 5:3174

ARBUTHNOT, JOHN
Jonathan Swift 3:1473

ARCHER, WILLIAM
William Shakespeare 2:1203
Robert Louis Stevenson 5:3078
Oscar Wilde 5:3152

ARNOLD, SIR EDWIN
Matthew Arnold 5:2856

ARNOLD, MATTHEW
Geoffrey Chaucer 1:97
John Milton 1:580, 595, 658
William Shakespeare 2:713, 1085
John Dryden 3:1319
Alexander Pope 3:1419
Thomas Gray 3:1602
Samuel Johnson 3:1748
Robert Burns 3:1827
John Keats 4:1918, 1919
George Gordon, Lord Byron
4:2017, 2046
Sir Walter Scott 4:2139
Samuel Taylor Coleridge 4:2178
Emily Brontë 4:2247
William Wordsworth 4:2323, 2325
Charlotte Brontë 4:2414, 2422
Thomas Babington Macaulay
4:2478
Thomas Carlyle 5:2690
Ralph Waldo Emerson 5:2744
Henry Wadsworth Longfellow
5:2776, 2782
Alfred, Lord Tennyson 5:2967
John Ruskin 5:3106

ARNOLD, THOMAS
Sir Francis Bacon 1:338
David Hume 3:1684
Matthew Arnold 5:2855

ASCHAM, ROGER
Geoffrey Chaucer 1:5

ASHE, T.
Robert Herrick 1:548

ATTERBURY, FRANCIS
Jonathan Swift 3:1471

AUBREY, JOHN
Sir Philip Sidney 1:126
Edmund Spenser 1:216
George Herbert 1:421
Ben Jonson 1:465

John Milton 1:605
William Shakespeare 2:672
Andrew Marvell 3:1254

AUBREY, W. H. S.
Henry Fielding 3:1515

AUSTEN, HENRY
Jane Austen 4:1883

AUSTEN, JANE
Sir Walter Scott 4:2145

AUSTEN-LEIGH, JAMES EDWARD
Jane Austen 4:1872

AUSTIN, ALFRED
Robert Browning 5:2911

BACON, DELIA
William Shakespeare 2:889

BACON, SIR FRANCIS
Sir Francis Bacon 1:325, 326

BAGEHOT, WALTER
John Milton 1:650
William Shakespeare 2:676
Alexander Pope 3:1411
Laurence Sterne 3:1566
Thomas Gray 3:1595
David Hume 3:1681
Edward Gibbon 3:1785
Percy Bysshe Shelley 4:1972
Sir Walter Scott 4:2152
Thomas Babington Macaulay
4:2483
William Makepeace Thackeray
5:2547
Charles Dickens 5:2630
George Eliot 5:2651
Robert Browning 5:2906
Alfred, Lord Tennyson 5:2986

BAILLIE, JOANNA
Sir Walter Scott 4:2141

BAILLY, JEAN SYLVAIN
Sir Francis Bacon 1:341

BAIN, ALEXANDER
Sir Francis Bacon 1:333
Robert Burns 3:1820

BAKER, DANIEL
George Herbert 1:435

BAKER, H. BARTON
Richard Brinsley Sheridan 3:1849

BAKER, SIR RICHARD
John Donne 1:376

BALDWIN, JAMES
John Webster 1:445

BALZAC, HONORÉ DE
Sir Walter Scott 4:2143
James Fenimore Cooper 4:2363

BANCROFT, GEORGE
Washington Irving 4:2456

BANCROFT, SIR SQUIRE
  Richard Brinsley Sheridan 3:1849

BARBAULD, ANNA LAETITIA
  Henry Fielding 3:1511
  Laurence Sterne 3:1551
  Samuel Johnson 3:1715
  Robert Burns 3:1817

BARHAM, R. H.
  Sir Walter Scott 4:2145

BARKSTEAD, WILLIAM
  William Shakespeare 2:1246

BARNFIELD, RICHARD
  Sir Philip Sidney 1:125
  Edmund Spenser 1:213
  William Shakespeare 2:1217

BARON, R.
  Ben Jonson 1:475

BARRIE, J. M.
  Robert Louis Stevenson 5:3076,
    3091

BASCOM, JOHN
  Robert Burns 3:1810

BASSE, WILLIAM
  William Shakespeare 2:671

BATES, KATHARINE LEE
  Nathaniel Hawthorne 5:2591
  Emily Dickinson 5:2844
  Herman Melville 5:2940

BAUDELAIRE, CHARLES
  Edgar Allan Poe 4:2288

BAUDOIN, J.
  Sir Philip Sidney 1:129

BAXTER, RICHARD
  George Herbert 1:423

BAYNE, PETER
  John Milton 1:580, 590, 596
  Samuel Taylor Coleridge 4:2182
  Charlotte Brontë 4:2415
  William Makepeace Thackeray
    5:2546
  Charles Dickens 5:2617
  Walt Whitman 5:3012

BAYNES, THOMAS SPENCER
  William Shakespeare 2:847

BEATTIE, JAMES
  John Milton 1:593
  John Dryden 3:1313
  Daniel Defoe 3:1374
  Alexander Pope 3:1406
  Henry Fielding 3:1510
  Thomas Gray 3:1585
  Samuel Johnson 3:1726
  Edward Gibbon 3:1772

BEAUMONT, FRANCIS
  Edmund Spenser 1:214, 217
  Ben Jonson 1:474

BEAUMONT, SIR JOHN
  Ben Jonson 1:467

BEDDOES, THOMAS LOVELL
  Percy Bysshe Shelley 4:1970
  George Gordon, Lord Byron 4:2022
  Robert Browning 5:2902

BEECHING, H. C.
  Richard Crashaw 1:535
  William Shakespeare 2:1234
  Andrew Marvell 3:1274
  John Bunyan 3:1284
  Thomas Gray 3:1596

BEERBOHM, MAX
  Oscar Wilde 5:3142, 3154

BEERS, HENRY A.
  John Milton 1:588
  William Makepeace Thackeray
    5:2554
  Nathaniel Hawthorne 5:2585

BELLOC, BESSIE RAYNER
  George Eliot 5:2659

BELOE, WILLIAM
  Henry Fielding 3:1519

BELSHAM, W.
  Alexander Pope 3:1421

BENSON, ARTHUR CHRISTOPHER
  John Milton 1:601
  Andrew Marvell 3:1269
  Thomas Gray 3:1604
  William Blake 4:2061
  Robert Browning 5:2899

BENSON, EUGENE
  Edgar Allan Poe 4:2286

BENSON, JOHN
  William Shakespeare 2:1217

BENTON, JOEL
  Edgar Allan Poe 4:2281

BERKELEY, GEORGE
  Alexander Pope 3:1417

BERRY, MARY
  Edward Gibbon 3:1766

BESANT, WALTER
  George Eliot 5:2660

BIERCE, AMBROSE
  William Shakespeare 2:718
  Oscar Wilde 5:3140

BIRCH, THOMAS
  John Milton 1:578

BIRRELL, AUGUSTINE
  John Milton 1:580, 603, 605
  Alexander Pope 3:1422
  Laurence Sterne 3:1556
  Samuel Johnson 3:1751
  Richard Brinsley Sheridan 3:1864
  William Hazlitt 4:2123
  Charles Lamb 4:2228
  Charlotte Brontë 4:2421
  Thomas Babington Macaulay
    4:2473
  Matthew Arnold 5:2857
  Robert Browning 5:2901

BLACK, JOSEPH
  David Hume 3:1679

BLACK, WILLIAM
  Oliver Goldsmith 3:1652

BLACKIE, JOHN STUART
  Robert Burns 3:1813
  Thomas Carlyle 5:2684

BLACKMORE, SIR RICHARD
  Edmund Spenser 1:215, 221
  John Milton 1:592
  John Dryden 3:1309
  Jonathan Swift 3:1471

BLACKWOOD, JOHN
  George Eliot 5:2658

BLAIR, HUGH
  John Milton 1:601
  William Shakespeare 2:709, 1046
  John Dryden 3:1333
  Daniel Defoe 3:1374
  Alexander Pope 3:1407, 1415,
    1419, 1423
  Jonathan Swift 3:1463
  Henry Fielding 3:1510

BLAKE, WILLIAM
  Geoffrey Chaucer 1:38

BLESSINGTON, MARGUERITE,
    COUNTESS OF
  Percy Bysshe Shelley 4:1965
  George Gordon, Lord Byron 4:2017

BLOCK, LOUIS J.
  Emily Dickinson 5:2846

BLOUNT, MRS.
  Alexander Pope 3:1402

BLUNT, WILFRED SCAWEN
  Oscar Wilde 5:3139

BOAS, FREDERICK S.
  Christopher Marlowe 1:208

BOILEAU, NICOLAS
  Edmund Spenser 1:220

BOLINGBROKE, HENRY ST. JOHN,
    VISCOUNT
  Sir Francis Bacon 1:338
  Alexander Pope 3:1416

BOLTON, EDMUND
  Ben Jonson 1:467

BORGHESI, PETER
  Geoffrey Chaucer 1:116

BORROW, GEORGE
  Daniel Defoe 3:1376

BOSWELL, JAMES
  John Bunyan 3:1286
  Jonathan Swift 3:1463
  Henry Fielding 3:1511
  Laurence Sterne 3:1549, 1556
  Thomas Gray 3:1587
  Oliver Goldsmith 3:1648, 1651,
    1654, 1656
  David Hume 3:1680, 1681, 1685
  Samuel Johnson 3:1710, 1723,
    1727, 1728
  Edward Gibbon 3:1765

BOTTA, ANNE C. LYNCH
  John Donne 1:377

BOURNE, HENRY RICHARD FOX
Sir Philip Sidney 1:128, 142

BOWLES, WILLIAM LISLE
Andrew Marvell 3:1254

BOYD, ANDREW K. H.
Anthony Trollope 5:2806

BOYESEN, HJALMAR HJORTH
William Makepeace Thackeray
5:2552

BOYLE, ROBERT
Sir Francis Bacon 1:340

BRADFORD, GAMALIEL, JR.
Anthony Trollope 5:2831

BRADLEY, A. C.
Christopher Marlowe 1:186
William Shakespeare 2:688, 1184
Percy Bysshe Shelley 4:2006
Robert Browning 5:2906

BRAMSTON, JAMES
Henry Fielding 3:1516

BRANDES, GEORGE
Sir Francis Bacon 1:331
Ben Jonson 1:467
William Shakespeare 2:1176, 1230

BREWSTER, SIR DAVID
Sir Francis Bacon 1:337, 341

BRIDGE, HORATIO
Nathaniel Hawthorne 5:2579

BRIDGES, ROBERT
John Milton 1:599
John Keats 4:1946

BRIGHT, HENRY
Nathaniel Hawthorne 5:2589

BRIMLEY, GEORGE
Alfred, Lord Tennyson 5:2974

BRINK, BERNHARD TEN
Geoffrey Chaucer 1:107

BRONSON, WALTER C.
Henry David Thoreau 4:2511
Emily Dickinson 5:2844

BRONTË, CHARLOTTE
Henry Fielding 3:1512
Robert Burns 3:1818
Jane Austen 4:1873, 1878, 1879
Sir Walter Scott 4:2146
Emily Brontë 4:2253
Charlotte Brontë 4:2413, 2419
William Makepeace Thackeray
5:2546, 2556
Charles Dickens 5:2629
Thomas Carlyle 5:2688
Ralph Waldo Emerson 5:2738
Matthew Arnold 5:2856
Alfred, Lord Tennyson 5:2973

BRONTË, EMILY
Emily Brontë 4:2247

BROOKE, CHRISTOPHER
William Shakespeare 2:1008

BROOKE, STOPFORD A.
Sir Francis Bacon 1:334
John Milton 1:590, 591, 596, 604
John Dryden 3:1334
Thomas Gray 3:1596
Percy Bysshe Shelley 4:1995
William Blake 4:2061
John Ruskin 5:3122

BROOME, WILLIAM
Alexander Pope 3:1419

BROUGHAM, HENRY, LORD
Samuel Johnson 3:1725
George Gordon, Lord Byron 4:2020
Thomas Babington Macaulay
4:2470, 2477

BROWN, JOHN
George Herbert 1:430

BROWN, T. E.
Ben Jonson 1:473
William Wordsworth 4:2330

BROWN, TOM
John Dryden 3:1308

BROWNE, IRVING
Sir Francis Bacon 1:330

BROWNE, JAMES P.
Henry Fielding 3:1508
Laurence Sterne 3:1550

BROWNE, WILLIAM
Sir Philip Sidney 1:126
Edmund Spenser 1:218, 228
Ben Jonson 1:467

BROWNELL, W. C.
George Eliot 5:2671
John Ruskin 5:3112

BROWNING, ELIZABETH BARRETT
Geoffrey Chaucer 1:49
John Donne 1:378
Ben Jonson 1:472
John Dryden 3:1315
Alexander Pope 3:1408
Robert Burns 3:1806
Jane Austen 4:1873
John Keats 4:1912, 1918
George Gordon, Lord Byron 4:2025
Samuel Taylor Coleridge 4:2176
William Wordsworth 4:2322
Charlotte Brontë 4:2421
Charles Dickens 5:2615
Thomas Carlyle 5:2686
Robert Browning 5:2894

BROWNING, OSCAR
Sir Francis Bacon 1:343
George Eliot 5:2655

BROWNING, ROBERT
Sir Philip Sidney 1:128
John Donne 1:379
Percy Bysshe Shelley 4:1970, 1983
George Gordon, Lord Byron 4:2025
William Wordsworth 4:2316
Mary Shelley 4:2389

BROWNSON, ORESTES AUGUSTUS
Ralph Waldo Emerson 5:2727

BRYANT, WILLIAM CULLEN
William Shakespeare 2:714
Robert Burns 3:1809
Richard Brinsley Sheridan 3:1854
Sir Walter Scott 4:2136
James Fenimore Cooper 4:2365
Washington Irving 4:2448, 2456,
2457
Charles Dickens 5:2615
Henry Wadsworth Longfellow
5:2775, 2782, 2784

BRYCE, JAMES
Anthony Trollope 5:2810

BRYDGES, SIR SAMUEL EGERTON
Jane Austen 4:1871

BUCHAN, JOHN
Walter Pater 5:3055

BUCHANAN, ROBERT
Sir Walter Scott 4:2136
Robert Browning 5:2905
Herman Melville 5:2937
Walt Whitman 5:3010

BUCKE, RICHARD MAURICE
Walt Whitman 5:3017

BUCKINGHAM, JOHN SHEFFIELD,
DUKE OF
Alexander Pope 3:1402

BUCKLAND, ANNA
Sir Philip Sidney 1:131

BUCKLE, HENRY THOMAS
Edward Gibbon 3:1776

BUCKNILL, JOHN CHARLES
William Shakespeare 2:1167

BULKLEY, L.
George Eliot 5:2658

BULLEN, A. H.
Christopher Marlowe 1:188

BULWER-LYTTON, EDWARD
Thomas Gray 3:1596
Oliver Goldsmith 3:1652
Charles Lamb 4:2224
George Eliot 5:2657

BUNYAN, JOHN
John Bunyan 3:1286

BURGES, SIR JAMES BLAND
Edward Gibbon 3:1767

BURKE, EDMUND
Sir Francis Bacon 1:332
William Shakespeare 2:1022
Oliver Goldsmith 3:1656

BURNETT, GEORGE
Sir Francis Bacon 1:332

BURNEY, CHARLES
John Dryden 3:1328
Samuel Johnson 3:1709
William Wordsworth 4:2319

BURNEY, FANNY
Alexander Pope 3:1403
Laurence Sterne 3:1557
Tobias Smollett 3:1622

Oliver Goldsmith 3:1653
Samuel Johnson 3:1708, 1728
Edward Gibbon 3:1765
Richard Brinsley Sheridan 3:1841

BURNS, GILBERT
Robert Burns 3:1803

BURNS, ROBERT
John Milton 1:582
John Dryden 3:1330
Robert Burns 3:1797, 1817, 1821

BURROUGHS, JOHN
Edward Gibbon 3:1777
Edgar Allan Poe 4:2281
Walt Whitman 5:3043

BURTON, JOHN HILL
Daniel Defoe 3:1374

BURTON, RICHARD
Tobias Smollett 3:1619
Charles Dickens 5:2624

BURTON, ROBERT
Edmund Spenser 1:229

BURY, J. B.
Edward Gibbon 3:1791

BUSHELL, THOMAS
Sir Francis Bacon 1:326

BUTLER, SAMUEL
Ben Jonson 1:468

BYROM, JOHN
Edward Gibbon 3:1765

BYRON, GEORGE GORDON, LORD
Geoffrey Chaucer 1:10
John Milton 1:582, 594
Alexander Pope 3:1408
Jonathan Swift 3:1463
Henry Fielding 3:1511
Laurence Sterne 3:1549
Thomas Gray 3:1594
Samuel Johnson 3:1716, 1723
Edward Gibbon 3:1766
Robert Burns 3:1803
Richard Brinsley Sheridan 3:1842,
1845
John Keats 4:1914, 1915
George Gordon, Lord Byron 4:2029
William Hazlitt 4:2100
Sir Walter Scott 4:2133, 2138,
2141
Samuel Taylor Coleridge 4:2168,
2174, 2175, 2185
William Wordsworth 4:2319, 2330

CAINE, HALL
John Milton 1:600
Laurence Sterne 3:1554
Richard Brinsley Sheridan 3:1843
John Keats 4:1925
Samuel Taylor Coleridge 4:2182

CAIRD, EDWARD
Thomas Carlyle 5:2693

CAIRD, JOHN
Sir Francis Bacon 1:360

CALDERWOOD, HENRY
David Hume 3:1689

CALVERT, GEORGE H.
John Keats 4:1926
Samuel Taylor Coleridge 4:2185

CAMDEN, WILLIAM
Edmund Spenser 1:214
Sir Francis Bacon 1:326

CAMPBELL, DR.
David Hume 3:1679

CAMPBELL, JOHN, LORD
Sir Francis Bacon 1:329, 336, 342

CAMPBELL, THOMAS
Sir Philip Sidney 1:126
John Donne 1:376, 378
John Webster 1:444
Ben Jonson 1:471
Richard Crashaw 1:516
John Milton 1:583
William Shakepeare 2:712
Andrew Marvell 3:1254
John Dryden 3:1314
Thomas Gray 3:1588
Tobias Smollett 3:1625
Robert Burns 3:1805

CAREW, THOMAS
John Donne 1:377

CARLETON, SIR DUDLEY
Sir Francis Bacon 1:325

CARLETON, WILLIAM
Henry Fielding 3:1520

CARLYLE, ALEXANDER
Tobias Smollett 3:1612
David Hume 3:1681

CARLYLE, JANE WELSH
William Makepeace Thackeray
5:2555
George Eliot 5:2657
Alfred, Lord Tennyson 5:2962

CARLYLE, THOMAS
Sir Francis Bacon 1:328
John Milton 1:584, 594
William Shakespeare 2:770
John Bunyan 3:1288
Jonathan Swift 3:1465
Henry Fielding 3:1511
Laurence Sterne 3:1549
Thomas Gray 3:1588
Tobias Smollett 3:1613
David Hume 3:1681, 1683
Samuel Johnson 3:1713, 1739
Edward Gibbon 3:1773
Robert Burns 3:1823
George Gordon, Lord Byron
4:2014, 2022
William Hazlitt 4:2098
Sir Walter Scott 4:2145, 2151
Samuel Taylor Coleridge 4:2173
Charles Lamb 4:2216
William Wordsworth 4:2318
James Fenimore Cooper 4:2362
Thomas Babington Macaulay
4:2469, 2477
Henry David Thoreau 4:2504
William Makepeace Thackeray
5:2545

Charles Dickens 5:2613
Thomas Carlyle 5:2684
Ralph Waldo Emerson 5:2723,
2729
Alfred, Lord Tennyson 5:2962,
2975

CARPENTER, FREDERIC IVES
Sir Philip Sidney 1:129
John Donne 1:379
John Webster 1:446, 449
Richard Crashaw 1:518
Robert Herrick 1:547
John Milton 1:588

CARR, J. COMYNS
William Blake 4:2076
Oscar Wilde 5:3143

CARROLL, LEWIS
William Makepeace Thackeray
5:2545
Alfred, Lord Tennyson 5:2963

CARY, HENRY FRANCIS
Thomas Gray 3:1588
Sir Walter Scott 4:2133

CATHER, WILLA
Walt Whitman 5:3019
Stephen Crane 5:3184

CAWTHORN, THOMAS
Henry Fielding 3:1519

CAXTON, WILLIAM
Geoffrey Chaucer 1:3, 4

CHALMERS, ALEXANDER
Tobias Smollett 3:1614

CHAMBERLAIN, NICHOLAS
Sir Francis Bacon 1:335

CHAMBERS, EDMUND K.
Andrew Marvell 3:1256

CHAMBERS, ROBERT
John Donne 1:379

CHANNING, E. T.
Oliver Goldsmith 3:1662

CHANNING, WILLIAM ELLERY
John Milton 1:583, 601
Henry David Thoreau 4:2506
Nathaniel Hawthorne 5:2590
Herman Melville 5:2935

CHAPMAN, GEORGE
Christopher Marlowe 1:166
Sir Francis Bacon 1:344

CHATEAUBRIAND, FRANÇOIS RENÉ,
VICOMTE DE
John Milton 1:579, 594, 599, 636

CHATTERTON, THOMAS
Oliver Goldsmith 3:1650

CHEEVER, GEORGE BARRELL
John Bunyan 3:1294

CHENEY, JOHN VANCE
William Blake 4:2060
Nathaniel Hawthorne 5:2584

CHESTERFIELD, PHILIP DORMER
STANHOPE, EARL OF
John Dryden 3:1306
Samuel Johnson 3:1726

CHESTERTON, G. K.
William Shakespeare 2:913, 1087
Alexander Pope 3:1453
Henry Fielding 3:1521
George Gordon, Lord Byron 4:2049
Thomas Carlyle 5:2719
Matthew Arnold 5:2859
Robert Browning 5:2927
Alfred, Lord Tennyson 5:2972
Robert Louis Stevenson 5:3080
Oscar Wilde 5:3145

CHILD, FRANCIS JAMES
Geoffrey Chaucer 1:11

CHIVERS, THOMAS HOLLEY
Edgar Allan Poe 4:2277

CHORLEY, G. F.
Jane Austen 4:1874

CHORLEY, HENRY F.
Charles Lamb 4:2223
Charlotte Brontë 4:2419

CHURCH, RICHARD WILLIAM
Edmund Spenser 1:295
Sir Francis Bacon 1:330, 333, 343,
365

CHURCHILL, CHARLES
Ben Jonson 1:470
Andrew Marvell 3:1254
John Dryden 3:1311
Alexander Pope 3:1406
Laurence Sterne 3:1550
Tobias Smollett 3:1611

CIBBER, COLLEY
John Dryden 3:1306, 1310
Alexander Pope 3:1420
Henry Fielding 3:1507

CIBBER, THEOPHILUS
John Milton 1:593

CLARKE, CHARLES COWDEN
Ben Jonson 1:472, 475, 476
Jonathan Swift 3:1488
Henry Fielding 3:1533
Laurence Sterne 3:1570
Tobias Smollett 3:1620
John Keats 4:1913

CLARKE, JAMES FREEMAN
William Shakespeare 2:908
Sir Walter Scott 4:2143

CLARKE, MARY COWDEN
Mary Shelley 4:2388

CLARKE, WILLIAM
Walt Whitman 5:3016

CLAYDEN, P. W.
William Shakespeare 2:1159

CLELAND, JOHN
Tobias Smollett 3:1621

CLEMM, MARIA
Edgar Allan Poe 4:2273

CLIVE, ARTHUR
Walt Whitman 5:3012

CLODD, EDWARD
Matthew Arnold 5:2861

CLOUGH, ARTHUR HUGH
John Dryden 3:1316
Robert Burns 3:1806
Ralph Waldo Emerson 5:2725
Henry Wadsworth Longfellow
5:2783

CLYMER, W. B. SHUBRICK
Jane Austen 4:1896
James Fenimore Cooper 4:2367

CODRINGTON, ROBERT
George Herbert 1:423

COKE, LADY MARY
Laurence Sterne 3:1549

COLERIDGE, HARTLEY
John Donne 1:378
John Dryden 3:1315
Thomas Gray 3:1588
Oliver Goldsmith 3:1652
Alfred, Lord Tennyson 5:2961

COLERIDGE, HENRY NELSON
Charles Lamb 4:2222

COLERIDGE, SAMUEL TAYLOR
Edmund Spenser 1:224, 255
John Donne 1:378
George Herbert 1:428, 429
Ben Jonson 1:471, 474, 475
John Milton 1:582, 594, 598, 623
Richard Crashaw 1:516
William Shakespeare 2:758, 933,
952, 986, 992, 1010, 1021,
1067, 1100, 1115, 1120, 1146,
1158, 1174, 1202, 1214, 1246
John Bunyan 3:1284, 1287
John Dryden 3:1332
Daniel Defoe 3:1375
Alexander Pope 3:1407
Jonathan Swift 3:1464, 1465
Henry Fielding 3:1512, 1520
Laurence Sterne 3:1551
Thomas Gray 3:1588
Edward Gibbon 3:1774
Samuel Johnson 3:1713, 1715,
1725
Richard Brinsley Sheridan 3:1841
George Gordon, Lord Byron
4:2014, 2022, 2031
Sir Walter Scott 4:2142, 2143
Samuel Taylor Coleridge 4:2168,
2169
Charles Lamb 4:2215, 2216
William Wordsworth 4:2331, 2336
Alfred, Lord Tennyson 5:2964

COLERIDGE, SARA
Richard Crashaw 1:516
Jane Austen 4:1873
Samuel Taylor Coleridge 4:2170
Charles Dickens 5:2626, 2629
Henry Wadsworth Longfellow
5:2782

Alfred, Lord Tennyson 5:2972,
2973

COLLIER, J. PAYNE
William Shakespeare 2:875

COLLIER, JEREMY
William Shakespeare 2:1022, 1083

COLLIER, WILLIAM FRANCIS
John Milton 1:605
Sir Walter Scott 4:2147

COLLINS, JOHN CHURTON
Geoffrey Chaucer 1:13
Christopher Marlowe 1:205
John Dryden 3:1318
Jonathan Swift 3:1493
George Gordon, Lord Byron 4:2050
Emily Dickinson 5:2844

COLLINS, WILLIAM
Ben Jonson 1:469
William Shakespeare 2:708

COLMAN, GEORGE, THE YOUNGER
Oliver Goldsmith 3:1650
Edward Gibbon 3:1767

COLVIN, SIDNEY
John Keats 4:1921

CONDELL, HENRY
William Shakespeare 2:701

CONDILLAC, ETIENNE BONNOT DE
Sir Francis Bacon 1:341

CONGREVE, WILLIAM
Ben Jonson 1:469
John Dryden 3:1306, 1310
Jonathan Swift 3:1471

CONINGTON, JOHN
John Dryden 3:1330

CONRAD, JOSEPH
James Fenimore Cooper 4:2368
Herman Melville 5:2939
Stephen Crane 5:3170

CONWAY, MONCURE DANIEL
William Blake 4:2072
Sir Walter Scott 4:2140
Henry David Thoreau 4:2504
Walt Whitman 5:3009

COOKE, GEORGE WILLIS
George Eliot 5:2666

COOPER, ELIZABETH
Geoffrey Chaucer 1:8

COPE, WALTER
William Shakespeare 2:951

CORSON, HIRAM
John Milton 1:603

COTTLE, JOSEPH
Samuel Taylor Coleridge 4:2171

COTTON, CHARLES
George Herbert 1:422

COURTENAY, JOHN
Samuel Johnson 3:1715

COURTHOPE, WILLIAM JOHN
  Christopher Marlowe 1:173
  John Donne 1:412
  Alexander Pope 3:1417
  Thomas Gray 3:1589
  Samuel Johnson 3:1724
  John Keats 4:1945
  Sir Walter Scott 4:2141

COURTNAY, W. L.
  Ralph Waldo Emerson 5:2735

COWLEY, ABRAHAM
  Edmund Spenser 1:220, 229
  Sir Francis Bacon 1:339
  Richard Crashaw 1:515

COWPER, WILLIAM
  Sir Philip Sidney 1:130
  John Milton 1:593
  John Bunyan 3:1286
  John Dryden 3:1313
  Alexander Pope 3:1406, 1422
  Jonathan Swift 3:1463
  Thomas Gray 3:1586
  David Hume 3:1682
  Samuel Johnson 3:1714, 1730
  Edward Gibbon 3:1767
  Robert Burns 3:1801

COXE, ARTHUR CLEVELAND
  Nathaniel Hawthorne 5:2587

CRABBE, GEORGE
  Geoffrey Chaucer 1:41
  Sir Walter Scott 4:2130

CRACROFT, BERNARD
  Sir Francis Bacon 1:329, 332

CRADOCK, JOSEPH
  Oliver Goldsmith 3:1649

CRAIK, GEORGE L.
  John Donne 1:378
  George Herbert 1:425
  Ben Jonson 1:476
  Richard Crashaw 1:517

CRAIK, HENRY
  John Milton 1:602
  Jonathan Swift 3:1470
  Henry Fielding 3:1516
  David Hume 3:1689
  Samuel Johnson 3:1722
  George Eliot 5:2656

CRANCH, C. P.
  Ralph Waldo Emerson 5:2741

CRASHAW, RICHARD
  Sir Philip Sidney 1:127
  George Herbert 1:427

CRAWFORD, F. MARION
  Richard Brinsley Sheridan 3:1848

CRAWFURD, OSWALD
  John Donne 1:379
  Ben Jonson 1:472
  Richard Brinsley Sheridan 3:1847

CROKER, JOHN WILSON
  Jonathan Swift 3:1473
  Richard Brinsley Sheridan 3:1846
  John Keats 4:1928

  Mary Shelley 4:2392
  Thomas Babington Macaulay
    4:2476, 2481
  Charles Dickens 5:2624

CROSLAND, CAMILLA TOULMIN
  Nathaniel Hawthorne 5:2585

CROSS, JOHN W.
  George Eliot 5:2650

CROSS, WILBUR L.
  Henry Fielding 3:1520
  Laurence Sterne 3:1582
  Tobias Smollett 3:1643
  Jane Austen 4:1903
  Emily Brontë 4:2251
  Charlotte Brontë 4:2421
  Nathaniel Hawthorne 5:2586
  Charles Dickens 5:2624
  George Eliot 5:2657
  Anthony Trollope 5:2809

CUMBERLAND, RICHARD
  William Shakespeare 2:739
  Oliver Goldsmith 3:1651

CUNNINGHAM, ALLAN
  Robert Burns 3:1806
  William Blake 4:2057

CURRIE, JAMES
  Robert Burns 3:1802, 1818

CURTIS, GEORGE WILLIAM
  John Milton 1:585
  Robert Burns 3:1810
  Jane Austen 4:1875
  Henry David Thoreau 4:2512
  William Makepeace Thackeray
    5:2547
  Nathaniel Hawthorne 5:2581
  Henry Wadsworth Longfellow
    5:2772
  Robert Browning 5:2894

DANA, CHARLES A.
  Walt Whitman 5:3022

DANA, RICHARD HENRY
  Washington Irving 4:2458
  Charles Dickens 5:2614

DANIEL, GEORGE
  John Donne 1:378
  George Herbert 1:428
  Charles Lamb 4:2218

DANIEL, SAMUEL
  Sir Philip Sidney 1:125
  Edmund Spenser 1:217, 228

D'AVENANT, WILLIAM
  Edmund Spenser 1:220

DAVIDSON, JOHN
  John Keats 4:1923

DAVIES, J. LLEWELYN
  Matthew Arnold 5:2866

DAVIES, JOHN
  William Shakespeare 2:671

DAVIES, THOMAS
  Ben Jonson 1:473, 474
  John Dryden 3:1324
  Oliver Goldsmith 3:1658

DAWES, RUFUS
  Ralph Waldo Emerson 5:2724

DAWSON, GEORGE
  Geoffrey Chaucer 1:99

DEFOE, DANIEL
  Geoffrey Chaucer 1:8
  Daniel Defoe 3:1366, 1374

DE LA MARE, WALTER
  William Shakespeare 2:1024, 1065,
    1087, 1120, 1155, 1195

DELANY, MARY
  Tobias Smollett 3:1621

DELANY, PATRICK
  Jonathan Swift 3:1460

DENHAM, SIR JOHN
  Geoffrey Chaucer 1:7
  Edmund Spenser 1:214

DENNIS, JOHN (1657–1734)
  Edmund Spenser 1:220
  William Shakespeare 2:865
  John Dryden 3:1309
  Alexander Pope 3:1416, 1423

DENNIS, JOHN (1825–1911)
  Robert Herrick 1:545
  John Milton 3:587
  Charles Lamb 4:2225

DE QUINCEY, THOMAS
  John Milton 1:584, 643
  William Shakespeare 2:767, 1055
  Daniel Defoe 3:1370
  Alexander Pope 3:1409
  Jonathan Swift 3:1466
  Samuel Johnson 3:1731
  Edward Gibbon 3:1767
  Robert Burns 3:1800
  John Keats 4:1916
  Percy Bysshe Shelley 4:1966
  William Hazlitt 4:2105
  Samuel Taylor Coleridge 4:2171
  Charles Lamb 4:2219
  William Wordsworth 4:2316
  Charles Dickens 5:2626

DESCARTES, RENÉ
  Sir Francis Bacon 1:339

DE VERE, AUBREY
  Edmund Spenser 1:283
  John Milton 1:597
  Robert Burns 3:1806, 1812
  John Keats 4:1912, 1917
  William Wordsworth 4:2326
  Robert Browning 5:2898
  Alfred, Lord Tennyson 5:2969

DIBDIN, CHARLES
  Ben Jonson 1:475, 476
  William Shakespeare 2:746
  John Dryden 3:1325
  Oliver Goldsmith 3:1658

DIBDIN, THOMAS FROGNALL
  Daniel Defoe 3:1367

DICEY, A. V.
  Richard Brinsley Sheridan 3:1851
  Thomas Babington Macaulay
    4:2498
  Anthony Trollope 5:2812

DICKENS, CHARLES
  William Shakespeare 2:1148
  Tobias Smollett 3:1616
  Washington Irving 4:2444, 2446
  William Makepeace Thackeray
    5:2546
  Charles Dickens 5:2629
  George Eliot 5:2657
  Henry Wadsworth Longfellow
    5:2772
  Robert Browning 5:2903

DICKENS, MAMIE
  Charles Dickens 5:2614

DICKINSON, EMILY
  Nathaniel Hawthorne 5:2583
  George Eliot 5:2650, 2660

DICKINSON, G. LOWES
  Oscar Wilde 5:3156

DIGBY, SIR KENELM
  Edmund Spenser 1:219, 235

DIGGES, LEONARD
  William Shakespeare 2:701, 703

D'ISRAELI, ISAAC
  Sir Francis Bacon 1:328
  Ben Jonson 1:471
  John Milton 1:605

DIXON, WILLIAM HEPWORTH
  Sir Francis Bacon 1:329

DOBELL, SYDNEY
  Emily Brontë 4:2250
  Charlotte Brontë 4:2426
  Thomas Carlyle 5:2685

DOBSON, AUSTIN
  Robert Herrick 1:545
  John Dryden 3:1317
  Alexander Pope 3:1413
  Henry Fielding 3:1509, 1514
  Tobias Smollett 3:1624
  Oliver Goldsmith 3:1673
  Henry Wadsworth Longfellow
    5:2772
  Robert Louis Stevenson 5:3077

DODGE, MARY ABIGAIL
  William Blake 4:2057

DODGE, R. E. NEIL
  Edmund Spenser 1:306

DOE, CHARLES
  John Bunyan 3:1281

DONNE, JOHN
  John Donne 1:377

DONNE, WILLIAM BODHAM
  Richard Brinsley Sheridan 3:1849

DONNELLY, IGNATIUS
  William Shakespeare 2:912

DORR, JULIA C. R.
  Charles Dickens 5:2629

DOUGLAS, LORD ALFRED
  Oscar Wilde 5:3144, 3150

DOUGLAS, GAVIN
  Geoffrey Chaucer 1:4

DOWDEN, EDWARD
  Sir Philip Sidney 1:129
  Sir Francis Bacon 1:343
  John Donne 1:379
  John Milton 1:580, 659
  William Shakespeare 2:1010, 1068
  John Bunyan 3:1299
  Jonathan Swift 4:1461
  Thomas Gray 3:1591
  Oliver Goldsmith 3:1671
  Robert Burns 3:1815
  Percy Bysshe Shelley 4:2001
  George Gordon, Lord Byron 4:2027
  Samuel Taylor Coleridge 4:2204
  Charles Lamb 4:2225
  William Wordsworth 4:2326
  Washington Irving 4:2448
  William Makepeace Thackeray
    5:2550
  Thomas Carlyle 5:2689
  Robert Browning 5:2908
  Alfred, Lord Tennyson 5:2993
  Walter Pater 5:3064
  John Ruskin 5:3108

DOYLE, ARTHUR CONAN
  Robert Louis Stevenson 5:3083

DOYLE, SIR FRANCIS HASTINGS
  John Milton 1:591
  Jane Austen 4:1881

DRAKE, JAMES
  William Shakespeare 2:1087

DRAKE, NATHAN
  Sir Philip Sidney 1:127
  Sir Francis Bacon 1:332, 336, 338
  John Donne 1:378
  John Webster 1:443
  Richard Crashaw 1:516
  Robert Herrick 1:543
  John Milton 1:589, 599
  William Shakespeare 2:755

DRAPER, JOHN WILLIAM
  Sir Francis Bacon 1:342

DRAYTON, MICHAEL
  Sir Philip Sidney 1:127
  Edmund Spenser 1:213, 218, 226
  William Shakespeare 2:702

DRUMMOND, WILLIAM
  Sir Philip Sidney 1:127
  Edmund Spenser 1:218
  John Donne 1:377
  Ben Jonson 1:464, 475

DRYDEN, JOHN
  Geoffrey Chaucer 1:18
  Edmund Spenser 1:214, 220, 226,
    227, 230
  John Donne 1:378
  Ben Jonson 1:468, 473, 475, 476
  John Milton 1:581, 592
  William Shakespeare 2:704, 705,
    706, 1074, 1113, 1207, 1208

John Dryden 3:1306, 1326, 1329,
  1332

DUFFERIN AND AVA, MARQUESS OF
  Richard Brinsley Sheridan 3:1844

DUNBAR, WILLIAM
  Geoffrey Chaucer 1:4

DUNLOP, FRANCES
  Robert Burns 3:1817

DUNLOP, JOHN
  Henry Fielding 3:1519
  Tobias Smollett 3:1614

DUNTON, JOHN
  George Herbert 1:422
  Daniel Defoe 3:1366

DUPORT, JAMES
  George Herbert 1:428

DUYCKINCK, EVERT A.
  Herman Melville 5:2942

DYCE, ALEXANDER
  Christopher Marlowe 1:181
  John Webster 1:449

EARLE, JOHN
  Sir Francis Bacon 1:337

ECHARD, LAURENCE
  John Milton 1:581

EDGEWORTH, MARIA
  Jane Austen 4:1880
  George Gordon, Lord Byron 4:2014
  Sir Walter Scott 4:2130, 2131,
    2145
  James Fenimore Cooper 4:2367
  Thomas Babington Macaulay
    4:2481

EDMUNDSON, GEORGE
  John Milton 1:599

EGAN, MAURICE F.
  Richard Crashaw 1:517

ELIOT, GEORGE
  Tobias Smollett 3:1615
  Jane Austen 4:1873
  William Wordsworth 4:2322
  Charlotte Brontë 4:2413, 2419,
    2422
  Nathaniel Hawthorne 5:2580
  Charles Dickens 5:2616
  George Eliot 5:2657
  Thomas Carlyle 5:2696
  Matthew Arnold 5:2861
  Robert Browning 5:2895
  Walt Whitman 5:3012
  Walter Pater 5:3056
  John Ruskin 5:3107

ELLIS, EDWIN J.
  William Blake 4:2078

ELLIS, HAVELOCK
  Christopher Marlowe 1:195
  William Shakespeare 2:714
  Henry David Thoreau 4:2510

ELLIS, ROBERT LESLIE
  Sir Francis Bacon 1:342

ELLWOOD, THOMAS
John Milton 1:577, 598

ELTON, OLIVER
Walt Whitman 5:3015

ELWIN, WHITWELL
Laurence Sterne 3:1562
Thomas Gray 3:1589
William Makepeace Thackeray
5:2558

ELZE, KARL
William Shakespeare 2:798

EMERSON, RALPH WALDO
Geoffrey Chaucer 1:10
Sir Francis Bacon 1:336
George Herbert 1:425, 426
Ben Jonson 1:472
Robert Herrick 1:544
John Milton 1:638
William Shakespeare 2:779
Jonathan Swift 3:1466
David Hume 3:1681, 1686
Samuel Johnson 3:1714
Edward Gibbon 3:1768
Robert Burns 3:1808
Sir Walter Scott 4:2139
Samuel Taylor Coleridge 4:2177
William Wordsworth 4:2318
Thomas Babington Macaulay
4:2473
Henry David Thoreau 4:2512
William Makepeace Thackeray
5:2546
Charles Dickens 5:2616
Thomas Carlyle 5:2684, 2700
Ralph Waldo Emerson 5:2724
Henry Wadsworth Longfellow
5:2783
Alfred, Lord Tennyson 5:2962,
2966
Walt Whitman 5:3021

ERDMANN, JOHANN EDWARD
Sir Francis Bacon 1:342

ESSEX, ROBERT DEVEREUX, EARL OF
Sir Francis Bacon 1:325

ETHEREGE, SIR GEORGE
John Dryden 3:1306, 1328

EVANS, HERBERT ARTHUR
Ben Jonson 1:473

EVANS, JOHN AMPHLETT
John Milton 1:587
John Dryden 3:1358

EVELYN, JOHN
Sir Francis Bacon 1:340

EVERETT, ALEXANDER HILL
Washington Irving 4:2445
Thomas Carlyle 5:2696

EVERETT, C. C.
Ralph Waldo Emerson 5:2740

EVERETT, EDWARD
John Milton 1:595
Washington Irving 4:2448, 2455,
2456

EYRE-TODD, GEORGE
Tobias Smollett 3:1617

F., J.
Emily Brontë 4:2251

FARQUHAR, GEORGE
John Dryden 3:1306

FARRAR, FREDERIC WILLIAM
Sir Francis Bacon 1:332
John Milton 1:599

FARRER, NICHOLAS
George Herbert 1:427

FAWCETT, MILLICENT GARRETT
Charlotte Brontë 4:2414

FELTHAM, OWEN
Ben Jonson 1:467

FELTON, CORNELIUS CONWAY
Washington Irving 4:2457

FENTON, ELIJAH
Alexander Pope 3:1422

FIELD, BARON
Robert Herrick 1:541

FIELD, MAUNSELL B.
Edgar Allan Poe 4:2275
James Fenimore Cooper 4:2361

FIELD, MICHAEL
Walter Pater 5:3049

FIELDING, HENRY
William Shakespeare 2:842
Alexander Pope 3:1420
Henry Fielding 3:1518

FIELDS, JAMES T.
William Makepeace Thackeray
5:2549, 2557

FISKE, JOHN
Henry Wadsworth Longfellow
5:2784

FITZGEOFFREY, CHARLES
Edmund Spenser 1:217

FITZGERALD, EDWARD
John Milton 1:596
Andrew Marvell 3:1257
Thomas Gray 3:1590
Jane Austen 4:1875
Sir Walter Scott 4:2146, 2147
William Makepeace Thackeray
5:2548, 2557
Nathaniel Hawthorne 5:2582
Charles Dickens 5:2618
Thomas Carlyle 5:2698
Ralph Waldo Emerson 5:2738
Anthony Trollope 5:2806
Robert Browning 5:2896
Alfred, Lord Tennyson 5:2972

FITZGERALD, PERCY
Oliver Goldsmith 3:1659
Charles Dickens 5:2614

FITZJEFFREY, HENRY
John Webster 1:443

FLECKNOE, RICHARD
Ben Jonson 1:467
William Shakespeare 2:704

FLETCHER, C. R. L.
Sir Francis Bacon 1:333
Oliver Goldsmith 3:1653
Samuel Johnson 3:1721

FORD, FORD MADOX
Oscar Wilde 5:3139

FORD, JOHN
John Webster 1:448

FORMAN, H. BUXTON
John Keats 4:1920

FORSTER, JOHN
Daniel Defoe 3:1370
Henry Fielding 3:1512
Charles Lamb 4:2230
Charles Dickens 5:2614
Robert Browning 5:2902, 2903

FORSYTH, WILLIAM
Henry Fielding 3:1513
Tobias Smollett 3:1617

FOSTER, JOHN
Edward Gibbon 3:1773

FOTHERINGHAM, JAMES
Robert Browning 5:2894

FOULIS, EDWARD
Geoffrey Chaucer 1:7

FOWLER, THOMAS
Sir Francis Bacon 1:329, 333

FOX, CAROLINE
Samuel Taylor Coleridge 4:2171
Charlotte Brontë 4:2414
William Makepeace Thackeray
5:2559
Ralph Waldo Emerson 5:2728

FOX, W. J.
Robert Browning 5:2901
Alfred, Lord Tennyson 5:2964

FOXE, JOHN
Geoffrey Chaucer 1:14

FRANCE, ANATOLE
William Shakespeare 2:1111

FRANCILLON, R. E.
George Eliot 5:2660

FREDERIC, HAROLD
Stephen Crane 5:3180

FREEMAN, EDWARD A.
Edward Gibbon 3:1777
Thomas Babington Macaulay
4:2479
Thomas Carlyle 5:2687
Anthony Trollope 5:2807

FRISWELL, JAMES HAIN
Anthony Trollope 5:2806
Alfred, Lord Tennyson 5:2968
John Ruskin 5:3107

FROUDE, JAMES ANTHONY
John Milton 1:586
William Shakespeare 2:713

Matthew Arnold 5:2860
Alfred, Lord Tennyson 5:2976

FULLER, MARGARET
George Herbert 1:436
Sir Walter Scott 4:2139
Samuel Taylor Coleridge 4:2177
Edgar Allan Poe 4:2282
William Wordsworth 4:2323
James Fenimore Cooper 4:2364
Thomas Carlyle 5:2684
Ralph Waldo Emerson 5:2738
Henry Wadsworth Longfellow
5:2787
Robert Browning 5:2895
Alfred, Lord Tennyson 5:2964

FULLER, THOMAS
Edmund Spenser 1:214
Sir Francis Bacon 1:326, 327
George Herbert 1:421
Ben Jonson 1:465, 468
William Shakespeare 2:672

GALT, JOHN
George Gordon, Lord Byron 4:2023

GALTON, ARTHUR
Robert Browning 5:2915

GARDENSTONE, FRANCIS GARDEN,
LORD
Tobias Smollett 3:1622

GARDINER, SAMUEL RAWSON
Sir Francis Bacon 1:329, 333, 338
John Milton 1:590

GARLAND, HAMLIN
Walt Whitman 5:3010
Stephen Crane 5:3186

GARNETT, EDWARD
Stephen Crane 5:3171

GARNETT, RICHARD
John Milton 1:603
John Bunyan 3:1290
Samuel Taylor Coleridge 4:2182
Emily Brontë 4:2248
Mary Shelley 4:2409

GARRICK, DAVID
Laurence Sterne 3:1549
Oliver Goldsmith 3:1647
Samuel Johnson 3:1726
Richard Brinsley Sheridan 3:1850

GARRIGUES, GERTRUDE
Samuel Taylor Coleridge 4:2199

GARTH, SIR SAMUEL
John Dryden 3:1310

GASCOIGNE, GEORGE
Geoffrey Chaucer 1:5

GASKELL, ELIZABETH
Emily Brontë 4:2248

GASSENDI, PIERRE
Sir Francis Bacon 1:339

GATES, LEWIS E.
Edgar Allan Poe 4:2308
Charlotte Brontë 4:2435
Thomas Carlyle 5:2695
Alfred, Lord Tennyson 5:3004

GAY, JOHN
Daniel Defoe 3:1374
Alexander Pope 3:1404, 1419
Jonathan Swift 3:1474

GEIKIE, SIR ARCHIBALD
Robert Burns 3:1820

GEORGE, ANDREW J.
Robert Burns 3:1816

GERVINUS, G. G.
Sir Francis Bacon 1:332
William Shakespeare 2:945, 1041,
1062, 1192, 1248

GIBBON, EDWARD
Alexander Pope 3:1419
Henry Fielding 3:1519
David Hume 3:1683
Edward Gibbon 3:1766, 1770,
1772, 1776
Richard Brinsley Sheridan 3:1851

GIFFORD, WILLIAM
William Wordsworth 4:2319

GILCHRIST, ANNE
Walt Whitman 5:3011

GILES, HENRY
William Shakespeare 2:1029
Oliver Goldsmith 3:1670

GILFILLAN, GEORGE
John Donne 1:378
George Herbert 1:429
Richard Crashaw 1:515, 519
Tobias Smollett 3:1616
Oliver Goldsmith 3:1657
Robert Burns 3:1800
Sir Walter Scott 4:2157
Samuel Taylor Coleridge 4:2187
Edgar Allan Poe 4:2293
Mary Shelley 4:2400
William Makepeace Thackeray
5:2559
Ralph Waldo Emerson 5:2741
Henry Wadsworth Longfellow
5:2776
Alfred, Lord Tennyson 5:2977

GILLIES, R. P.
Sir Walter Scott 4:2141

GISSING, GEORGE
Charles Dickens 5:2627, 2641

GLADSTONE, WILLIAM EWART
Richard Brinsley Sheridan 3:1844
Thomas Babington Macaulay
4:2492
Alfred, Lord Tennyson 5:2975

GODWIN, WILLIAM
Geoffrey Chaucer 1:31
Sir Philip Sidney 1:130
John Milton 1:582, 593, 603
William Shakespeare 2:710, 1116
Jonathan Swift 3:1472
Tobias Smollett 3:1613
Percy Bysshe Shelley 4:1977
Mary Shelley 4:2388
Washington Irving 4:2454

GOETHE, JOHANN WOLFGANG VON
John Milton 1:599
William Shakespeare 2:712, 1096,
1155
Oliver Goldsmith 3:1655
George Gordon, Lord Byron
4:2024, 2029, 2031
Sir Walter Scott 4:2133, 2145,
2146, 2148
Thomas Carlyle 5:2686

GOLDSMITH, OLIVER
Sir Philip Sidney 1:135
John Milton 1:601
John Dryden 3:1311, 1329, 1332
Alexander Pope 3:1403, 1418, 1422
Laurence Sterne 3:1556
Thomas Gray 3:1594, 1595
Tobias Smollett 3:1622, 1625
Oliver Goldsmith 3:1653
Samuel Johnson 3:1723

GOODRICH, SAMUEL GRISWOLD
James Fenimore Cooper 4:2361
Nathaniel Hawthorne 5:2578

GOSSE, EDMUND
Sir Philip Sidney 1:127
Sir Francis Bacon 1:334, 337
John Donne 1:376, 379, 394, 405
George Herbert 1:426
John Webster 1:446, 460
Ben Jonson 1:473, 475
Richard Crashaw 1:527
Robert Herrick 1:544, 548
John Milton 1:598, 600
William Shakespeare 2:864
Andrew Marvell 3:1267
John Bunyan 3:1290
John Dryden 3:1320, 1322, 1334
Alexander Pope 3:1413
Jonathan Swift 3:1471, 1472, 1475
Henry Fielding 3:1514, 1516
Laurence Sterne 3:1555
Thomas Gray 3:1593
Tobias Smollett 3:1618, 1634
Oliver Goldsmith 3:1653
David Hume 3:1681, 1684
Edward Gibbon 3:1777
Richard Brinsley Sheridan 3:1847
Jane Austen 4:1877
Percy Bysshe Shelley 4:1975
Sir Walter Scott 4:2144
Charles Lamb 4:2240
Emily Brontë 4:2253
Edgar Allan Poe 4:2281
Washington Irving 4:2449
William Makepeace Thackeray
5:2554
George Eliot 5:2656
Ralph Waldo Emerson 5:2740
Henry Wadsworth Longfellow
5:2780
Alfred, Lord Tennyson 5:2969
Walter Pater 5:3050
Robert Louis Stevenson 5:3076
John Ruskin 5:3111

GOSSON, STEPHAN
Geoffrey Chaucer 1:125

GOWER, JOHN
  Geoffrey Chaucer 1:2

GOWER, LORD RONALD
  Henry Wadsworth Longfellow
    5:2773

GRAHAM, GEORGE R.
  Edgar Allan Poe 4:2274

GRAHAM, HENRY GREY
  Robert Burns 3:1816

GRAHAM, P. ANDERSON
  Henry David Thoreau 4:2510

GRAHAM, RICHARD D.
  Emily Brontë 4:2251

GRAHAM, WILLIAM
  Percy Bysshe Shelley 4:1970
  George Gordon, Lord Byron 4:2019

GRANGER, JAMES
  Ben Jonson 1:470
  Robert Herrick 1:542
  Andrew Marvell 3:1254
  John Dryden 3:1312

GRANT, ANNE
  Oliver Goldsmith 3:1654
  Sir Walter Scott 4:2147

GRANT, JAMES
  Thomas Babington Macaulay
    4:2476

GRAY, ASA
  Sir Francis Bacon 1:330

GRAY, THOMAS
  Geoffrey Chaucer 1:22
  John Milton 1:582, 593
  William Shakespeare 2:708
  John Dryden 3:1307, 1311
  Alexander Pope 3:1402
  Henry Fielding 3:1509
  Laurence Sterne 3:1550, 1556
  Thomas Gray 3:1594, 1595
  Samuel Johnson 3:1723

GRAY, WILLIAM
  Sir Philip Sidney 1:127

GREELEY, HORACE
  Edgar Allan Poe 4:2275
  James Fenimore Cooper 4:2361
  Herman Melville 5:2940

GREEN, JOHN RICHARD
  Sir Philip Sidney 1:126
  Sir Francis Bacon 1:337, 338
  William Shakespeare 2:684
  John Bunyan 3:1290
  John Dryden 3:1332

GREEN, THOMAS
  John Milton 1:590

GREENE, GEORGE WASHINGTON
  Washington Irving 4:2459

GREENE, HERBERT EVELETH
  Jonathan Swift 3:1472

GREENE, ROBERT
  Geoffrey Chaucer 1:15
  Christopher Marlowe 1:165
  William Shakespeare 2:671

GREENWELL, DORA
  Sir Francis Bacon 1:338

GREGORY, GEORGE
  Tobias Smollett 3:1613

GREIN, J. T.
  Oscar Wilde 5:3153

GREVILLE, CHARLES CAVENDISH
    FULKE
  Thomas Babington Macaulay
    4:2470

GREVILLE, FULKE (LORD BROOKE)
  Sir Philip Sidney 1:125, 126, 130

GREVILLE, HENRY
  Thomas Babington Macaulay
    4:2480

GRIERSON, HERBERT J. C.
  Richard Crashaw 1:519

GRIFFIN, W. HALL
  Sir Francis Bacon 1:331
  Ben Jonson 1:474

GRISWOLD, RUFUS WILMOT
  John Keats 4:1927
  Edgar Allan Poe 4:2273
  Nathaniel Hawthorne 5:2580

GROSART, ALEXANDER B.
  Sir Philip Sidney 1:133
  George Herbert 1:423, 426
  Richard Crashaw 1:523
  Andrew Marvell 3:1255

GRUTER, ISAAC
  Sir Francis Bacon 1:331

GUEST, EDWIN
  John Milton 1:584, 590, 599

GUINEY, LOUISE IMOGEN
  George Herbert 1:426
  William Hazlitt 4:2103

GUIZOT, F. P. G.
  Edward Gibbon 3:1774

GWYNN, STEPHEN
  Robert Louis Stevenson 5:3081
  Stephen Crane 5:3183

HACKET, JOHN
  John Donne 1:376
  John Milton 1:604

HAGGARD, H. RIDER
  Daniel Defoe 3:1377

HALE, EDWARD EVERETT, JR.
  Robert Herrick 1:547
  Oscar Wilde 5:3151

HALES, JOHN W.
  John Donne 1:418
  John Milton 1:601
  William Shakespeare 2:1021
  Daniel Defoe 3:1373
  Thomas Gray 3:1594
  Jane Austen 4:1875
  Sir Walter Scott 4:2143

HALL, HUBERT
  Sir Philip Sidney 1:134

HALL, ROBERT
  David Hume 3:1685

HALL, S. C.
  William Hazlitt 4:2100
  James Fenimore Cooper 4:2362
  Washington Irving 4:2444
  Nathaniel Hawthorne 5:2579
  Charles Dickens 5:2625

HALLAM, ARTHUR HENRY
  Alfred, Lord Tennyson 5:2964

HALLAM, HENRY
  Sir Philip Sidney 1:132, 135
  Sir Francis Bacon 1:336
  John Donne 1:376, 378
  Ben Jonson 1:473
  Robert Herrick 1:544
  John Milton 1:594, 598, 600
  John Bunyan 3:1288
  John Dryden 3:1314, 1324, 1326,
    1327, 1329, 1330, 1333, 1334
  Jonathan Swift 3:1472
  Alfred, Lord Tennyson 5:2973

HALLECK, FITZ-GREENE
  James Fenimore Cooper 4:2365

HALLECK, REUBEN POST
  Sir Francis Bacon 1:335
  John Donne 1:380

HAMILTON, LADY ANNE
  Tobias Smollett 3:1621

HAMILTON, WILLIAM
  David Hume 3:1686

HANKIN, ST. JOHN
  Oscar Wilde 5:3143

HANMER, THOMAS
  William Shakespeare 2:1091

HANNAY, DAVID
  John Donne 1:379

HANNAY, JAMES
  Tobias Smollett 3:1621
  Edgar Allan Poe 4:2277
  William Makepeace Thackeray
    5:2548

HARBERT, SIR WILLIAM
  Sir Philip Sidney 1:125

HARDY, ARTHUR SHERBURNE
  Nathaniel Hawthorne 5:2590

HARPER, JANET
  Jane Austen 4:1877

HARRINGTON, SIR JOHN
  Sir Philip Sidney 1:127
  Edmund Spenser 1:218, 228

HARRIS, FRANK
  William Shakespeare 2:970, 980

HARRIS, JAMES
  Henry Fielding 3:1516

HARRISON, FREDERIC
  John Milton 1:597
  Henry Fielding 3:1520

Edward Gibbon 3:1780
John Keats 4:1959
Sir Walter Scott 4:2136
Emily Brontë 4:2251
Charlotte Brontë 4:2417
Charles Dickens 5:2639
George Eliot 5:2659
Thomas Carlyle 5:2693
Anthony Trollope 5:2822
Matthew Arnold 5:2866
Robert Browning 5:2894
John Ruskin 5:3126

HART, JOHN S.
George Herbert 1:425

HARTE, BRET
Charles Dickens 5:2627

HARVEY, CHRISTOPHER
George Herbert 1:427

HARVEY, GABRIEL
Sir Philip Sidney 1:129
Christopher Marlowe 1:166
Edmund Spenser 1:213, 216, 217,
227, 228

HAVERS, GEORGE
Sir Francis Bacon 1:339

HAWKINS, SIR JOHN
Henry Fielding 3:1519
Oliver Goldsmith 3:1648
Samuel Johnson 3:1711

HAWTHORNE, JULIAN
Daniel Defoe 3:1377
Anthony Trollope 5:2806
Herman Melville 5:2941

HAWTHORNE, NATHANIEL
William Shakespeare 2:682, 900
Samuel Johnson 3:1714
Robert Burns 3:1800
Sir Walter Scott 4:2132
Edgar Allan Poe 4:2285
Thomas Babington Macaulay
4:2470
William Makepeace Thackeray
5:2558
Nathaniel Hawthorne 5:2577,
2587, 2588, 2590
Charles Dickens 5:2614
George Eliot 5:2649
Henry Wadsworth Longfellow
5:2774, 2781
Anthony Trollope 5:2806
Robert Browning 5:2893
Herman Melville 5:2935, 2940
Alfred, Lord Tennyson 5:2963

HAWTHORNE, SOPHIA
Nathaniel Hawthorne 5:2588

HAYDON, BENJAMIN ROBERT
Richard Brinsley Sheridan 3:1846
John Keats 4:1912
William Hazlitt 4:2098
Charles Lamb 4:2219

HAYLEY, WILLIAM
Jonathan Swift 3:1463

HAYWARD, ABRAHAM
William Makepeace Thackeray
5:2556

HAZLITT, WILLIAM
Geoffrey Chaucer 1:43, 45
Sir Philip Sidney 1:139
Christopher Marlowe 1:178
Edmund Spenser 1:216, 256
John Donne 1:380
John Webster 1:444, 448
Ben Jonson 1:478
Richard Crashaw 1:516
Robert Herrick 1:543
John Milton 1:602, 625, 628
William Shakespeare 2:764, 933,
936, 945, 951, 956, 959, 969,
974, 980, 986, 999, 1013, 1019,
1028, 1033, 1039, 1065, 1075,
1098, 1115, 1131, 1145, 1155,
1167, 1174, 1183, 1199, 1202,
1210, 1218
John Dryden 3:1314, 1321
Daniel Defoe 3:1368
Alexander Pope 3:1436
Jonathan Swift 3:1465
Henry Fielding 3:1512, 1516, 1523
Laurence Sterne 3:1551
Thomas Gray 3:1588
Tobias Smollett 3:1615
Oliver Goldsmith 3:1655
Samuel Johnson 3:1716
Robert Burns 3:1804
Richard Brinsley Sheridan 3:1846
John Keats 4:1915
Percy Bysshe Shelley 4:1964, 1978
George Gordon, Lord Byron
4:2021, 2031, 2032, 2033
Sir Walter Scott 4:2148
Samuel Taylor Coleridge 4:2169,
2175, 2187
Charles Lamb 4:2216, 2229
William Wordsworth 4:2320, 2330,
2341
James Fenimore Cooper 4:2362
Washington Irving 4:2445

HAZLITT, WILLIAM CAREW
Robert Herrick 1:541, 547

HEADLEY, HENRY
George Herbert 1:424

HEALY, CHRIS
Oscar Wilde 5:3138

HEARNE, THOMAS
John Bunyan 3:1281
John Dryden 3:1306
Alexander Pope 3:1402

HEATH, RICHARD
John Bunyan 3:1291

HEINE, HEINRICH
William Shakespeare 2:992
William Hazlitt 4:2101
Sir Walter Scott 4:2138

HEMANS, FELICIA DOROTHEA
Sir Walter Scott 4:2130

HEMINGE, JOHN
William Shakespeare 2:701

HENDERSON, ANDREW
Tobias Smollett 3:1612

HENDERSON, ARCHIBALD
Oscar Wilde 5:3147

HENDERSON, THOMAS F.
Robert Burns 3:1820

HENLEY, WILLIAM ERNEST
Sir Philip Sidney 1:129
Robert Herrick 1:546
William Shakespeare 2:716
Henry Fielding 3:1515
Tobias Smollett 3:1619
Robert Burns 3:1816, 1820
George Gordon, Lord Byron 4:2026
William Hazlitt 4:2104
William Makepeace Thackeray
5:2569
Charles Dickens 5:2622
Henry Wadsworth Longfellow
5:2780
Matthew Arnold 5:2862, 2865
Robert Louis Stevenson 5:3075

HENRY, CHETTLE
Ben Jonson 1:467

HENRYSON, ROBERT
Geoffrey Chaucer 1:3

HERBERT, DAVID
Tobias Smollett 3:1622, 1624

HERBERT, EDWARD, LORD
George Herbert 1:421

HERBERT, GEORGE
George Herbert 1:426

HERFORD, C. H.
Mary Shelley 4:2390

HERRICK, ROBERT
Robert Herrick 1:547

HERVEY, JOHN, LORD
Alexander Pope 3:1420

HEWLETT, HENRY G.
William Blake 4:2074

HEYLYN, PETER
Sir Philip Sidney 1:129
Sir Francis Bacon 1:327

HEYWOOD, THOMAS
William Shakespeare 2:1269

HIGGINSON, THOMAS WENTWORTH
Jane Austen 4:1876
Edgar Allan Poe 4:2279
James Fenimore Cooper 4:2367
Henry David Thoreau 4:2508, 2510
Nathaniel Hawthorne 5:2583
Emily Dickinson 5:2838, 2843,
2846
Robert Browning 5:2901
Walt Whitman 5:3021

HILL, AARON
William Shakespeare 2:1140
Henry Fielding 3:1518

HILL, ADAMS SHERMAN
Jonathan Swift 3:1473

HILL, ASTRAEA AND MINERVA
Henry Fielding 3:1518

HILL, GEORGE BIRKBECK
Samuel Johnson 3:1754

HILLARD, GEORGE STILLMAN
Tobias Smollett 3:1623
Nathaniel Hawthorne 5:2579, 2589
Robert Browning 5:2893

HINES, JOHN A.
John Milton 1:588

HIPPISLEY, J. H.
Sir Philip Sidney 1:128

HOADLY, BENJAMIN
Daniel Defoe 3:1374

HOBBES, THOMAS
John Milton 1:604

HOGARTH, GEORGINA
Charles Dickens 5:2614

HOGG, JAMES
Sir Walter Scott 4:2132

HOGG, THOMAS JEFFERSON
Percy Bysshe Shelley 4:1968

HOLLAND, HUGH
William Shakespeare 2:701

HOLMES, NATHANIEL
Sir Francis Bacon 1:329
William Shakespeare 2:903

HOLMES, OLIVER WENDELL
Robert Burns 3:1808
Washington Irving 4:2444
Nathaniel Hawthorne 5:2580, 2581
Henry Wadsworth Longfellow
5:2773

HOLROYD, MARIA JOSEPHA
Edward Gibbon 3:1778

HOLT, JOHN
William Shakespeare 2:1209

HONE, PHILIP
Charles Dickens 5:2614, 2629

HOOD, THOMAS
Samuel Taylor Coleridge 4:2172

HOOLE, JOHN
Samuel Johnson 3:1709

HOPE, ANTHONY
Laurence Sterne 3:1557

HOPKINS, GERARD MANLEY
Geoffrey Chaucer 1:12
John Dryden 3:1320
Robert Browning 5:2905
Walt Whitman 5:3013
Robert Louis Stevenson 5:3078

HORNE, GEORGE
Samuel Johnson 3:1713

HORNE, RICHARD HENRY
Edgar Allan Poe 4:2278
Mary Shelley 4:2391
Robert Browning 5:2902

HORNER, FRANCIS
Sir Francis Bacon 1:332
Richard Brinsley Sheridan 3:1842

HOUGHTON, RICHARD MONCKTON
MILNES, LORD
John Keats 4:1925

HOUSMAN, A. E.
Matthew Arnold 5:2857

HOWELLS, WILLIAM DEAN
John Milton 1:597
William Shakespeare 2:717
Jane Austen 4:1876
Sir Walter Scott 4:2140, 2144
Emily Brontë 4:2252
Washington Irving 4:2451
Henry David Thoreau 4:2512
William Makepeace Thackeray
5:2553
Nathaniel Hawthorne 5:2579
Charles Dickens 5:2622, 2629
George Eliot 5:2658
Henry Wadsworth Longfellow
5:2781
Anthony Trollope 5:2808
Emily Dickinson 5:2840
Robert Browning 5:2905
Walt Whitman 5:3018
Stephen Crane 5:3172

HOWITT, WILLIAM
John Milton 1:579

HUDSON, H. N.
William Shakespeare 2:774, 965

HUDSON, WILLIAM HENRY
Sir Walter Scott 4:2163

HUGHES, JOHN
Geoffrey Chaucer 1:8
William Shakespeare 2:1130

HUGO, VICTOR
Ben Jonson 1:472
William Shakespeare 2:784, 1055,
1102

HUME, DAVID
Francis Bacon 1:327, 331
Ben Jonson 1:470
John Milton 1:582, 601
William Shakespeare 2:708
John Dryden 3:1311
Laurence Sterne 3:1556
David Hume 3:1689
Edward Gibbon 3:1770

HUMPHREY, OZIAS
Samuel Johnson 3:1708

HUNT, JOHN
David Hume 3:1686

HUNT, LEIGH
Geoffrey Chaucer 1:10, 59
Christopher Marlowe 1:168
Edmund Spenser 1:260
Sir Francis Bacon 1:332
John Milton 1:584
William Shakespeare 2:713
Andrew Marvell 3:1257
John Dryden 3:1315

Daniel Defoe 3:1371
Alexander Pope 3:1407
Thomas Gray 3:1596
Tobias Smollett 3:1612
Oliver Goldsmith 3:1666
Richard Brinsley Sheridan 3:1855
John Keats 4:1926, 1931
Percy Bysshe Shelley 4:1967, 1971
George Gordon, Lord Byron
4:2017, 2020, 2030
William Hazlitt 4:2098, 2104
Samuel Taylor Coleridge 4:2173,
2177
Charles Lamb 4:2220
William Wordsworth 4:2317, 2323
Charles Dickens 5:2616
Thomas Carlyle 5:2685
Robert Browning 5:2901

HUNT, THORNTON
Mary Shelley 4:2389

HURD, RICHARD
Edmund Spenser 1:238
Ben Jonson 1:473

HURDIS, JAMES
John Dryden 3:1313

HUTTON, LAURENCE
Charles Dickens 5:2624

HUTTON, RICHARD HOLT
Samuel Johnson 3:1721
Nathaniel Hawthorne 5:2592
Matthew Arnold 5:2868

HUTTON, WILLIAM HOLDEN
George Herbert 1:423
John Milton 1:605

HUXLEY, THOMAS HENRY
David Hume 3:1688
George Eliot 5:2650
Thomas Carlyle 5:2689

HUYSMANS, JORIS KARL
Edgar Allan Poe 4:2279

IDDESLEIGH, EARL OF
Jane Austen 4:1906

INGERSOLL, ROBERT G.
Walt Whitman 5:3015

INGLEBY, C. M.
John Milton 1:580
William Shakespeare 2:861

IRELAND, ANNIE E.
Robert Browning 5:2898

IRVING, DAVID
Robert Burns 3:1802

IRVING, SIR HENRY
William Shakespeare 2:1164
Richard Brinsley Sheridan 3:1848

IRVING, WASHINGTON
Sir Philip Sidney 1:130
William Shakespeare 2:675
Oliver Goldsmith 3:1650
Sir Walter Scott 4:2131
Washington Irving 4:2453
Nathaniel Hawthorne 5:2588

JACK, ADOLPHUS ALFRED
Jane Austen 4:1880

JACOBS, JOSEPH
George Eliot 5:2663

JAMES, HENRY, SR.
Thomas Carlyle 5:2686
Ralph Waldo Emerson 5:2749

JAMES, HENRY
Oliver Goldsmith 3:1675
Sir Walter Scott 4:2135
Edgar Allan Poe 4:2286
Henry David Thoreau 4:2508
George Eliot 5:2651, 2658, 2661
Nathaniel Hawthorne 5:2599
Ralph Waldo Emerson 5:2734
Anthony Trollope 5:2815
Matthew Arnold 5:2879
Robert Browning 5:2906, 2917
Walt Whitman 5:3011
Walter Pater 5:3050
Robert Louis Stevenson 5:3083

JAMESON, ANNA BROWNELL
Sir Philip Sidney 1:132
John Donne 1:376
William Blake 4:2057

JAMESON, J. FRANKLIN
Washington Irving 4:2454

JAPP, ALEXANDER HAY
Henry David Thoreau 4:2507

JEAFFRESON, JOHN CORDY
Percy Bysshe Shelley 4:1976

JEBB, R. C.
Alfred, Lord Tennyson 5:2970

JEFFERSON, THOMAS
Laurence Sterne 3:1558

JEFFREY, FRANCIS, LORD
Jonathan Swift 3:1477
Richard Brinsley Sheridan 3:1846
John Keats 4:1935
Sir Walter Scott 4:2138, 2141
William Wordsworth 4:2328, 2334
Washington Irving 4:2455
Thomas Babington Macaulay
4:2479
Charles Dickens 5:2627

JENYNS, SOAME
Samuel Johnson 3:1711

JESSOPP, AUGUSTUS
John Donne 1:376, 377

JOHNSON, CHARLES F.
Nathaniel Hawthorne 5:2585

JOHNSON, LIONEL
George Gordon, Lord Byron 4:2028
William Blake 4:2082
William Makepeace Thackeray
5:2550
Matthew Arnold 5:2863

JOHNSON, SAMUEL
Geoffrey Chaucer 1:9
Edmund Spenser 1:227
Ben Jonson 1:470
John Milton 1:578, 605, 616

William Shakespeare 2:725, 843,
939, 958, 973, 985, 999, 1019,
1023, 1032, 1039, 1061, 1064,
1084, 1113, 1119, 1139, 1153,
1174, 1209
John Dryden 3:1307, 1327, 1337
Alexander Pope 3:1427
Jonathan Swift 3:1483
Thomas Gray 3:1597
Samuel Johnson 3:1708

JOHNSON, W. H.
Matthew Arnold 5:2858

JOHNSTON, RICHARD MALCOLM
William Makepeace Thackeray
5:2557

JOLLY, WILLIAM
Robert Burns 3:1811

JONSON, BEN
Sir Philip Sidney 1:127
Christopher Marlowe 1:166
Edmund Spenser 1:214, 218, 219
Sir Francis Bacon 1:326
John Donne 1:377
William Shakespeare 2:671, 702,
704, 1061, 1201

JOWETT, BENJAMIN
John Bunyan 3:1285
Robert Browning 5:2893

JOYCE, JAMES
Oscar Wilde 5:3146

JOYCE, ROBERT DWER
Tobias Smollett 3:1621

JUSSERAND, J. J.
Sir Philip Sidney 1:131
William Shakespeare 2:828, 927
William Blake 4:2059

K., E.
Edmund Spenser 1:232, 234

KAMES, HENRY HOME, LORD
William Shakespeare 2:709

KAVANAGH, JULIA
Jane Austen 4:1878

KEATS, JOHN
Edmund Spenser 1:232
John Milton 1:583, 593
William Shakespeare 2:991
Tobias Smollett 3:1615
Robert Burns 3:1799, 1804
John Keats 4:1923
William Hazlitt 4:2100
Charles Lamb 4:2216
William Wordsworth 4:2319

KEBBEL, T. E.
Jane Austen 4:1875
James Fenimore Cooper 4:2384

KEIGHTLEY, THOMAS
John Milton 1:579, 601
Henry Fielding 3:1513

KEMBLE, FRANCES ANN
Jane Austen 4:1873
Sir Walter Scott 4:2146
Washington Irving 4:2443

Charles Dickens 5:2614
Alfred, Lord Tennyson 5:2961

KENNEDY, WALKER
Walt Whitman 5:3033

KENNETT, WHITE
Jonathan Swift 3:1457

KENRICK, WILLIAM
Oliver Goldsmith 3:1650

KENT, JAMES
Washington Irving 4:2446

KER, W. P.
Geoffrey Chaucer 1:110
John Dryden 3:1335
Samuel Taylor Coleridge 4:2180
Thomas Babington Macaulay
4:2475

KETTELL, SAMUEL
Henry Wadsworth Longfellow
5:2771

KING, HENRY
John Donne 1:375

KING, RICHARD ASHE
Jonathan Swift 3:1473

KINGSLEY, CHARLES
John Webster 1:451
John Milton 1:585
Charlotte Brontë 4:2421
Alfred, Lord Tennyson 5:2982

KIRK, JOHN FOSTER
William Makepeace Thackeray
5:2559

KIRKUP, SEYMOUR
William Blake 4:2056

KNIGHT, CHARLES
John Webster 1:444
William Shakespeare 2:1192
Samuel Taylor Coleridge 4:2186
William Makepeace Thackeray
5:2545

KNIGHT, WILLIAM
David Hume 3:1688

KNOX, VICESIMUS
Henry Fielding 3:1510
Laurence Sterne 3:1558

KOOPMAN, HARRY LYMAN
John Milton 1:587

LA FARGE, JOHN
John Ruskin 5:3113

LAMARTINE, ALPHONSE DE
John Milton 1:579, 595

LAMB, CHARLES
Sir Philip Sidney 1:126, 130, 131
Christopher Marlowe 1:167
Edmund Spenser 1:225
John Webster 1:447, 448
Ben Jonson 1:474, 475
William Shakespeare 2:1046
John Bunyan 3:1287
Daniel Defoe 3:1367, 1369
Alexander Pope 3:1403

Richard Brinsley Sheridan 3:1850
Percy Bysshe Shelley 4:1970
William Blake 4:2055
Samuel Taylor Coleridge 4:2170
Charles Lamb 4:2216
William Wordsworth 4:2319

LAMB, GEORGE
William Makepeace Thackeray
5:2549

LANCASTER, H. H.
John Ruskin 5:3113

LANDOR, WALTER SAVAGE
Geoffrey Chaucer 1:10
John Milton 1:599
John Dryden 3:1314
Daniel Defoe 3:1366
Thomas Gray 3:1594
Oliver Goldsmith 3:1650
David Hume 3:1691
Edward Gibbon 3:1768
Robert Burns 3:1805
John Keats 4:1917
Percy Bysshe Shelley 4:1967
George Gordon, Lord Byron 4:2024
Washington Irving 4:2448
Thomas Babington Macaulay
4:2479
Charles Dickens 5:2617
Robert Browning 5:2894
Alfred, Lord Tennyson 5:2962

LANG, ANDREW
Robert Herrick 1:545
John Bunyan 3:1290
Alexander Pope 3:1413
Henry Fielding 3:1515
Robert Burns 3:1812
Jane Austen 4:1894
John Keats 4:1913
Charlotte Brontë 4:2416
Nathaniel Hawthorne 5:2584
Matthew Arnold 5:2861, 2862
Robert Browning 5:2898, 2904
Alfred, Lord Tennyson 5:2969
Robert Louis Stevenson 5:3077,
3092

LANGBAINE, GERARD
John Webster 1:443
Ben Jonson 1:469
John Milton 1:576
John Dryden 3:1323

LANGFORD, JOHN ALFRED
John Donne 1:390

LANGTON, BENNET
Thomas Gray 3:1596

LANIER, C. D.
Walt Whitman 5:3023

LANIER, SIDNEY
Laurence Sterne 3:1556
Tobias Smollett 3:1617
John Keats 4:1927
Sir Walter Scott 4:2143
George Eliot 5:2650
Walt Whitman 5:3014, 3022

LANSDOWNE, GEORGE GRANVILLE,
LORD
Alexander Pope 3:1414, 1418

LARCOM, LUCY
Emily Dickinson 5:2843

LATHROP, GEORGE PARSONS
Henry Fielding 3:1513
Washington Irving 4:2461
Nathaniel Hawthorne 5:2583, 2590
George Eliot 5:2652

LATHROP, ROSE HAWTHORNE
Henry David Thoreau 4:2504

LATROBE, JOHN H. B.
Edgar Allan Poe 4:2275

LAWES, HENRY
John Milton 1:588

LAWRENCE, EUGENE
David Hume 3:1694

LEADMAN, WILFRID M.
Oscar Wilde 5:3161

LECKY, W. E. H.
Sir Francis Bacon 1:342
John Milton 1:603
Jonathan Swift 3:1467

LEE, SIDNEY
Richard Crashaw 1:518
William Shakespeare 2:1218

LEE, VERNON
Walter Pater 5:3052

LEE-HAMILTON, EUGENE
John Milton 1:591

LE GALLIENNE, RICHARD
Robert Herrick 1:546
Matthew Arnold 5:2861
Alfred, Lord Tennyson 5:2963
Walter Pater 5:3058, 3070
Oscar Wilde 5:3149

LELAND, CHARLES GODFREY
George Eliot 5:2650

LELAND, JOHN
David Hume 3:1685

LENTON, FRANCIS
Ben Jonson 1:467

LESLIE, CHARLES ROBERT
Sir Walter Scott 4:2130

LEWES, GEORGE HENRY
Christopher Marlowe 1:169
Jane Austen 4:1873, 1888
Emily Brontë 4:2250
Charlotte Brontë 4:2422, 2424
Charles Dickens 5:2636

LEWIN, WALTER
Henry Fielding 3:1515
George Eliot 5:2654
Walt Whitman 5:3023
John Ruskin 5:3108

LIGHTFOOT, J. B.
John Donne 1:376, 399

LILLY, WILLIAM SAMUEL
William Makepeace Thackeray
5:2553
Charles Dickens 5:2623

LINDNER, FELIX
Geoffrey Chaucer 1:85

LINGARD, JOHN
Sir Francis Bacon 1:328

LINTON, W. J.
Robert Herrick 1:547

LITTLEDALE, RICHARD F.
Anthony Trollope 5:2807

LLOYD, ROBERT
Thomas Gray 3:1586

LOCKER-LAMPSON, FREDERICK
William Makepeace Thackeray
5:2554
Anthony Trollope 5:2809

LOCKHART, JOHN GIBSON
Robert Burns 3:1806
John Keats 4:1924
Sir Walter Scott 4:2132
Samuel Taylor Coleridge 4:2168,
2185
William Wordsworth 4:2314
James Fenimore Cooper 4:2362
Charlotte Brontë 4:2419
Thomas Babington Macaulay
4:2480
Thomas Carlyle 5:2699

LODGE, HENRY CABOT
James Fenimore Cooper 4:2368
Nathaniel Hawthorne 5:2584

LODGE, THOMAS
Edmund Spenser 1:213

LONDON, JACK
Herman Melville 5:2940

LONGFELLOW, HENRY WADSWORTH
John Milton 1:586
William Shakespeare 2:714
Thomas Gray 3:1596
Robert Burns 3:1811
Jane Austen 4:1873
John Keats 4:1912
Edgar Allan Poe 4:2281
William Wordsworth 4:2320
Washington Irving 4:2447
Nathaniel Hawthorne 5:2578, 2586
Charles Dickens 5:2627
Herman Melville 5:2940
Alfred, Lord Tennyson 5:2968,
2972

LORD, WALTER FREWEN
William Makepeace Thackeray
5:2554
Anthony Trollope 5:2810

LOUNSBURY, THOMAS R.
John Milton 1:600
Henry Fielding 3:1509
Thomas Gray 3:1592
James Fenimore Cooper 4:2377
Robert Browning 5:2904

LOWELL, JAMES RUSSELL
Geoffrey Chaucer 1:51, 68
Sir Philip Sidney 1:128
Christopher Marlowe 1:199
Edmund Spenser 1:263
John Webster 1:444
John Milton 1:587, 599
William Shakespeare 2:788, 845,
1104, 1211
Andrew Marvell 3:1257
John Bunyan 3:1283
John Dryden 3:1331, 1353
Alexander Pope 3:1411
Jonathan Swift 3:1468
Henry Fielding 3:1509, 1514
Laurence Sterne 3:1553
Thomas Gray 3:1589, 1592
Tobias Smollett 3:1617
Robert Burns 3:1808
John Keats 4:1912, 1940
Samuel Taylor Coleridge 4:2203
Edgar Allan Poe 4:2276, 2286
James Fenimore Cooper 4:2364
Charlotte Brontë 4:2420
Washington Irving 4:2447
Henry David Thoreau 4:2518
William Makepeace Thackeray
5:2546
Nathaniel Hawthorne 5:2580,
2582, 2588, 2590
Charles Dickens 5:2630
Thomas Carlyle 5:2688, 2706
Ralph Waldo Emerson 5:2731,
2739
Henry Wadsworth Longfellow
5:2772, 2775, 2784
Herman Melville 5:2940
Alfred, Lord Tennyson 5:2975

LUCAS, E. V.
Oscar Wilde 5:3155

LYDGATE, JOHN
Geoffrey Chaucer 1:2

M., I.
William Shakespeare 2:671

MABIE, HAMILTON WRIGHT
Nathaniel Hawthorne 5:2585
Walter Pater 5:3052

MACAULAY, G. C.
Walt Whitman 5:3013

MACAULAY, THOMAS BABINGTON
Sir Francis Bacon 1:328, 349
John Milton 1:630
William Shakespeare 2:713
John Bunyan 3:1288, 1291
John Dryden 3:1329, 1332, 1347
Daniel Defoe 3:1375
Alexander Pope 3:1404
Jonathan Swift 3:1465
Oliver Goldsmith 3:1657
David Hume 3:1684
Samuel Johnson 3:1729, 1733
Edward Gibbon 3:1774
Richard Brinsley Sheridan 3:1847,
1851
Jane Austen 4:1873, 1880

Percy Bysshe Shelley 4:1970
George Gordon, Lord Byron
4:2031, 2036
Sir Walter Scott 4:2132
William Wordsworth 4:2320, 2331
Thomas Babington Macaulay
4:2477
Charles Dickens 5:2627
Thomas Carlyle 5:2687
Ralph Waldo Emerson 5:2730
Alfred, Lord Tennyson 5:2975

MACCALLUM, M. W.
William Shakespeare 2:1178

M'CARTHY, D. F.
Richard Crashaw 1:516

MCCARTHY, JUSTIN
Charles Dickens 5:2618
George Eliot 5:2649, 2653
Anthony Trollope 5:2807, 2810
Robert Browning 5:2897

MCCLURG, A. C.
Stephen Crane 5:3173

MCCOSH, JAMES
David Hume 3:1688

MACCULLOCH, J. A.
Walt Whitman 5:3021

MACDONALD, GEORGE
Sir Philip Sidney 1:128
Sir Francis Bacon 1:332
John Donne 1:391
George Herbert 1:425
Richard Crashaw 1:521
Robert Herrick 1:544
John Milton 1:586, 600
William Shakespeare 2:1108

MACHAR, AGNES MAULE
Robert Burns 3:1811

MACHEN, ARTHUR
Robert Louis Stevenson 5:3081

MACKAY, ANGUS M.
Emily Brontë 4:2248, 2265
Charlotte Brontë 4:2418

MACKAY, CHARLES
Samuel Johnson 3:1727
Robert Burns 3:1812

MACKENZIE, HENRY
William Shakespeare 2:1025, 1093
Robert Burns 3:1801

MACKENZIE, R. SHELTON
Laurence Sterne 3:1552

MACKINTOSH, SIR JAMES
Henry Fielding 3:1511
Laurence Sterne 3:1551
Samuel Johnson 3:1730
Richard Brinsley Sheridan 3:1845
Sir Walter Scott 4:2141

MACLEOD, DONALD
Sir Walter Scott 4:2134

MACMECHAN, ARCHIBALD
Herman Melville 5:2957

MACREADY, WILLIAM CHARLES
Jane Austen 4:1878
Sir Walter Scott 4:2145
Robert Browning 5:2893, 2902

MAETERLINCK, MAURICE
Ralph Waldo Emerson 5:2737

MAGINN, WILLIAM
William Shakespeare 2:959
John Keats 4:1911
George Gordon, Lord Byron 4:2022
Sir Walter Scott 4:2133
Charles Lamb 4:2217

MALKIN, BENJAMIN HEATH
William Blake 4:2061

MALLARMÉ, STÉPHANE
Edgar Allan Poe 4:2277

MALLET, DAVID
Alexander Pope 3:1402

MALLOCK, W. H.
Sir Walter Scott 4:2137
William Makepeace Thackeray
5:2551
Charles Dickens 5:2622

MALONE, EDMOND
Sir Francis Bacon 1:335
Alexander Pope 3:1403
Laurence Sterne 3:1549
David Hume 3:1680, 1683
Edward Gibbon 3:1765

MANGIN, EDWARD
Tobias Smollett 3:1614
Oliver Goldsmith 3:1654

MANNINGHAM, JOHN
William Shakespeare 2:969

MARSH, GEORGE P.
Sir Philip Sidney 1:135
Sir Francis Bacon 1:336

MARSHALL, FLORENCE ASHTON
Mary Shelley 4:2389, 2390

MARTIN, HELENA FAUCIT
Robert Browning 5:2903

MARTINEAU, HARRIET
William Wordsworth 4:2324
Charlotte Brontë 4:2414, 2422
Thomas Babington Macaulay
4:2471, 2473
William Makepeace Thackeray
5:2549
Charles Dickens 5:2618
Thomas Carlyle 5:2686, 2689
Robert Browning 5:2897

MARTINEAU, JAMES
Thomas Carlyle 5:2688
Ralph Waldo Emerson 5:2726

MARVELL, ANDREW
John Milton 1:592, 604
John Dryden 3:1307

MARX, KARL
Daniel Defoe 3:1377

MASON, GEORGE
Samuel Johnson 3:1715

MASON, WILLIAM
  David Hume 3:1681

MASSON, DAVID
  Sir Philip Sidney 1:130
  Richard Crashaw 1:516
  Robert Herrick 1:544
  John Milton 1:589, 596, 646
  John Bunyan 3:1288
  Daniel Defoe 3:1371
  Jonathan Swift 3:1467, 1485
  Laurence Sterne 3:1552
  Tobias Smollett 3:1617
  Jane Austen 4:1874
  John Keats 4:1913
  William Makepeace Thackeray
    5:2547, 2566
  Charles Dickens 5:2617

MASTERMAN, J. HOWARD B.
  George Herbert 1:426
  Richard Crashaw 1:518
  Robert Herrick 1:547
  John Milton 1:590, 591, 597, 601

MATHER, FRANK JEWETT
  Geoffrey Chaucer 1:114

MATHEWS, WILLIAM
  Sir Francis Bacon 1:332

MATHIAS, THOMAS JAMES
  John Dryden 3:1330
  Laurence Sterne 3:1550
  Tobias Smollett 3:1613

MATTHEWS, BRANDER
  Daniel Defoe 3:1373
  Richard Brinsley Sheridan 3:1850,
    1851
  Sir Walter Scott 4:2144
  Charles Lamb 4:2236
  Edgar Allan Poe 4:2284
  James Fenimore Cooper 4:2367
  Washington Irving 4:2452
  Henry David Thoreau 4:2510

MAURICE, FREDERICK DENISON
  Geoffrey Chaucer 1:11
  Sir Francis Bacon 1:332, 338
  John Milton 1:585
  Alexander Pope 3:1421
  Edward Gibbon 3:1776
  Samuel Taylor Coleridge 4:2178
  Thomas Carlyle 5:2688

MAYNADIER, G. H.
  Daniel Defoe 3:1397
  Tobias Smollett 3:1621

MAZZINI, GIUSEPPE
  George Gordon, Lord Byron 4:2040

MEDWIN, THOMAS
  George Gordon, Lord Byron 4:2015

MELVILLE, HERMAN
  James Fenimore Cooper 4:2365
  Nathaniel Hawthorne 5:2588

MELVILLE, LEWIS
  William Makepeace Thackeray
    5:2554

MEREDITH, GEORGE
  Ben Jonson 1:472
  John Milton 1:585
  William Shakespeare 2:927
  John Keats 4:1918
  Percy Bysshe Shelley 4:1971
  Samuel Taylor Coleridge 4:2177
  William Wordsworth 4:2323

MERES, FRANCIS
  Sir Philip Sidney 1:129
  Christopher Marlowe 1:166
  Edmund Spenser 1:226
  William Shakespeare 2:701

MERIVALE, HERMAN
  Thomas Carlyle 5:2698
  Robert Browning 5:2903

MERIVALE, J. H.
  William Hazlitt 4:2101

MERWIN, HENRY CHILDS
  Laurence Sterne 3:1554
  Walt Whitman 5:3019

MEW, CHARLOTTE M.
  Emily Brontë 4:2249

MEYNELL, ALICE
  Andrew Marvell 3:1259
  Emily Brontë 4:2252

MILL, JOHN STUART
  David Hume 3:1686
  Edward Gibbon 3:1774
  William Wordsworth 4:2324
  Thomas Babington Macaulay
    4:2479
  Thomas Carlyle 5:2689, 2698

MILLAR, J. H.
  David Hume 3:1682
  Washington Irving 4:2451

MILLER, HUGH
  John Keats 4:1927

MILLER, JOAQUIN
  Robert Burns 3:1809
  George Gordon, Lord Byron 4:2019

MILLS, ABRAHAM
  Sir Francis Bacon 1:332
  John Webster 1:448

MILMAN, H. H.
  Edward Gibbon 3:1780
  Thomas Babington Macaulay
    4:2477

MILTON, JOHN
  Edmund Spenser 1:214, 226, 229
  John Milton 1:576
  William Shakespeare 2:702, 944
  Andrew Marvell 3:1253

MINTO, GILBERT ELLIOT, FIRST
    EARL OF
  Richard Brinsley Sheridan 3:1851

MINTO, WILLIAM
  Geoffrey Chaucer 1:76
  Christopher Marlowe 1:170
  Sir Francis Bacon 1:333, 338
  John Donne 1:376, 377
  John Webster 1:445

  Ben Jonson 1:466, 472, 476
  John Milton 1:602
  Daniel Defoe 3:1372

MITCHELL, DONALD G.
  Sir Philip Sidney 1:127
  Sir Francis Bacon 1:331
  George Herbert 1:423
  John Webster 1:446
  Ben Jonson 1:472
  Robert Herrick 1:542, 545
  John Milton 1:587, 597
  Washington Irving 4:2458
  Henry David Thoreau 4:2511

MITCHELL, MARIA
  Nathaniel Hawthorne 5:2578
  Ralph Waldo Emerson 5:2725
  Matthew Arnold 5:2856

MITFORD, MARY RUSSELL
  Robert Herrick 1:544
  Andrew Marvell 3:1254
  Robert Burns 3:1803
  Jane Austen 4:1871, 1878
  Sir Walter Scott 4:2145
  Washington Irving 4:2447
  Charles Dickens 5:2616

MOFFET, THOMAS
  Sir Philip Sidney 1:136

MOIR, DAVID MACBETH
  Robert Burns 3:1806
  Percy Bysshe Shelley 4:1972

MONBODDO, JAMES BURNETT, LORD
  Henry Fielding 3:1519

MONROE, HARRIET
  Percy Bysshe Shelley 4:1974
  Walt Whitman 5:3017

MONTAGU, BASIL
  Sir Francis Bacon 1:328, 332, 336,
    337

MONTAGU, ELIZABETH
  William Shakespeare 2:732

MONTAGU, LADY MARY WORTLEY
  Alexander Pope 3:1405, 1416, 1422
  Jonathan Swift 3:1462, 1473
  Henry Fielding 3:1508
  Tobias Smollett 3:1622
  Samuel Johnson 3:1724

MONTAGUE, F. C.
  Jonathan Swift 3:1469

MONTGOMERY, JAMES
  John Milton 1:583, 602

MOODY, WILLIAM VAUGHN
  John Milton 1:581, 599, 601

MOORE, GEORGE
  Walter Pater 5:3054
  Robert Louis Stevenson 5:3083

MOORE, HELEN
  Mary Shelley 4:2402

MOORE, JOHN
  Robert Burns 3:1817

MOORE, THOMAS
Richard Brinsley Sheridan 3:1843, 1852
Thomas Babington Macaulay 4:2470

MORE, HANNAH
Henry Fielding 3:1510
Samuel Johnson 3:1708
Edward Gibbon 3:1767
Thomas Babington Macaulay 4:2469

MORE, PAUL ELMER
William Shakespeare 2:1240
William Hazlitt 4:2124
Charles Lamb 4:2244
Henry David Thoreau 4:2535

MORLEY, HENRY
Geoffrey Chaucer 1:102
Sir Philip Sidney 1:149
Sir Francis Bacon 1:336
Ben Jonson 1:474
Robert Herrick 1:547
John Milton 1:586
Jane Austen 4:1875

MORLEY, JOHN
Sir Francis Bacon 1:336
Thomas Babington Macaulay 4:2495
Robert Browning 5:2904
Walter Pater 5:3059

MORRILL, JUSTIN S.
Robert Herrick 1:541

MORRIS, CORBYN
Ben Jonson 1:470
William Shakespeare 2:1024

MORRIS, MOWBRAY
Charles Dickens 5:2630

MORRIS, WILLIAM
Geoffrey Chaucer 1:12

MORSE, JAMES HERBERT
James Fenimore Cooper 4:2366
Nathaniel Hawthorne 5:2584

MORTON, RICHARD
Andrew Marvell 3:1254

MOSELEY, HUMPHREY
John Milton 1:581

MOTLEY, JOHN LOTHROP
Thomas Babington Macaulay 4:2471
Nathaniel Hawthorne 5:2589

MOULTON, RICHARD G.
William Shakespeare 2:1078

MOXON, EDWARD
Charles Lamb 4:2219

MUIRHEAD, JAMES FULLARTON
Emily Dickinson 5:2850

MÜLLER, MAX
Alfred, Lord Tennyson 5:2972

MUNGER, T. T.
Sir Walter Scott 4:2132

MURPHY, ARTHUR
Henry Fielding 3:1521

MURRAY, DAVID CHRISTIE
Charles Dickens 5:2623

MYERS, F. W. H.
William Wordsworth 4:2332
George Eliot 5:2653

NADEL, E. S.
John Milton 1:596

NAPIER, MACVEY
Sir Francis Bacon 1:341

NASHE, THOMAS
Geoffrey Chaucer 1:6, 7
Sir Philip Sidney 1:125, 138
Edmund Spenser 1:213, 217

"NATHANIEL, SIR"
Herman Melville 5:2950

NAUNTON, SIR ROBERT
Sir Philip Sidney 1:126

NEELE, HENRY
George Herbert 1:424
Ben Jonson 1:471
John Milton 1:594

NETTLESHIP, JOHN T.
Robert Browning 5:2898

NEWCASTLE, MARGARET CAVENDISH, DUCHESS OF
William Shakespeare 2:719

NEWMAN, JOHN HENRY
John Dryden 3:1329
Thomas Carlyle 5:2698

NEWTON, THOMAS
John Milton 1:577

NICHOL, JOHN
George Herbert 1:441
Jonathan Swift 3:1479
George Gordon, Lord Byron 4:2033
Washington Irving 4:2448
Nathaniel Hawthorne 5:2589
Thomas Carlyle 5:2694
Henry Wadsworth Longfellow 5:2783

NICHOLS, THOMAS LOW
Herman Melville 5:2940

NICOL, JOHN
Sir Francis Bacon 1:330, 334, 343

NICOLL, HENRY J.
Sir Francis Bacon 1:329
William Makepeace Thackeray 5:2558

NICOLSON, WILLIAM
Sir Francis Bacon 1:338

NOBLE, JAMES ASHCROFT
John Milton 1:600
Jane Austen 4:1876
John Keats 4:1921
Emily Brontë 4:2248

NORDAU, MAX
Alfred, Lord Tennyson 5:2970
Walt Whitman 5:3019
John Ruskin 5:3110

NORMAN, HENRY
Henry Wadsworth Longfellow 5:2788

NORTHCOTE, JAMES
Oliver Goldsmith 3:1649

NORTON, CAROLINE
Richard Brinsley Sheridan 3:1843

NORTON, CHARLES ELIOT
William Blake 4:2058
Charles Dickens 5:2617
Ralph Waldo Emerson 5:2738
Henry Wadsworth Longfellow 5:2784

NORTON, JOHN
Andrew Marvell 3:1253

O'BRIEN, FITZ-JAMES
Herman Melville 5:2936

OCCLEVE, THOMAS
Geoffrey Chaucer 1:3

O'CONNOR, JOSEPH
Ralph Waldo Emerson 5:2734

O'CONNOR, WILLIAM DOUGLAS
Walt Whitman 5:3010

OGLE, GEORGE
Geoffrey Chaucer 1:9

OLDENBURG, HENRY
Sir Francis Bacon 1:339

OLDHAM, JOHN
John Milton 1:592

OLDMIXON, JOHN
Daniel Defoe 3:1366
Alexander Pope 3:1416

OLIPHANT, JAMES
Jane Austen 4:1905
Charlotte Brontë 4:2434

OLIPHANT, MARGARET
Richard Brinsley Sheridan 3:1860
Jane Austen 4:1879, 1880
George Gordon, Lord Byron 4:2029
William Blake 4:2059
William Hazlitt 4:2102
Charles Lamb 4:2226
Emily Brontë 4:2248
Mary Shelley 4:2391
Charlotte Brontë 4:2423
William Makepeace Thackeray 5:2551, 2561
Charles Dickens 5:2625
Anthony Trollope 5:2808
Robert Browning 5:2904
John Ruskin 5:3107

OLLIER, C. AND J.
John Keats 4:1914

OLNEY, HENRY
Sir Philip Sidney 1:135

ONDERDONK, J. L.
Stephen Crane 5:3174

ORMSBY, JOHN
Andrew Marvell 3:1263

ORR, ALEXANDRA
  Robert Browning 5:2905

ORRERY, JOHN BOYLE, EARL OF
  Jonathan Swift 3:1459

OSBORNE, FRANCIS
  Sir Francis Bacon 1:326

OSBOURNE, LLOYD
  Robert Louis Stevenson 5:3077

OWEN, ROBERT DALE
  Mary Shelley 4:2388

PALGRAVE, FRANCIS TURNER
  Sir Philip Sidney 1:132
  John Donne 1:379
  Richard Crashaw 1:518
  Robert Herrick 1:554
  John Milton 1:588
  Andrew Marvell 3:1256
  Sir Walter Scott 4:2139

PALMER, SAMUEL
  William Blake 4:2064

PANCOAST, HENRY S.
  James Fenimore Cooper 4:2369

PARKER, SAMUEL
  Andrew Marvell 3:1254

PARKER, THEODORE
  Ralph Waldo Emerson 5:2723,
  2730

PARKMAN, FRANCIS
  James Fenimore Cooper 4:2373

PARNELL, THOMAS
  Alexander Pope 3:1404
  Jonathan Swift 3:1462

PATER, WALTER
  William Shakespeare 2:953, 986,
  994
  Samuel Taylor Coleridge 4:2191
  Charles Lamb 4:2233
  William Wordsworth 4:2344
  Oscar Wilde 5:3148

PATMORE, COVENTRY
  John Keats 4:1923
  William Blake 4:2077
  Ralph Waldo Emerson 5:2734

PATMORE, PETER GEORGE
  John Keats 4:1930
  William Hazlitt 4:2099
  Charles Lamb 4:2221

PATON, LUCY ALLEN
  William Blake 4:2084

PATTEE, FRED LEWIS
  Henry David Thoreau 4:2512

PATTISON, MARK
  John Milton 1:580, 591, 596, 598,
  602, 603
  Tobias Smollett 3:1620

PAUL, C. KEGAN
  George Eliot 5:2650

PAUL, HERBERT
  Jonathan Swift 3:1499
  Laurence Sterne 3:1581

  Edward Gibbon 3:1778
  Charles Dickens 5:2624
  George Eliot 5:2660

PAYNE, WILLIAM MORTON
  Walt Whitman 5:3018
  Stephen Crane 5:3172

PEABODY, ANDREW PRESTON
  Henry David Thoreau 4:2512
  William Makepeace Thackeray
  5:2559
  Nathaniel Hawthorne 5:2591

PEABODY, W. B. O.
  Samuel Johnson 3:1718

PEACOCK, THOMAS LOVE
  Percy Bysshe Shelley 4:1970
  Samuel Taylor Coleridge 4:2184
  William Wordsworth 4:2320

PECK, G. W.
  Henry Wadsworth Longfellow
  5:2782

PECK, HARRY THURSTON
  Stephen Crane 5:3170

PEDRICK, J. GALE
  Sir Walter Scott 4:2141

PEELE, GEORGE
  Sir Philip Sidney 1:127
  Christopher Marlowe 1:166

PENNIMAN, JOSIAH H.
  Ben Jonson 1:474

PEPYS, SAMUEL
  Geoffrey Chaucer 1:7
  William Shakespeare 2:944, 969,
  1022, 1064, 1118, 1152, 1207

PERCY, THOMAS
  Oliver Goldsmith 3:1648

PERKINS, F. B.
  Charles Dickens 5:2618

PERRY, JENNETTE BARBOUR
  Walt Whitman 5:3020

PERRY, THOMAS SERGEANT
  John Milton 1:602

PHILLIP, W.
  James Fenimore Cooper 4:2368

PHILLIPS, AMBROSE
  Geoffrey Chaucer 1:8

PHILLIPS, EDWARD
  Christopher Marlowe 1:167
  Edmund Spenser 1:215
  Ben Jonson 1:468
  Robert Herrick 1:542
  John Milton 1:576
  William Shakespeare 2:705
  John Dryden 3:1308

PIERCE, FRANKLIN
  Nathaniel Hawthorne 5:2578

PINERO, ARTHUR WING
  Robert Louis Stevenson 5:3080

PINKERTON, JOHN
  John Dryden 3:1329

PIOZZI, HESTER LYNCH
  Daniel Defoe 3:1375
  Oliver Goldsmith 3:1648
  Samuel Johnson 3:1711
  Mary Shelley 4:2390

PLOWMAN, THOMAS F.
  Oscar Wilde 5:3137

POE, EDGAR ALLAN
  John Milton 1:589, 602
  William Shakespeare 2:1085
  Andrew Marvell 3:1256
  Daniel Defoe 3:1369
  Edward Gibbon 3:1775
  Percy Bysshe Shelley 4:1971
  Samuel Taylor Coleridge 4:2186
  Edgar Allan Poe 4:2272
  James Fenimore Cooper 4:2361,
  2364
  Washington Irving 4:2446, 2447
  Thomas Babington Macaulay
  4:2472
  Nathaniel Hawthorne 5:2580, 2586
  Charles Dickens 5:2625, 2626
  Thomas Carlyle 5:2687
  Ralph Waldo Emerson 5:2729
  Henry Wadsworth Longfellow
  5:2774, 2775
  Alfred, Lord Tennyson 5:2967

POLLARD, ALFRED W.
  Robert Herrick 1:559

POLLOCK, FREDERICK
  John Milton 1:587

POLLOCK, W. F.
  Jane Austen 4:1891

POLLOCK, WALTER HERRIES
  Anthony Trollope 5:2805

POLWHELE, JOHN
  George Herbert 1:427

POPE, ALEXANDER
  Geoffrey Chaucer 1:8
  Sir Philip Sidney 1:127
  Edmund Spenser 1:227, 231
  Sir Francis Bacon 1:327, 331
  Richard Crashaw 1:516
  John Milton 1:582, 592
  William Shakespeare 2:722, 836
  John Dryden 3:1307, 1310, 1311,
  1321, 1330
  Daniel Defoe 3:1366
  Alexander Pope 3:1401, 1402,
  1418, 1419, 1425
  Jonathan Swift 3:1459, 1462, 1473,
  1474

POPPLE, WILLIAM
  William Shakespeare 2:1089

PORSON, RICHARD
  Edward Gibbon 3:1772

PORTER, CHARLOTTE
  Robert Browning 5:2903

PORTER, NOAH
  Sir Francis Bacon 1:336
  Nathaniel Hawthorne 5:2582
  George Eliot 5:2657

PORTER, WILLIAM T.
Herman Melville 5:2936

POSNETT, HUTCHESON MACAULAY
John Milton 1:587

POWELL, THOMAS
Edgar Allan Poe 4:2274
James Fenimore Cooper 4:2369
Ralph Waldo Emerson 5:2730
Henry Wadsworth Longfellow
5:2776
Alfred, Lord Tennyson 5:2967

PRESCOTT, WILLIAM HICKLING
John Milton 1:579, 595
Robert Burns 3:1805
George Gordon, Lord Byron 4:2024
Sir Walter Scott 4:2143
Washington Irving 4:2456

PRESTON, HARRIET WATERS
Robert Browning 5:2902

PRESTON, MARGARET J.
John Keats 4:1927

PRESTON, MARY
William Shakespeare 2:940

PRICE, WARWICK JAMES
Emily Dickinson 5:2844

PRIESTLEY, JOSEPH
David Hume 3:1683

PRIOR, MATTHEW
Edmund Spenser 1:221, 230

PROCTER, BRYAN WALLER
Charlotte Brontë 4:2422
Nathaniel Hawthorne 5:2587

PROWSE, W. J.
Tobias Smollett 3:1623

PRYNNE, WILLIAM
Christopher Marlowe 1:166

PUFENDORF, SAMUEL
Sir Francis Bacon 1:340

PURNEY, THOMAS
William Shakespeare 2:707

PUSHKIN, ALEXANDER
Laurence Sterne 3:1551

PUTTENHAM, RICHARD
Geoffrey Chaucer 1:6

QUILLER-COUCH, SIR ARTHUR THOMAS
John Milton 1:600
William Shakespeare 2:1249
Laurence Sterne 3:1554
Sir Walter Scott 4:2132

RACKET, MRS.
Alexander Pope 3:1420

RADFORD, G. H.
William Shakespeare 2:956

RAE, W. FRASER
Richard Brinsley Sheridan 3:1844

RALEGH, SIR WALTER
Sir Philip Sidney 1:135
Edmund Spenser 1:228

RALEIGH, WALTER
Geoffrey Chaucer 1:121
Sir Philip Sidney 1:154
Ben Jonson 1:473
John Milton 1:588
John Bunyan 3:1283
Jonathan Swift 3:1477
Laurence Sterne 3:1557
Tobias Smollett 3:1635
Samuel Johnson 3:1729, 1759
Robert Burns 3:1816
Jane Austen 4:1901
Percy Bysshe Shelley 4:1976
Robert Louis Stevenson 5:3079

RAMSAY, ALLAN
Alexander Pope 3:1419

RAMSAY, CHEVALIER
Alexander Pope 3:1405

RAMSAY, H.
Ben Jonson 1:467

RANKE, LEOPOLD VON
Sir Francis Bacon 1:336
Thomas Babington Macaulay
4:2481

RANSOME, ARTHUR
Oscar Wilde 5:3166

RAVENSCROFT, EDWARD
William Shakespeare 2:1061

RAWLEY, WILLIAM
Francis Bacon 1:344

RAWNSLEY, H. D.
John Ruskin 5:3107

READE, CHARLES L.
George Eliot 5:2654

READE, COMPTON
George Eliot 5:2654

REED, HENRY
John Milton 1:589, 600

REID, T. WEMYSS
Emily Brontë 4:2250
Charlotte Brontë 4:2430

REID, THOMAS
David Hume 3:1685

REPPLIER, AGNES
Robert Herrick 1:542
Oscar Wilde 5:3150

REYNOLDS, HENRY
Edmund Spenser 1:229

REYNOLDS, JOHN
George Herbert 1:423

REYNOLDS, JOHN HAMILTON
John Keats 4:1929

REYNOLDS, SIR JOSHUA
Samuel Johnson 3:1713

RHYS, ERNEST
Christopher Marlowe 1:172
Robert Herrick 1:545
William Shakespeare 2:1001
Robert Burns 3:1815
Walt Whitman 5:3010

RICHARDSON, CHARLES F.
Henry David Thoreau 4:2509
Ralph Waldo Emerson 5:2740
Herman Melville 5:2938
Walt Whitman 5:3014

RICHARDSON, JONATHAN
John Milton 1:577

RICHARDSON, SAMUEL
Jonathan Swift 3:1460
Henry Fielding 3:1510, 1518
Samuel Johnson 3:1724
Robert Burns 3:1798

RICHARDSON, WILLIAM
William Shakespeare 2:1195

RIDDELL, MARIA
Robert Burns 3:1798

RIGBY, ELIZABETH
Charlotte Brontë 4:2423

RILEY, JAMES WHITCOMB
Robert Burns 3:1814
Henry Wadsworth Longfellow
5:2780

RIPLEY, GEORGE
Ralph Waldo Emerson 5:2732
Herman Melville 5:2941

RITCHIE, ANNE THACKERAY
Charlotte Brontë 4:2414
William Makepeace Thackeray
5:2559

RITSON, JOSEPH
Christopher Marlowe 1:167
Robert Burns 3:1802

ROBERTS, L. M.
Robert Burns 3:1801

ROBERTSON, ERIC S.
Henry Wadsworth Longfellow
5:2779

ROBERTSON, GEORGE CROOM
Sir Francis Bacon 1:343

ROBERTSON, J. LOGIE
Tobias Smollett 3:1617

ROBERTSON, JOHN MACKINNON
Edgar Allan Poe 4:2295
John Ruskin 5:3109

ROBERTSON, WILLIAM
Edward Gibbon 3:1771

ROBINSON, A. MARY F.
Emily Brontë 4:2256
Charlotte Brontë 4:2416

ROBINSON, HENRY CRABB
Edward Gibbon 3:1773
Jane Austen 4:1878, 1880
Percy Bysshe Shelley 4:1964
William Blake 4:2062
William Hazlitt 4:2097
Charles Lamb 4:2216
William Wordsworth 4:2314, 2330
Thomas Babington Macaulay
4:2469
Thomas Carlyle 5:2683
Ralph Waldo Emerson 5:2725

ROCHESTER, JOHN WILMOT, EARL OF
John Dryden 3:1308

ROE, EDWARD P.
Nathaniel Hawthorne 5:2584

ROGERS, HENRY
Andrew Marvell 3:1259

ROGERS, SAMUEL
Edward Gibbon 3:1767, 1776
Richard Brinsley Sheridan 3:1848
Percy Bysshe Shelley 4:1967
George Gordon, Lord Byron 4:2018

ROOSE, PAULINE W.
Walt Whitman 5:3039

ROSCOE, THOMAS
Henry Fielding 3:1517
Tobias Smollett 3:1613

ROSE, EDWARD
William Shakespeare 2:1013

ROSEBERY, LORD
Robert Louis Stevenson 5:3078

ROSSETTI, CHRISTINA
John Keats 4:1912

ROSSETTI, DANTE GABRIEL
Robert Burns 3:1800
John Keats 4:1913
Percy Bysshe Shelley 4:1973
William Blake 4:2057
Samuel Taylor Coleridge 4:2178
Emily Brontë 4:2250
Robert Browning 5:2904
Walt Whitman 5:3022

ROSSETTI, LUCY MADOX
Mary Shelley 4:2405

ROSSETTI, WILLIAM MICHAEL
Robert Herrick 1:544
John Milton 1:586
John Dryden 3:1318
Thomas Gray 3:1586
Oliver Goldsmith 3:1658
Robert Burns 3:1810
John Keats 4:1918, 1922
George Gordon, Lord Byron 4:2025
Sir Walter Scott 4:2140
Henry Wadsworth Longfellow
5:2777
Walt Whitman 5:3011, 3012

ROUSSEAU, JEAN JACQUES
Daniel Defoe 3:1374

ROWE, NICHOLAS
William Shakespeare 2:672, 719

ROWLEY, WILLIAM
John Webster 1:448

ROYCE, JOSIAH
David Hume 3:1703
George Gordon, Lord Byron 4:2029

RUSKIN, JOHN
Geoffrey Chaucer 1:11
Sir Philip Sidney 1:133
Edmund Spenser 1:232
Sir Francis Bacon 1:328
George Herbert 1:425

Samuel Johnson 3:1721
John Keats 4:1918, 1927
Sir Walter Scott 4:2147
Charles Dickens 5:2616
Robert Browning 5:2895
Alfred, Lord Tennyson 5:2967
Walt Whitman 5:3012
John Ruskin 5:3106

RUSSELL, W. CLARK
Emily Brontë 4:2250
Herman Melville 5:2937

RYMER, THOMAS
Edmund Spenser 1:229
John Milton 1:592
William Shakespeare 2:1075, 1120

S., I. M.
William Shakespeare 2:703

SAINTE-BEUVE, C. A.
Edward Gibbon 3:1776

SAINTSBURY, GEORGE
Geoffrey Chaucer 1:13
Sir Philip Sidney 1:129, 134
Christopher Marlowe 1:172
Edmund Spenser 1:319
Sir Francis Bacon 1:335, 339, 343
John Donne 1:401
George Herbert 1:426
John Webster 1:446, 448
Ben Jonson 1:466, 509
Richard Crashaw 1:531
Robert Herrick 1:545, 548, 562
John Milton 1:580, 588, 590, 591,
601, 602
William Shakespeare 2:802, 823,
1218, 1221
John Dryden 3:1320, 1325, 1356
Henry Fielding 3:1516
Tobias Smollett 3:1618, 1637
David Hume 3:1682
Samuel Johnson 3:1723
Edward Gibbon 3:1769
Richard Brinsley Sheridan 3:1848
Jane Austen 4:1877
John Keats 4:1957
Percy Bysshe Shelley 4:1975
George Gordon, Lord Byron 4:2026
William Blake 4:2087
William Hazlitt 4:2118
Sir Walter Scott 4:2161
Charlotte Brontë 4:2418
Thomas Babington Macaulay
4:2475
William Makepeace Thackeray
5:2554
George Eliot 5:2655
Thomas Carlyle 5:2699
Henry Wadsworth Longfellow
5:2799
Anthony Trollope 5:2809
Matthew Arnold 5:2865
Robert Browning 5:2900
Alfred, Lord Tennyson 5:2971
Walt Whitman 5:3023
Walter Pater 5:3051, 3054
John Ruskin 5:3111

SALMON, ARTHUR L.
Emily Brontë 4:2261

SALT, HENRY S.
Henry David Thoreau 4:2528
Herman Melville 5:2954

SANBORN, F. B.
Henry David Thoreau 4:2508

SANDERS, H. M.
Robert Herrick 1:542

SANDERSON, EDGAR
Sir Francis Bacon 1:337

SANDYS, GEORGE
Sir Francis Bacon 1:331

SANTAYANA, GEORGE
William Shakespeare 2:805
Ralph Waldo Emerson 5:2760
Robert Browning 5:2921
Walt Whitman 5:3044

SARGENT, W.
Tobias Smollett 3:1613

SAVAGE, RICHARD
Alexander Pope 3:1402, 1419

SCHELLING, FELIX E.
John Donne 1:398
Richard Crashaw 1:534

SCHERER, EDMOND
John Milton 1:602, 655
William Shakespeare 2:717
Laurence Sterne 3:1553
John Keats 4:1919
William Wordsworth 4:2325
George Eliot 5:2651
Thomas Carlyle 5:2690

SCHERER, WILHELM
John Milton 1:597

SCHLEGEL, AUGUST WILHELM
Ben Jonson 1:471
William Shakespeare 2:748, 933,
935, 940, 944, 951, 955, 958,
964, 969, 973, 979, 986, 993,
999, 1009, 1013, 1019, 1024,
1033, 1039, 1062, 1064, 1074,
1085, 1114, 1120, 1140, 1154,
1166, 1174, 1195, 1202, 1209
John Dryden 3:1321

SCHLEGEL, FRIEDRICH
Sir Francis Bacon 1:341
John Milton 1:593
David Hume 3:1683
Edward Gibbon 3:1773
George Gordon, Lord Byron 4:2020
Sir Walter Scott 4:2138

SCHUYLER, EUGENE
Tobias Smollett 3:1624

SCHUYLER, MONTGOMERY
John Keats 4:1956

SCOLOKER, ANTHONY
William Shakespeare 2:1083

SCOONES, W. BAPTISTE
Robert Herrick 1:545

SCOTT, JOHN
Sir Walter Scott 4:2133

SCOTT, R. PICKETT
Percy Bysshe Shelley 4:1978

SCOTT, SIR WALTER
Ben Jonson 1:471
John Milton 1:589
William Shakespeare 2:711
John Bunyan 3:1287
John Dryden 3:1323, 1325, 1327,
1328, 1333
Daniel Defoe 3:1378
Henry Fielding 3:1524
Laurence Sterne 3:1560
Tobias Smollett 3:1624, 1627
Oliver Goldsmith 3:1656, 1658
Samuel Johnson 3:1728
Robert Burns 3:1800
Richard Brinsley Sheridan 3:1846
Jane Austen 4:1872, 1878, 1881
George Gordon, Lord Byron 4:2016
William Wordsworth 4:2320
James Fenimore Cooper 4:2361,
2368
Mary Shelley 4:2393
Washington Irving 4:2453

SCUDDER, H. E.
Henry Wadsworth Longfellow
5:2794

SCUDDER, VIDA D.
John Milton 1:597
Jane Austen 4:1877
William Wordsworth 4:2328
George Eliot 5:2669
Alfred, Lord Tennyson 5:2974

SEARS, LORENZO
Richard Brinsley Sheridan 3:1852

SEDGWICK, ARTHUR GEORGE
Washington Irving 4:2450
George Eliot 5:2651
John Ruskin 5:3108

SEDGWICK, CATHARINE M.
Emily Brontë 4:2249
Charlotte Brontë 4:2422

SEDGWICK, HENRY D., JR.
William Makepeace Thackeray
5:2570

SEELEY, JOHN ROBERT
John Milton 1:586

SELWYN, GEORGE
Walt Whitman 5:3014

SERVICE, JOHN
Robert Burns 3:1829

SETOUN, GABRIEL
Robert Burns 3:1835

SEVERN, JOSEPH
John Keats 4:1911, 1927

SEWARD, ANNA
Laurence Sterne 3:1550
Samuel Johnson 3:1709
Sir Walter Scott 4:2130

SEWELL, WILLIAM
Thomas Carlyle 5:2687

SHACKFORD, MARTHA HALE
Emily Dickinson 5:2851

SHADWELL, THOMAS
Ben Jonson 1:468
John Dryden 3:1335

SHAIRP, JOHN CAMPBELL
John Milton 1:586
Thomas Gray 3:1590
Oliver Goldsmith 3:1657
Robert Burns 3:1818, 1819
John Keats 4:1920
William Wordsworth 4:2329
Thomas Carlyle 5:2698
Matthew Arnold 5:2861

SHAKESPEARE, WILLIAM
William Shakespeare 2:1112, 1246,
1247

SHANKS, LEWIS PIAGET
Oscar Wilde 5:3164

SHARP, JOHN
Thomas Gray 3:1585

SHARP, WILLIAM
Walter Pater 5:3057

SHAW, CUTHBERT
Tobias Smollett 3:1612
Samuel Johnson 3:1708

SHAW, GEORGE BERNARD
Christopher Marlowe 1:210
William Shakespeare 2:801
John Bunyan 3:1290
Oscar Wilde 5:3153

SHAW, THOMAS B.
John Webster 1:444
John Milton 1:584
Samuel Taylor Coleridge 4:2182

SHEFFIELD, EARL OF
Edward Gibbon 3:1780

SHEFFIELD, JOHN, LORD
Edward Gibbon 3:1779

SHELLEY, MARY
Percy Bysshe Shelley 4:1965, 1980
Mary Shelley 4:2387

SHELLEY, PERCY BYSSHE
Sir Philip Sidney 1:126
John Milton 1:583, 594
William Shakespeare 2:1140
John Keats 4:1912, 1924, 1925,
1926, 1936
George Gordon, Lord Byron 4:2021
Samuel Taylor Coleridge 4:2175
William Wordsworth 4:2320
Mary Shelley 4:2391

SHELLEY, SIR TIMOTHY
Mary Shelley 4:2387

SHENSTONE, WILLIAM
Samuel Johnson 3:1725

SHEPPARD, SAMUEL
John Webster 1:443

SHERARD, ROBERT H.
Oscar Wilde 5:3156

SHERIDAN, RICHARD BRINSLEY
Richard Brinsley Sheridan 3:1842

SHERWOOD, M. E. W.
William Makepeace Thackeray
5:2559

SHIRLEY, JOHN
Geoffrey Chaucer 1:3

SHORTER, CLEMENT K.
Emily Brontë 4:2251, 2253
Charlotte Brontë 4:2415

SICHEL, WALTER
Daniel Defoe 3:1373

SIDGWICK, HENRY
Matthew Arnold 5:2868

SIDNEY, SIR PHILIP
Geoffrey Chaucer 1:6
Edmund Spenser 1:226

SIGMOND, GEORGE GABRIEL
Richard Brinsley Sheridan 3:1856

SIMCOX, GEORGE AUGUSTUS
George Herbert 1:430
Richard Crashaw 1:517

SIMMS, WILLIAM GILMORE
Edgar Allan Poe 4:2280
James Fenimore Cooper 4:2370

SIMON, H.
Geoffrey Chaucer 1:63

SIMONDS, WILLIAM EDWARD
Laurence Sterne 3:1554

SINGER, S. W.
Robert Herrick 1:544

SKELTON, JOHN
Geoffrey Chaucer 1:13
Charlotte Brontë 4:2428

SMART, CHRISTOPHER
William Shakespeare 2:1118
Henry Fielding 3:1510

SMEATON, OLIPHANT
Tobias Smollett 3:1638

SMETHAM, JAMES
William Blake 4:2058

SMITH, ADAM
Alexander Pope 3:1420
Thomas Gray 3:1596
David Hume 3:1680
Samuel Johnson 3:1726
Edward Gibbon 3:1772

SMITH, ALEXANDER
Sir Francis Bacon 1:336
John Bunyan 3:1282
Nathaniel Hawthorne 5:2581
Charles Dickens 5:2617

SMITH, FREDERICK M.
Henry David Thoreau 4:2532

SMITH, GEORGE BARNETT
Robert Herrick 1:544
Tobias Smollett 3:1631
Jane Austen 4:1876

SMITH, SIR GEORGE MURRAY
Charlotte Brontë 4:2419
Emily Brontë 4:2254

SMITH, GOLDWIN
Andrew Marvell 3:1258
Jane Austen 4:1895

SMITH, HENRY JUSTIN
William Blake 4:2090

SMITH, SYDNEY
George Gordon, Lord Byron 4:2014
Sir Walter Scott 4:2147
William Wordsworth 4:2319

SMITHES, SIR THOMAS
Sir Philip Sidney 1:127

SMOLLETT, TOBIAS
Henry Fielding 3:1508
David Hume 3:1679
Samuel Johnson 3:1707

SMYTH, WILLIAM
John Milton 1:584
Tobias Smollett 3:1622

SNIDER, DENTON J.
William Shakespeare 2:974, 1034

SOMERSET, FRANCES THYNNE
HERTFORD, DUCHESS OF
Henry Fielding 3:1510

SOMERVILLE, WILLIAM
Alexander Pope 3:1421

SOTHEBY, SAMUEL LEIGH
John Milton 1:585

SOUTHEY, ROBERT
Sir Philip Sidney 1:126, 127
John Donne 1:378
Robert Herrick 1:543
John Milton 1:583, 589, 590
John Bunyan 3:1287
Henry Fielding 3:1512
George Gordon, Lord Byron
4:2021, 2031
Charles Lamb 4:2218, 2222
William Wordsworth 4:2314, 2319,
2330
Charlotte Brontë 4:2413

SPEDDING, JAMES
Sir Francis Bacon 1:329, 339
William Shakespeare 2:906
Charles Dickens 5:2628

SPEGHT, THOMAS
Geoffrey Chaucer 1:17

SPENCE, JOSEPH
Edmund Spenser 1:222
Alexander Pope 3:1418

SPENSER, EDMUND
Geoffrey Chaucer 1:5, 6, 7
Sir Philip Sidney 1:125

SPIELMANN, M. H.
John Ruskin 5:3106

SPINGARN, JOEL E.
Sir Philip Sidney 1:159

SPRAT, THOMAS
Sir Francis Bacon 1:327, 339

STAËL, MADAME DE
Henry Fielding 3:1519

STAFFORD, ANTHONY
Sir Philip Sidney 1:126

STANLEY, ARTHUR PENRHYN
Ben Jonson 1:466
John Bunyan 3:1289

STANLEY, HIRAM M.
Jane Austen 4:1902

STAPFER, PAUL
Sir Philip Sidney 1:135
William Shakespeare 2:880

STEBBING, WILLIAM
Tobias Smollett 3:1617

STEDMAN, EDMUND CLARENCE
John Webster 1:448
John Milton 1:597
William Shakespeare 2:1211
John Keats 4:1943
Edgar Allan Poe 4:2298
Nathaniel Hawthorne 5:2583
George Eliot 5:2652
Ralph Waldo Emerson 5:2750
Henry Wadsworth Longfellow
5:2779
Robert Browning 5:2896
Alfred, Lord Tennyson 5:2975
Walt Whitman 5:3010, 3026

STEELE, SIR RICHARD
Edmund Spenser 1:231
William Shakespeare 2:1008, 1022

STEEVENS, GEORGE
Samuel Johnson 3:1710

STENDHAL
Sir Walter Scott 4:2142

STEPHEN, SIR LESLIE
John Donne 1:380
John Milton 1:580, 604
Daniel Defoe 3:1384
Alexander Pope 3:1415, 1422, 1439
Jonathan Swift 3:1468
Henry Fielding 3:1536
Laurence Sterne 3:1572
Thomas Gray 3:1598
David Hume 3:1699
Samuel Johnson 3:1719, 1732,
1741
Edward Gibbon 3:1789
Percy Bysshe Shelley 4:1990
William Hazlitt 4:2109
Sir Walter Scott 4:2146, 2159
William Wordsworth 4:2349
Charlotte Brontë 4:2432
Thomas Babington Macaulay
4:2486
Nathaniel Hawthorne 5:2595
George Eliot 5:2681
Thomas Carlyle 5:2710
Ralph Waldo Emerson 5:2763
Anthony Trollope 5:2826
Matthew Arnold 5:2883

Alfred, Lord Tennyson 5:2997
Robert Louis Stevenson 5:3096
John Ruskin 5:3129

STEPHENS, ROBERT
Sir Francis Bacon 1:327

STERLING, JOHN
John Milton 1:583
Samuel Taylor Coleridge 4:2176,
2186
Thomas Carlyle 5:2700

STERNE, LAURENCE
John Bunyan 3:1286
Laurence Sterne 3:1555

STEVENSON, ROBERT LOUIS
Henry Fielding 3:1508, 1514
Robert Burns 3:1831
Sir Walter Scott 4:2137
Edgar Allan Poe 4:2283
Henry David Thoreau 4:2520
William Makepeace Thackeray
5:2550
Charles Dickens 5:2621
Herman Melville 5:2938
Walt Whitman 5:3032

STEWART, DUGALD
Sir Francis Bacon 1:336, 341
Robert Burns 3:1798

STILLMAN, WILLIAM JAMES
Henry Wadsworth Longfellow
5:2773
Robert Browning 5:2894
John Ruskin 5:3107

STOCKTON, FRANK R.
Daniel Defoe 3:1378

STODDARD, FRANCIS HOVEY
Jane Austen 4:1908
Sir Walter Scott 4:2145
Charlotte Brontë 4:2418
Nathaniel Hawthorne 5:2588
Emily Dickinson 5:2843

STODDARD, RICHARD HENRY
John Milton 1:587, 600
John Keats 4:1920, 1928
William Blake 4:2059
Herman Melville 5:2938

STOPES, CHARLOTTE CARMICHAEL
Sir Francis Bacon 1:369
William Shakespeare 2:936

STORY, ALFRED T.
William Blake 4:2086

STORY, JOSEPH
Washington Irving 4:2455

STORY, WILLIAM WETMORE
Sir Walter Scott 4:2148

STOWE, HARRIET BEECHER
George Eliot 5:2660

STRACHEY, JOHN ST. LOE
Herman Melville 5:2939

STRACHEY, LYTTON
William Shakespeare 2:810
Samuel Johnson 3:1733

STREET, G. S.
  Richard Brinsley Sheridan 3:1865

STRONG, AUGUSTUS HOPKINS
  John Milton 1:588, 598

STRONG, ISOBEL
  Robert Louis Stevenson 5:3077

STUART, LADY LOUISA
  Henry Fielding 3:1508

STUBBE, HENRY
  Sir Francis Bacon 1:331

SUCKLING, SIR JOHN
  Ben Jonson 1:465

SUMNER, CHARLES
  Nathaniel Hawthorne 5:2581
  Thomas Carlyle 5:2684
  Ralph Waldo Emerson 5:2724
  Henry Wadsworth Longfellow
    5:2771

SWIFT, DEANE
  Jonathan Swift 3:1461

SWIFT, JONATHAN
  John Milton 1:592
  John Bunyan 3:1286
  John Dryden 3:1310, 1329, 1333
  Daniel Defoe 3:1365
  Alexander Pope 3:1402, 1405, 1418
  Jonathan Swift 3:1459, 1479

SWINBURNE, ALGERNON CHARLES
  Geoffrey Chaucer 1:12, 98
  Sir Philip Sidney 1:161
  Christopher Marlowe 1:170, 183,
    185
  John Webster 1:445, 448, 452
  Ben Jonson 1:472
  Robert Herrick 1:558
  William Shakespeare 2:714, 1057
  Robert Burns 3:1815
  John Keats 4:1942
  Percy Bysshe Shelley 4:1975, 1989
  George Gordon, Lord Byron 4:2041
  William Blake 4:2071
  Samuel Taylor Coleridge 4:2195
  Charles Lamb 4:2226, 2228
  Emily Brontë 4:2259
  Edgar Allan Poe 4:2280
  Charlotte Brontë 4:2420
  William Makepeace Thackeray
    5:2550
  Charles Dickens 5:2618, 2643
  Matthew Arnold 5:2873
  Robert Browning 5:2897, 2898
  Alfred, Lord Tennyson 5:2976
  Walt Whitman 5:3036

SYLVESTER, JOSHUA
  Edmund Spenser 1:217

SYMONDS, JOHN ADDINGTON
  Sir Philip Sidney 1:127, 151
  John Webster 1:446, 449
  Ben Jonson 1:473, 481
  John Milton 1:602
  William Shakespeare 2:715, 1220
  John Keats 4:1923, 1927
  Percy Bysshe Shelley 4:1973

  George Gordon, Lord Byron 4:2032
  Robert Browning 5:2898
  Walt Whitman 5:3016, 3041
  Walter Pater 5:3056, 3057
  Robert Louis Stevenson 5:3080

SYMONS, ARTHUR
  John Donne 1:380
  William Wordsworth 4:2355
  Walter Pater 5:3061
  Robert Louis Stevenson 5:3095
  Oscar Wilde 5:3141

TAINE, HIPPOLYTE
  Sir Philip Sidney 1:131, 133
  Christopher Marlowe 1:170
  John Donne 1:379
  John Milton 1:586, 595
  John Bunyan 3:1296
  John Dryden 3:1317
  Daniel Defoe 3:1372
  Alexander Pope 3:1412
  Jonathan Swift 3:1478
  Henry Fielding 3:1530
  Laurence Sterne 3:1569
  Tobias Smollett 3:1629
  Oliver Goldsmith 3:1656
  Samuel Johnson 3:1718
  Robert Burns 3:1809
  Richard Brinsley Sheridan 3:1859
  Percy Bysshe Shelley 4:1973
  Alfred, Lord Tennyson 5:2968

TALFOURD, T. NOON
  Henry Fielding 3:1512
  Laurence Sterne 3:1551
  Tobias Smollett 3:1619
  William Hazlitt 4:2099

TATE, NAHUM
  William Shakespeare 2:706, 1138

TATHAM, FREDERICK
  William Blake 4:2056

TAYLOR, BAYARD
  William Makepeace Thackeray
    5:2548
  George Eliot 5:2660
  Alfred, Lord Tennyson 5:2972

TAYLOR, EDWARD (?)
  William Shakespeare 2:737

TAYLOR, SIR HENRY
  William Wordsworth 4:2322

TEMPLE, SIR WILLIAM
  Sir Philip Sidney 1:127
  Edmund Spenser 1:230
  William Shakespeare 2:927
  Jonathan Swift 3:1457

TEMPLE, WILLIAM
  Thomas Gray 3:1586

TENISON, THOMAS
  Sir Francis Bacon 1:340

TENNYSON, ALFRED, LORD
  John Milton 1:585
  Sir Walter Scott 4:2145
  Thomas Babington Macaulay
    4:2471
  Robert Browning 5:2893

TENNYSON, HALLAM
  William Shakespeare 2:718
  John Keats 4:1923
  Edgar Allan Poe 4:2279
  George Eliot 5:2649
  Walt Whitman 5:3019

TEXTE, JOSEPH
  Laurence Sterne 3:1555

THACKERAY, WILLIAM MAKEPEACE
  Alexander Pope 3:1410
  Jonathan Swift 3:1466
  Henry Fielding 3:1528
  Laurence Sterne 3:1552
  Tobias Smollett 3:1616
  Oliver Goldsmith 3:1652
  Sir Walter Scott 4:2132
  Charlotte Brontë 4:2420
  Washington Irving 4:2444
  Charles Dickens 5:2628, 2629

THAXTER, CELIA
  Charlotte Brontë 4:2415

THAYER, WILLIAM ROSCOE
  Thomas Carlyle 5:2695

THEOBALD, LEWIS
  William Shakespeare 2:838, 870
  Alexander Pope 3:1418

THIRLWALL, CONNOP
  George Eliot 5:2659

THOMPSON, FRANCIS
  Richard Crashaw 1:518, 532
  Alexander Pope 3:1414
  Robert Burns 3:1816
  Samuel Taylor Coleridge 4:2181
  Edgar Allan Poe 4:2285
  Thomas Carlyle 5:2697
  Robert Browning 5:2901

THOMPSON, JOHN R.
  Edgar Allan Poe 4:2276

THOMSON, CLARA
  Henry Fielding 3:1544

THOMSON, JAMES (1700–1748)
  Sir Philip Sidney 1:127
  John Milton 1:581

THOMSON, JAMES (1834–1882)
  Jonathan Swift 3:1468
  William Blake 4:2065
  Robert Browning 5:2895

THOREAU, HENRY DAVID
  Geoffrey Chaucer 1:56
  Thomas Carlyle 5:2704
  Ralph Waldo Emerson 5:2729
  Walt Whitman 5:3011

THORNBURY, GEORGE WALTER
  Ben Jonson 1:465
  William Blake 4:2057

THORPE, THOMAS
  William Shakespeare 2:1220

TICKNOR, GEORGE
  Sir Philip Sidney 1:130
  George Gordon, Lord Byron 4:2014
  William Hazlitt 4:2097
  Sir Walter Scott 4:2130

William Wordsworth 4:2315
William Makepeace Thackeray
  5:2559
Thomas Carlyle 5:2684
Henry Wadsworth Longfellow
  5:2783

TIREBUCK, WILLIAM
Charles Lamb 4:2229

TODD, MABEL LOOMIS
Emily Dickinson 5:2843, 2849

TOFTE, ROBERT
William Shakespeare 2:951

TOLAND, JOHN
John Milton 1:604

TOLSTOY, LEO
William Shakespeare 2:814, 1149

TONSON, JACOB
Alexander Pope 3:1415

TORREY, BRADFORD
Henry David Thoreau 4:2529
Nathaniel Hawthorne 5:2586

TOVEY, DUNCAN C.
Sir Philip Sidney 1:157
Thomas Gray 3:1593

TOYNBEE, ARNOLD
Thomas Carlyle 5:2700

TRAILL, H. D.
Alexander Pope 3:1449
Laurence Sterne 3:1580
Samuel Taylor Coleridge 4:2183
Anthony Trollope 5:2809
Matthew Arnold 5:2867
Stephen Crane 5:3181

TRELAWNY, EDWARD JOHN
Percy Bysshe Shelley 4:1969
George Gordon, Lord Byron 4:2019
Mary Shelley 4:2388

TRENCH, RICHARD CHENEVIX
John Donne 1:379

TRENT, WILLIAM P.
John Milton 1:581, 588, 591
Percy Bysshe Shelley 4:1977
Ralph Waldo Emerson 5:2739
Herman Melville 5:2939
Walt Whitman 5:3021

TROLLOPE, ANTHONY
Henry Fielding 3:1520
Charlotte Brontë 4:2416
William Makepeace Thackeray
  5:2550, 2557
Nathaniel Hawthorne 5:2602
Charles Dickens 5:2620
George Eliot 5:2654
Henry Wadsworth Longfellow
  5:2777
Anthony Trollope 5:2813

TROLLOPE, THOMAS ADOLPHUS
Charles Dickens 5:2614
Anthony Trollope 5:2806
Robert Browning 5:2894

TUCKERMAN, BAYARD
Sir Philip Sidney 1:131
Henry Fielding 3:1513

TUCKERMAN, CHARLES K.
Anthony Trollope 5:2806

TUCKERMAN, HENRY T.
Laurence Sterne 3:1564
William Hazlitt 4:2102
Charles Lamb 4:2223

TULLOCH, JOHN
John Bunyan 3:1282
Sir Walter Scott 4:2140
George Eliot 5:2654
Matthew Arnold 5:2856

TURNBULL, WILLIAM B.
Richard Crashaw 1:516

TUTIN, J. R.
Richard Crashaw 1:518

TWAIN, MARK
William Shakespeare 2:916
Sir Walter Scott 4:2136
James Fenimore Cooper 4:2380

TYERS, THOMAS
Samuel Johnson 3:1710

TYLER, ROYALL
William Shakespeare 2:711

TYNAN, KATHARINE
Oscar Wilde 5:3140

TYNDALL, JOHN
Thomas Carlyle 5:2691

ÜBERWEG, FRIEDRICH
Sir Francis Bacon 1:342
David Hume 3:1687

ULRICI, HERMANN
Ben Jonson 1:471

USK, THOMAS
Geoffrey Chaucer 1:1

VAN DYKE, HENRY
John Milton 1:603
John Keats 4:1954

VAUGHAN, HENRY
George Herbert 1:423

VAUGHAN, WILLIAM
Christopher Marlowe 1:166

VERITY, A. W.
Christopher Marlowe 1:189

VERPLANCK, GULIAN C.
Washington Irving 4:2454

VICTORIA, QUEEN OF ENGLAND
Charlotte Brontë 4:2420
Alfred, Lord Tennyson 5:2963

VINCENT, LEON H.
John Keats 4:1950

VOLTAIRE, FRANÇOIS MARIE
  AROUET DE
Sir Francis Bacon 1:348
John Milton 1:593, 613
William Shakespeare 2:1008, 1045,
  1083

Alexander Pope 3:1405
Jonathan Swift 3:1462

WALKER, ALBERT PERRY
John Milton 1:600

WALKER, HUGH
Robert Burns 3:1814
Emily Brontë 4:2251
Charlotte Brontë 4:2418
Matthew Arnold 5:2858
Alfred, Lord Tennyson 5:2977
Oscar Wilde 5:3157

WALLER, EDMUND
Sir Philip Sidney 1:127

WALPOLE, HORACE
Sir Philip Sidney 1:126, 135
Sir Francis Bacon 1:331, 338
John Milton 1:582
William Shakespeare 2:1201
John Dryden 3:1312, 1327
Alexander Pope 3:1418, 1420, 1422
Jonathan Swift 3:1461, 1475
Henry Fielding 3:1508
Laurence Sterne 3:1555, 1557
Thomas Gray 3:1585, 1594
Tobias Smollett 3:1612, 1623
Oliver Goldsmith 3:1658
Samuel Johnson 3:1708, 1714
Edward Gibbon 3:1770, 1771, 1772
Richard Brinsley Sheridan 3:1850,
  1851

WALSINGHAM, SIR FRANCIS
Sir Philip Sidney 1:125

WALTON, IZAAK
John Donne 1:375, 376
George Herbert 1:422, 427, 430

WALTON, JOHN
Geoffrey Chaucer 1:2

WARBURTON, WILLIAM
William Shakespeare 2:840
Alexander Pope 3:1403
Laurence Sterne 3:1556
Tobias Smollett 3:1622
David Hume 3:1682, 1683

WARD, ADOLPHUS WILLIAM
Geoffrey Chaucer 1:87
Sir Philip Sidney 1:161
Christopher Marlowe 1:171
John Webster 1:445, 447, 449
Ben Jonson 1:466, 475, 476
John Milton 1:589, 599, 603
William Shakespeare 2:929, 1005
John Dryden 3:1322, 1324, 1325,
  1326, 1327, 1328
Charles Dickens 5:2619

WARD, MRS. HUMPHRY
Walter Pater 5:3057

WARD, JOHN
William Shakespeare 2:671

WARD, MARY A.
Sir Philip Sidney 1:134
Emily Brontë 4:2266

WARD, THOMAS HUMPHRY
Sir Philip Sidney 1:161
Sir Francis Bacon 1:343
John Dryden 3:1322

WARD, WILLIAM
Ben Jonson 1:475

WARNER, CHARLES DUDLEY
Washington Irving 4:2462
Stephen Crane 5:3175

WARRE, F. CORNISH
Robert Herrick 1:568

WARTON, JOSEPH
Geoffrey Chaucer 1:10
William Shakespeare 2:1141, 1211
Alexander Pope 3:1405
Jonathan Swift 3:1477
Henry Fielding 3:1508

WARTON, THOMAS
Geoffrey Chaucer 1:23
Christopher Marlowe 1:177
Edmund Spenser 1:245
John Milton 1:589, 590
Thomas Gray 3:1586
Oliver Goldsmith 3:1647

WASHBURN, EMELYN W.
Sir Francis Bacon 1:336

WATKINS, JOHN
Richard Brinsley Sheridan 3:1848,
1849

WATSON, WILLIAM
John Milton 1:588
John Keats 4:1914
Samuel Taylor Coleridge 4:2184,
2186
Charles Lamb 4:2221
William Wordsworth 4:2326
Alfred, Lord Tennyson 5:2977

WAUGH, ARTHUR
Robert Browning 5:2901

WEBBE, WILLIAM
Geoffrey Chaucer 1:6
Edmund Spenser 1:226

WEBER, ALFRED
Sir Francis Bacon 1:343

WEBSTER, JOHN
John Webster 1:447

WEBSTER, NOAH
Samuel Johnson 3:1727

WEBSTER, WENTWORTH
George Herbert 1:426

WEEVER, JOHN
William Shakespeare 2:701, 1074

WEISS, SUSAN A. T.
Edgar Allan Poe 4:2276

WELLS, H. G.
Stephen Crane 5:3188

WELSH, ALFRED H.
John Donne 1:379
Henry David Thoreau 4:2509
Nathaniel Hawthorne 5:2584
George Eliot 5:2659

WENDELL, BARRETT
Edgar Allan Poe 4:2286
James Fenimore Cooper 4:2369
Washington Irving 4:2465
Henry David Thoreau 4:2512
Nathaniel Hawthorne 5:2585
Robert Browning 5:2899
Walt Whitman 5:3018

WESLEY, JOHN
Laurence Sterne 3:1558

WESLEY, SAMUEL
Edmund Spenser 1:220

WHALLEY, PETER
Ben Jonson 1:465
William Shakespeare 2:871

WHARTON, THOMAS
Thomas Gray 3:1596

WHATELY, ARCHBISHOP
Jane Austen 4:1886

WHIBLEY, CHARLES
Robert Burns 3:1821
Edgar Allan Poe 4:2305
William Makepeace Thackeray
5:2555

WHIPPLE, EDWIN P.
John Donne 1:377, 378
George Herbert 1:430
John Webster 1:444
Ben Jonson 1:466, 472, 474
John Milton 1:585
William Shakespeare 2:793
John Bunyan 3:1281
Henry Fielding 3:1518
Richard Brinsley Sheridan 3:1857
John Keats 4:1916
Percy Bysshe Shelley 4:1981
Emily Brontë 4:2249
James Fenimore Cooper 4:2366
Charlotte Brontë 4:2420
Washington Irving 4:2450
Henry David Thoreau 4:2509
William Makepeace Thackeray
5:2556
Charles Dickens 5:2616, 2620
Ralph Waldo Emerson 5:2736
Henry Wadsworth Longfellow
5:2785
Anthony Trollope 5:2807
Matthew Arnold 5:2864
Herman Melville 5:2938
Alfred, Lord Tennyson 5:2966
Walt Whitman 5:3014

WHISTLER, JAMES McNEILL
John Ruskin 5:3107

WHITE, ANDREW D.
Sir Walter Scott 4:2143

WHITE, HENRY KIRKE
Sir Philip Sidney 1:131
John Donne 1:378

WHITE, RICHARD GRANT
William Shakespeare 2:933
Richard Brinsley Sheridan 3:1862
Charles Dickens 5:2625

WHITFIELD, GEORGE
Laurence Sterne 3:1558

WHITMAN, SARAH HELEN
Edgar Allan Poe 4:2275

WHITMAN, WALT
William Shakespeare 2:716, 993
Robert Burns 3:1833
Edgar Allan Poe 4:2280
Thomas Carlyle 5:2691
Ralph Waldo Emerson 5:2725,
2733
Henry Wadsworth Longfellow
5:2778
Alfred, Lord Tennyson 5:2969
Walt Whitman 5:3022, 3023

WHITTIER, JOHN GREENLEAF
John Bunyan 3:1285
Robert Burns 3:1807
Robert Browning 5:2904

WHYTE, WALTER
William Makepeace Thackeray
5:2552

WILBERFORCE, WILLIAM
Sir Walter Scott 4:2147

WILDE, OSCAR
William Shakespeare 2:1086, 1221
Robert Browning 5:2899
Walter Pater 5:3059

WILKINSON, WILLIAM CLEAVER
George Eliot 5:2652

WILLIAMS, A. M.
Emily Brontë 4:2263

WILLIS, N. P.
Edgar Allan Poe 4:2273

WILLMOTT, ROBERT ARIS
George Herbert 1:425, 439

WILMER, L. A.
Edgar Allan Poe 4:2272

WILSON, ARTHUR
Sir Francis Bacon 1:326

WILSON, JAMES GRANT
Tobias Smollett 3:1625

WILSON, JOHN
John Webster 1:444, 447
John Milton 1:598
William Shakespeare 2:1052
John Bunyan 3:1281
Samuel Johnson 3:1728
Percy Bysshe Shelley 4:1970
William Hazlitt 4:2100
Sir Walter Scott 4:2146
Samuel Taylor Coleridge 4:2174
Charles Lamb 4:2222
William Wordsworth 4:2316, 2328,
2330
Thomas Babington Macaulay
4:2476, 2479
Alfred, Lord Tennyson 5:2965

WILSON, WALTER
Daniel Defoe 3:1374

WILSON, WOODROW
Edward Gibbon 3:1777
Thomas Babington Macaulay
4:2481

WINDHAM, WILLIAM
Samuel Johnson 3:1709

WINSTANLEY, WILLIAM
Christopher Marlowe 1:166
Edmund Spenser 1:215
Robert Herrick 1:542
John Milton 1:581

WINTER, WILLIAM
Richard Brinsley Sheridan 3:1847

WITHER, GEORGE
Edmund Spenser 1:219

WOLCOT, JOHN
Samuel Johnson 3:1711

WOLFE, THEODORE F.
Henry David Thoreau 4:2512

WOOD, ANTHONY à
Christopher Marlowe 1:167
Robert Herrick 1:542
John Milton 1:606

WOODBERRY, GEORGE EDWARD
William Shakespeare 2:817
John Bunyan 3:1298
Edgar Allan Poe 4:2303
Nathaniel Hawthorne 5:2608
Ralph Waldo Emerson 5:2737
Matthew Arnold 5:2856
Robert Browning 5:2918

WOODBRIDGE, ELISABETH
Ben Jonson 1:504

WOODHOUSELEE, ALEXANDER FRASER
TYTLER, LORD
Tobias Smollett 3:1613

WORDSWORTH, DOROTHY
Robert Burns 3:1798
Sir Walter Scott 4:2129
Samuel Taylor Coleridge 4:2168
William Wordsworth 4:2313

WORDSWORTH, WILLIAM
Geoffrey Chaucer 1:10
Edmund Spenser 1:216, 223, 232
John Milton 1:578, 582, 599
John Dryden 3:1313
Alexander Pope 3:1407
Thomas Gray 3:1587
Robert Burns 3:1799, 1804
John Keats 4:1911
Sir Walter Scott 4:2130, 2133
Samuel Taylor Coleridge 4:2168
Charles Lamb 4:2218
William Wordsworth 4:2327, 2332

WOTTON, SIR HENRY
Sir Francis Bacon 1:337
John Milton 1:589
William Shakespeare 2:1039

WRAXALL, SIR NATHANIEL WILLIAM
Henry Fielding 3:1511
Richard Brinsley Sheridan 3:1844

WRIGHT, WILLIAM
Charlotte Brontë 4:2415

WYATT, SIR THOMAS
Geoffrey Chaucer 1:5

WYCHERLEY, WILLIAM
Alexander Pope 3:1415

WYLIE, LAURA JOHNSON
Sir Philip Sidney 1:135
Samuel Taylor Coleridge 4:2187

WYNDHAM, GEORGE
Stephen Crane 5:3177

YEATS, W. B.
Edmund Spenser 1:321
William Shakespeare 2:809
Percy Bysshe Shelley 4:2004
William Blake 4:2078, 2089
Oscar Wilde 5:3140

YOUNG, ARTHUR
Edward Gibbon 3:1779

YOUNG, CHARLES MAYNE
William Wordsworth 4:2315

YOUNG, EDWARD
Ben Jonson 1:470
William Shakespeare 2:709
John Dryden 3:1311
Alexander Pope 3:1406
Jonathan Swift 3:1474

ZOUCH, THOMAS
Sir Philip Sidney 1:130

UNSIGNED
Edmund Spenser 1:228
John Donne 1:381, 387
George Herbert 1:424
Richard Crashaw 1:516
Robert Herrick 1:547
William Shakespeare 2:1246
John Dryden 3:1306
Jane Austen 4:1872, 1885
Percy Bysshe Shelley 4:1976, 1977
Mary Shelley 4:2398
Anthony Trollope 5:2810
Emily Dickinson 5:2838, 2839,
2840, 2841, 2845, 2846
Herman Melville 5:2938, 2941,
2944, 2945
Stephen Crane 5:3171, 3174, 3176